The Bible and
the Politics
of Exegesis

THE BIBLE AND
THE POLITICS
OF EXEGESIS

Essays in Honor of Norman K. Gottwald
on His Sixty-Fifth Birthday

David Jobling
Peggy L. Day
Gerald T. Sheppard
Editors

The Pilgrim Press   Cleveland, Ohio

Scripture quotations are from the Revised Standard Version Bible, copyright 1946, 1952, © 1971, 1973, Division of Christian Education of the National Council of the Churches of Christ in the United States of America, and are used by permission.

Book design by Jim Gerhard.
Cover design by Jim Gerhard.

Library of Congress Cataloging-in-Publication Data

The Bible and the politics of exegesis : essays in honor of Norman K. Gottwald on his sixty-fifth birthday / David Jobling, Peggy L. Day. Gerald T. Sheppard, editors.
    p.   cm.
  Includes bibliographical references.
  ISBN 0-8298-0913-9 (alk. paper) :
  1. Bible. O.T.—Criticism, interpretation, etc. 2. Sociology,
Biblical. 3. Politics in the Bible. 4. Bible. OT.—Study.
I. Gottwald, Norman K. (Norman Karol), 1926- . II. Jobling,
David. III. Day, Peggy Lynne. IV. Sheppard, Gerald T., 1946–
BS1171.2.B52   1991
220.6—dc20   91-27210
                                                       CIP

This book is printed on acid-free paper.

Printed in the United States of America.

10 9 8 7 6 5 4 3 2 1

The Pilgrim Press, Cleveland, Ohio

Contents

Preface   vii
Abbreviations   xi
Contributors   xv

Part One: Socio-Literary Readings in the Hebrew Bible

1. Psalms 9–10: A Counter to Conventional Social Reality   3
   Walter Brueggemann
2. What's So Strange About the Strange Woman?   17
   Claudia V. Camp
3. Psalm 139   33
   Robert B. Coote
4. "To Her Mother's House": Considering a Counterpart to the
   Israelite *Bêt 'āb*   39
   Carol Meyers
5. Micah—A Revolutionary   53
   George V. Pixley
6. "Enemies" and the Politics of Prayer in the Book of Psalms   61
   Gerald T. Sheppard
7. Exegetical Storytelling: Liberation of the Traditions
   from the Text   83
   Minka Shura Sprague

Part Two: The Bible in Comparative Perspectives

8. Israelite Religion and the Faith of Israel's Daughters:
   Reflections on Gender and Religious Definition   97
   Phyllis A. Bird

9. Prometheus, the Servant of Yahweh, Jesus: Legitimation and
   Repression in the Heritage of Persian Imperialism   109
   John Pairman Brown
10. Debt Easement in Israelite History and Tradition   127
   Marvin L. Chaney
11. Why is Anat a Warrior and Hunter?   141
   Peggy L. Day
12. The Evil Eye in the First Testament: The Ecology and Culture
   of a Pervasive Belief   147
   John H. Elliott
13. The Deuteronomic Law Code and the Politics of State
   Centralization   161
   Naomi Steinberg

Part Three: The Theory and Praxis of Biblical Scholarship

14. Revolutions in Reading the Bible   173
   Lee Cormie
15. Unresolved Issues in the Early History of Israel: Toward a
   Synthesis of Archaeological and Textual Reconstructions   195
   William G. Dever
16. New Constructs in Social World Studies   209
   James W. Flanagan
17. Sociological Criticism and Its Relation to Political and Social
   Hermeneutics: With a Special Look at Biblical
   Hermeneutics in South African Liberation Theology   225
   Frank S. Frick
18. Feminism and "Mode of Production" in Ancient Israel:
   Search for a Method   239
   David Jobling
19. Interpretation: Reading, Abduction, Metaphor   253
   Bruce J. Malina
20. Bible and Liberation in South Africa in the 1980s: Toward an
   Antipopulist Reading of the Bible   267
   Itumeleng J. Mosala
21. Mark's Gospel in the Inner City   275
   John J. Vincent

The Writings of Norman K. Gottwald   291

Notes   297

Preface

In 1979, there burst upon the world of biblical scholarship a book entitled *The Tribes of Yahweh*.[1] It was not like other books in the field. It was over nine hundred pages long, a scope usually reserved for introductions and commentaries of German provenance. Its subtitle called it a "Sociology," and it applied social-scientific method to the Bible with a seriousness unequaled since Max Weber. In its early pages, it raised the issue of "the social-class identity of the biblical scholar,"[2] suggesting that the neglect of sociology as a historical tool had everything to do with modern sociology—the sociology of learning in Western society, including the church. It systematically addressed feminist issues—not only the roles of women in early Israel, but also the problem of pronouns for God in scholarly writing. And it used for its dedication "an anonymous tribute to the people of Vietnam."[3] Nor did this book, which a prominent reviewer (one of our contributors) was to hail as one of the three main watersheds, after Julius Wellhausen and W. F. Albright, in modern biblical scholarship,[4] come from any of the usual publishers in the field. Rather, it came from the publishing arm of a Roman Catholic mission associated mainly with liberation theology.

In an interview soon after the publication, the author, Norman K. Gottwald, explained: "I came to write it out of my own social experience, growing up as a protected intellectual, and then thrown into the Civil Rights movement of the sixties and the protest against the war in Vietnam. Most of the religion I knew wasn't addressing those realities; I suspected that biblical religion had been different."[5] This explains not only the book's dedication and the circumstances of its publication, but also the fact that at that time Gottwald had for several years not held a regular, full-time teaching appointment. His was a new kind of scholarship that not only *accompanied* political engagement—many scholars were thus engaged in the civil rights and Vietnam times—but was at every level, in content, aims, and style, a *continuation* of that engagement. And even in 1979, the field gave little sign of being ready for it.

When Norman did, shortly thereafter, take up the permanent position he now occupies, as professor of biblical studies at New York Theological Seminary, it was not a typical one. One of our contributors expresses wonder

> that biblical scholarship's outstanding originator and theoretician in asserting the power of social, economic, and political influence in the time of scripture, has given himself to teaching, research, and fellow-laboring alongside workers in the seminary which as much as anywhere has committed itself to the city.[6]

New York Theological Seminary devotes itself to servicing urban ministry largely to nonwhite communities, and in a variety of languages. The majority of Norman's students are active ministers in the inner city. This work has led to extensive involvement, around the world, in the problems of ministry. Norman's scholarship is still a continuation of his political engagement.

The course of that scholarship, over nearly four decades, can be assessed from his bibliography (included at the end of this book). But in addition to his published works, other scholarly activities should be noted. In the major learned societies, especially the Society of Biblical Literature, he has been instrumental, as one of the main organizers of a series of working groups and seminars, in bringing social-scientific approaches to the center of scholarly activity. On a more local scale, he has taken initiative in the formation of influential groups of scholars in the Bay Area in the 1970s and in New York City in the 1980s. He has also served editorially on the boards of *Semeia* and of Almond Press's "The Social World of Biblical Antiquity" series.

When Norman, at the request of the late and greatly lamented John Hollar, of Fortress Press, wrote an introduction to the Hebrew Bible, he called it "A Socio-Literary Introduction,"[7] and this name encapsulates what has clearly been the major turn in his more recent work. That the book superbly rendered and advanced social-scientific work on the Bible was no surprise. More surprising was the care and thoroughness with which Norman took account of recent contributions to the *literary* study of the Bible. The literary and the social-scientific were, he saw, the two emerging paradigms in biblical studies, each in its own way challenging the dominance of historical criticism, and their articulation was a major agenda for the immediate future. "Exactly how," he asked, in an oft-quoted formulation, "does social reality inscribe itself in language and in literary creations?"[8] Several recent items in his bibliography indicate with what energy he has himself pursued this problematic.

Much has changed in biblical studies. The "drastic paradigm crisis"[9] that Norman diagnosed has become only more drastic, and some of its effects have been unsettling and hurtful. But it has also become exciting and stimulating, so that if our profession has become scarcely recognizable, it has also become much more personally and intellectually rewarding for many of us. In this transformation, the one we honor has had an enormous share. And it is not only we and our contributors who honor him. It is a happy and unanticipated coincidence for us who have prepared this book that its presentation coincides with the announcement of Norman's forth-coming presidency of the Society of Biblical Literature. What a change from the 1970s!

When we sent invitations to potential contributors, the most common response was, "He can't be anywhere near sixty-five yet!" Given the uncommon productivity and stress of his career, the years certainly seem to sit lightly on him. Perhaps staying on the cutting edge is a prescription for youthfulness! Through all, he has retained his humor and *Mensch-lichkeit*. In addition to being a revered leader and rewarding colleague, he is a genial friend. Long may he continue as all three! Thanks for everything, Norm!

DAVID JOBLING
PEGGY L. DAY
GERALD T. SHEPPARD

Abbreviations

With a few additions, abbreviations are the same as those given in *JBL* 107 (1988) 583–96. Any not included here should be sought there (e.g., names of biblical books, p. 584, or of Qumran scrolls, p. 585). Abbreviations of ancient sources are standard in the various fields (e.g., classics); cf. the remarks in *JBL* (p. 581).

AAR   American Academy of Religion
AB   Anchor Bible
AJA   *American Journal of Archaeology*
AJP   *American Journal of Philology*
AJSL   *American Journal of Semitic Languages and Literature*
AMEC   African Methodist Episcopal Church
ANEP   J. B. Pritchard (ed.), *The Ancient Near East in Pictures Relating to the Old Testament* (2nd ed.)
ANET   J. B. Pritchard (ed.), *Ancient Near Eastern Texts Relating to the Old Testament* (3rd ed.)
APOT   R. H. Charles (ed.), *Apocrypha and Pseudepigrapha of the Old Testament*
ASOR   American Schools of Oriental Research
b.   Babylonian Talmud
BA   *Biblical Archaeologist*
BAR   *Biblical Archaeologist Reader*
BARev   *Biblical Archaeology Review*
BASOR   *Bulletin of the American Schools of Oriental Research*

BCE	Before the Christian Era (cf. BC)
BWANT	Beihefte zur Wissenschaft vom Alten und Neuen Testament
BZ	*Biblische Zeitschrift* (new series)
BZAW	Beihefte zur *ZAW*
CAD	*The Assyrian Dictionary of the Oriental Institute of the University of Chicago*
CAH	*Cambridge Ancient History* (3rd ed.)
CBQ	*Catholic Biblical Quarterly*
CBQMS	Catholic Biblical Quarterly, Monograph Series
CE	Christian Era (cf. AD)
CIC	Corpus Iuris Ciuilis
CP	*Classical Philology*
Dtr	Deuteronom(ist)ic Historian
EI	*Eretz Israel*
ExpT	*Expository Times*
FGH	F. Jacoby, *Die Fragmente der griechischen Historiker*
FOTL	Forms of Old Testament Literature
GCS	Die griechischen christlichen Schriftsteller
Heb	Hebrew (versification of the Hebrew text, where it differs from the English)
HSM	Harvard Semitic Monographs
HTR	*Harvard Theological Review*
HUCA	Hebrew Union College Annual
IB	*Interpreter's Bible*
ICC	*International Critical Commentary*
ICT	Institute for Contextual Theology (South Africa)
IDB	G. A. Buttrick (ed.), *The Interpreter's Dictionary of the Bible*
IDBSup	Supplementary volume to *IDB*
IEJ	*Israel Exploration Journal*
Int	*Interpretation*
JAAR	*Journal of the American Academy of Religion*
JAC	*Jahrbuch für Antike und Christentum*
JAOS	*Journal of the American Oriental Society*
JB	Jerusalem Bible
JBL	*Journal of Biblical Literature*
JCS	*Journal of Cuneiform Studies*
JE	*Jewish Encyclopedia*
JFSR	*Journal of Feminist Studies in Religion*
JJS	*Journal of Jewish Studies*
JNES	*Journal of Near Eastern Studies*
JNSL	*Journal of Northwest Semitic Languages*

JPSV	Jewish Publication Society Version
JR	*Journal of Religion*
JRS	*Journal of Roman Studies*
JSOT	*Journal for the Study of the Old Testament*
JSOTSup	*JSOT* Supplements
JTS	*Journal of Theological Studies* (new series)
KAI	H. Donner and W. Röllig, *Kanaanäische und aramäische Inschriften* (3 vols.)
Kent	R. G. Kent, *Old Persian: Grammar, Texts, Lexicon* (2nd ed.)
KJV	King James Version
KTU	M. Dietrich, O. Loretz, J. Sanmartin, *Die Keilalphabetischen Texte aus Ugarit*
LXX	Septuagint
m.	Mishnah
ms(s).	Manuscript(s)
MT	Masoretic Text
MVAG	Mitteilungen der vorderasiatisch-ägyptischen Gesellschaft
n(n).	Note(s)
NAB	New American Bible
NEB	New English Bible
NRSV	New Revised Standard Version
OGIS	W. Dittenberger, *Orientis Graeci Inscriptiones Selectae*
OTL	Old Testament Library
OTS	*Oudtestamentische Studiën*
RAC	*Reallexikon für Antike und Christentum*
RB	*Revue biblique*
REB	Revised English Bible
RIDA	*Revue internationale des droits de l'antiquité*
RSV	Revised Standard Version
SBL	Society of Biblical Literature
SBLDS	SBL Dissertation Series
SBLSP	*Society of Biblical Literature Seminar Papers*
SBT	Studies in Biblical Theology
TBü	Theologische Bücherei
TDNT	G. Kittel and G. Friedrich (ed.), *Theological Dictionary of the New Testament*
TDOT	G. J. Botterweck and H. Ringgren (ed.), *Theological Dictionary of the Old Testament*
TEV	Today's English Version
TO	A. Caquot *et al.*, *Textes ougaritiques* (2 vols.)
TS	*Theological Studies*

UF	*Ugarit-Forschungen*
v(v).	Verse(s)
Vg	Vulgate
VT	*Vetus Testamentum*
VTSup	Vetus Testamentum Supplements
WMANT	Wissenschaftliche Monographien zum Alten und Neuen Testament
ZAW	*Zeitschrift für die alttestamentliche Wissenschaft*
ZTK	Zeitschrift für Theologie und Kirche
//	Synoptic Gospel parallels

Contributors

Phyllis A. Bird is Associate Professor of Old Testament Interpretation at Garrett-Evangelical Theological Seminary, Evanston, Illinois.

John Pairman Brown is retired. He formerly taught at the American University of Beirut and was Executive Director of the Northern California Ecumenical Council.

Walter Brueggemann is William P. McPheeters Professor of Old Testament at Columbia Theological Seminary, Decatur, Georgia.

Claudia V. Camp is Associate Professor of Religion at Texas Christian University, Fort Worth, Texas.

Marvin L. Chaney is Nathaniel Gray Professor of Hebrew Exegesis and Old Testament at San Francisco Theological Seminary, San Anselmo, and at the Graduate Theological Union, Berkeley, California.

Robert B. Coote is Professor of Old Testament at San Francisco Theological Seminary, San Anselmo, and at the Graduate Theological Union, Berkeley, California.

Lee Cormie teaches in the Faculty of Theology, St. Michael's College, and in the Toronto School of Theology, Toronto, Ontario.

PEGGY L. DAY is Associate Professor of Religious Studies, University of Winnipeg, Manitoba.

WILLIAM G. DEVER is Professor of Near Eastern Archaeology and Anthropology and Head of the Near Eastern Studies Department at the University of Arizona, Tucson.

JOHN H. ELLIOTT is Professor of Theology and Religious Studies and Director of the Honors Program in the Humanities at the University of San Francisco, San Francisco, California.

JAMES W. FLANAGAN is Archbishop Paul J. Hallinan Professor of Catholic Studies in the Department of Religion, Case Western Reserve University, Cleveland, Ohio.

FRANK S. FRICK is Professor of Religious Studies at Albion College, Albion, Michigan.

DAVID JOBLING is Professor of Old Testament Language and Literature at St. Andrew's College, Saskatoon, Saskatchewan.

BRUCE J. MALINA is Professor in the Department of Theology at Creighton University, Omaha, Nebraska.

CAROL MEYERS is Professor of Biblical Studies and Archaeology in the Religion Department, Duke University, Durham, North Carolina.

ITUMELENG J. MOSALA is Professor of Old Testament and Black Theology at the University of Cape Town, South Africa, and is currently Research Fellow and Tutor at Wesley House, Cambridge, England.

GEORGE V. PIXLEY is Professor of Bible at the Seminario Teológico Bautista, Managua, Nicaragua.

GERALD T. SHEPPARD is Professor of Old Testament Literature and Exegesis at Emmanuel College, University of Toronto, Toronto, Ontario.

MINKA SHURA SPRAGUE is Professor of New Testament and Biblical Languages at New York Theological Seminary, New York City.

Naomi Steinberg is Assistant Professor of Hebrew Bible at DePaul University, Chicago, Illinois.

John J. Vincent is Director of the Urban Theology Unit, Sheffield, England.

The Bible and
the Politics
of Exegesis

PART ONE

Socio-Literary Readings in the Hebrew Bible

1   *Psalms 9–10*

A Counter to Conventional Social Reality

Walter Brueggemann

Norman Gottwald's scholarship has impinged upon our common work in crucial ways. He has placed us all in his debt, including those who do not easily follow his lead. I am pleased to register my debt through this essay. Two aspects of Gottwald's work have been in my purview for this essay. First, Gottwald has well argued that acceptance of "the final form of the text" (as in canon criticism) does not preclude a social analysis of the text, but requires it, so that we can attend to the interest and disputes that have received canonical articulation.[1] Second, Gottwald has shown that scriptural texts, like all texts, grow out of socio-economic-political reality and voice those realities, and cannot be understood apart from those realities.[2] He has been criticized (rightly in my judgment) for not treating text and social reality in a more dialectical fashion; he has, nonetheless, taught us critical lessons concerning the reality-base of a textual voice. In this essay, I will propose a rereading of Psalms 9–10 that is, in my judgment, decisively illuminated by Gottwald's scholarship.

I

Psalms 9–10 together constitute an acrostic poem, though in the middle section the acrostic is somewhat disturbed.[3] The acrostic is nonetheless clear enough, so that these psalms constitute a single poem (as is reflected in the LXX numbering). Though the psalm is conventionally identified as a Song of Thanksgiving, it is in fact much more complicated.[4] I will argue that these psalms together constitute the conflicted conversation that arises inevitably in an unequally organized society where the reality of Yahweh is taken into account. That conflicted conversation, however, is here presented from the perspective of the one who nowhere else is permitted any social voice.[5]

The poem of Psalms 9–10 begins as a Song of Thanksgiving that describes and celebrates a past powerful deliverance wrought by God (9:2–17). In this unit, the speaker has found an assertive voice, using a first person pronoun five times (vv. 2–3),[6] and returning to the same self-assertion twice more (v. 15).[7] The speaker's powerful voice both celebrates a new situation already in hand (vv. 2–3) and anticipates a new situation yet to be enacted by God (v. 15).

The one addressed in these verses, indeed the true subject of the song, is Yahweh. In vv. 4–7, Yahweh is directly addressed six times, each time as the subject of a powerful, active verb that describes Yahweh's action already witnessed by the speaker.[8] The actions for which Yahweh is celebrated are of two kinds. On the one hand, there are various destructive actions: "destroyed, blotted out, rooted out." On the other hand, the more powerful cluster of active verbs concerns judicial activity: "maintained my just cause," "gave righteous judgment," and perhaps "rebuked." It may be that even the destructive actions credited to God are done by court decree, for a verdict in court may indeed "blot out" and "root out," that is, render publicly null and void.[9] Thus the accumulation of these verbs may celebrate a day the speaker had in court, a day of total vindication.

This sense of thanksgiving is reinforced in more formal, distanced language in vv. 8–9, wherein Yahweh is described in the third person with the five terms *mišpāt*, *špṭ*, *ṣedeq*, *dyn*, and *měšārîm*. Thus the speaker celebrates the fact that in court, Yahweh is not only an equitable judge, but is a free agent who is not in the pocket of the wicked; God is able to take independent action, even against the presumably strong one in behalf of the weak ones.[10] Westermann has shown that the complaint psalm characteristically involves three parties.[11] In this poem, the decisive party is Yahweh, who governs powerfully and equitably. Yahweh is the one who takes all the decisive actions. It is Yahweh, executor of judgment, whose actions determine the social position and possibility of the other two parties. The speaker's counterpart, the "enemy" (vv. 4, 7) (who is the helpless "outsider" to this textual world) is variously identified as "the nations" (vv. 6, 16, 18), the "wicked" (plural, v. 18), and the "wicked" (singular, vv. 6, 17). There seems to be no stable identity of the "enemy" in this poem, as indeed there is not generally.[12] In any case, the "enemy" is not an active, vocal party to this poem; the poem does its best, as we shall see, to commit an act of social nullification of the enemy. The poem is crafted to exclude the enemy from any significant action and any determinative speech. The poem intends to render the "enemy" impotent and irrelevant.

We gain our best clue to who the "wicked" might be if we notice the identity of the third party, presumably the one who speaks in the poem, the "I" of vv. 2–3, 15. Five terms are used to describe the speaker and the ones with whom the speaker identifies and on whose behalf the poem is rendered. This is the voice of the "oppressed" (*dak*, v. 10), the "poor, afflicted" (*'ănāwîm* or *'ăniyyîm*, vv. 13, 19), the "one who suffers" (*'ŏnî*, v. 14), and the "needy" (*'ebyôn*, v. 19). This cluster of words makes clear that the speaker (and those for whom the speaker speaks) are the socially vulnerable and marginal. Thus the poem is the voice of the marginated, the ones without power, resources, or authority who are vulnerable in the face of their adversaries. They have, however, found recourse in the juridical reliability of Yahweh, whose verdicts make unequal social relationships viable. It is only in this courtroom under the governance of Yahweh that the usual power relations between the strong and the weak are interrupted, transformed, and rectified, so that the weak and marginal speak here as they are permitted to speak nowhere else.

The poem is intentional and powerful in building a picture of social reality by clustering pejorative terms. On the one hand, there are "enemies, nations, wicked." On the other hand are the "oppressed, afflicted, suffering, needy, and poor." Thus the psalm deftly proposes a disputatious framing of social reality and social power. Given that framing, the poem asserts that it is only in the court of Yahweh that the second party gets a fair hearing against the first, stronger party that usually dominates court proceedings. That is a passionate theological affirmation. When one asks, however, where this peculiar court of Yahweh is convened that renders such unusual and equitable verdicts, the answer is, this odd court is convened *in the poem* and *only in the poem*. This is what makes the poem so urgent. It becomes a script and practice of counter social reality that does not seem to pertain outside the poem. This does not make the poem untrue. It only makes the poem more urgent. The thanksgiving voiced in these verses concerns precisely distorted (even if routine) social relations that have been rectified by the reality of Yahweh. The season of this alternative court extends, in the first instance, only through the life span of this voiced poem. When the poem ends, this odd court is adjourned.

II

The guarantee of this surprisingly rectified mode of social relations depends on the resolve, attentiveness, and faithfulness of Yahweh, without whom the usual exploitative patterns of social relations would not be broken. In v. 13, there is a pivotal juxtaposition of "remember" (*zkr*) and "forget" (*škḥ*). Everything turns on the assurance, here given vigorous affirmation, that God *remembers* and does not *forget*. The pronominal object of *zkr* is presumably Yahweh's "saving deeds" (*ǎlîlôt* in v. 12, cf. *niplā'ôt* in v. 2). In our context, these "saving deeds" perhaps refer to legal precedents whereby Yahweh has overturned conventional court rules that favor the strong. Yahweh remembers those precedents and knows how to continue to act in the same ways. Conversely, "forget" has as its object the cry of affliction that Yahweh has heard and continues to heed and honor. This parallelism thus affirms what is most crucial about Yahweh for this speaker:

> *saving deeds* are "remembered,"
> *cries of the afflicted* are "not forgotten."

These two are interrelated, for it is the *cries* of wretchedness that evoke the *deeds* of saving.[13]

The verb *zkr* is used negatively in v. 7; Yahweh has destroyed the memory of the enemy. Yahweh is clear concerning what is to be remembered. The enemy and their cities have been nullified; that is, the names are blotted out, removed from public identity and from membership in the community (v. 6). They are made to be socially irrelevant, declared by the court to be null and void. Conversely, the term "forget" is used again in v. 19 positively. The needy are not forgotten.

Verse 19 seems to be a careful, positive counterpart to the negative assertion of v. 7. Whereas the memory of the strong enemy is nullified (v. 7), the needy are not forgotten but remembered (v. 19). Both verses, v. 7 (negatively) and v. 19 (positively), use the adverb *neṣaḥ*, but to contrasting effect. The enemy is voided *lāneṣaḥ*; the poor are not forgotten *lāneṣaḥ*. Both verses use the verb *'bd*, one negatively and one positively. The memory of the enemy has perished (*'bd*, v. 7); the hope of the poor does not perish (*'bd*, v. 19). The uses of *zkr* (vv. 7, 13) and of *škḥ* (vv. 13, 19) portray a social reversal whereby the powerful wicked have been nullified and the marginal have been given a guaranteed social position. Both received a future that is improbable in normal social transactions. The thanksgiving of vv. 2–19 celebrates a social inversion made possible because of Yahweh, but visible and concrete in the world of politics and economics, made visible by this daring poem. There is much for which to give thanks. Thus the genre of Thanksgiving Song becomes a vehicle for articulating a radically different mode of social relationship. The intent is not simply thanksgiving, but the voicing of new modes of social power.

III

The psalm, of course, does not end at v. 19, but moves into more interesting and agitated speech. Already in vv. 14–15, the confidence of the Song of Thanksgiving has begun to erode. The verdict of Yahweh, decisive as it is, is not enduring. The power of the wicked ("the enemy," "the nations") is enormously resilient. One might have thought, and Yahweh might have intended, that the affirmation of vv. 8–9 would put an end to the destructive work of the wicked. Our own social experience, however, reminds us that the defeated, delegitimated forces of exploitation have a remarkable way of regrouping and reemerging with power and as threat.[14] It is because of that reemergence that the Song of Thanksgiving of vv. 2–19 turns to fresh and urgent appeal to Yahweh.

The petition of v. 14 is not yet very intense, and vv. 14–15 already assume a good resolution of the conflict that will culminate in praise.[15] The petition, however, becomes much more urgent in 9:20—10:2. It is as though the verdicts and assurances of 9:2–19 have not occurred, and the poor are again deeply at risk. Thus the voice of *thanksgiving* gives way to the voice of urgent *petition*. In 9:19 the poor have enormous hope. By 10:2, however, the same poor are in deep jeopardy, because the wicked (10:2, singular) has reappeared in the poem, and in the social reality of the speaker. This urgent petition begins with a powerful summons to God: "Arise!" The tone of the imperative suggests that the confident and reassuring verdicts of the remembered past have been discarded by the judge who made them.

The motivation to support that strong imperative is presented in a chiasm (vv. 20–21). In vv. 20–21 are two imperatives, "judge" (in *niphal*) and "put in fear." The petition asks Yahweh to do again what was earlier celebrated, to pursue and execute judgment against the exploiters. The two verbs are framed by the double use of *'enôš* with jussive verbs. That is, the ones critiqued are only human. They have therefore no right to dominate social relations. The prayer is that the threatening ones would be returned to their proper, modest social position, for they have forgotten that position and have claimed for themselves power, authority, privilege, and preeminence that never legitimately belongs to human persons.[16]

The appeal to Yahweh in 10:1 contrasts the present conduct of Yahweh with the previously celebrated conduct of Yahweh. In 9:10 Yahweh was a "stronghold in times of trouble." Now in 10:1, the same phrase is used to assert that Yahweh is absent in times of trouble; when Yahweh is absent, the wicked will devour the poor. Everything depends on Yahweh's presence, and now Yahweh is hidden. In 10:1 "stand afar off" (*běrāhôq*, which has no precise parallel in 9:9) may serve as a contrast to "not forsaken" (v. 11). That is, the God who is *afar off* has indeed forsaken the poor when they are in jeopardy. Thus both lines of 10:1 voice a strong contrast to the assurance of 9:10–11. In the contrast between 9:10–11 and 10:1, the poem closely connects *actual social relations* and the *theological reality* of God's presence or absence. The prospect for the well-being of the vulnerable in social relations depends on the initiative, attentiveness, and activity of Yahweh. Without Yahweh, the poor and afflicted are without an avenger (v. 13) and have no hope (v. 19), for "man" prevails (9:20). By 10:2, the poem has made clear that everything in social relations depends on the presence or absence of Yahweh. When Yahweh is absent, social relations will take their inevitably destructive course, which the weak cannot resist. When Yahweh is present, as Yahweh may be because of urgent petition, conventional destructive relations are overcome and new social possibilities may emerge.

IV

In 10:3–9, the psalm takes a curious and unexpected turn. The previously identified but silent adversary is permitted to speak. A new voice speaks, one usually not heard in such a psalm, and certainly not heard heretofore in this psalm. It is the voice of the "wicked" (singular), the one who previously has been "enemy, nations, wicked" (plural).

The wicked is permitted to say and forced to say what he might prefer not to say out loud. He is required to speak what he truly intends. His actions are characteristically indirect, hiding his true intentions in ideological self-justification. Now his speech, directly quoted, goes behind the pretense to speak the unvarnished truth.[17] We are given three alleged quotes from the wicked:

(1) "There is no God" (v. 4). This statement is not presented as a direct quote, but the verbs in v. 3 ("boast," *hll*; "curse," *brk*; "renounce," *n's*) suggest self-asserting speech.[18] The wicked one acts through speech.[19]

(2) "He thinks in his heart, 'I shall not be moved;[20] throughout all generations I shall not meet adversity' " (v.6).

(3) "He says in his heart, 'Thou wilt not call to account' " (v.13, cf. v. 4).

All three statements are dismissals of God and assertions of self-sufficiency and autonomy. The speaker of these lines imagines he is free to do whatever he wants.

We have seen in 9:2–19 that social relations are powerfully different because Yahweh has decisively intervened as a third party. These statements attributed to the "wicked" are statements that dismiss that third party as an effective player in the drama of social interaction. The statements are insistences that social relations include only two parties, the wicked and the weak. There is no third party to intervene or to disrupt that simple, direct, and predictable transaction. The subject of these statements is "God." The intent, however, is to articulate a social reality without the inconvenient theological element of Yahweh.

We notice that all three statements are either alleged or implied. That is, they are not and do not claim to be direct, actually verbalized statements, for no one would have dared to speak so. In fact, they are not speeches or claims made by the wicked. They are rather statements attributed to the wicked but made by someone else. They are assigned and attributed speeches. Thus, in the rhetoric of this psalm, the wicked are not in fact permitted to speak for themselves but are at the mercy of those who seize the chance to speak for them. This remarkable rhetoric strategy of the psalmist places the wicked in an odd and unusual circumstance. The wicked (who are also the strong) are accustomed to speaking for themselves so that they may carefully choose what they say and what they deliberately withhold—what they want to leave unsaid. That is, their selective, self-serving speech can keep them from telling the truth about their social intentions.

Moreover, because the wicked are also the strong, the wicked are accustomed not only to speaking for themselves; they also determine when the weak are permitted to speak and what they are permitted to say. Characteristically, the wicked (= strong) control social conversations. They govern not only their own speech, but also the speech of their fragile, intimidated adversaries.

What has happened in this poem is that the wicked have lost their control of the social conversation. They no longer decide what will be uttered or who will speak; now, perhaps for the first time, the strong are at the mercy of the weak, who are free to construe conflicted social dynamics in a very different way. Instead of the usual self-justifying, mystifying ideology of the wicked, we now get a critical exposé of the actions and intentions of the wicked. Their actual intent is now placed in their own mouths as a harsh self-indictment.

The alleged statements of the wicked (in vv. 4, 6, 13) are surrounded by rhetoric that contextualizes their alleged statements, and by observed behavior that supports the adversarial construal of the speech and intent of the wicked by the weak.

The supportive rhetoric is of two kinds. First, there is a series of words alluding to speech: "boast" (*hll*), "curse" (*brk*), "renounce" (*n's*) (v. 3); "puff" (*pyḥ*, v. 5); "curse" (*'lh*), "deceit" (*mirmâ*), "tongue of mischief and iniquity" (v. 7). This cluster of words suggests that the wicked are so strong and influential that they can manipulate social processes, social symbols, social communication, and social decision making in ways that further victimize the weak.[21] They have social power to arrange social relations to their own advantage.

Second, destructive speech is matched by their usurpatious actions. Thus there are these phrases, "greedy for gain" (v. 3), "sits in ambush," "murder the innocent," "watch for the hapless" (v. 8); "lurks in secret," "lurks that he may seize," "seizes the poor" (v. 9). The picture that emerges is of rapacious violence.

In this dramatic portrayal of the wicked, we have a convergence of three facts that are held together by the daring rhetoric of the poet: (1) the visible *exercise of destructive social relations in the economic realm*, (2) the *exercise of speech* as the primary way in which social power is destructively manipulated, and (3) an implicit *theological disclaimer* that removes Yahweh from the world of social reality. Violent action, manipulative speech, and nullification of God work together to permit a certain kind of social world in which the powerful are free to do what they want for their own interest. This convergence is not an occasional act of brutality, but is a systemic, ideological practice of perverse social relations. The violent acts and manipulative speech are possible only when social reality is reduced to only two unequal partners. When there are only two, the weak have no chance against the ruthless strong.

V

The world as socially ordered in 10:3–9 is no doubt a polemical construal, but it is not an unknown or unrecognizable world. It is a world that everywhere exists when social relations involve only these two partners. In that brutalizing world, the wicked do not need to proceed by overt acts of ambush, lurking, and seizing. Over time, they are able to proceed by the power of their ideology.[22] When that ideology has nullified God, so that only two parties are left, it is "natural" and "obvious" that symbiosis of the power of the strong and the vulnerability of the weak is ordinary, permanent, and eventually normative. Indeed, in the reduced world it is the only imaginable mode of social relations; that is, the power of the strong controls the weak. The ideology of the strong assaults the weak until the victims of wrong social relations accept the world as defined by the perpetrators.[23] Thus unchallenged power is eventually accepted as legitimate.

That mode of social relations prevails almost everywhere—except in this psalm and in like assertions of counterreality. In such assertions, the ideology of the wicked is given full, albeit hostile, voicing in order that the ideology of the strong may be exposed, critiqued, and overthrown. Thus I propose that vv. 3–9, when taken alone, are a fairly standard script, albeit kept invisible and unvoiced for uncritical social relations. This psalm is an extraordinary act of counterspeech and counterpower. It seizes the conventional, usually unquestioned, script of the strong, states it, mocks it, and overrides it, so that the psalm itself is a moment of social inversion and even social control for those who normally are left without speech and without power.

There can hardly be any doubt whose voice sounds in this psalm. It is the voice of the oppressed, the afflicted, the suffering, the needy, the poor, who are endlessly pursued until they cease to exist. Although usually denied voice, they nonetheless speak boldly in this psalm. They have finally, through this poem, gained the floor, and they speak without interruption. Indeed, they will not let anyone else speak, for they know that if the wicked begin to speak, their ideology will again usurp social relations. The marginal have spoken first in celebration of the "third party" (Yahweh) who changes social relations (9:2–19). Then they have issued a plea for the continued presence of that third party (9:20–10:3). Then they have mockingly reiterated the speech of the powerful, who reduce social relations to two parties and by their speech eliminate the dangerous third party (10:3–9).

After their mocking attribution of speech to the strong, the weak ones now return to their own situation and their own social insistence (10:10–18). In vv. 10–11, the voice of the poor candidly reports their intimidated response to the ideological onslaught of the wicked. The marginal had almost succumbed to the assertions and definitions of the wicked. That is, they had well-nigh accepted the portrayal of social reality offered by the wicked in 10:3–9 (cf. Ps 73:10–14). The poor had nearly yielded to the self-serving ideology of the wicked. The poor experienced a failure of nerve, and the courageous rhetoric of 9:2–19 was almost abandoned. The poor are crushed and fallen, that is, ready to submit without a struggle.

We have seen the arrogant wicked who "thinks in his heart," who has evil purposes he wants kept hidden. In v. 11, we now are permitted access to the hidden thinking of the vulnerable. The dispute between the wicked and the poor concerns the reality of God. What is "hidden" has to do with the autonomy of the powerful and the despair of the poor. The latter think:

> God has forgotten,
> God has hidden his face,
> God will never see it. (v. 11)

The first phrase echoes 9:19, only now that vigorous, confident assertion has become a despairing resignation. What was vigorously affirmed in

9:19 is now reluctantly abandoned. The wicked have won the battle for the imagination, and the thoughts of the poor have come to mirror and replicate the thoughts of the wicked.[24] The wicked have imagined God away, and the poor now accept that verdict. The world without God (who is hidden, v. 11, cf. v. 1) is a hopeless world for the poor. The poor accept the ideology of the powerful.

In v. 12, however, the psalm takes a most unexpected turn. The psalm might have ended in v. 11 in defeat and resignation. Verse 12, however, is discontinuous from the forlornness of v. 11. The powerful petition of vv. 12–13 must have been a surprise to the wicked, who had counted on the resignation of their victims in vv. 10–11. It must equally have been a surprise to the poor, who, in the same verses, had indeed lost hope. Indeed, the imperative of v. 12 is an inexplicable non sequitur after vv. 10–11.

That, however, is exactly the work of the psalm as a political act. It is the psalm as a voice of inexplicable hope, surely rooted in an unquenchable sense of Yahweh as a third party in social relations, that in its utterance creates a new social possibility that did not exist before or outside this utterance. It is the political work of the poet, by an act of daring rhetoric, to create a new social possibility by negating the dominant ideology of vv. 3–9 and by countering it with a liberated imperative.[25]

The imperative of v. 12 begins at the same place as did the imperative of 9:20: "Arise!" In 9:20, however, the imperative follows a statement of hope, a conviction of not being forgotten (9:19). Now, however, the same imperative follows an admission of hopelessness and a sense of being forgotten by God (10:10–11). The imperative of v. 12 is inexplicable, except as an act of political counterimagination rooted in theological passion.[26] Any other explanation of the unexpected imperative is perforce ruled out, because any other explanation seeks to accommodate the dominate ideology that the strong must prevail and that Yahweh is no social agent. Imaginative, liberated rhetoric precludes conventional explanations, primarily because this rhetoric arises outside the field of acceptable explanation and posits a genuine *novum*, new politically, rhetorically, and theologically.

The name of Yahweh is regularly on the lips of the speaker (9:2, 8, 10, 11, 12, 14, 20, 21, 10:1). That name has been absent in the speech of the wicked (10:3–9), who want to eliminate Yahweh politically and rhetorically.[27] The alleged rhetoric of the wicked speaks only of "God," who is easier to eliminate than is "Yahweh."[28] Now in v. 12, the name of Yahweh is again invoked as an active, decisive agent. In the remainder of the psalm, God is addressed directly, whereas the wicked speak of God only as a remote third party who is assumed not to be present to the conversation. In vv. 14–18, the address is completely to Yahweh. The rhetoric is saturated with "thou" (as in vv. 5–7); Yahweh is again a real agent who controls decisive verbs. The verbal form is matched by pronominal suffixes that place Yahweh at the center of the poem.

This passionate rhetoric waits on Yahweh to intrude decisively into skewed social relations, to act decisively against the wicked, who imagine they are autonomous. The object of God's concern is the afflicted (v. 12), the fatherless (v. 14), the meek (v. 17), the fatherless and oppressed (v. 18); that is, the socially marginal, powerless, and vulnerable. The hope of this voice is for justice. Appeal is made through a majestic political metaphor of enthronement, which echoes 9:8 (v. 16).

The text is a script for an alternative construal of social relations. In this script, Yahweh is an active agent. Moreover, by the end of the psalm, the wicked have been eliminated as an active force and are only the object of God's terrible intention (v. 15). The intrusion of Yahweh into social relationships decisively transforms the prospect of both the wicked and the poor.

This text is itself a practice of alternative politics. It is not mere wishful thinking, nor is it a description of what happened elsewhere. The psalm itself, each time it is boldly uttered in its criticism, polemic, celebration, and anticipation, is the place of redefined power relations.[29] In the rhetoric of this psalm, it is impossible to sort out what is theological (for Yahweh is a function of counterpolitics) and what is political (for social conflict is a function of Yahweh's purpose and presence).[30] Everything depends on the psalm as an act of political imagination. Without the psalm, Yahweh would never be present, and social relations would forever be the two-party transaction envisioned by the ideology of the wicked. The psalm creates a possibility for energy, courage, hope, and imagination that orders political power differently.

VI

This reading of Psalms 9–10 suggests that the (repeated) utterance of the poem is indeed a political act. The psalm asserts a shaping of the social process that contradicts the conventional ideology of the powerful. Although the psalms may indeed make a theological point—namely, that there is a God to whom to appeal against the nullification of that God by the ideology of the powerful—the practical, and I believe intended, effect of the psalm is to create a zone of social possibility outside the ideology of the powerful.

In this reading, we may reflect on three issues that derive from Gottwald's work. First, reading the "final form of the text" does not preclude but requires social scientific criticism in order to hear the text. What is canonized is not a settled consensus of theological affirmation, but a conflictual conversation in which the wicked and the poor hold contrary views of the reality and pertinence of God. It is the ongoing conflict that is canonized. Moreover, in canonical form, what is normative is that both sides of the social-theological dispute are rendered through the polemical, critical voice of the poor. In this reading of social reality, the poor not only (finally) have their say, but they also are permitted to construe the say of the wicked. This final form no doubt counters other "forms" of rendering social reality in which the decisive say is said by the powerful. The final form of the text thus protests against and offers an alternative to conventional social renderings. The convergence of "final form" and "countersay" is unavoidable in reading this text critically.

Second, the religious claim of the text arises from concrete socio-economic-political reality. One could hardly imagine this text being framed without direct and intimate connection to social reality. Indeed, any reading of the poem, such as genre analysis, that ignores this interface to social reality will likely miss hearing the psalm.[31] The God-question is situated exactly in a social dispute between the wicked who say "There is no God" and the poor who say "God has forgotten," and yet who voice an urgent imperative to that same God who has forgotten. The dispute about God is clearly not an innocuous religious question, but a life-and-death dispute about the nature of social reality, social power, and social possibility.

Third, however, Gottwald's characteristic premise that the text arises from social reality is, in my judgment, not sufficiently dialectical.[32] If the text only arises from social experience, I imagine that the text might have ended in 10:11, when the poor accept the claims of the wicked. Psalm 10:12, however, breaks beyond such social experience and voices a genuine *novum* that is the work of the text. Thus I suggest that not only does the text receive its voice of advocacy from social reality, but it also speaks its countervoice back against social reality in a way that contradicts accepted social reality and therefore social power. This latter maneuver makes clear that the text cannot be explained solely from social reality. There is no doubt that the text is a function of social experience. Gottwald allows, but does not greatly appreciate, that the text also leads reality, so that reality is a function of the text. How or why the text is capable of this free, unfettered say is beyond our work here. That question leads through the affirmation that the text is a political act, to questions of revelation and imagination.

This rereading is informed, as best I understand it, by questions Gottwald has taught us. In appraising his work, we may ask whether Gottwald's questions matter and whether we read differently because of his work. They do, and we do! As a result, the conventional ideology does not have a final say in this text, nor in our reading of it.

2 What's So Strange About the Strange Woman?

Claudia V. Camp

In spite of decades of scrutiny and several major publications,[1] the figure of the Strange Woman, the *'iššâ zārâ/'iššâ nokriyyâ*, of Proverbs 1–9 remains mysterious in terms of its significance within Israel's religious thought. Central to this mystery is the fact that the terms *zār/nokrî* have a variety of (sometimes overlapping) meanings in the Hebrew Bible. They can refer to persons of foreign nationality,[2] to persons who are outsiders to one's own family household,[3] to persons who are not members of the priestly caste,[4] and to deities or practices that fall outside the covenant relationship with YHWH.[5] The recognition that neither *zār* nor *nokrî* necessarily refers to a foreigner (in the literal sense of that word) has led to somewhat diverse scholarly conclusions on the sense of the terms. Humbert takes the rather minimalist perspective that in many cases they simply refer to another person; hence the *'iššâ zārâ* is "the wife of another." Snijders, on the other hand, finds a broad sense of deviation, faithlessness, and the unknown: the *'iššâ zārâ* represents all one must utterly avoid. Which of these connotations, or which combination of connotations, applies to Proverbs?

THE STRANGE WOMAN IN THE POSTEXILIC PERIOD

Several years ago, I proposed a social setting for the Strange Woman, along with Woman Wisdom, in early postexilic Palestine.[6] In this setting, I argued, the figure functioned symbolically, synthesizing several of the meanings of "strangeness" as they related to the ethos and worldview of the time. Two major issues were at stake for the returned exiles. One was

17

the need for family stability, in both the material and symbolic senses of that phrase; a functional family household was needed to accomplish the tasks of survival in a rebuilding society, *and* clear evidence of family identity was needed to establish claims to land and political power in a divided and contentious community. The second issue was the need to promulgate pure and proper worship of YHWH, unadulterated by foreign cultic practice. The two issues were closely linked, and indeed reached moments of crisis, because of the practice by some members of the *Golah* of marrying into foreign families. Foreign marriage (we will consider further on whether it was always a question of wives) not only brought the danger of foreign gods, but also threatened the stability of the authority structure: intermarriage for the sake of upward mobility could bring outside challenges to the power of the leadership group and, further, call into question whether this group could maintain power over the generations if inheritances passed out of the families of "pure Israelites." Especially relevant here are the railings of Ezra and Nehemiah against the *nāšîm nokriyyôt* (Ezra 10:2, 10–11, 17–18, 44; Neh 13:26–27). The punishment called for by these men was exclusion from the *qāhāl*, with its attendant forfeiture of property and civic status, a fate similar to that expressed by Prov 5:7–14 for assignation with the Strange Woman. There is also postexilic prophetic material that helps locate the Proverbs poems in the early postexilic period and, specifically, ties the problem of exogamy to the problem of the goddess cult. Zechariah 5:5–11 is a vision of a woman with a name sounding much like Asherah (*hāriš'â*, "Wickedness"), flown to Babylon in an ephah. Isaiah 57:3–13 depicts an adulteress/prostitute with some features similar to the Strange Woman in Proverbs. In terms reminiscent of Prov 2:17, Mal 2:10–12 enjoins against men divorcing the wives of their youth in favor of "the daughter of a foreign god."

Given this background, I suggested, the Strange Woman of Proverbs could be understood as a multivalent symbol. She is strange both in the sense of being an adulteress, whose breaking of social boundaries disrupts the stability of the family household, and in the sense of being a foreign national, who introduces the dangers of foreign worship and of ramification of power and wealth outside the community. The imagery of the adulteress predominates, however, in Proverbs 1–9, and thus I concluded that this connotation was the dominant and originary one in the figure's history, that it was the aspect of deviant sexuality that gave her the power to function as "an archetype of disorder at all levels of existence."[7] The interpretation of the *zārâ* as a "foreign woman" was, then, secondary, emerging significantly in the course of Nehemiah's and Ezra's marriage reforms.

In a recent paper, however, although arguing again forcefully for a postexilic *Sitz im Leben* for the Strange Woman, Joseph Blenkinsopp puts exclusive emphasis on the problem of exogamy as it relates to foreign worship as the *raison d'être* for this figure.[8] In addition to the biblical evidence already noted, Blenkinsopp also cites the attribution of the Proverbs' instructions to Solomon, whose single sin was "his addiction to foreign women (*nāšîm nokriyyôt*, 1 Kgs 11:1–8)." These led him to violate the deuteronomic law against intermarriage and fall prey to the inevitable consequence of syncretism (Deut 7:3–4). Proverbs 1–9 is thus formulated as "a cautionary instruction of Solomon based on his own experience." In Blenkinsopp's view, moreover, the prophetic material also leads to an identification of intermarriage and syncretism as Proverbs' sole concern. He claims that the prophets' focus was on goddess worship. Thus the description of the strange woman "corresponds closely to the 'orthodox' perception of non-Israelite cults involving a female deity," and trades on "the well-established connection in the Israelite tradition between sexual seduction and the allure of foreign cults." This fact, plus the analogy of the Proverbs instructions to Solomon's problem with foreign women, indicates to Blenkinsopp that foreign worship, not "sexual irregularity," is the primary issue.

There are a number of problems with limiting the meaning of *zārâ/nokriyyâ* to "foreign woman" in Proverbs, some of which may be adduced from the summary of my own argument for multivalence above and others to which I will draw attention below. There are, however, two larger critical issues at stake here that may call into question not only aspects of Blenkinsopp's argument, but some of my own previous work as well. The first is the problem of dating this material in the early postexilic period— the early fifth (my preference) to no later than the very early fourth century (the somewhat wider scope indicated by Blenkinsopp). If this dating is correct, then I think that Blenkinsopp's emphasis on the exogamy/foreign worship issue is indeed *apropos*; and there is no reason to assume, as I have done, that adultery was the originary and dominant connotation of the Strange Woman's strangeness. However, I would now like to suggest that I am seeing a concatenation of evidence that may force us toward an even later date for the Proverbs poems, at a time when intermarriage and idolatry were not the overriding concerns they were early on, as evidenced by Ben Sira's lack of attention to them. Although the evidence is not conclusive, it bears consideration as an alternative socio-historical reconstruction. Central to such a reconstruction is a revised understanding, that I will offer below, of the purported cultic activity of Woman Stranger in Proverbs 7.

A second difficulty lies in the fact that neither my own nor Blenkin-sopp's analysis has been sufficiently critical with respect to the imagery of sexuality. Thus, the full ideological range of the figure of Woman Stranger has yet to be articulated. An analysis of this figure as a metaphor, "woman is a stranger," will extend and refine both Blenkinsopp's and my own previous attempts at interpretation.

THE STRANGE WOMAN AND HER "CULT"

Two recent studies on "sacred prostitution" help to clarify the identity of the woman in Proverbs 7. Phyllis Bird's examination of harlotry as a metaphor in the Hebrew Bible[9] establishes conclusively that the zônâ (cf. 7:10; 6:26; 23:27) is never associated with cultic activity and that even qĕdēšâ means simply "consecrated woman" ("hierodule," in Bird's terminology), among whose varied functions may or may not have been ritual sex. Thus, she concludes, the association of sex and foreign cult in the Hebrew Bible is polemical, not necessarily descriptive, a piece of rhetoric initiated by Hosea.

Although Bird does not discuss Proverbs 7, extension of her argument allows us to draw two corollary inferences. First, we are relieved of any necessity to interpret the motives of the woman "dressed as a harlot" (šît zônâ, 7:10) as involving ritual sex for purposes of her own fertility or as an act of service to a goddess of love and/or fertility. On the other hand, given the fact that Hosea's polemical rhetoric became increasingly natural-ized over time in Israelite thought,[10] we cannot deny the possibility that the illicit sexuality rendered in Proverbs functioned, in part, as a cipher for the breaking of covenant faith with Yahweh. The question of whether ritual sex associated with a goddess cult was involved remains open to investigation.[11] Bird's careful analysis of the mixture of literal and allegor-ical sex-language in Hosea provides a model for interpreting the multiva-lence of the Strange Woman: not only must references to human sex acts be distinguished from theological rhetoric, but polemic that hurls ac-cusations of illicit sex must be distinguished from descriptions of actual activity.

In another recent article, Karel van der Toorn independently argues against the existence of "sacred prostitution" in ancient Israel.[12] He pro-poses a novel interpretation of the Strange Woman in Proverbs 7 as a basically honest Israelite matron who turns in desperation to an isolated act of harlotry in order to raise money to pay a vow to the Temple. Although I find this particular thesis implausible and his argumentation for it unpersuasive, van der Toorn's work does provide a clue that might explain the woman's reference to her sacrifices and vows in 7:14:

> Sacrifices of peace offerings (*zibḥê-šĕlāmîm*) are upon me;
> today I fulfill (*šillamtî*) my vows.

The question of how to translate the tense of *šillamtî* has been a crux for interpreters, the assumption being that if she has already offered her sacrifice (14a), but has yet to "fulfill her vows" (14b), then the implication is she has made a vow of ritual sex in honor of the goddess, which she plans to fulfill with the young man.

The significant move made by van der Toorn is to associate the vow instead with a typical act of Israelite piety,[13] which is, however, being funded by extraordinary means. Although, as I have noted, the scenario of a proper Israelite matron picking up some pocket change with a little harlotry on the side seems improbable, his instinct to associate Prov 7:14 with *biblical* rather than foreign ritual is attractive. Indeed, further investigation reveals that, in spite of widespread acceptance of some sort of fertility-worship theory,[14] this aspect of the Strange Woman's speech can be easily and well explained by reference to the biblical laws.

C. H. Toy noted long ago that the "sacrifices of peace offerings" (*zibḥê-šĕlāmîm*) is an instance of the sacrificial feasts described in Lev 7:11–21. "In the present instance its occasion is a vow which has just been fulfilled,"[15] which must be eaten on the day of the offering or the next (Lev 7:16). Unmentioned by Toy is the fact that the levitical law also requires that the flesh of the sacrifice be eaten by persons in the state of ritual cleanness (7:19–20). Thus, when the Strange Woman invites the young man for sexual activity to take place either the night before the sacrifice or the next night, between the two days of feasting, she invites him to commit with her a crime whose penalty is that "that person shall be cut off from his or her people" (*wĕnikrĕtâ hannepeš hahî' mē'ammêhā*, Lev 7:20).[16] Proverbs describes a similar fate for the man who associates with Woman Stranger (Prov 2:22; 5:14). As one of the wicked, he will be "cut off" (*yikkārētû*), in this case "from the land" (2:22), and in "utter ruin in the *qāhāl* and *'ēdâ*" (5:14), that is alienated from the people.[17]

The concept of ritual uncleanness associated with sexual activity—though here with a quite different motivation—is also found in the deuteronomic legislation, where the payment of a vow to the Temple with "the hire of a harlot (*'etnan zônâ*) or the wages of a 'dog' " is regarded as an abomination to YHWH (*tô'ăbat YHWH*) (Deut 23:18 [Heb 19]).[18] In Leviticus, it is the act of sex itself that ritually defiles, whereas in Deuteronomy the problem lies in the persons' deviance from prescribed sociosexual roles.[19] The overlap and distinction between what might be seen as two primary symbols—that of "stain" in the former text and "deviation" in the latter—would be an interesting object of scrutiny.[20] That particular investigation of "sexual cultics" lies mostly outside our present scope, though I will suggest at least one implication of it below. Of significance for this moment is the fact that *both* of these pieces of legislation apply to the vow of Woman Stranger in Prov 7:14. We have already seen that she proposes to defile—ultimately defile—both herself and the young man with sex during the period of feasting. But now we also see that she has paid or will pay her vow to the Temple (the sequence matters nowhere near as much as past commentators have fretted) with the "hire of a harlot."

With these two links between the Strange Woman's words and biblical cultic regulations rather firmly established, another somewhat more tenuous one may be suggested. The sensual attraction in the woman's speech is enhanced, in 7:17, with the allure of a bed perfumed with "myrrh (*mōr*), aloes (*'ăhālîm*), and cinnamon (*qinnāmôn*)." Although, on the one hand, this is typical love-talk such as that found in Ps 45:9 (the royal lover's robes are "fragrant with myrrh and aloes and cassia") and Cant 4:14 (the beloved is compared to a garden of spice and fruit, including "myrrh and aloes"), the background of cultic violation already invoked suggests another allusion as well. In Exod 30:22–33, a recipe is provided for the "holy anointing oil" to anoint the cultic objects and to consecrate the priests, "Aaron and his sons." The oil is to be made of myrrh, cinnamon, aromatic cane, cassia, and olive oil; that is, with two of the Strange Woman's three ingredients. The connection might seem stretched but for the following line that concludes the legislation on oil:

> Whoever compounds any like it or whoever puts any of it on an outsider (*zār*) shall be cut off from his people (*wĕnikrat mē'ammāyw*).

Here, as elsewhere in the priestly writings, our variegated term *zār*, when applied to persons, means "outsider to the priesthood, layperson."[21] The penalty for disobedience, being "cut off from one's people," clearly connects this law, however, with the levitical legislation on peace-offerings and hence with the *zārâ* of Proverbs 7.

If Prov 7:14 is related not to foreign worship but to defilement of the Israelite cult, an unexpected twist is added to our mysterious Strange Woman, and the question of her socio-historical setting is further complicated. Whatever the merit of the argument that interprets this figure as a foreigner and goddess worshiper, we now find that she is also a violator of not just one, but a whole series of Israelite cultic laws as well. In this reading, then, she appears not as a foreign woman, but as an Israelite, though a peculiarly and intentionally deviant one. The "foreign worship" interpretation is, moreover, undercut, insofar as 7:14 had provided the only explicit reference to such presumed practices in Proverbs 1–9.

Now, if the Strange Woman poems are dated in the fifth to early fourth century, it may well be the case that intermarriage and its attendant possibility of syncretism are the underlying issue in Proverbs, even if the references are allegorical rather than explicit. But this revised interpretation of Prov 7:14 puts a hitch in that proposed dating, as well as in the ethnicity of the female figure. The poet of chapter 7 clearly assumes that readers will be familiar with both deuteronomic and priestly legislation and, indeed, will see them as pieces of a single fabric that can be wrapped around this female figure. Thus we see an author who is a student and interpreter of Torah and, more specifically, one with a special investment in pieces of legislation dealing with cultic purity. It is unlikely, then, that Proverbs 7 can be dated before the time of Ezra, and it may be considerably later.[22] More than ever, the editor of Proverbs appears as a prototype for Ben Sira, by whom the interlocking of Torah, cult, and wisdom will be finally, fully expressed.

WOMAN STRANGER AS METAPHOR

A fuller understanding of the function of the Strange Woman figure may be available by analyzing it as a metaphor. The metaphor can be expressed as "Woman is a Stranger," wherein the "system of commonplaces" or "metaphorical paradigm" associated with each term, woman and stranger, interact to produce a new semantic entity.[23] We must be clear, however, that "woman" is defined in quintessentially male terms, namely, as "one with whom one has some form or another, socially sanctioned or not, of sexual relationship." The question of what makes the Strange Woman strange centers around the sexual behavior of her and her partner. Although the significance of sexuality is not entirely a literal one in this material, I will suggest that it functions far more complexly and powerfully than as a mere allegory for faithless worship. Because of the repeated scholarly emphasis on this aspect of the metaphor, it is worth beginning with a reevaluation of the relationship of strangeness to exogamy and foreign cults.

A cursory overview of Israelite thought on this matter in fact reveals a wide variety of dynamics among these ideas. In Deut 7:2–5, and likewise in 1 Kings 11, although the *functional* connection between intermarriage and religious syncretism is made, the *symbolic* connection between marriage to foreign women and worship of a foreign deity is not. Because marriage is fundamentally a mechanism for control of women's sexuality, however, even this seemingly gender-neutral act already overdetermines sexuality in a peculiar way: the sort of sexual activity that would normally be legitimate, sex within marriage, is delegitimated when it occurs with the "wrong" women, namely, strange (= foreign) ones.

It would seem at first glance that the concern for exogamy in Malachi and Ezra-Nehemiah does no more than reiterate that of Deuteronomy. However, even their seemingly "literal" reference to sexuality, in the form of social regulation, already shows evidence of a gender bias that casts it in the direction of the ideological symbol it will become: unlike Deut 7:2–5, which legislates against any sort of spousal exchange, "giving your daughters to their sons or taking their daughters for your sons," the postexilic material is concerned primarily with foreign *wives*.[24] There are several possible explanations for this shift. In general, because wives become part of the husband's family, there is more danger in this situation of foreign religious practices being imported into the community than when an Israelite daughter leaves her father's household. This fact does not explain, however, the difference between Deuteronomy and the later material. More specifically, the focus on wives in the postexilic literature may represent a sociological situation in which Judean men were marrying foreign women but not giving their daughters as brides to foreign men, perhaps because the foreign brides brought as dowries actual land holdings titularly claimed by members of the *Golah* community. A third possibility, which does not exclude either of the first two, is that we are already finding at work the presence of a gender ideology in which woman *qua* woman has become the symbol of the strange.

If this conceptual move has not been made (or has been made only implicitly) in Ezra and Nehemiah, it is certainly obvious in Proverbs, where the "strange women" of the two former writers are poetically condensed into *the* Strange Woman. Along these lines, I would reevaluate Blenkinsopp's important reference to the sin of Solomon as a basis for the Proverbs' instructions, an allusion also made in Neh 13:26. Although 1 Kings 11 makes the causal connection between foreign women and foreign worship, thus reinforcing a crucial division between what is proper to Israel and what is not, Proverbs makes the metaphorical connection between woman and the strange, thus identifying woman as that which is not proper to Israel. Ethnic distinction has been assimilated to and named by gender distinction.

A comparison of Proverbs with the pre- and postexilic prophets must also be made to appreciate the variety of metaphorical linkages between sex, strangeness, and idolatry. In the preexilic prophets and in Third Isaiah (chap. 57), an act of illicit sexuality, wanton adultery, serves as an allegory for religious infidelity. Accusation of actual human sexual activity as part of this foreign cultic practice is, however, a polemical move whose validity cannot be determined.[25] It is important to bear in mind that, with our new understanding of Prov 7:14, the book of Proverbs gives no clear indication of such activity.

We must also be clear that the form of the sex/worship relationship in both Malachi and Proverbs departs drastically from its appearance in the preexilic prophets. For the earlier prophets, the female figure did not represent either a foreign woman or a foreign goddess. To the contrary, Gomer can only be understood as an Israelite and, thus, as an allegory for the people of Israel who join themselves with a foreign deity (indeed, as in the case of Malachi, a male deity). The people are thus represented in female form (perhaps a derogatory comment in itself), and a wanton one at that, but intermarriage is not an issue (even though it may have been a causal force!).

In Malachi, both the gender dynamic and the symbolic dynamic change. Here the people are imaged as male, rather than as female.[26] This shift in the gender dynamic is presumably due to a social situation in which literal Judean men were marrying literal foreign women, a practice that had to be stopped. Foreign worship is still presumably an issue, but the focus is as much on the cause—intermarriage—as it is on the effect. Indeed, except for the allusion to one's foreign wife as "the daughter of a foreign god," the problem of foreign worship is nowhere explicit in Malachi. I would suspect, in fact, that the basis of the concern for syncretism in both Malachi and Ezra-Nehemiah is their perception of a more pervasive cultural danger than simply the foreign cult. The concern is for maintaining family and community identity, and rights to inheritance and power, at least as much as it is for pure worship of Yahweh. It is undoubtedly too cynical to say that the theological motive functions solely as an ideological justification for more material interests, but it certainly is no more than one part of the mix. In any case, no longer do we have an act of sociosexual deviance, adultery, functioning as a *symbol for* religious deviance. Rather, we have an act of communal deviance, intermarriage, functioning as a *cause of* religious deviance. We have thus returned at this point to the logic of the "sin of Solomon": the thread from 1 Kings 11 to Malachi is clear, but it is not that of the other prophets.

The female imagery in Proverbs creates a different dynamic yet. It is still the case, as in Malachi, that the Israelite addressee is imaged as male, rather than as female. It may also still be the case that the exogamy that leads to polytheistic worship is at issue. There is a significant difference, however, between the portrayal of women's alien status in Malachi and that in Proverbs. Whereas the prophet's *bat-'ēl nēkār* is no more than a woman, even if she is seen to represent a foreign cult,[27] Woman Stranger of Proverbs is a full-blown force of evil, an evil that manifests death in sexual form. Unlike the earthly daughter of a strange god, who awaits the pleasure of her prospective husband, Woman Stranger accosts, deceives, and seduces.

In this regard, the shift in subject in the otherwise similar imagery in Mal 2:14 and Prov 2:17 is instructive. In Malachi, the active partner is the man, who is condemned for being faithless to "the wife of your youth" (*'ēšet nĕ'ûrêkā*), who is "your companion and your wife by covenant" (*ḥăbertĕkā wĕ'ēšet bĕrîtekā*). The contextual connection of this judgment with the preceding one against those who marry daughters of a foreign god, and thereby are "faithless to one another, profaning the covenant of our fathers" (2:10), makes clear that the prophet (or at least his editor) viewed faithlessness to one's wife as a form of covenant infidelity, given its motivation (a foreign wife) and its consequence (foreign worship) in this particular social setting. The same train of thought occurs in Prov 2:17, but the gender dynamic shifts. Here it is the *'iššâ zārâ*, not her partner, who forsakes the "companion of her youth" (*'allûp nĕ'ûrêhā*) and forgets "the covenant of her God" (*bĕrît 'ĕlōhêhā*).[28]

How should we understand the gender and symbolic dynamics in Proverbs 2? It seems, first of all, an exercise in irrelevance to imagine the Judean poet castigating a foreign woman who forgets her marital vows and/or her devotion to her (foreign) deity. Alternatively, taken out of context, it is possible to construe this verse allegorically, with the woman forgetful of her marital covenant representing the Israelite community acting in covenant faithlessness. Such an understanding is hard to square with the context, however, which assumes a male listener who is being persuaded against a future liaison with a female who has forgotten (in parallel) her youthful companion and the covenant of her God. Although the identification of marital and religious faithlessness is similar to that in Malachi, Proverbs' focus on female agency, rather than male, suggests that decisions about exogamy—over which women had little control—are not the main concern. In sum, it is difficult to construe this particular text as representing anything other than an Israelite wife who is faithless to her husband. The issue at stake here is not marriage to the proper wife or even faithfulness to one's wife. Rather, the issue is social control of women's sexual behavior.

We are forced, then, to consider a second of the connotations of *zār/ nokrî*, that of the outsider to the family household, which is, in fact the dominant imagery in Proverbs 1–9. The woman is depicted as *zārâ* because, as an adulteress and prostitute, she acts in ways that are alien to the family structure, a structure that itself is a fundamental defining feature of what is "our own," not-strange.[29] If we eliminate 7:14 as evidence for a foreign cultic practice, all the language of sexuality in Proverbs 1–9 has sociosexual deviance—prostitution and adultery—as its primary referent.

One could argue, as Blenkinsopp does, that the allusion to Solomon in Prov 1:1, as well as the allegorical use of sexuality in the preexilic prophets and Third Isaiah, should lead us to the conclusion that, in the wisdom book too, religious fidelity, not sex, is at issue. The problem with such a conclusion is that, unlike in those prophets, Proverbs never makes explicit the association with foreign worship, whereas, to the contrary, faithfulness to one's wife, adultery, and harlotry are discussed in literalistic (if not fully literal) ways (see especially the poem on marital fidelity [5:5–19]; the contrast between the prostitute and the adulteress [6:26]; and the description of the consequences for "going in to the wife of another" [6:27–35]). Perhaps we might assume that an Israelite of this day would "naturally" make the connection between these images and foreign worship. But we must also assume that an Israelite of this day would have been concerned with such matters as establishment and preservation of the family name and inheritance rights, and of status and power within the community, all of which are threatened by deviant sexual activity by the women in a man's household.

In Proverbs 7, strangeness, not of nationality but of gender, is given its fullest expression. We must be clear, however, that neither Proverbs 2 nor 7 is attempting to describe the actions of a particular given woman. The language of deviant sexual behavior *is* being used symbolically, but not as a mere cipher for deviant worship. Rather, it is a symbol of the forces deemed destructive of patriarchal control of family, property, and society. Because control of women's sexuality is a sine qua non of the patriarchal family, it is no accident that the forces of "chaos" are embodied in a woman who takes control of her own sexuality.

Indeed, it would seem that the purpose of this poem is to project into a single figure the greatest evil imaginable, even at the expense of realistic description, by portraying an improbable combination of sexually deviant activities. That the Strange Woman in Proverbs 7 (cf. 2:17) is about to commit an act of adultery against her own husband seems clear, an act that in itself is bad enough. But this is adultery of the worst kind—no passionate love affair (however improbable that may have been in any case), but calculated, anonymous sex with a stranger, and an innocent lad at that. Indeed, we learn of her marital status only at the end of her speech; it is with her wantonness that we are first impressed. Notice, however, that she is *not* a professional prostitute, but is only "dressed" as one.[30] Had she been a "pro," the sage's depiction of utter evil would have been undercut, for the professional prostitute does have a place in a patriarchal world, even if it is a liminal one. Unprotected by any man, she is also unobligated to any man; she is the "institutionally legitimated 'other woman.' "[31] Far more dangerous is the woman who exists within the boundaries of male-controlled sexuality, but who decides for herself to opt out of them. Such is the wife *šît zônâ* in Proverbs 7.[32]

There is yet one more piece to the puzzle of sexuality and strangeness that will complete our picture of woman embodied in the full paradigm of sexual evil. The one who is *zār* can be not only foreign, not only outside the family, but also outside the priesthood. In a general sense, of course, all women are *zārôt* on this level. Once again, however, the Strange Woman is portrayed as an active creator of her own alien status, engaging in sex during the feast of her peace offering, bringing her harlot's hire to the Temple to pay her vows, and compounding the priestly anointing oil to perfume her illicit sexual encounter.

Given how fully the meanings associated with sexuality and strange-ness are articulated and interwoven in Proverbs 1–9, it becomes important to ask to what extent and in what manner any of these represent a socio-historical "reality." I have already suggested the possibility that, whatever concerns our poet-editor has for exogamy and foreign worship, they may not reflect the same sort of immediate crisis as that confronting the writers of the fifth and very early fourth centuries. Given the shift in imagery from the "real" foreign women of Malachi and Ezra-Nehemiah to the almost mythical figure in Proverbs, it seems possible that the latter book may express less of a current situation and much more of an increasingly mythicized *memory* of a time when, as it were, the bad women were really bad. Because of the chronological telescoping effected by myth, however, one era of the past becomes conflated with another and with the present as well. Thus "memories" of the foreign women who led our ancestors astray at Baal-Peor, the foreign women who turned Solomon's heart from God,[33] and the "daughter of a foreign god" who caused Malachi to castigate our fathers' (grandfathers'?) generation meld into an image of all that is dangerous to us in the present and future. In such an interpretation of Proverbs, it is not so much a matter of illicit sex serving as an allegory for dalliance with strange gods, but rather of a female image that evokes this metonymic memory and thus functions as a symbol for every danger that threatens the well-being of the community (as defined, of course, by those in charge).

The socio-historical veracity of the association of strangeness with adultery and harlotry must be assessed in an analogous way. Against van der Toorn, I think it is unlikely that we should imagine a social situation in which married women regularly engaged in acts of harlotry. Although it is certainly true that laws are often enacted to counter some existing practice, what information we have about the postexilic period suggests to me that in Proverbs 7 we are confronting not a social reality of wanton wives but rather a sociopsychological reality of men threatened by a multiply stressed social situation, including internal religio-political power struggles, economically oppressive foreign rule, and the pressures of cultural assimilation. We might describe the psychological dynamics in this way: The need to maintain familial and social stability in the face of enormous disruptive forces created in the male leaders and thinkers of the community a fear of chaos that was projected into an external, but nonetheless imaginary, object of fear, the woman who goes strange in the sense of deciding to stand outside the family structure as defined by its sexual roles and restrictions.

Finally, the sage's close association with, if not membership in, the priestly caste completes the linkage of Woman, Strangeness, and Sex. Precisely because all women are *zārôt* to the sons of Aaron, Woman becomes a "natural" target on which to project evil. But, just as Woman Stranger's vile adultery is not a depiction of women's actual activities, so also her deliberate violations of cultic regulations do not represent the acts of a flesh-and-blood woman. Rather, they represent the worst forms of defilement our priestly sage can imagine. Along with the accusations of wanton adultery, this depiction of the cultic violator must be taken as polemical, not descriptive, an expression of male anxiety as one generation attempts to pass its ideology of control to the next.[34] Although, in the biblical laws, defilement can come in many forms, from both men and women, here Woman—particularly in her sexual nature—becomes the embodiment of defilement. The metaphor has now been fully realized, but also reified: Woman is Strange.

DEATH, YHWH, AND THE STRANGE WOMAN

One final step is necessary to reveal the depth and significance of this ideological move, and that is to suggest its theological dimensions. We must consider the relationship of Woman Stranger to Death and Sheol in light of their connection to YHWH. A rather unexpected connection—of Isaiah 28 to Proverbs 1–9—provides the basis for our reflection. This chapter of Isaiah is notable for its concentration of wisdom vocabulary, most obviously its reference to "teaching knowledge" (v. 9) and its description of YHWH as "wonderful in counsel, and excellent in wisdom" (v. 29). More specifically, however, Isaiah 28 contains a series of images and vocabulary that are later used in connection with the strange woman and strange man[35] of Proverbs. The Lord's message is said to come "on jabbering lips and in another tongue" (bĕla'ăgê śāpâ ûbĕlāšôn 'aḥeret, Isa 28:11). In Proverbs, YHWH does not need to speak in an alien language, for Woman Stranger's smooth lips and tongue offer a quite comprehensible message.[36] The imagery of the snare is also prominent in both pieces of material. Because of the people's failure to listen to YHWH's warnings, Isa 28:13 claims that the divine word will cause them to "go, and fall backward, and be broken, and baited (wĕnôqĕšû) and snared (wĕnilkādû)." In Proverbs, the word pair yqš/lkd, both in the niphal, is repeated most exactly in a reference to the effect of becoming surety for a strange man (6:2; cf. 6:5), but the imagery of bond (môsēr, emended) and snare (pāḥ) also helps to create one of the sage's most powerful warnings against the Strange Woman (7:22–23).

The most important point for our purposes is that Isaiah 28 contains one of the few scattered places outside of Proverbs where the word pair zār/nokrî occurs.[37] The chapter describes a situation in which the leaders of Ephraim, likened to drunkards (vv. 1, 3, 7–9),[38] make "a covenant with Death, an agreement with Sheol" (vv. 15, 18). Because of this, YHWH will rise up

> to do his deed—strange (zār) is his deed!
> to work his work—alien (nokriyyâ) is his work! (28:21)

It is not only this word pair that anticipates the Proverbs poems; so also does Isaiah's mythicized Death-Sheol language that is so similar to its use in Prov 2:18; 5:5; 7:27; and 9:18, where the house of Woman Stranger— who forgets "the covenant of her God"—is imaged as in the maw of Mot.[39]

The continuity of imagery between Isaiah and Proverbs helps to call our attention, however, to a very significant difference between them. In Isaiah it is YHWH who speaks a fatal word in a foreign tongue, whereas in Proverbs this word issues from the enticing mouth of Woman Stranger. Similarly, Isaiah portrays the deity doing the strange deed and working the alien work in response to the people's covenant with Death and Sheol, whereas Proverbs moves the burden of strangeness to the Deadly One herself. I would suggest, then, that we see in Proverbs manifestation of a pattern of postexilic theological thought in which evil, whether in the form of strange deeds or deadly words, is removed from the character of the deity, and responsibility ascribed to a quasi-human, quasi-mythical incarnation of evil. The language of death, shades, and Sheol, which may have had its origin in the cult of a goddess (so Blenkinsopp) or some other chthonic deity (so McKane), is transformed in Proverbs to articulate a force—defined here as female—that will ultimately split the religious cosmos of Judaism and Christianity into a dualistic moral system in which women can come out on only one side.

3   Psalm 139

Robert B. Coote

The Psalms, like much of the Hebrew scriptures, preempt the voice of the poor. About half of the psalms copy the plea of the exploited. In the form of traditional speech, such pleas could be hyperbolic, derivative, and formulaic. Still, the plaintiff's grave desperation retains its face value, notwithstanding his conviction that God is just. With law and order in the grip of the powerful, the exploited had nowhere to turn for acquittal and justification but to their god. The plea of the wrongly accused, charged, punished, and persecuted constitutes the root and essential moment of the Psalms, even if under the patronage of the powerful.

The basic stages of the Psalter's formation are readily discernible. The process is best outlined in reverse. Something like the present collection provided sung prayers for the service of the Persian and Herodian temples. The Levitical service prescribed in Chronicles depended on Psalms 2–89 more or less as we have them: this set of psalms is organized according to the three sons of Levi; and 11QPs[a], containing only psalms from Psalms 90–150 with additions, seems to confirm that the latter part of the Psalter, "Books" IV–V as such, may be something of a coda (despite quotations in Chronicles from them). The Levitical service included an earlier set of psalms, 2–41, 51–72, 86 (possibly minus a handful), belonging to the service of the first temple of the house of David, the great majority of which are pleas of the exploited. There is little reason to doubt that this collection began with David himself, who, as many might once have believed, added insult to injury by exploiting not just the poor but their cry. If so, the ascription "to/of (the house of) David" indicates use by the house of David, and perhaps more often than not by David himself, and conceivably, though of less significance, composition by David himself.

Such a historical outline makes sense, more or less, of the "Davidic" psalms up to Psalm 86, the Davidic temple collection to which the colophon in Ps 72:20 applied and of which the Persian-period Levites in the name of David availed themselves. How then are we to understand the history of the psalms "to/of (the house of) David" in Psalms 90–150? Do they also stem mostly from the cult of the first temple, or are they later examples or imitations of the prevailing type in the earlier collection? If they are Davidic in the same sense as those in Psalms 2–89, why do they fall outside the Levitical frame centered on Psalms 50–51? Except when there are linguistic clues, as has often been argued in the case of Psalm 139, I don't know how to answer these questions. The one thing to be noted is an apparent symmetry or near symmetry: there appear to be about *thirty-six* psalms ascribed to (the house of) David prior to the Levitical core (3–41)[1] and about *thirty-six* such psalms within and after the Levitical core, consisting of *eighteen* before the colophon (51–65, 68–70)[2] and *eighteen* after the colophon (86, 101, 103, 108–110, 122, 124, 131, 133, 138–145).

This symmetry suggests that the Levitical core is to be understood as nested in the midst of rather than at the end of its Davidic matrix. This understanding, of course, ignores the ad hoc nature of a number of the Davidic headings (e.g., Psalms 122 and 133)[3] and must concern a late stage in the composition of the Psalter. However, one aspect of the symmetry probably does stem from the earlier Davidic collection; in *both* sets of thirty-six, the overwhelmingly predominant type of prayer is the plea. In each group, about five out of every six psalms is of this or a related type. It is likely that the psalms "of (the house of) David," however capricious the use of that heading over the centuries, always consisted predominantly of pleas of the exploited, this largely in contrast to the rest of the Psalter.

The consistency of this observation depends on the analysis of the particular psalms and raises the issue of the politics of interpreting psalmic pleas. There is a tendency—churchly and, less so, academic—to avoid the simplicity of the genre and its offensive references to conflict by translating such psalms in terms of a genial piety,[4] by complicating their genre, and by softening or misconstruing their imagery. Psalm 139 is a notorious instance. The realization that Psalm 139 is a plea occurs sporadically in the literature but in the midst of more widely shared assumptions suggesting or implying that it is not, or is only partially so.[5]

The explanatory note in *The New American Bible* is representative of this tendency:

Psalm 139: A hymn to God's omnipresence and omniscience, in the form of a meditation in which the psalmist ponders the truths that the Lord sees and knows him. . . . He therefore resolves to abhor the wicked and to live sincerely in God's sight. . . . The current Hebrew text is rather poorly preserved.[6]

The last sentence is true, the rest dubious and misleading. The text is well enough preserved to indicate a less genial reading, especially if its acerbity is not sweetened by benign translations of "poorly preserved" sections.

The psalm has four stanzas, and the quickest way into the spirit of the psalm is to jump to the last (vv. 19–24). Some of the translation that follows represents paraphrase or guesswork; ellipses mark places where there is insufficient reason to venture a translation.

> Kill the wicked, God!
>> Get rid of the murderers!
> Who perjure themselves . . . ,
>> Who give false testimony under oath.
> I *hate* those who hate you, Yahweh,
>> And I detest those who attack you.
> I hate them with a consummate hatred—
>> Your enemies are my enemies.
> Investigate me, God, and know my mind,
>> Test me and know my . . .
> Note that I do not follow the villain's way,
>> And hence guide me in the way that lasts.

The plaintiff (assumed male) is more agitated than hymnic and meditative. He is under indictment and fears for his life—just as is the case in the most common genre of psalm. He knows he is innocent. He has been had by the people who do the building, hiring, renting, lending, bossing, and bribing. No one is going to risk further trouble with the bosses by taking his side. He has nothing going for him except—and this is the point of the psalm, which has only one main point—his conviction that the god of his judicial cult knows he is innocent.[7] Whether that is going to help him, we do not know. All we know, to judge from the psalm, is that that is all he has.

So that is all he talks about in the first three stanzas—some forty lines of "God knows me, so God must know I'm innocent, because I *am* innocent, and God knows it better than I." In the first stanza (vv. 1–6), God has conducted his own trial, which supersedes and invalidates the trial the plaintiff faces.

> Yahweh, you have investigated me and known me:
>> You have known my sitting and rising,
>> You have perceived my purpose from a distance,

> My going and staying you have propounded,
>   With all my ways you are familiar.
> Before a word gets to my tongue,
>   You know the whole thing, Yahweh.
> You have stuck close in front and behind,
>   And set over me the palms of your hands.
> Knowing [like that] is beyond me,
>   Too lofty for me to manage.

God is Perry Mason or Rumpole of the Bailey on the bench itself. The last two lines imply that if God's brief on the plaintiff is better than the plaintiff's own, his accusers come in a poor and ignorant third.

Prompted by thoughts of ways and heights, the plaintiff's frantic imagination takes him in the second stanza (vv. 7–12) through the cosmic course of judgment.

> Where could I get away from your breath?
>   Where could I flee your (judicial) favor?
> If I go up to the sky, you are there [fortunately].
>   If I lie flat in the underworld—you again [fortunately].
> If I lift the wings of dawn [in the east]
>   And settle beyond the sea [in the west],
> There also your hand guides me,
>   Your right hand retains hold of me.
> And when I say [there in the underworld],
>   "Ugh, darkness compresses me,
>   And night squeezes around me"—
> Even darkness is not too dark for you,
>   And the night is like the day.
> (Like darkness like light.)

The plaintiff roves to the greatest height, then to the greatest depth. He sees himself as the sun, or in the company of the sun, circuiting the sky, then setting to begin its nightly course through hell. There in the darkness God becomes the sun, the ultimate torch, the plaintiff's guide and advocate as well as judge (as normally in ancient Palestinian conception), the one who sees all, even in the world's darkness.

While in hell and facing impending condemnation—and with it dishonor, shame, ignominy, reproach, and disgrace socially tantamount to death—the plaintiff recalls secret times and places, tokens of the parts of his existence beyond his own ken, dark to himself, but essential to the self-esteem at the core of his plea. The latter section of this third stanza (vv. 13–18) presents the most difficult text in the psalm.

> You created my kidneys,
>   You . . . me in my mother's womb.
> I thank you, for . . .

Marvelous is your work [in me],
  As my life knows well.
Not even my bones were hid from you
  When I was made in secret.
I became multicolored cloth deep in the earth
  Yet your eyes viewed me folded up.
In your book were all of them,
  The [future] days shaped were recorded, . . .
How valuable are your purposes for me, God,
  How firm are their chief points:
Let me number them—they are more than the sand;
  When I reach the end/when I awaken,
I am still with you.

"Marvelous" alludes to the miracle of pregnancy and birth. The colored cloth apparently represents the bloody fetus and placenta. The key element is the first, the kidneys. These are the seat of thinking, intending, and willing, much like the "mind" ("heart") in the fourth stanza. The plaintiff's life and actions, innocent (*ṣaddîq*) in contrast to those of his wicked (*rāšāʿ*) and murderous accusers, originated in his kidneys, which head the stanza on the invisible because they stand for what is most at issue, the psalmist's intention and action, and whether these are right or wrong, innocent or guilty. Jeremiah 12:2 describes the falsehood he is up against: "Yahweh, you are near their mouths but far from their kidneys" (cf. Ps 7:9 and Jer 11:20, 17:10, 20:12).

By the end of the third stanza, the plaintiff has reached the end of his journey through hell. Having come full circle, he lies distraught but resolute just below the eastern horizon, awaiting the "judgment at the gate" taken at dawn. He approaches the moment of wakening following the rite of incubation, a significant feature of many psalmic pleas, including, for example, the first two in the entire collection, Psalms 3 and 4. He has come far enough to glimpse the light at the end of the tunnel, but what kind of end will he find? Will he come to an end, and fail to rise with the sun vindicated, or will he awaken to a new day, born again, his innocence triumphant over his accusers? It's them or him, and it's now or never.

"Kill them!" "I hate them!" "*You* investigate me, God." The plaintiff is not meditative. Oppressed, distressed, and harassed, he is crying out one last time to his one constant and truthful patron, to the judge who sits on the final court of appeals, to God, who takes no bribes. He makes his last plea to the only one who can make the plaintiff's circuit, "his way" (possibly "case"), last into daylight and beyond.

Who makes this plea? He is in the process of losing "in the gate," about to go under in the place where legal judgments are handed down,

rules are made, decisions are taken, rights are confirmed and violated—
where the haves, those on the way up, and those on the take are taking
care of the have-nots. Most of the people in the gate could hardly do
otherwise; they have to make a living in this town like anybody else.

Psalm 139 may be partly metaphorical, but the burden of proof lies
with whoever would suggest so. Complaint genres in preindustrial cultures
are known for exaggeration, but the categorical cry of the victimized
comes through, nevertheless. The God of Psalm 139 is not omni- this or
that. The tone of such terms is wrong. The God of Psalm 139 is the last
resort and is appealed to as such with an acuity and longing to match any
other of the plaintiff psalms "of (the house of) David." This is the starting
point for comprehending Psalm 139, and it poses the question regarding
what sense it makes to go much beyond this starting point in interpretation, for the psalm in its textual obscurity warns against too dense an
interpretation. In its simplicity, it remains sufficient for those whose plea
it voices, and is already difficult enough for those against whom it is
directed to bear and respond to with integrity.

4

"To Her Mother's House"

Considering a Counterpart to the Israelite Bêt 'āb

Carol Meyers

At the heart of Norman K. Gottwald's monumental contribution to biblical scholarship, *The Tribes of Yahweh*,[1] is an analysis of the social structure of ancient Israel. The tribe, as the focus of his concern with the premonarchic era, is considered on its own terms as the primary subdivision of Israelite society. Gottwald then examines in great and perceptive detail the secondary and tertiary subdivisions of Israel: the *mišpāhâ*, or "protective association of families"; and the *bayit/bêt 'āb*, "the extended family." Another prominent feature of his book is the assertion that tribal Israel was relatively egalitarian, in comparison with contemporary Canaanite society. His careful examination of this aspect of ancient Israel is noteworthy for its sensitivity to the social status of all members of society, including women.[2]

In light of these two core interests and concerns of Professor Gottwald's scholarship, it is fitting that this study, which considers a female perspective on the tertiary subdivision of ancient Israel according to his analytical scheme, be part of a volume that seeks to honor him. As one who has been deeply influenced by his work, especially by his sociological approach to biblical studies, I am pleased to be able to participate in this celebration of his illustrious career.

The expression "father's house," which is found dozens of times in the Hebrew Bible, has long been recognized as referring to some aspect of the social configuration of Israelite life. The Hebrew term *bêt 'āb*, and sometimes its elliptical variant *bayit*, usually function as technical terms for a specific subunit of the community of Israel. Yet the scholarly discussion

39

of this terminology has virtually overlooked the fact that in several places in the Hebrew Bible there appears a related term, *bêt 'ēm* ("mother's house/household"), that may signify the same entity as does *bêt 'āb*. "Mother's house" is found in the story of Rebekah in Genesis, in the book of Ruth, and in the Song of Songs. In addition, Proverbs contains several references to a household or house in association with a woman. These occurrences of "mother's house" are striking in view of the overriding importance of "father's house" in the Hebrew Bible, and the term merits consideration on its own.

The commentaries on the texts containing "mother's house" cannot avoid noting this phrase. Yet they tend to treat it variously by considering it an aberration, by seeing it as a reference to a harem or "women's quarters" in a house, by understanding it to be used if the father is dead or in reference to the female side of the family, by viewing it as a way of saying that a girl is running home to mommy, or, in some of the early commentaries, by perceiving in it a relic of an original primitive matriarchy. None of these suggestions involves serious attention to the female perspective of the term's context nor consideration of the possibility that *bêt 'ēm* may itself be a technical term that serves as a counterpart to the far more common *bêt 'āb*.

It is worth noting that the not unexpected failure of biblical scholarship to take seriously the term "mother's house" is the result of the presence of androcentric bias.[3] That bias exists at several levels—in the ancient texts themselves and also in both the traditional and the contemporary interpretative processes.[4] Feminist biblical critics readily acknowledge the male bias of the texts—the male authorship of most, if not all, biblical books and also the overriding interest of those books in the public, masculine world of the polity Israel, with its preponderance of male leaders—its kings, prophets, priests, sages, and soldiers.[5] The other areas of androcentrism are less prominent but must also be recognized. The ancient translators and tradents injected their own male biases,[6] which tend to be perpetuated in contemporary historical-critical analyses by the unexamined patriarchal assumptions of modern interpreters.[7] Consequently, recovering the remnants of women's deeds and words, which are the clues to the nature of women's lives in the biblical past, must involve an approach that is conscious of the obstacles of androcentrism at all these levels.[8]

RELEVANT ASPECTS OF THE *BÊT 'ĀB*

In ancient Israel, effective membership in society for nearly everyone involved the basic unit of society—Gottwald's tertiary level—the *bêt 'āb*. This phrase, literally translated "house of the father," involves both spatial/

material and kinship/lineage concerns. Despite the apparent simplicity of the term, it is not always possible to identify on the basis of biblical texts exactly what it signifies. The problems in delineating what is meant by *bêt 'āb* arise from the fact that it is sometimes used in a metaphoric sense for the pseudokinship structures that biblical writers have imposed upon their understanding of the people Israel.[9] Hence the phrase sometimes can be found in reference to the primary level of social organization (tribe, *šēbeṭ/ maṭṭeh*) and perhaps even to the secondary level (clan [?], *mišpāḥâ/'elep*).

The confusion exists also because of the levels of redaction of the biblical sources representing various chronological periods of Israelite history. The configurations of all of the subdivisions of Israelite society certainly changed over time. The terminology for the units thus had to be fluid, indicating different understandings of the various subunits at different times. For example, the experience of exile caused considerable adaptation in the structural organization of both the exiled Judeans and those who remained in Yehud. The traditional language for social units took on new meanings.[10] Because this was a formative epoch for the formation of the biblical canon, it was inevitable that sixth-century usages of centuries-old terms should affect the nomenclature of the older texts being collected and edited during and after the Exile.

However flexible it may have been in representing various aspects of family and multifamily lineages, the fundamental grounding of *bêt 'āb* in reference to the smallest unit of Israelite society is what is relevant here. In its core usage as a term for the household unit in ancient Israel, it included both biologically related individuals as well as those with affinal or other ties. It was in effect a living group as much as a kinship group.[11] The "father's house" achieved its basic configuration in the rural communities in which it functioned at the time of Israelite beginnings and probably throughout much of the succeeding centuries; and its importance was integrally related to its role as the basic economic unit, producing virtually all of what was needed for the subsistence of its members.

Although the term "extended family" is sometimes used to refer to the *bêt 'āb*, that designation seems too limiting, in that *bêt 'āb* in its economic aspect included structures (buildings), property (land and equipment), and animals as well as people.[12] Thus "family household" is a preferable translation, because it incorporates the basic kinship orientation of a multigenerational family while allowing for the various functions of the household—residency, economic production, social activity, cultic practices, and so on.[13]

The dynamics of life in the self-sufficient family household involved a wide variety of agrarian tasks necessary for survival. Except perhaps for metal tools and implements, individual households produced all the necessities of daily life—food, clothing, simple wooden tools, and plain, utilitarian vessels. Providing these essentials involved a carefully orchestrated division of labor among all family members, male and female, young and old. Clearly, the survival of the household as a whole depended upon the contributions of all its members.

Because we are about to examine several passages identifying the *bayit* with the mother, it is important to note that the female's role in the household production system was no less important than the male's. Women participated in agricultural tasks, were responsible for the processing of crops into comestibles, made most of the clothing and probably also the baskets and the ceramic vessels, managed the activities of children and grandchildren (and of servants, hired workers, sojourners, if present), to say nothing of their role as progenitors. In such situations, households typically are characterized by internal gender balance rather than gender hierarchy.[14]

The word *internal* is critical here. Whereas outward forms of status and recognition may indicate male privilege, the dynamics within domestic units may be quite different, with women even dominating the multifarious facets of economic life, and also of social and parenting activities, that take place within the family household.[15] Because the public record of ancient Israel, like that of most traditional societies, is so androcentric, aspects of female power within the Israelite household can rarely be seen. Yet the relative invisibility of female power does not mean it did not exist, and occasionally it can be glimpsed even in the male-oriented canon.[16]

GENESIS 24:28

The longest chapter in the book of Genesis contains the endearing story of how Rebekah became the wife of Isaac. Sometimes called the Wooing of Rebekah, or the Courtship of Rebekah, the narrative chronicles the journey of the trusted yet unnamed servant of Abraham to the city of Nahor in Mesopotamia, where he identified Rebekah as a suitable wife for his master's designated heir, made the nuptial arrangements, and accompanied the bride-to-be back to Palestine, to the Negeb, where Isaac was awaiting her arrival. Embedded in this long and vivid account is the well-known incident of Rebekah at the well, in the course of which Abraham's emissary asked who the helpful maiden was and whether he and his entourage of camels might lodge in "her father's house," whereupon she hurried home to tell "her mother's household" (v. 28) what had happened.

Most commentators relate the appearance of "mother's household" to the ambiguity in the Genesis story about whether Rebekah's father Bethuel was still alive.[17] Although Bethuel is mentioned in vv. 13, 24, and 50, he plays no role in the story. Indeed, some suggest that, in v. 50, the appearance of Bethuel cannot be original.[18] Yet it should be noted that Rebekah does not respond to the servant's inquiry about room in her "father's house" with any demurrer about his being dead. Either way, *bêt 'āb* in v. 23 seems to stand as an indicator of her family household, regardless of who the senior male happened to be. Thus, "mother's household" in v. 28 must be considered as an alternate expression for the same societal unit, and not as a function of the particular configuration of Nahor's family. Ironically, the Syriac of v. 28, with its androcentric bias, assumes just that in reading "father's house" for "mother's house."

The appearance of *bêt 'ēm* in the Rebekah story must be considered in light of several relevant features of the Genesis 24 narrative, which probably has not received the attention it deserves.[19] In its present form, chapter 24 has its own integrity and stands in relative isolation, despite its context within the Abrahamic story and genealogy.[20] Although it depends on the reader's knowledge of the preceding Abraham stories, Genesis 24 has its own complex plot, developed through an intricate series of dialogues and speeches. Because of these features, it can perhaps be classified as a novella,[21] one as compelling as any in Hebrew scripture.[22]

The story unfolds through the initial agency of Abraham's servant and concludes with Isaac taking Rebekah as his wife. Yet the prominence of the second matriarch in this story, as well as in other passages in Genesis, should not be overlooked. Indeed, because of her role in Genesis 24 as well as the extensive recounting of her collusion with Jacob to secure the birthright for her preferred son, Rebekah emerges as the most fully portrayed matriarch. She is also the only one of the foremothers to whom an oracle is given directly from Yahweh (Gen 25:23). Furthermore, in comparison with the delineations of the other matriarchal figures in Genesis, Rebekah appears as a much more active and autonomous individual. The very language of the passages concerning her involves a far more dynamic vocabulary than the language used for her mother-in-law or daughters-in-law. Rebekah "came out" (24:15), "went down" (24:16), "let down her jar" (24:18), "emptied her jar" (24:20), "ran" (24:28), "arose, and rode upon the camels" (24:61). A similar vocabulary of activity accompanies the birthright story in Genesis 27.

Not only does Rebekah outshine the other matriarchs, but also she in a sense is equated with the foremost patriarch of all, Abraham. She will leave behind the same "country," "kindred," and "father's house" (24:4, 38) as did her father-in-law in the momentous opening of the patriarchal epoch in Gen 12:1. The Rebekah story echoes the language of the divine call to Abraham. Similarly, Abraham's remarkable departure from his homeland, signified by the verb *hlk* ("go," "go forth"; see Gen 12:1, 4), is mirrored and intensified by Rebekah's departure. The key verb "to go" appears seven (!) times in the Rebekah story, thereby emphatically conveying the notion that the shift in her life course is of the same ilk as Abraham's momentous departure from Haran.[23] Finally, Rebekah is blessed, as the future "mother of thousands of tens thousands" and of the descendants who will "possess the gate of those who hate them" (24:60), in much the same way that Abraham is repeatedly blessed.[24]

The prominence of Rebekah, in the second generation of Israel's proto-history, in a way compensates or substitutes for the relative absence of Isaac stories in Genesis as well as for the relatively weak portrayal of Isaac in the few places he appears. Isaac practically disappears between the extensive biography of Abraham and the many episodes recounted for Jacob.[25] In many ways, Isaac functions more as a symbol, as a passive representative of God's covenantal promise that Abraham will have a child to inherit the land to which he has journeyed, than as a character in his own right.

The several stories involving Rebekah as an active individual thus overshadow the sparse accountings of Isaac. For the transition between the first father Abraham and Jacob = all Israel, Rebekah's role as mother of nations looms larger than that of her husband as father of nations. Hence Genesis 24 can be considered a woman's story in that it showcases the matriarch who dominates the central generation of the ancestry sequence of Genesis. It is Rebekah who supplied the "vitality of the line."[26]

RUTH 1:8

Perhaps the most prominent narrative about women in Hebrew scripture is contained in the book of Ruth. One of only two biblical books to bear a woman's name, Ruth presents the struggle of two women to survive. For much of the story, Naomi and Ruth are without men; they take risks, they make their own decisions, they shape their own destinies, and their success is celebrated by women (4:14). This novella or historical short story,[27] however it may serve the interests of the Davidic genealogy, is a story about women that can legitimately be called a women's story.[28]

Still, some feminist scholars[29] resist claiming Ruth or Naomi as heroines. Instead, they insist that the motivations of both women are patriarchically driven and ultimately serve only the interests of men in providing them with heirs and so preserving the male line. Such critiques are problematic in that they anachronistically assume individual autonomy for ancient Israelites and so deny that women's lineage concerns served all

Israel, not only males.[30] Thus they should not detract us from the female orientation of this beloved and beautifully crafted tale.

In the first scene of the story, Naomi finds herself in a strange country bereft of her husband and her two sons. Hearing that the famine in the land of Judah, which had originally driven her and her family away from home, has subsided, Naomi decides to leave Moab. She starts on the journey to her homeland along with her Moabite daughters-in-law, Orpah and Ruth. Suddenly, she turns to the two younger women and urges them, in an extended and poignant dialogue, not to be part of her return (*šûb*), but rather to effect their own return (*šûb*) to their own people and religion (1:15). Naomi initiates this dramatic exchange (which results in Orpah's heeding her plea, but in Ruth's rejecting it with her memorable and poignant statement of loyalty, "Whither thou goest . . ." [1:16, KJV]) with the exhortation "Go, return each of you to her mother's house" (*bêt 'immāh*) (Gen 1:8).

In dealing with this "surprising"[31] term, scholars typically note that it would be more common to have the widowed women return to their father's house, as does Tamar in Gen 38:11 ("remain a widow in your father's house") or as is indicated for a priest's widowed daughter in Lev 22:13.[32] The ancient versions adumbrate this reluctance to accept the existing MT on its own merits: the Alexandrinus LXX reads *patros*; Syriac has "parents"; and other LXX manuscripts have some variant of "fathers."[33] Thus both the ancient and current responses exhibit androcentric bias, basing their consideration of the phrase on male norms. The fact that the phrase "mother's house" appears here in a brilliant, resoundingly female tale should help us to refocus the investigation of what it signifies so that it may stand on its own as a legitimate social term.

SONG OF SONGS 3:4 AND 8:2

The Song of Songs, or Canticles, is surely the most famous collection of love poetry in the Western world. It is also the only biblical book probably spoken more by women than by men. Despite the traditional ascription of authorship to Solomon, which probably occurred at the time of editing because his name is mentioned several times in the work,[34] the author or authors remain anonymous. Yet, according to the signification of the speakers in the poem itself, 53 percent of the text is spoken by females, as opposed to the 34 percent uttered by males.[35] A female voice begins the collection of love poems and also ends it;[36] the female speaker clearly dominates this extraordinary book.

Not only is a woman's voice heard more directly in the Song than anywhere else in the Hebrew Bible; but also its major character is a woman, and women form much of the supporting cast of characters. References to other females far outnumber mentions of men. Furthermore, female emotions are presented more prominently than are those of the male. Although there is no definitive proof for female authorship, some of the love lyrics that comprise the Song are so fundamentally feminine in texture and tone that the possibility that at least some parts of this book are a woman's composition must be entertained.[37] The question of the author's gender aside, the treatment of gender is virtually unique in the Hebrew Bible. There is little gender stereotyping, with the woman being at least as assertive as, if not more so than, the man in the pursuit and celebration of her beloved.

The mutuality of the lovers notwithstanding, the female voice and female characters dominate. Furthermore, in a striking reversal of conventional language, traditional masculine imagery is employed by the poet to portray the female rather than the male. Through the use of military terms and also of certain animal metaphors, the female is repeatedly depicted in figurative language that associates her—and *not* the male—with strength, might, aggression, and even danger.[38] The woman more than the man is connected with images of power.

In the context of this series of poems characterized by the prominence and power of females, the use of the term "mother's house" to signify the female's family household should come as no surprise. This phrase occurs twice in the Song, in 3:4 and in 8:2,[39] when the female expresses how dear her beloved is by speaking of bringing him "to her mother's household."[40]

In the first occurrence, the phrase is followed by a parallel reference to the mother's "chamber" (*ḥeder*). This use of a spatial term need not mean that the preceding *bêt 'ēm* is also spatial. Rather, "chamber" intensifies, focuses, and clarifies the female orientation of its parallel.[41] For it is not simply a bedroom, it is "the chamber of her that conceived me," an amplification highlighting the mother's procreative role.

The second instance of "mother's house," in 8:2, involves textual variants that again illustrate the androcentric bias of the ancient translators as well as of modern commentators. This verse, like 3:4, involves a parallel, which reads *tĕlammĕdēnî* in the MT. This word could be translated either "she teaches (or instructs) me" or "you (masc.) teach (or instruct) me." The translations that understand the former possibility,[42] acknowledging "mother" to be the referent, are to be preferred, given the female orientation of this verse and of the entire book, and also for other reasons to be discussed below.

The Hebrew word *tlmdny*, however, takes on other meanings in some of the versions. The LXX, Vulgate, and Peshitta all delete it and instead offer translations that would represent an expanded and quite different Hebrew: *wĕ'el-ḥeder hôrātî* ("to the room of the one who bore/conceived me"). This phrase, clearly influenced by the parallelism of 3:4, has been adopted by a number of influential English translations.[43] Furthermore, as might be expected, many modern critics favor the versions over the MT,[44] if they have not already decided that *tlmdny* is masculine and that the male lover or even God, and not the mother, must be doing the teaching.[45]

All of these suggestions, both modern or ancient, resist the intensification of "mother's house" in the MT by a word signifying, as does the other reference to *bêt 'ēm* in 3:4, a maternal role, in this case the giving of instruction. The appropriateness of "mother's house" being associated with the mother as one who teaches can be justified on the basis of anthropological paradigms considered in relation to biblical data as well as in recognition of the relevance of certain wisdom texts in Proverbs.[46] The readings of ancient and modern biblical scholarship should not be allowed to blur the way in which woman/mother, household, and instruction are linked in the MT.

WOMEN AND WISDOM IN PROVERBS

Although the phrase "mother's house" does not appear in Proverbs, several key passages bring together the figure of a woman and the house/ household that is hers. These passages are found in each of the three main sections of Proverbs: in the provocative and enigmatic image of Woman Wisdom in the introductory section (Proverbs 1–9), in several related proverbs in the collections that follow, and in the famous acrostic poem (31:10–31) that lauds woman and in so doing brings the book of wisdom to an apt conclusion.[47]

In 9:1, as the culmination of the complex series of passages that personify an abstract wisdom (*ḥokmâ*) as a woman, Woman Wisdom is depicted as having "built her house," setting it up on the much discussed and debated "seven pillars of wisdom."[48] In the succeeding verses, she is depicted as managing her household, serving food, and also providing "insight."

In two related verses in the collections that follow, woman and wisdom are again associated with the building of a house.[49] The MT of 14:1 reads either "Wise women (*našîm*) build their houses" (although "house" is singular in Hebrew) or "The wisdom of women builds her house." The difficult Hebrew has led most translators, ancient and modern, to delete "women" from this verse.[50] Yet "women" surely belongs with the combined themes of wisdom and house. In the case of 24:3, the other passage in the collections mentioning house and wisdom, "woman" is not actually part of the text. Still, the fact that this verse echoes the house-building language of 9:1, and merges it with the imagery of Wisdom filling treasure-houses with wealth (8:21), indicates that the wisdom by which a house is built is female wisdom.[51]

Finally, the worthy woman poem of 31:10–31 describes a woman skillfully and righteously managing all aspects of a complex household. She directs the members of the household in their various responsibilities. She participates in the actual physical labor involved in a variety of household tasks, especially that of textile production. She is in charge of her household's acquisition of property and in its participation in the market economy of the day. In performing all of these functions, she provides moral leadership for the members of her domain as well as for others who should take notice of her exemplary qualities.

In the process of enumerating the attributes, probably idealized, of an Israelite woman who is clearly a mother (because her children are mentioned in v. 28 and perhaps also v. 15), the poem connects her with "her household" (bêtāh) twice in v. 21. Thus "mother's household" is represented, although the phrase as such does not occur. Furthermore, "wisdom" is an explicit part of the vocabulary of the poem, in v. 26, where she is said to speak "with wisdom." Also in v. 26 she is connected with instruction (tôrâ), as is the mother of Cant 8:2. The phrase "teaching of kindness" picks up on the association of the mother with instruction— "your mother's teaching"—found in 1:8 and 6:20 and 23. Altogether, the maternal instructional role is mentioned four times in Proverbs, once more than is the equivalent paternal teaching role.

The prominence of the interwoven motifs of woman, household, and instruction for both the personified Wisdom of Chapters 1–9 and the human woman of chapter 31 is noteworthy, particularly because these two sections provide a female-oriented framework for the entire book. Because of the structural and thematic linkage of these two sections, Woman Wisdom may indeed be modeled after a real, albeit idealized, woman, rather than, or in addition to, the attributes of deity, mythological or Yahwistic, involved in that personification.[52]

One could hardly call Proverbs a woman's book, with all its admonitions being directed from father to son. However, despite this male "axis of communication,"[53] the female-wisdom-teaching-house combination does frame and define the book. In addition, the discourse of the long introduction is strikingly concerned with women: "Talk about women and women's speech occupies an astonishing amount of the text—men, preoccupied with speech, talking about women and women's speech."[54] It is no wonder, then, that "mother's house" is found, albeit elliptically, in Proverbs as well as in Genesis, Ruth, and the Song of Songs.

DISCUSSION

Each of the parts of the Bible in which the term "mother's house" is found has its own integrity; each features a unique style, setting, date, and function. Yet, examining the various contexts of *bêt 'ēm* reveals that, distinct and different as they are from each other, they also share certain fundamental characteristics.

A woman's story is being told. This is most obvious for the Song of Songs and is surely true for Ruth, feminist objections notwithstanding. The Rebekah story too, despite its location in the patriarchal narratives, showcases the second matriarch, who overshadows her husband. Even Proverbs, where our phrase is only elliptically present, contains more of women's voices than is usually recognized.

A wisdom association is present. For Proverbs, this is self-evident; for the other passages it is less clear. Yet both Genesis 24 and Ruth have certain features of biblical wisdom,[55] and the Song of Songs is likewise often grouped with wisdom literature.[56]

Women are agents in their own destiny. Although it is often assumed that gender hierarchies in ancient Israel precluded female autonomy, all the women in these passages assume active agency. To a greater or lesser extent, they initiate or decide on actions that affect the course of their lives.

The agency of women affects others. Rebekah's participation in the decision to leave her household is the prelude to *her* prominence, more than Isaac's, as parent of all Israel. Ruth and Naomi become progenitors of the house of David.[57] In Proverbs, Woman Wisdom is close to Yahweh in status— present at creation, existing everywhere, source of instruction (*tôrâ*); and the worthy woman is solely responsible for the well-being of her own household and also that of others in need. The woman in the Song does not have such broad influence, but the lyrically drawn emotional power she has over her beloved represents in its own way the enormous strength, and also the essence, of female power in its effect on others.

The setting is domestic. Although this may seem obvious, because the word *bayit* is part of the phrase being considered, it is a point to be emphasized. No matter how broad the ramifications of the women's deeds, the women are related to the household's activities. Even Woman Wisdom's cosmic role is couched in the metaphor of the house she builds and the table over which she presides.

Marriage is involved. Arranging a marriage is explicit in the Rebekah and Ruth stories, and it is implicit in the Song. Proverbs offers a somewhat different perspective: the worthy woman is obviously married, and Woman Wisdom functions somewhat as a divine consort.[58]

The significance of these features can be summarized by emphasizing that all involve a female perspective on issues that elsewhere in the Hebrew Bible are viewed from the male perspective that dominates scripture. The term "mother's house" has drawn us into the internal or household setting that circumscribed the life activities of virtually all Israelite women (and probably also of most Israelite men). Within that setting, women's voices were heard, their presence was valuable and valued, and their deeds had a profound influence on others.[59]

That influence went beyond the family household. The marriage aspect of the passages considered is salient in this regard. Israelite women apparently had a role equal to if not greater than their husbands in arranging the marriages of their children, although this is not always easy to discern under the androcentrism of the texts. But Rebekah's mother clearly plays a role, as later does Rebekah herself; Naomi of course instigates Ruth's conjugal pairing; and the woman of the Song, in bringing her beloved to the "mother's house," the place of her own birth and of her mother's "teaching," is no doubt involving her mother in her love arrangements. It cannot be assumed, in texts where fathers are said to secure marital liaisons, that they are acting on their own.

In forming marriages, alliances are formed between one bêt 'āb and another, or between mišpāḥôt, or even between tribes. Marriages, although intensely personal, private, and domestic, also have a critical suprahousehold dimension and thus are public arrangements[60] with economic if not political implications. The woman's role in effecting nuptial agreements involved perspicacity and diplomacy,[61] features of wisdom exemplified on a national level by Solomon and his affairs of state, and thus was not a trivial aspect of family and communal existence.

To consider once more the term "mother's house"—its appearance may be startling in an androcentric document such as the Bible, but its existence as a meaningful term in Israelite society should not be unexpected. It may be rare and surprising in the written word, but would not have been so in life as lived. As anthropologists have discovered, the male-oriented, formal record of any society does not stand in a one-to-one relationship with informal reality, in which women are also powerful actors in daily affairs and in family decisions on matters ranging from the mundane to the momentous. The biblical angle of vision rarely lets us view the female role. Yet in some instances, as in the survival of "mother's house" as a counterpart to the usual term for family household as the fundamental unit of society, the wisdom and power of women in ancient Israel become fleetingly visible.

5   *Micah—A Revolutionary*

George V. Pixley

Norman Gottwald has done biblical scholars and believers the great service of putting God's kingdom in the hills of Canaan during the tribal period of Israel's history, pulling it out of the ethereal reaches of the mind where it floated in most theology. What we believed as Christians struggling for justice, and what we suspected as scholars who were acquainted with Buber[1] and Mendenhall,[2] *The Tribes of Yahweh* confirmed. And in the process of confirming the validity of our suspicions that Israel was more than a primitive people gifted with religious genius, *Tribes* rounded out the picture and filled in its political and economic implications. Or at least it posed the questions about such implications, thus setting the agenda for much work to come.

One of the tasks set before us by a revolutionary understanding of Israel's origins is to pursue the aftereffects of this early revolution on the life of the nation Israel. It is especially significant to seek for signs of the survival of the revolutionary doctrines and practice in the prophets of Israel who claimed to speak for Yahweh, the God who brought Israel out of bondage in Egypt. Yet the scholarly consensus points to not one prophet who was a revolutionary. In light of Israel's origins, this consensus is in need of review. In the modern church and academy, the prophet who sets the norm is Amos, a powerful preacher who denounced the evils of Israelite government, judicial practice, religion, and business. His oracles were addressed to the mighty, mostly threatening them with destruction in the name of Yahweh, sometimes offering hope if they repented and changed their ways. In short, Amos was a reformer,[3] as were Isaiah and John the

53

Baptist, so far as we can tell. But, I suggest, this is not the only model of prophecy we find in the Bible. Micah ought to be read as a revolutionary. This is not to preclude the possibility that other prophets may also have been revolutionaries. It is only to begin the task of looking at the prophets for evidence that they were influenced by memories of the early revolutionary movement among the tribes of Israel.

MICAH CENSORED

The key to opening up the preaching of Micah is the oracle in 2:6–11. This saying deals explicitly with the efforts his opponents made to silence him and his associates (v. 6, "Do not preach," is plural), and to find prophets who would be willing to preach about "wine and strong drink" (v. 11). The oracle raises a number of questions, and its interpretation is complicated by the fact that it has itself been the victim of censorship,[4] which resulted in a great deal of textual corruption.[5] Prophetic scholarship of the last two centuries has developed techniques for reconstructing censored, corrupt texts, but with this particular text the results have been disappointing. This is because scholars and translators have proceeded on the assumption that Micah was a reformer, and this assumption has guided the use of ancient versions and the generation of modern conjectures to arrive at a text that can be translated for use in modern churches. It is that consensus that I believe ought to be challenged in the light of the sort of sociological research pioneered by Gottwald.[6]

The fundamental question is, Whom is the prophet addressing in the saying that "the house of Jacob" considers improper? When the prophet calls for his audience to "Arise and go, for this is no [time] to rest" (v. 10), is he addressing the landowners of 2:1–5 (the translators' consensus), or is he calling on "my people," the peasants of the land, to take up arms and no longer tolerate their oppression? I suggest that the latter is the more probable answer.

Although v. 8 poses several very difficult problems, it is clear that the subject is "my people" in both MT and LXX. Yet most translators emend this with no textual basis, to make "my people" the object of the aggressions of the landholders. The Vulgate is an honorable exception to the rule on this point, although its overall interpretation follows the consensus. If MT and LXX are to be followed, the Judahite peasants are said either to rise up as an enemy or to arise against the enemy. In either case, it is the peasants who are the active agents, not the landholders addressed in 2:1–5.

A revolutionary reading of the oracle can find support in the LXX of v. 9, thus obviating the need for conjectural emendation. LXX reads:

"Therefore, the rulers of my people shall be torn from the homes of their leisure; because of their evil deeds they shall be thrown out." "Rulers" stands as a translation of an original *něśî'ê*, which MT gives as *něšê* ("women"). If, however, "my people" stands, as it usually does in Micah, for the peasants of the countryside, it makes little sense to accuse the landholders of tearing their women out of their "houses of leisure." The verb in MT is second person plural imperfect, allowing us to reconstruct, with the help of LXX, "You shall throw the rulers of my people from the homes of their leisure."

My proposed reconstruction/translation of this text is as follows:

6. Do not preach—they preach—
   Do not say such things:
   that shame will not be stopped.
7. Should this be said, House of Jacob?
   Is the Spirit of Yahweh shortened?
   Are not these His works?
   Are my words not good for him who acts uprightly?
8. Of old my people used to arise against the enemy,
   today you shall rip off tunics and garments,
   making the prisoners of war pass by safely.
9. You shall cast out the rulers of my people
   from their houses of leisure;
   because of their evil deeds you shall expel them forever.
10. Arise! Go!
    For this is no time to rest;
    because of the filth you shall destroy,
    and the ruin shall be painful.
11. If a man walking on air invents lies—
    "I shall preach of wine and drink"—
    such will be the preacher of this people!

This rendition requires no departures from the MT in the framework of the oracle. The body requires some difficult moves in vv. 8 and 9. One, perhaps the most uncertain, is the rendering of *'etmûl/mimmûl* by the contrasting pair "of old/today." The only major emendation is in v. 9b, but it is supported in a general fashion by LXX (the third person passive of LXX becomes in this reconstruction a second person active). Compared with recent Spanish versions and with the RSV, this proposal is conservative in the use of emendations to the MT.

MICAH'S ASSESSMENT OF JUDAH AND JERUSALEM

The scholarly consensus about the book of Micah follows Bernhard Stade's 1881 proposal that the primary collection is contained in chaps. 1 to 3. The rest of the book, according to this consensus, probably contains some sayings authentic to the eighth-century prophet embedded within a mass of sayings added from various sources. Because we wish to identify the stance of the prophet himself, we must begin by analyzing the sayings that are most likely his own, setting aside the material in the last chapters.[7]

An oracle of judgment in 3:9–12 denounces "you heads of the house of Jacob and rulers of the house of Israel" who, as it turns out, are the rulers of Jerusalem. The prophet accuses them of "building Zion with blood and Jerusalem with wrong." They have used their Yahweh religion as a false security, trusting that, because Yahweh's temple is in their midst, no evil will befall them. The oracle culminates in Micah's pronouncement:

> Therefore, because of you, Zion shall be plowed as a field;
> Jerusalem shall become a heap of ruins,
> and the mountain of the house a wooded height. (3:12)

It might be helpful to contrast this threat to Jerusalem with an analogous threat in Isa 1:21–26. Isaiah believes that Jerusalem was originally a faithful city, but has become a place of murderers. This could be taken as another way to speak of a city "built with blood," but the threat that follows the denunciation shows that the analysis is in fact different. Isaiah expects that the purifying fire of Yahweh's wrath will remove the dross, after which the city will again be called a faithful city. Micah's assessment is more radical, and so is his "solution": Jerusalem will become a plowed field and a heap of ruins. Thus Judah will be saved by the rooting out of the structural cause of its evil.

Another difference between these two analogous sayings may also be significant. Isaiah makes Yahweh the direct agent of the purifying judgment on Jerusalem: "Ah, I will vent my wrath on my enemies, and avenge myself on my foes" (Isa 1:24). The judgment in Micah's oracle is impersonal: "Zion shall become . . ." In both cases the prophets may be thinking of a foreign invasion. Such an invasion could well be viewed by Isaiah as Yahweh's action. And it would not be unusual for God's action to be veiled in impersonal terms like Micah's. On the other hand, it is just possible that Micah avoided appealing to Yahweh's action in order to prevent the peasants whom he addressed from assuming a passive stance, "leaving it to Yahweh."

The ruling classes usually understand that appeals to God's actions in history do not mean a historical passivity on their own part. They are used to acting in history, to guiding the events of their nations. If they are religious, their belief in providence does not lead them to withdraw from their accustomed aggressiveness. On the other hand, those who pastor the poor know that their impotence has conditioned them to passivity about history. For the poor, history is a sphere where others take the initiative. And religious belief tends to reinforce this natural passivity. If Micah had the poor of the land ("my people") as his audience, this would be sufficient reason to silence God's action.

The destruction of Jerusalem and of the cities of the Shephelah (1:10–16) is nowhere attributed to Yahweh. It is, of course, natural to assume that the prophet believed that it was Yahweh behind the impending judgment. Most interpreters in the twentieth century assume that the prophet expected the invading Assyrian forces to be the instrument of Yahweh's judgment. It is in fact a natural assumption. It is what Isaiah understood to be the case (Isa 10:5–15). It might also be what Micah had in mind. But let us note that nowhere does he say this. Why do our interpreters not suggest the alternative proposal that the prophet is calling on the peasants to stage a revolution to destroy the cities? Surely, in the light of the experience of the tribes of Israel in the late second millennium (if we have been right in our interpretation of that experience), a Judahite prophet could well see the hand of Yahweh's judgment in a popular uprising to destroy oppressive cities, just as surely as in an Assyrian invasion.

An important saying to reinforce the analysis of Jerusalem as the problem is Mic 1:5. RSV translates as follows:

> All this for the transgression of Jacob
>   and for the sins of the house of Israel.
> What is the transgression of Jacob?
>   Is it not Samaria?
> And what is the sin of the house of Judah?
>   Is it not Jerusalem?

Like many interpreters, RSV follows LXX in the next to last line. MT reads, "What are the heights (*bāmôt*) of Judah? Are they not Jerusalem?" RSV here follows O. Procksch's suggestion in Kittel's *Biblia Hebraica*, which rests on the assumption that Judahite scribes suppressed the prophet's radical analysis that Jerusalem was in its very existence the problem of Judah. Alt[8] felt that v. 5b (after "Samaria") was an addition, but Procksch's and RSV's solution seems more likely. The prophet, from the perspective of the peasant population of Judah, finds that it is the parasitic cities (not just Samaria and Jerusalem, but also Gath, Lachish, Mareshah, and Adullam, too) that are the root of the problem. If we are correct in following LXX in 1:5, we can better understand why the solution proposed by Micah in 3:9–12 is the destruction of the city of Jerusalem.

In 2:1–5 we find the oracle that was the basis of Alt's essay. The prophet denounces a process of expropriation of the lands of the free peasants in Judah. His denunciation is independently confirmed by Isaiah of Jerusalem, who laments about those who "add field to field, until there is no more room, and you are made to dwell alone in the midst of the land" (Isa 5:8). By the eighth century, a historical process of accumulation of lands in the hands of urban landowners was apparently far advanced, so much so that even a city dweller such as Isaiah was aware of it as social cancer.

For Isaiah this issue was one among many. For Micah it was the heart of the nation's illness. And Micah was able to see beyond the problem toward its solution:

> Behold, against this family I [Yahweh] am devising evil,
>   from which you cannot remove your necks. . . .
> In that day they shall raise a lament against you, . . .
> "We are utterly ruined;
>   the portion of my people is measured by the rod [LXX];
> there is none to hinder its being turned back.
>   Our fields are divided up."
> Therefore you will have none to cast the line by lot
>   in the assembly of Yahweh. (2:3–5)

Alt gave us the solution to this text. It has been corrupted, as was to be expected, but LXX is quite helpful in recovering it. The assembly of Yahweh, in any case, stands in both MT and LXX, and it refers, as Alt correctly saw, to a distribution of land of the sort attributed to Joshua in the Israelite tradition. This (re-)distribution is more understandable on my assumption that the prophet calls for insurrection than it is on Alt's assumption that the judgment of God will come in the shape of an Assyrian invasion.

WAS A PEASANT REVOLUTION CONCEIVABLE IN EIGHTH-CENTURY JUDAH?

The narrative texts of the history of Judah give no indication of a revolutionary movement at this time. That proves nothing. The Deuteronomistic History is a history of the kings of Israel and Judah, more than of the nation. A peasant uprising that left no permanent changes in the political configuration of Judah likely would not be recorded by Dtr. On the positive side, we must allow that the very mention of an assembly of Yahweh to redistribute the land is evidence of utopian dreams in the countryside of Judah at that time.

These utopian dreams rested on a subversive popular memory. The stories of the exodus from Egyptian bondage and victory over various invading forces, by means of popular armies led by Deborah, Gideon, and

Jephthah, were still alive in the urban centers, and were surely present also in the countryside. Probably in these circles the stories were less assimilated to the vision of national unity under the kings, which was the standard urban vision. The versions we have in the Hebrew Bible today were originally "expropriated" from the popular memory by the urban elite. Who knows how much more was preserved in the villages of Judah?

What were the political conditions in the countryside of Judah during Micah's lifetime? Gath, Lachish, Azekah, and the other cities of the western slope of the Judean hills were the scene of several Assyrian invasions between 734 and 701, and during this time the kings of Jerusalem lost their control over all of this territory. It was incorporated into various Philistine city-states and Assyrian provinces. Assyria's interests in Palestine were focused on this coastal area, which could serve as a buffer against invasion from Egypt into Asia. Egypt was a potential threat, and firm control over the cities of Philistia and Judah was in the Assyrian interest of preventing such a threat from materializing. In 734 Tiglath-Pileser III reached Gaza. In 720 Sargon II reached "the river of Egypt," where he destroyed the border post of Rapihu. He returned in 711 and converted Ashdod into an Assyrian province, bringing enough people from Assyria to establish a population base for Assyrian control of the area. The reorganization of these territories was completed with the invasion of Sennacherib in 701, when a whole system of provinces was established based on the Philistine cities. Hezekiah was stripped of his Judean possessions and reduced to Jerusalem and its immediate surroundings.

From this brief summary (based on various essays in Alt's *Kleine Schriften*) one can see that the peasant area that Micah knew was not under the stable control of Jerusalem. Neither did it pass definitively into Assyrian hands until Sennacherib's invasion. It is this sort of unstable administrative situation that often provides the context for peasant unrest. Perhaps there were one or more insurrections against the urban landowners of Jerusalem or the Assyrian provincial capitals or both. In this context we could also understand the mysterious allusion in Mic 2:8 to prisoners of war.

The main interest of Dtr and the Chronicler in Hezekiah, a king during Micah's time, was in his reform. Hezekiah's objective seems to have been the consolidation of Jerusalem's position at the head of the nation. In the religious realm, this led to the removal of the *bāmôt*, local sanctuaries where Yahweh and other deities received worship. Hezekiah sought to take advantage of the defeat of the kingdom of Israel and the fall of its capital Samaria to make Jerusalem the capital of a new Israel. For this reason he "purified" the cult in the Jerusalem temple to make it more acceptable to

Israelites, eliminating accretions of doubtful legitimacy like the bronze serpent attributed to Moses.

The centralization had military, judicial, and fiscal, as well as religious, implications. It may be supposed that the enforced closure of local sanctuaries and administrative centers caused some resentment among the peasant population. The king had unilaterally closed revered places of festivity. This, combined with the weakening of the military garrisons in small cities like Gath, could well have rendered insurrection a plausible social alternative.

CONCLUSION

Norman Gottwald spoke for many of us in Latin America when he gave a systematic reading of the origins of the tribes of Israel in a peasant movement in the land of Canaan. His contribution is essential, but it is not enough. We must learn to read the entire history of Israel (and of America) as a history of the struggle of peasants (most of whom among us were and are also Indians) to become the agents of their own history.[9] Insofar as we are Christian believers, we must also carry out the project implicit in Gottwald's work of reading the Bible from the perspective of the poor.

In this essay, the attempt has been made to read Micah as a spokesperson for peasant insurrection. Much more can and must be said about Micah. What has been said here is sufficient, I believe, to make it at least as plausible to interpret Micah as a revolutionary as it is to reconstruct the mutilated text of his sayings to make him a reformer in the line of Amos. In fact, further work may well prove that much in this small prophetic book becomes clear when read with this assumption.

The fact that the peasant insurrection in eighth-century Judah failed to achieve its objectives of creating an autonomous peasant society does not make the effort insignificant. Most peasant movements in history have failed. If we look at the long run, all historical movements are in the nature of things destined to eventual failure. This is the nature of historical existence, the only sort of existence we know. But life is in the struggle. Victory is important when we struggle for conditions that will support life for all. But victory is not everything. The struggle itself is life. "Your mercy (*hesed*) is better than life itself" (Ps 63:4). And we know the mercy of God in the struggle for worthy conditions of life for all, where God's loyalty and mercy sustain us.

6   *"Enemies" and the Politics of Prayer in the Book of Psalms*

Gerald T. Sheppard

A persistent debate in the modern study of Psalms concerns how to interpret prayers that imprecate "enemies," "the wicked," "evildoers," and other antagonists. Key problems include the question of who are the enemies, why they remain unnamed within the prayers themselves, and what role such prayers actually played both in ancient society and, finally, in the later formation of scripture. This essay will first offer an analysis of the sociopolitical role of prayer in the biblical prehistory, and will then explore some theological implications that derive from the retentions and alterations of that same tradition history within the canonical context of Jewish and Christian scripture. One hermeneutical aspect of this essay is to show how even a canonical approach to theological interpretation still needs and benefits from the type of social-scientific analysis that Norman Gottwald has impressively pursued.

AN OVERVIEW OF THE DEBATE
ABOUT ENEMIES IN THE PSALMS

One of the most common problems in the study of Psalms has been how to evaluate references to enemies and the accompanying graphic imprecations. The wish for violence against these enemies, whether God is summoned or the supplicant volunteers to retaliate, may seem harsh, childish, or "primitive." Commentators before the last century usually considered most of the enemies to be historical persons in the time of David. In the modern critical period, Bernard Duhm was perhaps the last major scholar who sought systematically to identify each reference to an enemy with particular historical persons. However, the prevalence of "enemies" even in some psalms where the psalmist seems content and at peace (e.g., Psalm 92) led Duhm to conclude, "It appears to belong to the invention of piety that one considers certain people as enemies. . . . Likewise, piety has its customs." In contrast, postexilic Judaism was, according to Duhm, preoccupied with the parties and politics of the new Jewish state, and, consequently, psalms from this period reflect a very different type of internal enemy against the pious rulers of the nation or against the administration of the Second Temple.[1]

By the late nineteenth century—especially in the works of W. M. L. de Wette, J. G. von Herder, and Hermann Gunkel—the study of the cultic forms and functions of prayers, as well as the psychological-aesthetic nature of prayer itself, called for a radical change in the conception of enemies in the psalms. Gunkel found in the stylized and historically ambiguous depictions of enemies a sign that these prayers were composed for reuse by different persons and under a variety of specific historical circumstances. The "formulaic" quality of many statements about enemies proved that the poet often "assigned less value to the external events than to psychological impressions (den seelischen Eindrücken)."[2] Even if someone originally wrote a lament with quite specific enemies in mind, later usage of that psalm could blunt certain historically specific language in the psalm through slight modifications introduced by its ritualized recitation.

Gunkel also sought to make some general observations about the external conditions evoking the use of these psalms. In his 1904 Ausgewälte Psalmen, Gunkel suggested, "The predominant situation of the lament psalms is sickness."[3] In his view, at least sixteen psalms seemed to have illness as their primary concern. Relying on social-scientific conclusions in Lévy-Bruhl's Die geistige Welt der Primitiven (1927), Gunkel concluded that in "primitive" societies sick persons experience the whole world as an enemy and commonly find demonic powers at work all around them. The biblical psalms are exceptional in their lack of reference to demons. According to Gunkel, irrational anger at the world and the demonic for illness had in ancient Israel been replaced by a rational theory of sickness as the result of sin. Although God ultimately allowed or caused the illness, the relation of human enemies and sin to the illness played an integral role. Gunkel drew heavily on the case of Job and his friends as paradigmatic.[4] In general, Gunkel saw three categories of enemies in the psalms: (1) those related to illness and misfortune, (2) enemy nations, particularly in the exilic period, and (3) antagonistic heathen among whom Jews lived in the postexilic period.

Several problems remained unresolved in Gunkel's study. Almost no scholars granted that all of his sixteen psalms of sickness really should belong to that category.[5] Othmar Keel has cogently criticized the vagueness in Gunkel's account of how illness was logically related in prayer to the accusation of enemies or to an indictment of enemies for folly or for abandoning faith in God.[6] Sigmund Mowinckel, Gunkel's student, sought to clarify this relationship in his *Psalmenstudien* by arguing that '*āwen* in the psalms was, in fact, a technical term for magic and witchcraft, and that the *pō'ǎlê* '*āwen* are workers in magic and witchcraft, the enemies of the psalmist. Mowinckel explained this tendency by appeal to economic inequalities exacerbated by a *"kapitalistisches"* system in the monarchial period. The prayers in this period reflect a response of the lower classes, who regularly depict these "witches" as wealthy and in positions of leadership (cf. Psalms 37, 49, 52, 62, 73).[7] Hempel observed a major problem with this proposal, namely, that we lack in the psalms the expected word for "those who use witchcraft" *měkaššēpâ* (cf. Exod 22:17), a term corresponding to the Akkadian usage in the expression *nišu u mamit*, "witchcraft and magic(?)."[8] Mowinckel's argument for such a technical use of the common Hebrew term '*āwen* cannot be easily defended and has not gained wide acceptance.

H. Birkeland, Mowinckel's student, pursued this same question extensively in various studies, but put even greater emphasis than did his mentor on the role of the king. He concluded that most of the psalms were royal psalms, so that the "enemies" must consistently be "non-Israelites," or in the postexilic period, "gentile" nations.[9] Birkeland based his case on the evidence of about twenty psalms where the antagonists are clearly outsiders; then he assumed that similar stereotypical language found elsewhere implies the same circumstances even with the absence of clear reference to other nations. No modern commentary on Psalms has taken Birkeland's final conclusion seriously, and evidence of an all-encompassing royal enthronement festival in Israel remains a matter of controversy. The diverse expressions of the psalms themselves work against any singular categorical solution to the identity of the enemies. The problem is made only more obvious by strained explanations, such as that of G. Widengren: "The so-called 'misery-description' in the royal psalms of lamentation reflect the mythical situation, when the god finds himself imprisoned in the nether world, surrounded by wild, demonic creatures."[10]

More recent, full-scale studies are those of L. Delekat, O. Keel, and Steven J. L. Croft.[11] Delekat took the extreme position that most of these prayers about enemies really belong to the traditions of a person's seeking "refuge" from those who might seek revenge. He has profoundly stated a question to which we will return—one that, in my view, the other studies similarly fail to answer: "When the ones praying and their enemies . . . are private persons, why do they turn to God for protection instead of the civil courts (*weltliche Gericht*) and how do they think of this protection?"[12] Delekat's own proposal suffers from overly subtle argumentation for what would have had to be a remarkably understated feature, and he fails to explain why a concern with a place of refuge would actually solve the range of problems described in the lamentations themselves.[13]

Rejecting Delekat's position, Keel has sought to find an answer in a fresh assessment, found originally in Gunkel's work, of how prayer can be used to express in externalized, commonplace language deeply painful psychological or pious impressions associated with suffering. He tries to focus more specifically than Gunkel on the content and the inner logic of the psalms themselves within the life setting of an ancient pious recitation of a prayer. As proof of a lack of proper attention to content, he notes that no one has even yet offered a study of the term *rāšā'* ("wicked") in the psalms. From a social-scientific perspective, Keel stresses the prevalence of xenophobia in ancient societies, and finds in the patterned and heated expressions against the enemies signs of social-psychological conflict between groups both within and outside of Israel. Although the psalmist might, of course, be under real attack by some personal enemies, Keel concludes:

> One would misunderstand the psalms, however, if one believed that in their depictions of the enemies there was contained nothing more than a natural conflict between persons. By means of projection the temptations of the ones praying (for example, doubt in the reliability of Yahweh) are transferred to the antagonists, and, as such, they are experienced as impinging (or intruding) on those praying. Precisely because the one praying addresses his need to Yahweh, this will be continuously modified.[14]

By describing many if not most references to enemies as evidence of pious, psychological projection derived from the psalmist's own unconscious self-criticism, Keel finally rationalizes these occurrences in a thoroughly modern way. Even if such an explanation might account for the pervasive occurrence of this feature in the psalms, there would still remain the need for a sociopolitical and religious estimate of how these appeals to the enemy made sense both to those who pray in this manner and to people who were indicted by such prayers. This latter concern becomes all the more necessary if, as we shall show, these prayers were traditionally spoken out loud and intended to be overheard by friends and enemies alike. In that case, they do not belong to the rhetorical resources characteristic of a private and individualized catharsis, but express their complaints and desires publicly; therefore, these surface features of prayer presume a correspondence somehow to known persons, places, and events.

Croft's study, without showing awareness of Keel's work, takes up Keel's concern for the need of word study. After a sustained criticism of Birkeland's treatment of enemies as chiefly opposition to the king by other nations, Croft offers an impressive effort to distinguish between use of the terms 'ōyĕbîm ("enemies") and rĕšā'îm (the "wicked") in the psalms. He concludes that "enemies" in the psalms "always" pose a direct threat to the "I" of the prayer. Conversely, "in many but not all of the psalms discussed" Croft finds that "the wicked" pertains to those who have turned from God without threatening the psalmist.[15] At a minimum, Croft confirms that the psalms may carefully employ terms for "enemies" with referential precision and distinction. He recognizes that appeals in a psalm to such word pairs as the righteous and the wicked echoes vocabulary in wisdom literature, refined by a "common tradition of faith" known as much outside the psalms as within them.

Despite its many strengths, Croft's conclusion that "the wicked," in contrast to "the enemies," do not attack the "I" of the psalms, cannot be sustained consistently. He admits, for example, that in Psalm 34 the wicked are implicitly indicted for persecuting the one praying and for that reason are called "evildoers" in verse 17. So, too, Psalm 112 includes in its description of the wicked the confidence that the psalmist will "see" the downfall of "his adversaries," clearly assuming that "the wicked" belong to this same group. Though Croft states too rigidly the semantic rules governing the use of these two terms, he confirms the value of such word study in the psalms and, of more importance, shows more explicitly than most past scholars how often individual psalms presuppose that the enemy belongs to his or her own community. Moreover, Croft sees clearly that psalms belong to a complex process of public, oral, and written transmission.[16] He excels in his general description of the liturgical situation in which listeners made sense of these ancient prayers, but he fails to explore carefully enough the implications of this system for the role of "the enemies" within it.

PSALMS AND ENEMIES IN GOTTWALD'S "SOCIO-LITERARY APPROACH"

Since the publication of his *The Tribes of Yahweh* in 1979, Norman Gottwald has sought to consider more fully the literary formation of scripture and what consequences these changes in literary presentation might entail for any sociopolitical interpretation. The title of his 1985 introduction underscores just this point: *The Hebrew Bible: A Socio-Literary Introduction.*

Although Gottwald has not backed away from his consistent focus on the social and political "reality," the adjectival phrase "socio-literary" in the title indicates his renewed interest in the literary significance of "the Bible." Instead of focusing exclusively on social-scientific reconstructions of liberating "foundational events" and the recurrence of a subversive memory about these events within the biblical prehistory, Gottwald here discusses the "shape" of subcollections and of whole books. The appeal to the "shape" of a text recalls a similar usage in both the New Literary proposals of Northrop Frye and the canonical approach of Brevard Childs.[17] Gottwald's treatment of biblical books includes, also, overviews of structuralist, narrative, and other studies that assume a strong synchronic orientation to biblical texts.

Gottwald states emphatically in his introduction that his goal now is to find a "common ground" between literary and social-scientific criticism.[18] The main question raised by the literary dimension is: "Exactly how does the social reality inscribe itself in language and in literary creations?"[19] Gottwald argues that what both literary criticism and social-scientific criticism share in common is a concern with "structure" that can, in turn, be correlated to a pattern of "social reality" within the human experience. The effort to describe "social reality" may best convey the goal of Gottwald's analysis of each biblical book in his *Introduction*, not least in his interpretation of Psalms.

A problem initially for Gottwald is where to locate his discussion of Psalms within his introduction. This problem is compounded by the fact that his aim is so impressively encyclopedic. In Part I, "The Text in Its Contexts," Gottwald discusses methodologies, material culture, and the literary history of the Bible. Here references to Psalms occur primarily as illustrations of the plurality of observable "contexts," including the oral level pursued by form criticism, as well as the later written, canonical context. Parts II–IV put these "contexts" into a sociopolitical chronology, dividing history into different epochs according to the major social configurations of Israel: "Intertribal Confederacy" ("Revolutionary Beginnings"), "Monarchy" ("Counterrevolutionary Establishment"), and "Colonial Recovery" (with some reemergence of premonarchical revolutionary Yahwism as described in Part I).

Within the framework of these three major periods of historical and socioeconomic development, Gottwald gives only passing attention to the role of psalms, as well as proverbs, in the monarchical period. He notes simply that as "finished books" Psalms and Proverbs "are manifestly of postexilic date."[20] Of the preexilic psalms, he mentions royal psalms (2, 18, 20–21, 45, 72, 101, 110, 132), as well as certain preexilic proverbs ("among the collections in Prov 10:1—31:31"). These traditions do "reveal preexilic monarchic references and codes of conduct typical of high court officials" and, accordingly, "are very instructive about the general ethos and culture of the upper class circles who prospered under the centralized institutions of kingship."[21] In other words, traditions from the books of Psalms and Proverbs are described for these early periods only in terms of an elitist and counterrevolutionary ideology.

Only in the final postexilic epoch of "Colonial Recovery" does Gottwald return to a more sympathetic examination of the psalms, with a mixed assessment of their ideological import. Here I think one of his strengths is a recognition of the changing socioeconomic roles that psalms might have played from their origins in the monarchical period to their later function in the literary context of the book of Psalms. He recognizes that the incorporation of older psalms from the earlier period of the monarchy into the book of Psalms implies a change in their use from preexilic to postexilic programs of worship. The alteration of older cultic pieces when they became part of "a written collection as literature was a major one," because "much of the actual cultic functioning of the psalms, both early and late, has been lost or obscured." In the literary formation of the book of Psalms, Gottwald notes a further tendency to make the older communal prayers available for "private 'devotion' or 'study,'" including the possibility of comparing different biblical passages with each other."[22]

Gottwald further elaborates the implications of the literary formation of the book of Psalms by observing different consequences for inner-biblical interpretation within the book itself and within scripture as a whole. For example, the psalms become part of a wider "thematizing" within scripture, so that Gottwald can speak of a "linking" of the psalms with both the written Mosaic Torah and the biblical prophets. He describes Psalms 1 and 2 as an "introduction" to the book of Psalms and provocatively proposes a number of internal relationships between groups of psalms within the context of the book of Psalms as a whole. Gottwald's endeavor contributes at this point directly to the debate over the composition-history or canonical context of the book of Psalms. In my view, he pursues these implications in his treatment of the book of Psalms far more thoroughly than he does for some other books, for example, the book of Isaiah.[23]

Gottwald's goal lies beyond merely a concern with either exploring various socioeconomic dimensions in the tradition history of the psalms or describing "the shape" of the literary composition of the book of Psalms itself. What he most wants to achieve belongs to the final section in his presentation on Psalms, under the title, "Sociohistoric Horizons of the Psalms."[24] Here he identifies the "common ground" between the social-scientific and the literary descriptions. Above all, he singles out the problem of who constitutes concretely and politically the voice of the suffering one who prays in the psalms, and who are the enemies against whom such prayers are so often directed.

For Gottwald, the late historicizing titles that link certain psalms to events in the life of David as presented in 1 and 2 Samuel might mislead one into finding a warrant for "individualizing" or "psychologizing" the psalms. He argues that even in the postexilic usage, "David stood for the righteous leader of the community" and was, therefore, "not an object of purely past historical and personal speculation."[25] Further, the collecting of older psalms into written "books" obscured or obliterated any record of their originating socioeconomic settings. This loss of information pertinent to the prehistory of the prayers in the psalms has often led later interpreters to a false view of them as expressing concern for only private fears, illnesses, or the harm done by interpersonal shaming or witchcraft. Instead, Gottwald argues that in the psalms " 'rich' and 'wicked' are often spoken in the same breath" as a sign that the social dimension of the privileged has been retained even in the biblical psalms. Moreover, Gottwald proposes that "this wealth of language about socioeconomic conflict" should be "compared with and illuminated by speeches of the prophets and proverbs of the wise." Hence, the psalms and the prophets can be seen to express the same "world of socioeconomic oppression."[26]

On this same basis, Gottwald challenges the tendency of Christian scholars to treat the prophets as "ethical" champions over against the cultus and priests who are unfairly assumed to represent only "legalism" and social conformity. If language of the psalms and the prophets belongs to the same "world of socioeconomic oppression" with its opposition to "the *pauperization of the populace*," then the priests themselves must have been supportive of these prayers by oppressed people. Though priests required the sanction of the ruling elite, they still sought to be genuinely responsive to those whom the elite oppressed. Consequently, they were in "a difficult spot." Gottwald speculates that priests may have sought "to ameliorate the worst abuses by giving cultic support to the wronged even when the courts failed and by helping to build and disseminate a community climate for the defense of traditional rights." Finally, he conjectures that this tension in the social setting of the cult "may be one reason for the vagueness of language in the laments, because to have been more explicit might have brought further recriminations and penalties on the worshippers and priests alike." From the fact that thanksgiving songs, though fewer than lamentations, are also found in the psalms, Gottwald surmises that "sometimes the actions of oppressors were blocked and frustrated . . . [despite the ruling elite's] determination to smash the tribal landholding system."[27]

This treatment of Psalms is, in my view, one of the best examples of Gottwald's effort to hold literary description and social-scientific analysis together. He challenges literary approaches that underestimate the significance of specific social factors in textual production, or seeks, on a literary-canonical level, to describe how that knowledge about that social-scientific etymology still retains influence in the realism of the present biblical text within scripture. Although Gottwald explores in only a limited manner the frequent loss, alterations, or even reversals in the semantic transformation through tradition history leading to the biblical text, he still reminds us that the retentions of reference to a flesh and blood social world of justice and injustice in the ancient past can prove as illuminating of the biblical text as other appeals to the realism implicit solely in the later purely literary "shape" of a biblical book.

By identifying the enemies in the psalms frequently as the ruling elite or their sympathizers, Gottwald is able to explain plausibly why they would not be named and hence how the priests, who depend on support from the ruling elite, could often join with the populace in worshipful protest. Underlying Gottwald's observation is the assumption that the prayers are heard in public, and, therefore, those who pray take a political risk of response from the "enemies" who overhear, or hear about, these prayers. Though I would want to add several other dimensions to Gottwald's insight about the later association of the psalms with events in the life of David, including the messianic reorientation of royal psalms and other aspects of Psalms within the intertext of scripture, my concern in this essay will be restricted to the implications of references to enemies and, more specifically, those who are assumed to be antagonists within the immediate society of those who pray.

ENEMIES WHO OVERHEAR: SOME FURTHER SOCIAL-SCIENTIFIC CONSIDERATIONS

There have been some substantial anthropological studies of prayers and their reference to enemies in preindustrialized, peasant societies. These studies often highlight the recurring pattern of an individual's "blaming" of other persons within society. As in the psalms, prayers by persons in peasant societies rarely explain misfortune by appeal to either impersonal circumstances or poor planning. This evidence points to what sociologist F. G. Bailey calls one of the "limitations" of the "cognitive map" of peasant societies.[28] "Outsiders," even if they become "officials," are usually viewed as enemies or probable enemies. Likewise, peasants who become rich are commonly assumed to have "cheated" to do so. At a minimum, we are forewarned that the identification of enemies and the rationale for identifying them in ancient Israel's prayers may, at times, have little relation to "moral" outrage. Although social injustice may, indeed, provide a legitimate basis for accusation, xenophobia and the limits of one's cognitive map may also create a search for enemies alien to our modern notion of a just and proper indictment.

Furthermore, in peasant societies the "enemies" frequently include one's peers who become unfriendly, aloof, inhospitable, uncaring, or openly antagonistic. Likewise, the psalms are replete with comments about betrayal by friends, neighbors, and family. There is hope that God will protect the one praying from those "who speak peace with their neighbors, while mischief is in their hearts" (28:3). False witnesses are described as hypocrites who once relied upon the one praying when they themselves were sick (35:11–14). There is the fear that someone who amasses wealth easily becomes pompous and aloof to the needs of erstwhile friends (49:6–20, esp. v. 16). The psalms vividly describe wicked people in the immediate society who surreptitiously abuse widows, sojourners, and orphans because they think God will not take notice of their crimes (94:4–7). Psalm 86 presents a graphic picture of the poor who seek help from such "ruthless men" (v. 14). The enemies seem to be a common topic of prayer partly because social experience confirms that even in one's own neighborhood, "the wicked sprout like grass and all evildoers flourish" (92:7). So, if psalms often consider ruling authorities enemies, as Gottwald emphasizes, they just as often assume the enemy is a peer, a neighbor, or a member of the family.

We must also be careful not to assume that antagonism against ruling authorities in public prayer is uniquely characteristic of biblical psalms. Anthropologist I. M. Lewis reminds us that "ritual relates to the existing economic and social order in a way which is neither simple nor straightforward—nor, above all, is its thrust always in the same direction."[29] Though we normally think of cults as oriented toward supporting established authorities, Lewis observes that even official royal rituals "which primarily protect and hallow the existing power structure may, however, contain rebellious episodes."[30] Lewis observes the general rule that a single public liturgy can contain prayers both of support for the ruling elite and outrage over oppression and abuses of power by those in authority. For example, in the ancient Babylonian Akitu-festival, the king receives blessing and honor, but also ritually confesses his innocence, assuring the god, Marduk, that he "did not smite the cheek of the people under your [the god's] protection." The presiding cult functionary responds by slapping the king's face and pulling harshly on his ears. Tears by the king are a favorable sign to the public.[31]

For an explanation of such ritual behavior, Lewis draws on the studies of African tribal rituals by anthropologist Max Gluckman to show that "songs of hate and unedifying scenes of ritualized violence achieve their apotheosis in a glorious paean of praise celebrating the existing order despite its habitual inequalities and injustices."[32] Prayers of protest against authorities may, following Trotsky and Marxist theories, after the "early" Marx, often seem to serve primarily as a mode of ritualized catharsis and, in fact, to dissipate the will to take revolutionary action. However, Lewis acknowledges another, even if less common, occurrence, namely, that "such ritualized rebellions were frustratingly titillating and led eventually to a greater and more fundamental cataclysmic explosion."[33] Although the ritualized expressions of violence may usually dissipate and neutralize the desire actually to retaliate, to punish, or to take power from another person, the prayer does not preclude the possibility of action either on the part of the one who prays or, as I want to call more to our attention, on the part of those who overhear. These studies confirm that ritual prayers are spoken out loud or "sung" in public; therefore, people accused in the prayers are often present, able to overhear them or at least to hear about them from others who are present.

Furthermore, we may observe that, for the psalms, Gunkel presupposes too readily that the oral use of prayer requires an oral memory with no dependence on a written record, so that the oldest units of traditions must be short.[34] From the preservation of ancient Near Eastern prayers and on the basis of anthropological studies, we now know that the fact that a prayer occurs in written form in no way betrays a necessary transition away from orality. We can assume neither that written traditions always move in the direction of an increasingly learned style in contrast to more primitive oral types of literature, nor that written traditions by their very nature presume a tendency toward silent or privatized usage. Just as Augustine was shocked to find Ambrose reading a text in silence, so we are reminded that the Hebrew verb for reading, qr', signifies principally "to call out," "read aloud," or "to recite." Recent studies have shown that up until the modern period virtually all "reading" of written texts would have been articulated out loud.[35]

For prayer, this same observation applies. Within the Bible, the account of Hannah's prayer in 1 Samuel 1 is the only full account of someone offering an individual lament in a holy city. In that narrative, Hannah came to "the house of the Lord" to ask for a child because she was barren. Eli sat by the doorpost at the time she made her vow, which was part of her prayer. She, then, "kept on praying" but "in her heart." At this point, Eli "watched her mouth," noticing that "only her lips moved, but her voice could not be heard" (vv. 12–13). For that reason alone, Eli accuses her of being drunk. Hannah asserts she is not drunk, but this extraordinary circumstance has occurred because "I have only been speaking all this time out of my great anguish and distress." Clearly, the tradition assumes that Eli's inability to overhear the prayer is exceptional rather than normal. As in the case of Job, prayers are not considered in general elsewhere in the Old Testament to be secretive, silent, or private exercises. The capacity of a prayer to be overheard is a characteristic rather than an incidental feature of it.

This social and political dimension of the prayer has begun to be recognized by both Gottwald and Croft, but remains one of the most underestimated features in psalm study today. In Claus Westermann's often cited form-critical study of psalms, he puts emphasis on three parties involved: (1) the one praying, (2) God, and (3) the enemy. In this model, the enemy stands as a distant object of the prayer, someone unaware of the psalmist's defiant voice to God.[36] On this point, I am proposing the opposite circumstance, namely, that prayers are assumed to be overheard or, later, heard about by friends and enemies alike; and, furthermore, "enemies" mentioned in these prayers, as often as not, belong to the very same social setting in which one prays. The presence of overhearing "enemies" is integral to the prayer situation and influences the perceived function of prayer socially, rhetorically, religiously, and politically.

Just as Gunkel looked to the book of Job as a model of lamentation, we find there a confirming illustration of this position. Job is joined in mourning by "friends" (2:11). His opening lamentations are overheard and evaluated by them. Early on, as his friends become antagonistic, Job voices his disappointment in them: "My comrades are fickle, like a wadi" (6:15; cf. 6:21). The word 'ōyēb, "enemy," occurs in only three places in the book. Two of the occurrences belong to an argument in which Elihu appears to quote from Job's own words found in 13:24. In that instance, Job claims that God "counts me as his enemy" (cf. 33:10). Conversely, Job's accusations of God seem to treat God as his "enemy." The remaining reference to "enemy" belongs to Job's rebuttal of his friends, accompanied by the petition "Let my enemy be as the wicked, and let him that rises up against me be as the unrighteous" (27:7). In this context, "enemy" is clearly aimed at his friends who came originally to comfort him, but have stayed to torment him with accusations. The "friends" at the beginning of the book have become by its end Job's "enemies." This scenario also explains that an overheard lament traditionally may contain threats and instruction to the enemies, as here in Job. A similar case occurs in the so-called confessions of Jeremiah, where once again family and friends have either deserted him or become active antagonists (cf. Jer 9:4–5, 12:6). Likewise, even God has dealt unfairly with him, overpowering him in a manner that resembles sexual abuse (cf. Jer 20:7). These prayers are not portrayed as silent agonies, but complaints and indictments shared with an audience to which the enemies belong.

Applying this insight to the psalms, I find three principal ways in which the enemy is indirectly addressed in these prayers: (1) as someone whom the psalmist, through overheard prayer, implicitly exposes in public and from whom protection is now sought; (2) through indictments or threats against the enemy; and (3) by harsh commands, advice, or instruction given to the enemy, often in hope for the conversion of the enemy.

Public exposure and protection. Here we return to Delekat's question "When the ones praying and their enemies . . . are private persons, why do they turn to God for protection instead of the civil courts and how do they think of this protection?" My answer is that a prayer that is overheard does, in fact, offer some effective protection from an enemy. Alternatively, for example, a person might impugn an enemy through gossip and shunning, seek illicit revenge, name the enemy in a public curse, or bring a case against the enemy in the courts. Each of these stategies entails different political consequences and different real possibilities of protection. Although taking someone to court, for instance, might in certain cases be plausible and efficient, in many other circumstances courts might not consider some charges and could offer little valuable redress in others. Gottwald recognizes well that the authorities who control the courts might be exposed and threatened effectively in prayers. Furthermore, prayer, as the anthropological evidence confirms, may be less risky in its denunciation of the elite than would some other type of public discourse or court action. The hope by the elite for a cathartic effect may provide one reason for tolerance.

Prayer provides protection for the supplicant in various ways. For one, exposure of an enemy, even though not explicitly named, brings an end to abuse denied or endured in silence. Especially in a tight-knit peasant society, these prayers about enemies undoubtedly invited those "in the know" to interpret the prayer in ways that could make obvious who the enemies were and what was the nature of their wrongdoing. The prayers could easily be "reused" to some effect by other parties. From the content of the psalms, we can see that the situation itself is presumed to be common knowledge already. So, in Psalm 41 an individual describes the "enemies" (vv. 3, 6–7, 12) who "come to visit me." Yet they are full of mischief and "go out . . . to tell it abroad," adding poignantly, "Even my bosom friend in whom I trusted, who ate of my bread, has lifted his heel against me" (v. 9). Elsewhere, the psalmist points to the irony of a time when he or she had comforted someone "as though it were a friend or my brother . . . like one mourning for his mother," but now the same person "fights against me" (Ps 35:14). Besides expressing frustration that there are no comforters and that the family no longer recognizes the one who prays, a fear is expressed in Psalm 69 that "I am the subject of gossip for those who sit in the gate." Elsewhere one observes, "Because of my foes I am the particular butt of my neighbors, a horror to my friends, those who see me on the street avoid me" (Ps 31:11–13; cf. the "empty folly" of the enemy in v. 6). Prayer is assumed to be only one moment in a larger web of intriguing words and actions in which the psalmist is fully involved. Indictments in prayer offer some protection for the psalmist because they expose actions taken by others and implicitly threaten further exposure and recognition of the same by everyone who overhears or hears from others present about the prayer.

Moreover, the words of prayer are distinguished from words used in gossip and can, consequently, be unusually blunt and graphic. In this regard, prayer becomes a significant alternative to gossip because, unlike gossip, it makes God the primary listener, maintains the intimacy of that discourse by not naming the enemy, and directly asks God, rather than neighbors, to respond in word and deed in behalf of the petitioner. As prophets are protected, despite their denunciations, by claiming that their words are God's rather than their own, the psalmist can argue that only God is directly addressed rather than the public. Just as the prophet when speaking prophetically cannot properly be charged with sedition, the psalmist when praying cannot properly be accused of gossip. In so doing, each finds protection while they publicly expose enemies, despite the need for those who overhear to interpret the ambiguous words in terms of specific parties.

Another protection sought by the psalmist through prayer is found in the actions that might be taken both by God and by those who overhear. The psalmist obviously hopes that prayer will evoke God's mercy and ensure that "the righteous will surround me" (Ps 142:7). The biblical psalms of lamentation and praise are filled with asides to those who overhear to join in prayer, to take up shouts, or even to repeat specific pious formulas.[37] In this way, prayer offers the prospect of protection both by God and by other persons who overhear and who join both in prayer and care for the one who suffers. Also, an assumption in the prayer is that those who overhear ought to be able to discern a fit between the words of the prayer and the discrete circumstances of the one praying in terms of specific persons and events. In the complaint of Psalm 38 about "enemies" (v. 19), the claim is made that "my friends and companions stand aloof from my plague, and my kinsmen stand afar off" (v. 11). This complaint presupposes that one's intimates should come near at the time of prayer and show themselves as publicly supportive. Prayers, therefore, become a unique political event that tests the loyalty of friends who must choose to stand either near or afar off. The prayer undermines the potential of secret treachery on the part of the enemy, because friends who are true sympathizers become alert to the perceived presence of an enemy.

Finally, there is some protection in the hope that the prayer itself might lead the enemy to repent and stop the wrongdoing. Although the address of prayer to God explains why the enemies do not need to be named, it also provides an opportunity for the enemies to save face, to alter their actions, or perhaps even to seek face to face reconciliation and reparation (see below, "Harsh commands, advice, and instruction to the enemy"). This circumstance stands in contrast to the real possibility of naming an enemy within prayer, as shown in the case of Neh 6:14. Furthermore, the commonplace ambiguity in the accusations of prayer hint at the possibility that the psalmist can resort to more explicit condemnation and other means of protection or remedy. Such prayers employ a less confrontative strategy than other possible verbal indictments on the part of the psalmist and, consequently, guarantee more protection for the one praying than some other type of discourse and action.

Indictments and threats. Frequently in the psalms we find appeals to God for judgment, and threats or hateful wishes directed against the enemies. God may be asked to slay the wicked (e.g., Ps 139:19), or a blessing is offered to whoever will do the same (e.g., Psalm 137). A hope for the destruction of the wicked and their families is common (e.g., Psalm 109). God's vengeance on the enemy provides an occasion to rejoice (e.g., Ps 58:9–10). These expressions seem less related to any specifically comtemplated action on the part of the psalmist than to the vivid expression of anger and wish for protection or retaliation. Perhaps one underestimated implication of the overhearing of such prayers by the enemy is the degree to which the threat itself might be an effort indirectly to persuade the enemies to change their thoughts or course of action. So, in the prophets, Jonah hesitates to deliver a threat to the Ninevites because he suspects they might repent and begrudges any blessing God might grant them. This role of the prophetic threat is, of course, assumed in Jonah to be characteristic of prophecy in general. So, too, the consequences of the prophetic threat that Isaiah brings against Hezekiah in Isaiah 38 is, by God's response to the king's response in the form of a sincere prayer, delayed by fifteen years. Likewise, the indirect threat aimed at an enemy in prayer by its very public nature allows the possibility of the enemy's repentance, reconciliation, reparation, or the abatement of offensive actions.

More rarely, a prayer may contain an indictment reminiscent of a juridical charge. Psalm 55 complains bitterly of "the enemy" who causes "the oppression of the wicked" (v. 3). The supplicant is well into the prayer when a sudden and shocking revelation occurs:

> It is not an enemy who taunts me—
>   then I could bear it;
> it is not an adversary who deals insolently with me—
>   then I could hide from him.
> But it is you, my equal, my companion, my familiar friend.
>   (vv. 12–13)

This announcement of a friend who has become like an enemy is given plaintive depth by the further assertions: "We used to hold intimate conversations together, as we walked with the throng at the house of God" (v. 14). This past companion who worships at the same place is now accused of attacking his own friend, violating the covenant, and acting as one with words "smoother than butter, yet war was in his heart" (vv. 20–21). The social context suggests that the person indicted is present and overhears the prayer and should be convicted by its rhetoric.

The formula of accusation "But it is you" (wĕ'attâ 'ĕnôš) occurs elsewhere in the prophets commonly as part of the accusation within juridical parables. For example, after Nathan tells David a parable and the king offers his judgment of the protagonist, the prophet responds, "You are the man!" ('attâ hā'îš; 2 Sam 12:7). Similarly, in Isa 3:13–14 the prophet addresses the leaders in Judah, "It is you (wĕ'attem) who devoured the vineyard!" This text has been displaced editorially from its original position with the rest of a juridical parable now found still preserved in Isa 5:1–7.[38] Psalm 55 shows at least the possibility of an accusation that surprises the friend who is unwittingly in attendance at the time of the prayer. This usage of prayer parallels exactly the use of a juridical parable by which someone is invited surreptitiously to make a judgment that, immediately, proves to be his or her own self-condemnation. Here a friend stands nearby and, therefore, supports and joins in the prayer of a lamenter. By staying close to the lamenter, the friend implicitly judges that the description of abuse is sufficient to deserve the severity of the prayer's complaint. Suddenly, the lamenter exposes the friend ("it is you") and capitalizes on the friend's unwitting self-condemnation. In this sophisticated manner, the friend is here exposed publicly as one who has, in fact, acted as an enemy.

Accordingly, the threats and wishes for opposition to the enemy in the prayer are heard as applicable to real situations rather than viewed as merely psychological projections. Besides specific indictments—for example, "You have caused friends and neighbors to shun me" (Ps 88:8, 18)—there are specific threats; for example, "May his memory be cut off from the earth" (109:13). The intensity of these accusations probably corresponds to the intensity of perceived pain, suffering, and need. If one takes seriously the degree of anguish that gives rise to these prayers, as well as the presence of the enemy so often within the community, then we must take seriously how violent ordinary life must have seemed for the ones who prayed these prayers. This violence points not only to the life-threatening power of the rich over the poor, but also to abuse within families, and between erstwhile friends and neighbors. The psalms suggest that contentment and harmony were fragile elements within the society for diverse reasons. Although threats expressed in silence toward an enemy may seem extreme to modern ears, they may become more understandable if they are overheard and pertain also to family violence, sexual abuse, and internecine conflicts that are common even today and increase when other economic injustices in society become more extreme. Although the expressed wishes for violent revenge are rhetorical, polemical, and sometimes exaggerated in tone, they should, nonetheless, be seen to reflect real feelings of hostility in response to an equally intense sense of pain and violation on the part of the petitioners.

Harsh commands, advice, and instruction to the enemy. In some of these psalms we find instructions to the enemy. Psalms often address the supportive members of the congregation in this same way. Prayers may contain admonitions, for example: "Love the Lord, all you his saints! . . . Be strong and let your heart take courage" (31:23–24, cf. 32:6). Instructive descriptions may be offered, with blessings and condemnation of certain actions: "Blessed is the man who makes the Lord his trust" (40:4; cf. 62:8) and "Behold the wicked man conceives evil" (7:14–16; cf. 10:2–11; 14:1–6; 17:10–12). Didactic teaching, including the use of proverbs, occurs throughout the psalms and resonates even in introductory invocation: "I will instruct you and teach you the way you should go" (32:8–11; cf. 37:1–40; 49:1–20; 78:1–72).

Other psalms indirectly address the enemy as well as any potential enemies among those who overhear. Prayers may contain statements in the second person, in the form of a command: "Depart from me" (6:8–10; cf. 35:19) or a repartee: "You would confound the plans of the poor, but

God is his refuge" (14:6). The opening verses of Psalm 52 have exactly this same tone, with the rhetorical question "Why do you boast, O mighty man?" In Psalm 62 the enemies are addressed at the outset: "How long will you assail a person, will you batter your victim, all of you?" (v. 3). Then those tempted to join with the enemies are instructed: "Put no confidence in extortion and set no vain hopes on robbery" (v. 10). These statements fulfill some of the promise expressed in Ps 51:13: "I will teach transgressors your ways, that sinners may return to thee." Here is seen a side benefit of public prayer. The evildoer and the potential enemy may learn from the prayer and be admonished to alter his or her actions. Similarly, Ps 94:8–11 with its proverbs assumes the same role for prayer, that the wicked and foolish might gain insight through overhearing these well-said prayers. This is so, too, in Job; immediately after calling his friends enemies (27:7), Job volunteers to "teach you according to the hand of God" (v. 11) and offers a description of the wicked man who will not prevail (vv. 13–23) in a manner similar to that of the psalms.[39]

ENEMIES WHO OVERHEAR:
A CANONICAL APPROACH

The preceding investigation has primarily been a social-scientific assessment of prayer in ancient Israel. In his *Introduction*, Gottwald highlights some implications of the collecting of these psalms into a book, and of its role within a later canonical context of scripture. He argues that much of the biblical prehistory of these prayers is retained in this later scriptural presentation. My study will conclude with some further suggestions about how the originating sociopolitical situation is partially retained, but also how the scriptural presentation subverted, reoriented, or semantically transformed other moments in the same prebiblical traditions when they became a part of scripture.

1. When the ancient prayers were collected, they often gained secondarily an association with familiar biblical figures, and a few were given historicizing titles that play directly upon episodes in the life of David depicted in 1 and 2 Samuel. Consequently, most prayers in the book of Psalms are now presented in relation to a specific set of individuals (e.g., Moses, Solomon, David, Korah, Asaph). One effect of the historicizing titles is that *the reader* can sometimes know the identity of an unnamed enemy in David's use of a prayer both by the title and by appeal to the narratives in 1 and 2 Samuel (e.g., Absalom, Psalm 3; Cush, Psalm 7; Saul, Psalms 18 and 57; Abimelech, Psalm 34; Doeg the Edomite, Psalm 52; Philistines, Psalm 56). The titles permit readers of the prayers in scripture to "overhear" them in a way similar to how they were once overheard in

their biblical prehistory. Here, to a degree, the older living situation of prayer is retained and perpetuated in the later book of Psalms.

The psalms now contribute, within scripture, to the realistic depiction of David's activity of prayer, distinct from or in collusion with other rhetorical or physical responses of David to his enemies. Once again, prayer is seen as one option, or even as an alternative to other possibilities of discourse. As in Psalm 73, the one praying thought in response to the words of the enemy, "I will talk on in this way." But such use of words would have been "untrue," and, though prayer seemed "a wearisome task," the psalmist felt differently when he or she "went into the sanctuary" (vv. 15–17). So, the decision to use prayer rather than, or in conjunction with, some other forms of discourse is not self-evident, and entails a critical decision within faith. Admittedly, these depictions do not offer us "history" in the narrow modern sense, but as a part of scripture they can be heard as witness to God's revelation regarding the politics of prayer within history. From the standpoint of canonical context, we see that social-scientific knowledge of these ancient prayers can continue to illuminate those elements retained in the book of Psalms and refines the nature of the biblical witness to prayer itself.

2. Gottwald grants that the formation of the prayers in a book of scripture obscured or altered some elements of the originating prehistory. He warns against a tendency by some scholars to find in the association of psalms with named individuals a warrant for merely pietistic or individualistic interpretations of them. Our study may help us appreciate why complaints even about illness are often accompanied by accusations of enemies. In their own way, the psalmists assumed that "illness" is never just a "private" medical problem.[40] Today, we are even more aware of how illness can be related to stress, malnutrition, inhumane conditions of labor, lack of uncontaminated water, and so forth. Additionally, how society responds to the one who prays about an illness is another test of those who overhear.

Each of these features points again to a larger socioeconomic setting, so that illness, rather than being a private matter, belongs to the entire social fabric, in both the ancient period and in the present. As a contemporary example, whether Jewish and Christian believers will touch someone with AIDS, will stand near or afar, and how they will address the enemies who contribute through carelessness or prejudice to that suffering, are all questions that pertain to the testimony of the psalms regarding the theology and the politics of prayer.

Furthermore, because "David stood for the righteous leader of the community," Gottwald warns against either naive historical or psychological speculation. In this same direction, the presentation of David as speaking prophetically in the psalms shows a further semantic transformation of the older prayers (cf. 2 Sam 23:1-2; 1 Chr 25:1-3; 2 Chr 20:14, 24:19; Acts 2:29-30; Matt 22:43; Luke 12:36). As parts of the book of Psalms, the older prayers can now be read both as commentary on the Torah and as promises that find their fulfillment, for Christians, in how the sufferings of the oppressed participate in the redemptive sufferings of Jesus on the cross. This prophetic and messianic dimension in the context of scripture resists any reduction of the psalms to merely ancient examples of individual prayers.

3. Alongside Gottwald's proposal that the unnamed enemies were frequently members of the ruling elite, our study shows that the "enemies" could just as often be neighbors, friends, or members of the family. The prayers point, in my view, to a world of intimate enemies not so different from our own. Only in the recent period have churches begun to acknowledge the all too common occurrence of violence associated with addictions, incest, child abuse, date rape, sexism in the school and workplace, racism, and the abuse of wives by husbands. This admission might help us hear, for example, Psalm 55 as a resource in connection with the abuse of wives.[41] That these prayers were meant to be overheard invites any reader of scripture to ask not only "What prayers should I pray?" but also "What prayers might others pray about me?" The role of such prayers overheard would, furthermore, represent a form of discourse that does not perpetuate denial. Instead, it would show an awareness that accusations of an intimate enemy can take a variety of forms, in the determination to stop the violence and, at times, in the hope of some face-saving repentance and reparation. The complaint need not end in prayer, but at least the one praying is challenged to become fairly articulate to God about the injustice in order to name it and to instruct those who stand nearby, even when the enemy may be included in that group.

4. Gottwald, furthermore, suggests that we can "illuminate" the language of the psalms by linking it to the speeches of the prophets. In my view, this position finds its best support by appeal to the later canonical context of scripture. This context is constructed by dependence upon an intertextuality that requires interpretive links between different collections of biblical tradition, regardless of how anachronistic these links may be from a modern historical point of view. Such an intertextuality may blur social-scientific distinctions between different periods. One may question whether there is any constant and fixed "world of economic oppression" in the history of Israel, or if the social situation and referential import of the religious language of the postexilic psalter coincides originally and

historically with the speeches of the preexilic prophets. For example, I would argue that many original possibilities once implicit in the term "enemies," including petty attitudes due to the limits of a peasant's "cognitive map," have been reoriented semantically when the earlier prayers are read as parts of the book of Psalms. In the interpretation of Psalms in the context of a later scripture, we find correlative information about enemies in the prophets (as Gottwald suggests) and in other parts of scripture as well. For one instance, the blunt antagonism against enemies in the psalms as scripture should be read within the larger intertext of admonitions to be kind to enemies in the Torah (Lev 19:17, 18; Exod 23:4–5) and in the Solomonic Wisdom books (Prov 24:17; 28:17). This larger context helps us understand, from a Christian perspective, how the teaching of Jesus about kindness to enemies finds its warrants in Jewish scripture and is not a "Christian" corrective to the "Old" Testament. Within Christian scripture, the Torah, Prophets, and Wisdom still warrant idiomatically how language about "enemies" in the book of Psalms belongs to the full human witness of the text to God's revelation of the gospel and the role of prayer within it.

5. Finally, this investigation helps us realize that prayer is always "political," as is especially obvious if it is overheard and serves as one form of public discourse in comparison with others. We may argue that prayer even when spoken in private is a political activity. Prayer requires an economic use of times and places. Prayer seeks to articulate reality, attribute aspects of reality to God, summon God to act, and nurture courage to persevere or provoke changes in the conduct of the one who prays. The question is, strictly speaking, not whether a prayer is political, but what politics pertain to this or that particular prayer. Even in silent prayer, an assumption is usually present that something transformative is happening in the solitude of prayer. For all of these reasons, the choice between piety and politics, rights and ritual, is always a false one, from a socioeconomic as well as a theological perspective. This observation stands despite the common criticism of hypocrisy in prayer, when people pray according to one theo-political agenda but conduct their lives in a way that collaborates with or even promotes the very evils condemned in these prayers.

In sum, the core of this essay has been a social-scientific consideration of prebiblical prayers that later become parts of the biblical book of Psalms. In the final emphasis on the canonical context, my aim is to help define the arena in which theological interpretation of scripture takes place. Only a few features have been considered in terms of a canonical approach.[42] At a minimum, in a theology of prayer that uses scripture as its authoritative guide, the occurrence of "enemies" in the psalms reminds us of the political background integral to all language of prayer. These observations show how the intertextuality of the book of Psalms confirms the caution of Dietrich Bonhoeffer that such prayers do not depend merely on the imagination of the heart (including social and political analysis) but ultimately seek to be an expression informed by the Word of God.[43] There is, also, the perceptive reminder by Childs that the "righteousness" underlying these prayers is not an "ideal" norm indicative of a "works righteousness."[44] Instead, "righteousness" and "justice" in the psalms both belong to the vocabulary of faith in the covenant that God freely established with Israel in association with acts of divine deliverance. For that reason, we are reminded that, as scripture, "these confessions functioned within Israel's worship as a declaration of loyalty to a prior claim."[45] In my view, it is this loyalty to a "prior claim" that requires of us a careful adjudication of modern social-scientific insight. Only by accepting that challenge can we in late modernity begin to understand profoundly how the book of Psalms as scripture still provides a normative witness to the politics of prayers for Jews and Christians alike.

A Christian response to these matters should, at the outset, acknowledge the independent value of Jewish scripture for Christian theology. Only with that full awareness may Christians seek, then, to hear properly the witness of Jewish scripture as "Old Testament" within the larger context of Christian scripture. In the latter case, Christians must look to the cross and its import for our understanding of the gospel. There are many great dangers if that effort loses its footing in the gospel, which is its true subject matter—if one finds, for example, a simple identification of "Jews" as the enemies of Jesus, or if the cross is seen as a warrant for masochism or other worldly acquiescence to injustice, or if the suffering of Jesus is viewed as a romantic, triumphalist apotheosis of pain. This important theological issue far exceeds the limits of this one essay. Its solution lies, in my view, in the direction of Bonhoeffer's challenge that Christians must learn from the New Testament witness how "the crucified Jesus teaches us to pray the imprecatory psalms."[46] This way of framing the question requires a careful consideration of both the continuity and the discontinuity that Christianity must maintain with its priceless legacy in Judaism and Jewish scripture.

7 Exegetical Storytelling

Liberation of the Traditions from the Text

Minka Shura Sprague

> Now we see through a mirror by means of a
> reflected image;
> then we shall see face to face
>
> (1 Cor 13:12)

Paul's words are as true for those of us who tell stories and do exegesis as they are for all of human existence. In his unique use of the language of optics and reflection, the apostle describes the limited perception of the human viewpoint. It is when *telos* comes, he says, that humanity can perceive through the partial to the whole, can see "face to face."

Paul speaks precisely here of the one, limited image that is received by one who views reflective glass. He does not modify the verb of perception with an adverb to describe the sight. Instead, he uses the prepositional phrase *en ainigmati* to describe the way the glass is cut, the way the mirror works. It is not that we see "dimly" or "darkly," as the English translations state. Rather, the apostle suggests, human perception at any given moment is like looking at one facet of a piece of refracted glass, a mirror, a prism. It is only when *telos* comes that the view from all the facets may be seen.

Exegetical methods and hermeneutical keys yield textual reflections in the same way that each facet of a prism yields one image of many. So, too, stories are told and retold. Each story, each exegetical analysis, yields an image of the text. None of these images is dim or murky, yet none of them is a complete view of the text. Each story, each method, is something of a true reflection, yet none sees the text "face to face."

In the story and discussion that follow, exegetical methodologies have been used as the facets of a prism for the retelling of the Noah cycle from Genesis. The story bears the imprint of exegetical analysis as well as its own hermeneutical viewpoint. Exegesis serves as the liberator of the traditions. Informed by exegesis, the traditions are freed from their canon-

83

ical context to be retold as a story willing to speak to contemporary issues in a later time.

The story I will tell and the discussion that follow offer one reflected image of the use of exegetical methodology and biblical storytelling. They serve as a model for the claim that exegesis and storytelling may be political acts of liberation in and of themselves.

THE STORY
"NOAH SPEAKS: BEGINNING AGAIN"

I did not choose to sail or fish upon return. My days upon the waters had been sufficient. I chose soil with something of relief.

"This is where we began," I said to myself, "and this is where we will begin again." I put myself, my wife, and my sons upon the soil.

"In the beginning," I mused, "we were told to serve it and preserve it. This time, I will dig deeply into it. I will till it."

I chose soil. I put myself, my wife, and my sons upon it. I set my face to the face of the ground.

I had known both life and death upon those waters. I lived with the ceaseless stirring of movement between life and death upon those waters.

I set my face to the face of the ground, for there was a stability to the soil that was good to my touch. There was a settled rhythm to the soil that was good to my soul. Season to season, creation and her rhythms brought life and death as the constants of human existence. The vines grew tall and produced fruit while the soil lay still beneath my feet.

My generations are continuous with those of Adam, yet separate and distinct. Like Adam's generations, we are creatures of the sixth day. With the cattle, the creepers, and birds of the air, we are God's own creation, called forth in the likeness of God—male and female, blessed by God and named "humanity" by God. By womb of woman and father's loin to son, my generations are related to the generations of Adam. With these generations, God calls us by the name of *hā'ādām*, "humanity."

Between us, however, stands the grief of God. Because of this grief, the flood.

Because of this grief, I watched creation herself disappear. For forty days, the cattle, the creepers, the birds of the air, and I watched her go. All of us, called into life on the sixth day. All of us watched her die. For the grief of God.

Because of this grief, my generations stand within the sign of God's rainbow.

I had no idea I was the only one. I had no idea of the extent of God's grief. I had no idea of the implications of God's words when they came to me, "I have determined to make an end of all flesh."

To this day, I am not quite sure of how or what it was that I did right. I am very old. I do not know what found me favor in the eyes of the Lord. Somehow, more than five hundred years old and the father of three sons, I was blameless in my generation, the generation of God's grief.

To this day, I do not know the human violence that caused God to regret creation. I do not know the every imagination of the thoughts of human hearts that God recognized as evil. I only know that the sight and sound and smell of humanity grieved God to the heart.

I only know God said, "I will blot out humanity whom I have created from the face of the ground, humanity and beasts and creeping things, and birds of the air, for I am sorry that I made them."

I *do* know that I did not fully comprehend God's words when they came to me. Whatever I had done to be blameless and find favor in God's sight was hardly the issue when they came.

I did not understand these words. I simply took them as they were.

God said, "I have determined to make an end of all flesh, for the earth is filled with violence through them. Behold, I will destroy them with the earth."

Nor did I know how to build when the words of the Lord came to me.

"Make yourself an ark of gopher wood. Make rooms in the ark, and cover it inside and out with pitch," God said.

Fortunately, for my sake, God's instructions were precise and comprehensive.

"This is how you are to make it," God added. "The length of the ark is to be three hundred cubits, its breadth fifty cubits, and its height thirty cubits. Make a window for the ark, and finish it to a cubit above. Set the door of the ark in its side. Make the ark with lower, second, and third decks."

The words that followed were astonishing. I was thinking of the construction, of course—where I might find the best of gopher wood and just how huge three hundred cubits might be. My mind was running to details as fast as it could go—how to get decks one atop the other and how to boil down the pitch for the painting, once construction was done. How to *do* the construction? Who could help? I was lost somewhere in the imagination of lumber and tree sap and the cutting of windows and doors when I realized that God had more to say.

"For behold," God said, "I will bring a flood of waters upon the earth, to destroy all flesh in which is the spirit of life from under heaven. Everything that is on the earth will die."

The words that I had accepted struck home. My mind stood still. "All flesh?" I said to myself incredulously. "*All* flesh? Everything?" I asked.

"Everything that has in it the breath of life, the spirit of life? The very breath and wind of God's own creation? Everything, every living thing on earth? Will die?"

The words struck home. My mind stood still. And my heart broke for the grief of God.

My mind abandoned the details of construction. My heart lay in pieces on the floor of my soul. I was shattered from the inside out.

Then God promised, "I will establish my covenant with you."

There was no time for my heart to mend. "All flesh?" echoed among its shattered fragments. There was no time to think.

The instructions came down. First, I was to build the ark according to God's design and specifications. Then, I was to bring my wife and sons, my sons' wives aboard. I was also to bring aboard the ark a male and female pair of every sort of all flesh—birds and animals and creeping things of the ground. I was to find and gather every sort of food that is eaten and take it aboard as well. Lastly, there were to be seven pairs of clean animals on the ark, a pair of the animals that are not clean, and seven pairs of the birds of the air.

I stored the instructions into the shattered recesses of my mind and soul. My heart cried out to God, "Why me?"

God replied, "For I have seen that you are righteous before me in this generation."

The generation of God's grief.

There was no time. There was no time for fretting about how life is lived righteously. There was no time for thinking how mammoth the task seemed to be. There was no time for mourning for creation herself. God had been clear; I had seven risings of the sun and moon–shinings in which the job was to be done.

"In seven days," God said, "I will send rain upon the earth forty days and forty nights. Every living thing that I have made I will blot out from the face of the ground."

The sun rose and the moon shone seven times. The task was done. My sons and my wife and my sons' wives came aboard. Male and female and two by two, the animals and birds and everything that creeps upon the ground made their ways among the decks of the boat. I prayed that the pitch would seal and shoved us all away from the earth itself.

"Goodbye," I said to everything I had ever known.

In the six hundredth year of my life, in the second month, on the seventeenth day of the month, on that day all the fountains of the great deep burst forth, and the windows of the heavens were opened. Rain fell upon the earth forty days and forty nights.

The flood continued forty days upon the earth. The waters increased and bore up the ark, and the ark rose high above the earth. The waters prevailed and increased greatly upon the earth. The ark floated upon the face of the waters. The waters prevailed so mightily upon the earth that all the high mountains under the whole heaven were covered. The waters prevailed above the mountains, covering them fifteen cubits deep.

"All flesh?" I had cried out.

Yes, all flesh.

All flesh died that moved upon the earth—birds, cattle, beasts, all swarming creatures that swarm upon the earth, and every human. Everything on the dry land in whose nostrils was the spirit of life died.

God blotted out every living thing that was upon the face of the ground, humans and animals and creeping things and birds of the air; they were blotted out from the earth.

The waters prevailed upon the earth a hundred and fifty days. I watched creation herself float away. I thought I had lost the sight of the face of the ground forever.

But God remembered. God remembered me and all the beasts and all the cattle that were with me in the ark.

God made a wind blow over the earth, God's very own breath and spirit-wind, and the waters subsided. God closed the fountains of the deep and the windows of the heavens. God restrained the rain from the heavens. The waters abated, and we came to rest upon the mountain of Ararat.

I was ready. I was hungry for soil. I yearned to feel my feet planted upon the face of the earth herself.

The moment the forty days were passed, I opened the window of the ark and sent a raven to fly forth. With that raven, I sent my breath, my own spirit-wind, to watch the waters subside.

The raven did not return.

My spirit grew weak. I forced myself to breathe.

I waited seven moon-risings more.

This time, I sent a dove from the window of the ark. "See if the waters have subsided from the face of the ground," I spoke in hope to the dove.

The dove found no place to set her foot. She returned to the ark. The waters were still upon the face of the earth.

Moon-shining and sun-rising, I watched another seven days. Those seven days, I was slow and still. My age was heavy on my frame those seven days. Slow and still, I worked to breathe. Slow and still, I walked those days with the wonder of a child.

"Seven days to call creation forth," I thought.

I walked those seven days measuring my breath. Plants and vegetation, fruit trees bearing fruit, a third day. Lights in the firmaments of the heavens for signs and seasons, days and years, a fourth day. Sweet-water and salt-water creatures and every winged bird according to its kind, a fifth day.

Like a child, I worked and watched and waited. I felt the wind of my soul against my hope. Five hundred years I lived before the sight, the sound of my firstborn child. Seven days to bring creation forth. Seven days to walk. Five hundred years were nothing like as long as those seven days.

Cattle, creeping things, beasts of the earth, humanity—a sixth day.

I took the seventh day as Sabbath-rest. In Sabbath-rest, I found a mended heart. In Sabbath-rest, I felt my breath flow free in my ancient bones. In the Sabbath-rest of the seventh day, I became a child of hope.

I sent forth the dove.

"Again!" I cried out with my Sabbath-rest hope. "Fly again! Return with a sign from the face of the ground!"

It was nearly nightfall when she returned. In her mouth she held a freshly plucked olive leaf. I knew that the waters had abated from the earth.

We made ready to land in seven days as well. These seven moon-shinings and sun-risings flew with a speed of their own. Once so carefully measured, my breath was hard to catch.

"Inhale," I said quietly to myself, and held the olive leaf in the palm of my hand.

When the seven days had come and gone, so too my dove. I sent her forth after these seven days. She did not return.

It was the six hundred and first year, in the first month, the first day of the month in which I removed the covering of the ark and saw that the face of the ground was dry. In the second month, on the twenty-seventh day of the month, the earth herself was dry and God sent us forth.

"Go forth," God said. "Bring with you every living thing that is with you of all flesh—birds and animals and every creeping thing that creeps on the earth—that they may breed abundantly on the earth, and be fruitful and multiply upon the earth."

Creatures of the fifth and sixth day, we went forth from the ark—the few of us formed from 'ādāmâ, every beast, every creeping thing, every bird. Everything that moves upon the earth went forth from the ark.

When my feet touched earth, my soul sang in thanksgiving to the Lord. With my insteps caressing the rich, dry loam of creation, I set my hands to fashion an altar to the Lord.

I took of every clean animal and every clean bird, and offered sacrifice on the altar to the Lord.

I held my breath. My mind stood still. My heart remembered. My once-shattered soul remembered how God's words struck home. All I could remember was the sound of God's voice around the words of destruction of all flesh.

I remembered the destruction of all flesh. The sound. The smell. The still.

In the stillness, I offered sacrifice and waited upon God.

In the stillness, the odor of the offering was pleasing to the Lord.

God remembered, too.

God remembered and offered to establish covenant. Again, God's words were for all flesh. This time, God's words promised life for all flesh upon the earth.

"I will never again curse the ground because of humanity, for the imagination of the human heart is evil from its youth," God vowed. "Neither will I ever again destroy every living creature as I have done. While the earth remains, seedtime and harvest, cold and heat, summer and winter, day and night, shall not cease."

So it has been. Seedtime and harvest, summer and winter, day and night come and go as I till this soil, as the vines rise to the heavens. So it has been by the vow, the covenant of the Lord. So, also, it has been for the human heart, still foolish and violent and evil in its imagination from its youth.

This has been so from the beginning. Upon this soil, the face of this fertile ground, the perversity of human imagination is still evident in my family's ways.

The generations of Adam and my generations share this truth, this human reality. This truth, that the human heart is evil in its imagination from its youth, is a hard truth. For those of us who live within the sign of God's rainbow, it is at its best an embarrassing reality, an embarrassing truth.

The covenant of the Lord accepts this truth. God's own grief stands between Adam's generations and my family's ways.

Death stands between the generations of Adam and my family's ways—the loss of breath and spirit and wind, death of God's creation and God's creatures. Death of all flesh.

And God's covenant stands between our generations.

"Behold," God said, "I establish my covenant with you and your descendants after you and with every living creature that is with you. I establish my covenant with you, that never again shall all flesh be cut off by the waters of a flood, and never again shall there be flood to destroy the earth."

God even promised to remember the memory: "This is the sign of the covenant which I make between me and you and every living creature that is with you, for all future generations: I set my bow in the cloud, and it shall be a sign of the covenant between me and the earth.

"When I bring clouds over the earth and the bow is seen in the clouds," God vowed, "I will remember my covenant which is between me and you and every living creature of all flesh. The waters shall never again become a flood to destroy all flesh. When the bow is in the clouds, I will look upon it and remember the everlasting covenant between God and every living creature of all flesh that is upon the earth. This is the sign of the covenant which I have established between me and all flesh that is upon the earth."

I did not choose to sail or fish upon return.

"This is where we began," I said, "and this is where we will begin again."

I chose soil. I set my face to the face of the ground.

It is this face of earth herself from which my generations arise. It is this face of the ground from which my vines grow tall. It is this face of earth herself from which God's rainbow springs—the rainbow within which my generations live. It is this rainbow that bears God's promise that there will never be such generations of God's grief.

ANALYSIS: A LITERARY LOOK
AT THE STORY ITSELF

Traditions. "Noah Speaks: Beginning Again" retells most of "the Noah cycle" found in Gen 5:28–10:1. The story opens and closes with Noah as tiller of the soil (Gen 5:28, 9:20) and depends upon 6:5–9:17. Noah's words interpret but do not retell the tradition in 9:21–29. The story does not consider Noah's birth and naming in 5:28–31.

Characters and point of view. In the Noah cycle of stories, God is the principal character in both action and voice. The point of view of all the Genesis stories, however, is impersonal; narration in Genesis occurs in an unidentified third person singular voice. The story depends upon Noah's existence, but he serves as the object of God's action and design.

In "Noah Speaks," God is still the principal character of the story, and Noah remains the object of God's action and design. Noah's voice in monologue, however, shifts the story's point of view and creates the illusion that Noah is the principal character. In fact, Noah's words recount a story in which his action is in response to that of God.

Conversation and sequence of events. God's voice speaks the only narrated words in the Genesis account. These words have moved from the biblical page onto Noah's lips in the story. Both Noah and God speak, and the illusion of dialogue is created. Actually, Noah is in conversation with the reader. His voice describes the events and recounts God's words. In the monologue narrative, Noah is able to respond and react to God's action without conversing with God directly. Noah's response and reaction carries interpretation of the biblical account. His assertion, "I had no idea . . . ," for example, answers the often-asked questions: "What exactly was God so angry about?" and "What did Noah do right?"

The sequence of events in the Genesis story is essentially preserved. Genesis 9:20 serves as a framework *inclusio*, limiting the story to the Noah cycle. Noah is allowed, however, knowledge of the stories that precede him, particularly the creation stories of Gen 1:1–2:3 and 2:4–25. For example, he speaks of *'ādām* and *'ădāmâ*. And his wait for the bird's return deliberately echoes the story of the days of creation.

Language. God's words from Genesis are recounted as faithfully as possible from the RSV translation of the Hebrew Bible. The exception to this is that "God" or "the Lord" have been substituted for masculine personal pronouns. Apart from the words reserved for God's voice, the bulk of the language of "Noah Speaks" belongs to the retelling of the story, characterized by the storyteller's own language and interpretation interwoven with Hebrew idioms in translation.

EXEGESIS AS LIBERATOR FOR STORY

The methodologies of grammatical, rhetorical, and canonical criticism liberate the traditions from their biblical context and permit their retelling as story.

Retranslation of the Hebrew terminology and careful use of Hebrew idioms frees the biblical story from its patriarchal theology and context. God has names instead of gender. The relationship of "humanity" to "earth" may be specified. Where English cannot precisely render the Hebrew meaning, the Hebrew words themselves may be used. The language of agriculture—"tilling" and "the soil"—may be used with reference to "the face of the ground"; at the same time, "to till" is rejected as an adequate translation of *'bd* in Gen 2:15.

Canonical criticism provides the unit of material for rhetorical work. Without attention to source-criticism, the story accepts the canonical cycle. "Community shapes text and text shapes community," Donn Morgan observes.[1] The retelling of the canonical cycle values this truth and seeks to free the tradition from the values and theology that brought it into

Genesis in the first place. "To speak of canon is to speak of text and community in dialogue," Morgan adds.[2] The retelling of Noah takes the canon and shapes it into a new story for fresh dialogue in another community.

Canonical criticism provides the framework and grammatical criticism the word-work that allows for rhetorical-critical exegesis. In this approach, "rhetorical criticism" stands much closer to Phyllis Trible's "focus upon an intrinsic reading" than to Burton Mack's "rhetoric as argumentation." Rhetorical criticism is here a "new historiography, an approach to texts with an eye to social histories."[3]

The "intrinsic reading" of Genesis that yields "Noah Speaks" is a study of the patterns and particularities of the biblical language from an identifiable hermeneutical point of view. "Although it employs learned procedures, principles and controls," Trible states, "the methodological approach resides in the realm of art."[4] This is how it can be so: "In great variety, language plays with imagery, sounds, style, and viewpoints to yield particular distinctions, subtleties and nuances. Analysis of such literary and stylistic features is the study of form and content as a key to meaning. In general, the practice of rhetorical criticism relates to literary criticism by accenting the unique as a major clue for interpreting a text."[5]

How does the Bible speak to humanity's life in creation in environmentally precarious times? This is the hermeneutical question that underlies the "intrinsic reading" of the Noah cycle. Once asked of the text, the form and content yield keys for its meaning. Noah's seven-day waits suddenly echo the creation account of Gen 1:1–2:3. The story of the Flood emerges as re-creation; the details of the original creation story stand in high relief. What is *not* in the text becomes obvious; God's grief at human ways acquires poignancy. The other seven human beings in the story fade into the background. God's covenantal promise becomes a divine reminder.

The "intrinsic reading" of the text—with grammatical criticism at its heart, canonical criticism as its frame—liberates the text from its traditions. Exegesis allows the liberation of the language, its patterns, and particularities within the confines of the "learned procedures, principles and controls" that Trible names.

Each exegetical methodology provides a reflected image of the text. The story bears these reflected images as a prism bears rays of light through each facet. The story retold offers one new clear, though partial and particular, view of the text.

The one reflected view of exegetical storytelling offers advantages in several ways. The advantage of exegesis is its ability to set the text free from the community that formed its words at the same time that the context of this formation is honored. Exegetical methodology insures the value of community, context, language, and canon.

The advantage of storytelling lies in story's ability to quicken the human heart. The story carries the exegesis for all to hear. Noah's story can speak to the human soul in a way that word-studies cannot. Story is happy to carry the fruit of the exegete's love of the text.

The advantage of exegesis refracted in story lies in its well-being in all communities. Story is already "at home" in the biblical field, as well as in the church and in the synagogue. Exegetical storytelling offers scholarship to the congregation, a quickened heart to the scholarly world. Finally, story is "at home" in the world among those wary of institutionally religious ways. Into these wary human hearts, exegetical storytelling may bring the Bible anew.

PART TWO

The Bible in
Comparative Perspectives

8 Israelite Religion and the Faith of Israel's Daughters

Reflections on Gender and Religious Definition

Phyllis A. Bird

As a contribution to the project of applying social scientific perspectives and methods to the study of the Hebrew Bible, a project deeply indebted to our honoree, I have attempted in various ways over the past decade and a half to "place" women in the social world of ancient Israel.[1] These efforts to reconstruct the lives of Israelite women and locate them within the fabric of an ancient patriarchal society have confronted me increasingly with questions about the nature of the enterprise and its presuppositions.[2] I have been brought by my latest work to focus on questions of definition and boundaries, questions raised by attempting to view social institutions and relationships through women's eyes or with attention to women's participation and experience.

The question of definition is focused in this essay by the question of religion. In shifting attention from "the place of women in the Israelite cultus" to "the faith of Israel's daughters,"[3] I found myself asking repeatedly what I was looking for and how I would recognize it. I needed a theory of religion to guide my search and provide a grid that would help me locate women's religious practice. Standard works on ancient Israelite religion offered little help in their textually oriented and (evolutionary-) historical treatments, whose compilations of diverse data on ritual practices, cultical personnel, and theological concepts lacked clear articulation of a guiding concept or sense of a unified whole. They also gave little, or no, attention to women, either as participants in communal rituals or as engaged in distinctive religious practices.[4] Anthropological treatments of religion offered the kind of systemic analysis I sought, but they too lacked

97

awareness of women as religious subjects, employing categories that either
excluded or marginalized women's contributions and offering little help in
identifying and interpreting women's religious practice.[5] In my search for
society-encompassing constructs and in my attempts to interpret individual actions and beliefs, I found repeatedly that women's practice either did
not fit the conventional categories of analysis or transgressed the boundaries (spatial and conceptual). Asking the question of women's religious
practice and belief entails a shift of perspective that affects both the
contours and the content of the phenomenon known as "Israelite religion."

This essay is an attempt to identify some of the issues of definition that
arise from this shift of perspective. It originated in an effort to present to a
general audience some of the fruits of my current research on women's
religious lives in ancient Israel.[6] It is not a presentation of results but of
questions along the way, questions I will introduce in the same manner
that they presented themselves to me, namely, in consideration of particular examples.

In my attempts to reimage Israelite religion so as to bring women fully
into focus, I have drawn largely upon anthropological studies of contemporary women's religious practice in which descriptions of actions are
accompanied by the interpretations of actors and observers.[7] I begin with
four examples that illustrate in different ways and in different contexts
problems of defining or classifying religious activity involving women.

The first is an account of a funeral in an Iranian tribal village, which
the anthropologist Erika Friedl characterizes as an "open-air religious
ceremony":

> During a funeral . . . women function as mourners, crying and singing around
> the body in the cemetery, while the men dig the grave. As soon as the body is
> buried and the prayers begin—in other words, as soon as the ceremony takes
> on a *distinctly religious* character—the women must leave.[8]

My next two examples come from a study of the religious lives of
elderly Jewish women, mostly Kurdish immigrants from Iraq, who frequented a Day Center in Jerusalem in 1984–85. The author, Susan Starr
Sered, characterizes the women as illiterate and uneducated, in a community where religion in its dominant, male expression is highly literate and
book oriented. According to Sered, women and men in the Sephardic
village culture represented by these women occupy different religious
worlds, "sometimes diametrically opposed, sometimes complementary,
sometimes overlapping."[9]

The first example from Sered's study concerns the major holidays, in
particular Passover, which Sered's informants considered the ultimate

religious holiday. Their preparations began months in advance and centered on cleaning and food preparation, both rooted in biblical prescriptions but shaped by later custom. In their cleaning, the women go far beyond the law that requires the removal of forbidden grain and other substances. "Investing weeks creating an immaculate house is one of the most important measures of a pious woman," according to Sered. "Even when the women moan and groan about the work," she says, "there is a definite element of pride in their ability and willingness to carry out a divine command in what they perceive to be the correct, female manner."[10]

Food preparation plays a central role in women's "celebration" of all major holidays, according to Sered. When asked what they or their ethnic group did on Passover, Purim, Hanukkah, and so forth, the women's answers always pertained to food or food preparation. "Food is the central symbol of each holiday for the women," Sered concludes, and "food preparation is the most important *ritual* activity . . . they perform."[11] One of the women's most difficult Passover tasks was cleaning the rice (eaten by Sephardic Jews during Passover, in contrast to Ashkenazic practice). The women sort through the rice grain by grain (sometimes as much as ten to fifteen kilos for a large extended family), repeating the process for a total of seven times. This "unnecessary" repetition, Sered argues, was understood as "a form of worship." "These women believed that sorting the rice pleases God in much the same way that it pleases God to hear prayers or Psalms of praise."[12]

A second example from Sered's study relates to tombs. "The old women who frequent the Day Center" see themselves, Sered reports, "as the spiritual guardians of their extended families." "As young and middle-aged women they tended and cared for their families, and in old age this role has become spiritualized." "Seeing themselves as the link between the generations," she says, "old women are responsible for soliciting the help of ancestors whenever their descendants are faced with problems such as illness, infertility, war, or economic troubles." "Guarding over, petitioning, visiting and negotiating with ancestors [who may be biological ancestors, or "mythical" ancestors such as saints and biblical figures] is an important part of their religious lives." The women "remember" their ancestors in a variety of rituals, including lighting candles on the Festival of the New Moon (a festival that is hardly acknowledged by the men but is celebrated by all of the women) and visiting cemeteries and holy tombs.[13] At the tombs, they typically kiss and caress the structure and cry—in a manner Sered describes as "ritualistic." In the old country, the women would often stay all night, but are prevented from doing so now by the government, which supervises the tombs.[14]

My final example is an excerpt from an interview with a 20–year-old maid in Salé, Morocco, recorded by the Moroccan sociologist Fatima Mernissi.[15] It concerns a visit to a *marabout*, a North African saint's shrine, often at the site of the saint's tomb.

> Q: *Do you go to the Marabout often?*
> A. Yes, quite often. For example, I prefer to go there on the days of *Aïd* [religious festivals]. When one has a family as desperate as mine, the shrine is a haven of peace and quiet. I like to go there. . . . I stay there hours, sometimes whole days.
> Q: *The day of Aïd it must be full of people.*
> A: Yes, there are people, but they are lost in their own problems. So they leave you alone. Mostly it's women who cry, without speaking, each in her own world.
> Q: *Aren't there any men at the shrine?*
> A: Yes, but men have their side, women theirs. Men come to visit the shrine and leave very quickly; the women, especially those with problems, stay much longer.
> Q: *What do they do and what do they say?*
> A: That depends. Some are happy just to cry. Others take hold of the saint's garments and say, "Give me this, oh saint, give me that."[16]

I have chosen this final example from contemporary sources because of similarities to the tomb visits of the Iraqi Jewish women, but also because of resemblances to the biblical story of Hannah at the sanctuary in Shiloh (1 Sam 1:1–28, esp. vv. 9–18), weeping in deep distress, without words, praying in her heart for a child, and making a vow (a typical form of women's devotion in Islam). Although this example is not primarily concerned with religious boundaries and definitions, it illustrates the way in which women use general or male-dominated religious institutions and occasions for their own purposes to suit their own peculiar needs, investing them at times with their own rituals and meanings (as when the Jewish women light candles at the tombs or throw unlighted candles through the grating where they are prevented from direct access to the tomb).[17]

The *marabout*, or the local sanctuary in Israel, is a place where a woman can go according to her own needs and opportunities. Her visits may coincide with a communal festival, especially where a pilgrimage is involved (in which case we should probably speak of a regional, rather than a local, sanctuary). Her visits are not determined, however, by calendrical observances and prescriptions—that is, by feasts of the agricultural year, related primarily to men's cycle of labor—except in dependence on men's obligations. Within the total spectrum of religious observances, individual pilgrimages to shrines and visits to graves appear to play a more important role in women's religious lives than in men's. Thus a practice that may be secondary or peripheral for men may be central for women.

In the case of Hannah, the occasion for the visit to the sanctuary was the annual pilgrimage of her husband Elkanah. This pilgrimage is usually understood to have been one of the three mandated feasts when "every male" was to "appear before the Lord" (Exod 23:17), although it may have been a clan festival.[18] In either case, it is the man's obligation that determines the visit, but it entails family participation of wives and children, all of whom share in the sacrificial meal. Hannah, however, uses this occasion to bring her desperate distress to the attention of the deity and to make her vow. She must certainly have prayed often and fervently for a child in her home, but she apparently regarded the sanctuary at Shiloh as an especially efficacious place for her petition—a place where the deity was felt to be present in a special way, just as the saint's spirit is understood to be present in the *marabout*.[19]

Two of my examples concern ancestors, saints, and tombs, with which women appear to have a special affinity. The association of women and tombs is not limited to modern Judaism and Islam. Peter Brown notes the attraction of women to tombs in his book on the cult of the saints in Latin Christianity. He comments that throughout the Mediterranean world (of late antiquity) the cemetery was the only place where women could find respite and protection.[20] Ancient Israel, however, or at least the tradition canonized in the Hebrew Bible, had no place for the cemetery or for ancestors in its worship. Both ancient Israel and later Judaism attempted to draw a firm line between the world of the living and the world of the dead. The God of Israel was a God of the living, not of the dead (Ps 88:5–6; Isa 38:18–19; cf. Matt 22:32 // Mark 12:27 // Luke 20:38). Attempts to communicate with the dead were condemned and mediums banished (1 Sam 28:3, 7–19). Tombs are desacralized in the Hebrew Bible—but they persist in the landscape to emerge in aetiological notices (Gen 35:8 [Deborah]; Judg 16:31 [Samson]; Josh 24:30 [Joshua]); incidental remarks ("you will meet two men by Rachel's tomb" [1 Sam 10:2]); and prophetic denunciations of practices that "provoke the Lord" ("sitting inside tombs" [Isa 65:4]).

Sered's report of the women's rituals relating to graves and her interpretation of their actions suggest a number of questions about the *religious* meaning of graves and ancestors in ancient Israel and the relationship of women to such actions and beliefs. I can only touch on these, noting first of all that the women's "devotion" to the ancestors reported by Sered finds no basis in ancient or modern (Israelite/Jewish) religious prescriptions; in fact, it is discouraged. This should alert us to the possibility of ritual activities and religious beliefs that receive no mention in our texts but nevertheless play a significant role in the lives of ancient Israelite women—

or men. Popular practice and belief that is not seen as directly threatening may go unreported—the more so, one may speculate, if identified with women.

The question of ancestral cults or a cult of the dead in ancient Israel needs to be raised again,[21] and more particularly the question of women's roles in such cults. Earlier reconstructions of Israelite religion that found its origins in a cult of the deified ancestor typically argued that women had little or no place in Israelite religion, because only a male heir could perform the essential duty of representing and propitiating the deceased ancestor.[22] Such reasoning appears sound insofar as continuity of "name" or lineage is the primary concern of the cult; but Sered's report of the Iraqi women's understanding of themselves as the link between the generations, "mothers" of the deceased as well as the living, gives us reason to ask whether women, precisely in their role as mothers (the one role singled out for equal honor with men), might have had a role in an ancestral cult alongside the male head of the household or lineage.

The suggestion by Karel van der Toorn that the teraphim should be understood as ancestral images, in the sense of a deified ancestor, raises further interesting questions about women's role in such a family cult.[23] Although the account of Rachel's theft of the teraphim (Gen 31:19, 30–35) clearly identifies them/it[24] as belonging to her father, it is interesting to note that the only two narrative references to teraphim in the Hebrew Bible place them in women's hands (Michal in 1 Sam 19:13, 16).[25]

Attention to women's religious practice raises questions of religious definition and boundaries in relation to family or ancestral cults, regional and local cults, magic, and mediation. In general, women appear to be identified primarily with local rather than national or centralized forms of religious expression, and with "folk" practice (often viewed as "superstition") rather than the learned tradition. For ancient Israel, we need to ask about the existence, form, and function of a family cult alongside the national or pan-tribal cult of Yahweh: How were family and national cult related?[26] What role did women play in family or household cults? Was the family cult necessarily an ancestral cult?

The importance of regional sanctuaries has long been recognized, although the question of distinct regional cults has usually been relegated to the premonarchic period. The meaning of these sanctuaries, however, as well as the local shrines (*bāmôt*: "high places") denounced (in Deuteronomistic circles) as places of pagan worship, needs to be reexamined with reference to women's practice and women's religious needs. Mernissi's account, which can be paralleled elsewhere in the Muslim world, suggests that visits to local shrines, pilgrimages, and individual acts of petition and dedication related to particular needs were favored by women and better suited to the general rhythms and the exigencies of their lives than were the major communal rites and celebrations.

A variant of this shrine-oriented pattern of seeking supernatural aid might be seen in visits to mediums or seers. It is difficult to assess the evidence for gender-differentiated involvement in such practices, partly because the activity is generally discouraged or condemned by religious elites and partly because of inadequate sources and problems of terminology.[27] The predominance of women as mediums and clairvoyants has been noted in many cultures, as well as the prominence of women as participants in ecstatic cults.[28] Women are more commonly accused of sorcery and identified as witches;[29] they are also popularly viewed as more inclined to the use of magic. The issues involved in this assemblage of marginal or quasi-religious practices are too complex for discussion here. What requires note, however, is that the criteria that are often used to distinguish these types of activity from recognized and/or approved religious practice often coincide with common distinctions between male and female realms or patterns of action.

Women's practice cannot simply be identified with magic or mediums or local cults, because it transgresses these boundaries. However, because it is so frequently characterized by practices that are normally located at or outside the limits of normative/male-defined religion, focusing on women draws attention to the problematic character of these limits. This may be illustrated by another class of evidence that refers to women's world, at least symbolically, but whose meaning remains uncertain precisely because it cannot be neatly located by conventional categories of classification. That is the small terracotta figurines of a naked female found throughout Iron-Age Palestinian sites. Variously described as images of a goddess or of a pregnant/fertile woman, as objects of veneration, amulets, or toys, they have baffled interpreters because of their anomalous distribution. They are found both in domestic sites, occurring singly in private houses, *and* in collections associated with sanctuaries, especially of the extramural/peripheral type.[30] We are uncertain of their function or name, and we cannot connect them with certainty to anything in the biblical text. They challenge the conventional boundaries between sacred and secular, domestic and foreign cult, orthodox (Yahwistic) and idolatrous practice.

Another kind of question about definitions and boundaries is illustrated by my first example. Here we see a case in which women play an essential, and ritually elaborated, role as mourners in a communal ceremony; but only the prayers, recited by the men, are understood as religious. Nevertheless, Friedl characterizes the ceremony as a whole as "religious." On what basis is that assessment made? From whose point of view? Friedl describes the women of this village as holding essentially the same views as the men concerning the requirements of religion (in this case Islam). Because of their inability to fulfill the gender-blind demands in an optimal manner, the women generally considered themselves to be "bad Muslims" and even "heathens," concurring in the men's low assessment of their religious character.[31] A cycle of low expectations, lack of religious training, and obstacles to full participation in communal religious practices centered in the mosque worked to reinforce women's religious marginality. Unlike their urban counterparts, they had no religious rituals or activities of their own to complement men's rituals from which they were almost completely excluded.[32] It appears likely, then, that both the women and the men viewed the prayers alone as religious.

One of the questions raised by this example concerns the extension of religion into the "secular" realm or the realm outside the sanctuary or recognized holy place.[33] Common means of extending the realm of the holy into the realm of the profane include prayers and blessings that invoke the deity, actions of sacred persons or religious experts, and use of sacred objects or texts. Do these special actions or symbols transform the entire event into a religious event, or does it become "religious" only at the point where explicitly religious language and symbols are introduced?[34]

There is a deeper question, I think, about the assessment of religious meaning in the gender-differentiated actions of the funeral ceremony that is not adequately answered by identifying the religious element with the prayers alone. It concerns the definition of "religion" and "religious," and the ability or right to define. The view that identifies the prayers as the religious element of the ceremony represents a narrow definition of religion identified with a set of formal practices or symbols. There is, however, a wider area of practice, feeling, and cognition characterized by understandings of social obligation and welfare, of duty to family, community, nation, or people, of "right" action or conduct pleasing to God, that might be subsumed under a broader definition of religion. Sered draws on such an understanding in interpreting the actions of her informants as "religious."[35] Following her lead, we might ask in a broader way how the women mourners understood their role: As a duty—or as a "natural" response, as something needed by the deceased? As required or desired by God? One might argue that the women's sense of the necessity and appropriateness of their culturally specified part in the funeral ceremony was functionally equivalent to that of the men in the performance of their culturally specified actions.[36]

Insofar as lamentation and prayers are both required rituals of the burial ceremony and are recognized as such, the formal distinction between "religious" and "not religious" loses some of its force, although it does not disappear completely. If we were to ask further about the women's own understanding of their role, we might discover that although acknowledging the men's monopoly of the religious symbols, they themselves accord these symbols less weight than do the men. When the men complain that the women have little religious "sense" or sensibility, they may be confirming that in fact the women have less involvement and/or investment in the symbolic world controlled by the men. We must consider the possibility that the distinction between the sacred and the profane falls at a different place or carries different weight or implications for women than it does for men in the same society.

I realize that the question of who defines what is religious can be understood as meaningless or moot. The obvious answer is that the society defines in the complex way that societies create culture and institutions, generate myths, values and rules of conduct, and in general construct and maintain a worldview. To say that society defines, however, means in ancient Israel, and in modern Iran, that men define, because the means of creating and enforcing common cultural understandings lie in the sphere of male activity and male control. If the public sphere, the sphere of the society's overarching and integrating institutions, is not exclusively a sphere of male activity, it is still a sphere dominated by males and male interests; and if women play a significant role in transmitting and inculcating the society's perspectives and values and may thereby affect the shape of those cultural understandings, they still lack control of the means for developing a distinctive voice or vision of their own. A fundamental characteristic of patriarchal societies is asymmetry of gender-differentiated roles and institutions. The primary spheres of male and female activity are not strictly complementary; rather, the public sphere, dominated by males, encapsulates and penetrates the domestic sphere through its laws, religious values, and worldview.

I have already suggested one way in which this male power of definition may need to be qualified—not at the level of content, but in the degree of authority or ultimacy accorded to it and in the relative weight given to various constitutive elements. Although I would maintain that men and women in the same society do not hold different worldviews, women's perspective on, and investment in, that common worldview is conditioned by their different location within it and by the degree to which they possess freedom and power to manipulate its symbols.[37]

The society defines what is religious and what is not, just as it determines the content of religious belief and the forms of religious practice; and it is the historian's or anthropologist's first duty to articulate the meaning of this institution or aspect of culture in a manner that would "make sense" to members of that society. But the effort of "making sense" is always a creative act, whether done from the inside or the outside. The outside observer invariably brings to the task views and understandings alien to the society being observed. There is a sense, then, in which any society or institution viewed from the outside is defined by the observer. "Religion" is a construct imposed on the ancient society by a modern observer who attempts to understand and delineate its referent by comparing it with similar phenomena in other societies. The historian or anthropologist has a unique freedom, as an outsider, to see what no member of the society can see, to achieve an overview, but also to discern tensions and cleavages that may not be recognized or articulated from within, that may be felt but never formulated.

The contribution of feminist criticism has been to identify gender as a critical factor in the social and symbolic construction of the world and to analyze its role in the distribution of power and honor. In the case of the funeral, the question of religious definition—the shape and boundaries of the sacred realm—leads to recognition of a fundamental asymmetry in the men's and women's roles, both of which are essential to the performance of the ceremony. The element of the ceremony or ritual process that makes it "religious" is reserved to males, but the ceremony requires the contributions of both men and women—both of which take ritual form. Funerals require mourners (perhaps even more than prayers); and cross-culturally, women play a prominent specialized role in mourning, which may acquire professional status and involve special training. This phenomenon is well attested in the Hebrew Bible (Jer 9:17 [Heb 16], 20 [Heb 19]; 2 Chr 35:25) and is illustrated by tomb paintings from Egypt and sculptured reliefs on a royal sarcophagus from Byblos.[38]

The role of women in relation to feasts (which generally have some religious occasion) may be seen as analogous to their role in funerals, except that it is more clearly confined to the preparatory stages, with spatial and temporal separation of the men's and women's actions—especially in those cases where the sacred meal is consumed only by men, or in which only the men's segregated eating is ritually elaborated.[39] It is not clear what sort of ritual actions may have been performed at sacred meals in early Israel, if any (the symbolic actions may have related only to the sacrifice).

Both funerals and festival meals celebrated in the home represent a class of ceremonies located outside the sanctuary or cult site. In these celebrations, the domestic and public realms meet and overlap (or interpenetrate). Men bring the prayers, blessings, and ritual actions of the sanctuary into the home or kinship gathering,[40] whereas women contribute actions that are elaborations or extensions of their normal roles and activities within the household. The professional mourner represents a specialization of the woman's "natural" role as grieving mother. These gender-differentiated actions also extend to actions related to the sanctuary. Elkanah sacrifices annually; Hannah dedicates her child and annually brings him a little robe that she has made for him (1 Sam 2:19): two forms of devotional action—or fulfillment of obligation. Are both religious? Of equal value?

Forms of religious observance that take place apart from sanctuaries and without a recognized religious specialist are difficult to assess. Here the line between religion and magic, sacred and profane is less sharply or clearly drawn. But it is precisely here that women are most involved.[41] Even more difficult to evaluate, however, are activities involving only women, or centered on women's experience and performed in women's space, such as rituals of birth and menarche. In Mesopotamia there is evidence for the Old Babylonian period of a class of priestesses associated with the midwife in a birth ritual, but this cultic association—or the religious function assumed by the midwife—seems to have been lost in the subsequent period.[42] In Israel the midwife has no religious function, though blessings associated with birth suggest a religious association.[43]

I have only touched on the issues that are raised in trying to place women in religious systems defined by male participation and male constructions of meaning. The problems involve both placement and interpretation of women's roles and activities. The limited examples I have offered suggest that women may respond in quite different ways to their exclusion or marginalization in a male-defined system.[44]

For ancient Israel, I believe it is essential to recognize gender-differentiated roles, activities, and experience as a fundamental characteristic of religious as well as social, political, and economic life, and to recognize asymmetry as a fundamental feature of these relations. Religion defined in male terms or according to male models has difficulty placing women and assessing their piety, whether it imitates men's, in which case it rarely achieves parity, or assumes distinctive female forms, which may either go unacknowledged or be identified with foreign or heterodox cults. The whole question of religious pluralism *within* a national Yahweh cult is just beginning to be explored in relation to evidence for Asherah as a symbol operating within Israelite Yahwism. Women's religion cannot be equated with goddess worship, but there is sufficient evidence to suggest that women's religion did represent a significantly differentiated form of religious expression within Yahwism, which must be studied along with other forms of pluralism in the religion of ancient Israel. To speak of the faith of Israel's daughters means at the very least to reexamine the boundaries of the religion we have reconstructed and to make room for more differentiated forms of piety than we have hitherto imagined—with attention given to hierarchies of power in a gender-differentiated system of roles and offices.

9 Prometheus, the Servant of Yahweh, Jesus

Legitimation and Repression in the Heritage of Persian Imperialism

John Pairman Brown

> "Today you will be with me in Paradise"
> (Luke 23:43)

Jerusalem, in the time of Jesus, was at the frontier of two empires. Although it was the Roman empire that executed Jesus, the saying in Luke, like other New Testament materials, acquires fresh light from Parthian imperial symbolism. This essay will (1) sketch the historical succession of the imperial idea; (2) show that within that history Jesus appears as the successor to Greek and Hebrew rebel-victims under Persian rule—Prometheus and the Servant of Yahweh—but also as one to whom both Roman and Persian imperial titles were ascribed; (3) show that Rome knew Persian symbols of legitimation, mostly as exotic, and developed native functional equivalents; (4) show that Oriental-Persian modes of repression continued in Rome substantially unchanged.[1]

The Crucifixion took place far to the west, under the rule of Tiberius (14–37 CE), brooding on the Palatine or at Capri. Closer at hand was Artabanus III the Parthian (about 12–38 CE, with gaps[2]) in his winter palace at Ctesiphon on the Tigris (Strabo 16.1.16). For a while, his rival Vonones was interned by the Romans nearby, in Syria or Cilicia, no doubt as a check on the incumbent (Josephus *Ant.* 18.52; Tacitus *Ann.* 2.58). In 35 CE, Artabanus wrote to Tiberius demanding Vonones' treasure and impertinently offering to annex the former empires of Cyrus and Alexander (Tacitus *Ann.* 6.31). A Roman put the two empires on a par, *duo imperia summa Romanorum Parthorumque*, and a Greek called them "rivals" (*antipaloi*).[3]

At Rome, crucifixion was "the slaves' punishment," *seruile supplicium*.[4] It is already a paradox, then, that Jesus should have been so executed as "king of the Jews." In a Jewish context, "paradise" could only refer to the Garden of Eden (so translated in the LXX of Gen 2:8; thus Rev 2:7, "the tree of life in the paradise of God"). But the Davidic king is not said to restore Eden for his people, and Luke does not again take up Paul's theme of Christ as a greater Adam (cf. 1 Cor 15:22).

With the Old Persian kings, crucifixion in some form was the punishment of pretenders to the diadem. Darius says that he "impaled" four rivals.[5] The exact meaning in the Old Persian is unclear, but the Babylonian version (as we will see) looks back to the boasts of the Assyrian kings. In it, he says of Fravartish the Median, "Then upon a stake (*za-ki-pi*) at Ecbatana did I affix him."[6] *zakīpu*, "stake," is from *zkp*, "lift up." One that alters the Aramaic decree of another Darius at Ezra 6:11 shall have a beam pulled out from his house, "and he is to be lifted up (*zkyp*) and fastened on it"; the participle recalls the Akkadian noun, which recurs in the Syriac Gospels, where "cross" is regularly *zkyp*. Again, in the Old Persian empire, the "paradise" is a hunting-park, the prerogative of king and satrap. Thus, in Iranian context, Luke 23:43 has an excellent specific sense: although Jesus is executed as a pretender to some diadem, he is in fact its legitimate wearer.

Norman Gottwald whom we honor saw early Israel as a reaction to Egyptian imperialism and Canaanite feudalism. I see later Israel in the light of Persian imperialism and its successors, a position much better documented. Even so there is debate, for example, regarding how far Roman imperialism was consciously intended.[7] Here I study techniques of control, which are more accessible than the motives of rulers. I take up two parallel continuations of the Achaemenid empire (560–330 BCE): its direct descendants, the Arsacid (250 BCE–228 CE)[8] and Sassanid (226–651 CE) dynasties; and its indirect descendant, Rome, via the Seleucid kingdom and Carthage. Ideal items of the Iranian heritage will be those embedded in Persian loanwords,[9] or calques, however transformed, on the very scene of the former empire. The Eastern empires regularized their techniques of control in the face of resistance by less autocratic states. The triumph of those techniques lay in their adoption by the West through the transformation of states once democratic (Athens, a great exactor of tribute) or oligarchic (Carthage, Rome) into capitals of empire.

The ongoing vitality of imperial techniques in their Roman form is surprisingly attested by Edward N. Luttwak, both Roman military historian and American strategic analyst, in his comparison of the two situations:

> We [Americans], like the Romans, face the prospect not of decisive conflict, but of a permanent state of war, albeit limited. We, like the Romans, must

actively protect an advanced society against a variety of threats rather than concentrating on destroying the forces of our enemies in battle. Above all, the nature of modern weapons requires that we avoid their use while striving to exploit their full diplomatic potential.[10]

Translate, "nuclear deterrence." Again, on the dilemma of tying down troops to police remote frontier regions (for example, Judaea then, and South Korea now), Luttwak notes:

> It is for this reason [the need of quick response] that American troops must be stationed in the theater itself, with the resultant diseconomy of force, regardless of the obvious political functions that these deployments also serve.[11]

In the extensive literature on Iranian parallels to biblical and apocryphal texts[12] I briefly note two items. First, Morton Smith[13] has laid out striking parallels between a poem of Zarathustra and the Hebrew doctrine of creation. The Avestan text is a series of questions addressed to Ahura Mazda: (1) "Which man has held the earth below and the heavens (*ząmcā adā nabåscā*) from falling?";[14] compare, "Who has . . . marked off the heavens with a span, enclosed the dust of the earth in a measure?" (Isa 40:12). (2) "Which craftsman created the luminous bodies and the dark spaces (*raocåscā daṭ tomåscā*)?" (*Yasna* 44.5); compare, "I form light and create darkness" (Isa 45:7).[15] The questions of priority and relationship have barely been addressed.

Second, Iranian demonism downgrades Sanskrit *deva*, "god." Xerxes overthrew the sanctuary (unknown) of certain false gods, *daivā*; so Avestan, *daēva*.[16] Often the Syriac Gospels translate Greek *daimonion* by the Iranian loanword *daywa'* (e.g., Matt 9:33–34).[17] Because the Gospel *daimonion* represents the co-optation of the psyche by an outside social structure like the "Legion" of Mark 5:9, the political rejection of the *daivā* continues.[18]

THE SUCCESSION OF EMPIRES

The Romans saw themselves as inheritors of Near Eastern imperialism:

> The Assyrians were the first of all races to hold world power (*rerum potiti sunt*); then the Medes, Persians and Macedonians. Then through the defeat of the two kings Philip and Antiochus, not long after the overthrow of Carthage, imperial control (*summa imperii*) passed to the Roman people.[19]

This text picks up an old historico-mythical scheme of four or five successive realms; it still corresponds fairly closely to reality. At Dan 2:36–45 it is combined with the motif of four successive ages of metal, which in Hesiod appears apart from world empire.[20] Appian[21] says that Scipio at the fall of Carthage in 146 BCE thought of the fall of Troy, Assyria, the Medes, Persia, Macedon, and in some future, of Rome herself. A Greek historian

(Dionysius of Halicarnassus 1.3.3) lists previous empires—the Assyrian, Median, Persian, Macedonian, and the Successors—and adds, "But Rome is the first and only one to have made the rising and setting of the sun the boundaries of its *dynasteia*."

Actually, he is applying an old Oriental theme to Rome. Esarhaddon defines his realm as "from sunrise to sunset," *TA na-pa-ah* ^{d}*šam-ši a-di e-reb* ^{d}*šam-ši.*[22] A Greek orator (Aeschines 3.132) says that Xerxes claimed to be "despot of all men from the rising sun to the setting." So Mal 1:11, probably of the Persian period, proclaims: "From the rising of the sun to its setting my name is great among the nations" (and so Ps 50:1, 113:3). The Romans relished the phrase; Sallust (*Cat.* 36.4) speaks of the *imperium populi Romani* "at a time when all peoples from sunrise to sunset, overcome by its arms, obeyed it" (*cui cum ad occasum ab ortu solis omnia domita armis parerent*).[23] This is the imperial background to Jesus' boast: "Many will come from east and west and sit at table with Abraham, Isaac, and Jacob in the kingdom of heaven" (Matt 8:11).[24] When Muhammad made the same boast, "To Allah belong the East and the West" (*Quran* 2.142), it was shortly to acquire imperial reality also. In a parodistic passage, James Joyce says of Queen Victoria, "For they knew and loved her from the rising of the sun to the going down thereof, the pale, the dark, the ruddy and the ethiop"[25]—a learned improvement of "the empire on which the sun never sets."

The Greeks knew little of the Assyrian and Babylonian empires. In Israel, institutions of their occupation were blurred over by the two centuries of Persian control. Thus the forms of Near Eastern imperialism inherited by the West passed through a Persian phase. A nice example is the name given over the centuries to various functionaries: the "ruler of a thousand," in Greek *chiliarch*. Darius set over his army rulers of a thousand and ten thousand (Herodotus 7.81). Sapor speaks of a *hzrwpt*, where the Iranian appears in Greek as *azarapateis* and in Rabbinic as *gzyrpty.*[26] There was one such par excellence, an Artabanus under Xerxes, "master of the royal audience" and commander of the king's bodyguard of a thousand.[27] Alexander took over the office, and Antipater installed his own son Cassander as chiliarch (Diodorus 18.48.4–5). The Hebrews also had rulers of a thousand (Exod 18:21). Rome had a roughly comparable rank in the *tribunus militum*, commander of a tenth of a legion, or six hundred men, in Greek given the honorific Seleucid title *chiliarch.*[28] From all these sources, the little romanized militia of Herod Antipas in Galilee had chiliarchs (Mark 6:21), merely transcribed in the Old Syriac, as the Nabataean army has a *klyrk'?*[29] A midrash in an imaginary military hierarchy of six has the *klyrkws* next to bottom;[30] the "chiliarchs" of Rev 6:5, 19:18 are in equally vague context. But in John 18:12 and Acts 21–24 the *chiliarchos* is an actual Roman soldier (the Vulgate correctly has *tribunus*), who thus in Palestine is stepping into the boots of his Persian, Seleucid, and Aramaean counterparts.

I offer a final point of precision. Where we say "[Old] Persian," the Greeks very often have "Median": thus "the battle at Marathon of Medes against Athenians" (Thucydides 1.18.1). The Greeks cannot have mistaken their enemy; Medians were the line troops.[31] Further, Western texts favor Median linguistic forms over Persian.[32] Thus the name of the *satrap* in Greek and Hebrew always has an internal dental consonant followed by *r*.[33] The Old Persian is *xšaçapāvā*, "kingdom-protector," whereas the Median Fravartish took the name *Xšathrita*, which implies Median *xšathra*, "kingdom," as in Avestan.[34] It was the Median form that survived into the Sassanid period; for in the great trilingual inscription of Sapor (about 260 CE),[35] the Parthian has *ḫštrp* and the Middle Persian *štrp*. Thus the Persian-speakers who won the kingship and wrote the inscriptions were a minority, whereas Medes staffed and named the imperial offices, fought the battles, and shaped the future of the language.

THE REBEL VICTIMS

In the Hellenistic world, hidden currents of sympathy worth further study flowed among resistance movements. Joseph Vogt[36] thinks that the slave revolt of Eunous in Sicily (136–132 BCE) had relations to the Seleucid kingdom and was likely "influenced by the Maccabean war of liberation." Eunous was a follower of the "Syrian goddess," that is, Atargatis; he called himself "Antiochus" and the rebels "Syrians."[37] Toynbee[38] compares the Gospels to Plutarch's biographies of Hellenistic and Roman popular leaders. With Matt 8:20 // Luke 9:58, "Foxes have holes (*phōleoi*), and birds of the air have nests; but the Son of man has nowhere to lay his head," he compares the saying of Tiberius Gracchus: "The wild beasts that roam over Italy have a hole (*phōleos*), to each is its lair or nest; but the men who fight and die for Italy have no share in anything but air and sunshine" (Plutarch *Gracchi* 9.4).

I propose that in an earlier period, symbolic figures of victimization and rebellion under Persian imperialism—likewise joined by hidden currents of sympathy—appear in Aeschylus' Prometheus and the Suffering Servant of Second Isaiah. Podlecki[39] sees the *Prometheus Bound* as a critique of tyranny in the Greek city-states. But its Zeus, the "new tyrant among the gods" (*PV* 310), is a more universal figure; the scene is Scythia, the play includes two surveys of what is in effect the Persian empire (*PV* 408ff., 705ff.) Io's tormentor Argos, with his "crafty eye" (*PV* 569), is reminiscent of the "King's Eye," or intelligence service.[40] The more we meditate on Zeus' attributes in the play, the more parallels we find to the Great King. Above all, the running critique of tyranny in the *Prometheus Bound* agrees with the critique of tyranny that Herodotus puts in the mouth of the Persian Otanes.[41]

A recent touring Vatican art exhibit included a black-figured Laconian vase of about 555 BCE attributed to the Arkesilas painter.[42] Prometheus is tied to a column at right while the eagle attacks his chest; at the left, Atlas holds up a starry sky. The two antagonists of Zeus are punished together as in Hesiod (*Theog.* 517–25) and Aeschylus. The Catholic context irresistibly defined the scene as a crucifixion, complete with the carrion bird that in the old curse (see below) preys on the defenseless body.[43]

The nineteenth century read Aeschylus' play as an attack on *all* authority, political and religious. Shelley, in the Preface to his *Prometheus Unbound*, refused the theme of "reconciling the Champion with the Oppressor of mankind" and plainly identifies omnipotent Jupiter, responsible for "thrones, altars, judgment-seats, and prisons," with the Christian God.[44] Marx, in the Preface to his doctoral thesis,[45] calls Prometheus "the most eminent saint and martyr in the philosophical calendar." A cartoon of 1843 on the censoring of the *Rheinische Zeitung* shows Marx as Prometheus, chained to a printing press.[46] Posted to the press is a canceled page of the journal; the chain leads up to the leg of a heavenly throne. Marx's heroic figure is surrounded by lamenting Oceanids, done in the style of the odalisques of Ingres. His liver is being attacked by the crowned Prussian eagle, also tethered to the throne; a long line of carrion birds in the sky await their turn.

One theological reaction to the revival of Prometheus was to reject whatever atheists accepted, at the cost of having to swallow Aeschylus' Zeus as a portrait of God. Thus Karl Barth writes enigmatically on Rom 7:7:

> Under the scrutiny of law men became sinners . . . ; for in the end human passion derives its living energy from that passionate desire, *Eritis sicut Deus!* . . . Can there be any affirmation of passion that outstrips the passion with which Prometheus robs Zeus of his fire and uses it for his own advantage?[47]

Hans Küng spells out the underlying thought when he rejects the rebellion of "rising up defiantly against the power of the gods, like emancipated, autonomous Prometheus."[48] Environmentalists do better justice to the genuine ambivalence of the tragedy when they accuse Prometheus of the crime of bringing the primordial technology of fire to earth.

The New Testament suggests an ambiguous parallel between Christ and Prometheus. The risen Jesus tells Paul, "It hurts you to kick against the goads" (Acts 26:14). This quotes exactly a classical Greek proverb;[49] less closely, Oceanus advises Prometheus not to "offer your limbs to the goads" (Aeschylus *PV* 323). But in our times, the Christian-Marxist dialogue, over against Barth and his followers, has fully engrafted Prometheus onto Christ.[50] Thus we read in the enormous work of the atheist Ernst Bloch:

> Prometheus, through his poet Aeschylus, became as it were the founder of his own religion, one which did not of course blossom out. It had to remain unblossomed in the spirit of its rebellion, firstly because a social mandate such as that of Moses against the Pharaoh, of Jesus against Caesar, was lacking.[51]

The Czech theologian Jan Milič Lochman—in words now applicable to the former Soviet tyranny—demands a place for Prometheus in theology, in three areas: (1) challenging the idea of God as "an inhuman superstructure imposed on humanity from above"; (2) revealing that inertia in face of God's promise of liberation is as great a sin as *hybris*; (3) pointing to grace as that which "mobilizes human creativity," a driving force for "Promethean existence."[52]

Toynbee sees the "creative power of suffering" as equally illustrated by Prometheus, the Suffering Servant, and Christ, but misses the imperial settings.[53] Jesus was crucified by order of the Roman governor.[54] But the New Testament writers, for whom it was dangerous to underline that fact, explained it by Hebrew antecedents—above all, by Isaiah 53 (with the other Servant poems) and Psalm 22.[55] C. H. Dodd sees certain Hebrew texts as a substructure of New Testament theology, with Isaiah 53 and Psalm 22 at the heart of one of four groups, in each of which the writers remain "true to the main intention" of the Hebrew text.[56] We may add that Psalm 22 has vocabulary links to Second Isaiah: the human figure is a "worm" (Ps 22:7, Isa 41:14); "all the ends of the earth" (Ps 22:28, Isa 45:22) will turn to God.

What are the Hebrew poems *about*? It is arbitrary to interpret them in terms of sickness or leprosy and then make the adversaries metaphorical. The Greek translators long before Jesus found a crucifixion in them: thus Psalm 22:17c LXX, "they have pierced my hands and feet," where the Hebrew is unclear.[57] The "dogs" of Psalm 22:17a are naturally interpreted as carrion feeders around their helpless prey. The New Testament citations make the best sense if their authors *correctly* interpreted the Hebrew poems as arising from a situation of imperial oppression like their own—and in fact, as we shall see, its ancestor. Isaiah 53 is certainly of the Persian period, and Psalm 22 will fit there. A century of scholarship summed up by North[58] asked only who the Servant was, not what happened to him or who did it. If we do ask, we will most naturally conclude that the Servant poems are images, self-censored but recognizable, of the *crucifixion under the Persians of an ideal figure representing Israel.* Thus Toynbee, in comparing the Servant with Prometheus and both with Christ, was a better historian than he realized.

SYMBOLS IN THE SELF-LEGITIMATION OF PERSIAN IMPERIALISM

Here we survey modes in which the Old Persian empire defined its own status, modes in part handed down to successor states. By its subjects, those symbols were seen in a double light—as illegitimate claims to be rebelled against, but also as the basis of counterclaims in rebellion.

"No other lord but me." What are called "treaties" between unequal parties, in the ancient Near East best documented in the Hittite realm, demand exclusive loyalty from the weaker party. Thus Suppiluliuma (ca. 1350 BCE) speaks to a vassal: "You, Hukkanas, recognize as regards lordship the Sun [the Great King of Hatti] alone."[59] Esarhaddon speaks to numerous vassals (ca. 650 BCE): "Another king, another lord, you shall not set over yourselves."[60] Darius states loyalty as a *fait accompli*: "This country Persia . . . by the favor of Ahuramazda and of me, Darius the King, does not feel fear of [any] other."[61] Hebrew "covenant" formularies are modeled on such "suzerainty" treaties;[62] the demand for exclusive loyalty stands already in the Decalogue, "You shall have no other gods before me" (Exod 20:3). In one text, Rome inherited the exact Near Eastern formula. By some route, it appears in an inscription containing the loyalty oath of the Cypriotes to Tiberius (14 CE):

> . . . and to propose the voting [of divine honors], along with the other gods, *solely* to Rome and to Tiberius Caesar, son of Augustus, Augustus, [space for the insertion of *Autokrator* "Emperor" if that title should be voted him], and to the sons of his blood; *but to no others at all.*[63]

By the same formula, Jesus refuses loyalty to Satan (Matt 4:10) and Mammon (Matt 6:24); also, "Render to Caesar . . . render to God" (Mark 12:17) is not a comparison but a contrast. The high priests chose the other side: "We have no king but Caesar" (John 19:15).[64] Thus the competing loyalties to God and to Caesar were expressed by both sides *in the same formula* from the same source.

Court ceremonial: investiture, prostration. These, after an abortive graft onto Rome in the time of Julius Caesar, remained exotic—but well known and the basis of native developments. In the New Testament, Christ is assimilated to the *Roman* emperor by several formulas;[65] at Rev 19:11–16 we are in the *Parthian* realm. It is a vision of Christ as the "Word of God" with: (1) many diadems on his head; (2) a sword coming out of his mouth; (3) on his robe and thigh a name written, "King of kings and Lord of lords." Also at Rev 19:4, (4) the elders prostrate themselves (*proskynein*) before God. Artabanus III, in a Greek inscription of 21 CE, calls himself "Arsaces king of kings";[66] Darius, in a newly found statue from Susa, has his name and title "King of kings" in four languages on the *robe* that covers his *thigh*![67] Matthew Bridges, in the hymn "Crown him with many crowns," saw Revelation 19 as an investiture (taking "crowns" for *diademata* from the KJV, which assimilated the text to the *British* monarchy). Monobazus was invested as king of Adiabene (ca. 45 CE) in Iranian style with three elements: the diadem, the signet, and the "*sampsēra*" (Josephus *Ant.* 20.32). The last is Iranian for "sword," rare in Greek[68] but well known in Aramaic.[69] Sapor had a *spsyrdr*, "sword-bearer," in the Greek *spathophoros*,[70] replacing the spear-bearer and bow-bearer of Darius.[71] Thus the Hebrew elements of Revelation 19, like the "rod of iron" (Ps 2:9), have been grafted onto a pictorial representation of the *Parthian* king. Such an image is called in Old Persian *patikarā*; elsewhere I have shown how it comes to denote "idol" in Aramaic *ptkr'* and LXX Greek *patachron*.[72]

The emblem of the Persian king's authority was the *diadēma*, a cloth headband. Darius, on the Behistun relief, apparently wears a diadem over a tiara.[73] The diadem was adopted by Alexander and Seleucus, and continued by the Parthian kings, where the Surena invested the new king with it (Arrian *Anab.* 7.22; Tacitus *Ann.* 6.43). The "kingly crown" that Shakespeare has Antony offer Caesar was really a *diadēma*; the proposal that Caesar be styled *rex* rested on a convenient Sibylline prophecy that "the Parthians could only be conquered by a king" (*Parthos nisi a rege non posse uinci*, Suetonius *Julius* 79.2–3). That would have made Rome one more monarchy on the Parthian-Seleucid model—the only one available. The emperors were so far above wearing the diadem themselves that they bestowed it on Armenians and such: Tiberius early in his career on Tigranes II, Nero on Tiridates.[74] The recognition of royal authority in one wearing the diadem was the act of *proskynēsis*. In 66 BCE, Tigranes I came to Pompey on horseback with the diadem over his tiara; Pompey made him dismount, and he then threw off his diadem and did obeisance (*proskynein*) to the Roman (Dio Cassius 36.52.3). When Cinnamus the pretender in 37 CE recognized Artabanus III as king, he first did obeisance (*proskynēsās*) and then transferred the diadem from his own head to the other's (Josephus *Ant.* 20.65).

The verb *proskynein* suffered a shift in meaning, which in spite of other theories[75] is best explained by a shift in Persian ceremonial. Originally it must have meant "blow a kiss": just that is done by an inferior to the king in a relief from Persepolis.[76] As social differences widened, the act became prostration and carried the Greek verb with it.[77] Darius' five colleagues had to jump off their horses before performing it (Herodotus 3.86.2). At first Greeks rejected *proskynēsis*, but in spite of resistance, Alexander took it over from Persian court ceremonial.[78] Persian style so imposed itself that the verb, no doubt with the sense "fall prostrate," is standard in Matthew's Gospel for respect shown to Jesus. It was appropriate that Satan, perhaps with Ahriman somewhere in his background, should ask Jesus to "fall down and worship him" (Matt 4:9). It was even more appropriate that Magi, looking for the king of the Jews, "fell down and worshiped him" (Matt 2:11), for a council of "wise men and Magi" also played a key role in the designation of the *Parthian* king (Strabo 11.9.3).

One more tableau of the Parthian court appears in the *Hymn of the Soul* (or of the Pearl), which Kruse assigns to Bardesanes.[79] The court is defined as the "gate of the king of kings," as the Ottoman court was the *Sublime Porte*. Xenophon (*Anab.* 1.9.3) knows that noble Persian youth were educated "at the gates of the King." The same idiom appears at Esth 2:19, "the king's gate."[80]

The "paradise."[81] The forested game-park was an Iranian institution, taken over by Hadrian for a functional purpose, which otherwise in the West acquired solely religious connotations. Xenophon found several such in his march upland (*Anab.* 1.2.7, 2.4.14, etc.). Briant[82] sees them as bestowing attributes of the king on the satrap, and with their villages constituting models of land development, *vitrines idéologiques*. Much more than pleasure-parks,[83] they were the forest reserves of the Middle East, royal monopolies for building temples and fleets. When Nehemiah requests from Artaxerxes a logging permit to "Asaph keeper of the king's *pardes*" (Neh 2:8), this can only be the Lebanese cedar forest, controlled by Hiram of Tyre six centuries earlier. Hadrian put boundary markers on the living rock designating certain species as his monopoly;[84] what was then the forest edge is today treeless shale. In theory, the king had planted the forest; Cyrus the younger claimed himself to have planted trees in the "paradise of Sardes."[85] In reality, the forests were far older—on Lebanon the postglacial climax vegetation. A Greek scientist describes cedars on the "mountains of Syria" that three men cannot surround, and even bigger in the "paradises"; a Scythian forest had been "immune from cutting for four successive generations" (Theophrastus *Hist. Plant.* 5.8.1; Curtius 8.1.13).

The word probably appears in an Old Persian inscription as *paradaya-dam* "pleasant retreat(?)."[86] In Avestan, it names the "enclosure" to be built around a man who has defiled himself by carrying a corpse, *pairi.daēząn pairi.daēzayąn,* "they shall heap up an enclosure."[87] Only the king who in theory planted it may cut it; Artaxerxes must set an example to his own soldiers of cutting down a tree for firewood (Plutarch *Artax.* 25.2). It was an act of war for another to cut it.[88] In the third millennium BCE, the cedar forest of Lebanon was thought guarded by the monster Humbaba; Gilgamesh, like the Assyrian kings after him, went west, overcame the guardian and cut the trees.[89] The garden of Eden was truly a "paradise" long before the LXX so named it, because Yahweh himself had planted it (Gen 2:8) along with the cedars of Lebanon (Ps 104:16). The "paradise of pomegranates" (Cant 4:13) on Lebanon is the sexuality of the beloved. The "hanging paradise" of Babylon was built for Nebuchadrezzar's Median wife, homesick for her native mountains.[90] When Paul was "snatched up to Paradise" (2 Cor 12:4), it was to a place otherwise inaccessible. Of the four rabbis who entered Paradise, three came to a bad end (*b. Ḥag.* 14b). It was the ultimate promise that "one will open the gates of paradise" (*T. Levi* 18:10). Only the elect are "the heirs who will enter *Firdaws*" (*Quran* 23.10–11); this Iranian symbolism built into the sacred book of Islam laid the foundation for its ultimate acceptance in Iran. In the Iranian context that the word demands, Jesus could be represented as making no more audacious claim to authority than "today you will be with me in Paradise."

"King of kings." This formula remained Oriental, although it acquired religious connotations. There is a magisterial treatment by Schäfer.[91] The title[92] is attested in Egypt for both gods and kings since Ahmose (1580–1550 BCE), and in Assyria since Tukulti-Ninurta I (1246–1209 BCE) and down to Esarhaddon,[93] though never as fixed royal titulature.[94] With the Achaemenids it is invariable; Darius begins his inscriptions by calling himself *xšāyathiya xšāyathiyānām.* Normally, in Old Persian, the genitive would precede,[95] so that the title was likely taken over from Akkadian via (unattested) Median usage; it is echoed by Aramaic[96] and Greek[97] inscriptions. It was adopted in Greek by the Arsacids in their coins and rare inscriptions (*OGIS* 430, 432); Pompey refused that title to the Parthian, and Suetonius says that the *regum . . . regem* joined in mourning Caligula's death (Plutarch *Pomp.* 38.2; Suetonius *Calig.* 5). Among the Sassanids, the normal order was restored with the genitive first. The Iranian original is masked in the inscriptions by Aramaic ideograms;[98] but it is transcribed by a Roman historian,[99] who records the battle cries on Roman and Sassanid sides in a siege of 359 CE at which he himself was present:

> Nostris uirtutes Constanti Caesaris extollentibus ut domini rerum et mundi, Persis Saporem *saansaan* appellantibus et *pirosen,* quod "rex regibus imperans" et "bellorum uictor" interpretatur.

"Our men were extolling the virtues of Constantius Caesar as 'lord of all things and of the world,' while the Persians were praising Sapor as *saansaan* and *pirosen*, which mean 'king ruling over kings' and 'victor in battle.' " In this Middle Persian, the phonetics are already reduced, as in Byzantine Greek *segansaa*[100] and modern Persian *šāhān-šāh*. The ruler-formulas of the two empires are set in absolute confrontation.[101]

What does the title mean? Schäfer contrasts it with "song of songs," which must mean "song pre-eminent among songs, song *par excellence*."[102] It is natural with Ammianus to accept the literal sense "king ruling over vassal kings," demanded in the Rabbinic extension of Rabbi 'Aqiba: "Know before whom you are to give account; before the *King of the kings of kings*" (*m. 'Abot* 3.1). It underlines a political reality: the Achaemenids were unable to supplant tributary kings and left them in place as satraps; Aeschylus calls Xerxes' generals "kings subordinate to the Great King" (Aeschylus *Pers.* 24). It shows that name is being honored above substance: Antony called his sons by Cleopatra "kings of kings" and gave them lands he did not control—Armenia, Media, and Parthia to his son Alexander (Plutarch *Ant.* 54.4). It underlines the pretension of kinglets like Septimius Odainath of Palmyra.[103] The romantic Diodorus (1.47.4) puts "king of kings" on the monument of his "Osymandyas" (really the Ramesseum of Thebes)—the basis for Shelley's sonnet "I met a traveler from an antique land." Silver Latin poetry adopts the form *dux ducum* for Agamemnon or Jason (Ovid *Her.* 8.46; Seneca *Medea* 233); it is picked up by the Vulgate at 1 Chr 7:40; and in Hebrew transcription appears in a Midrash on Num 3:32 "prince of princes" (*Num. Rabbah* 7.3).

Elsewhere "king of kings" is again a divine title. In the *Suppliants* of Aeschylus (cf. v. 524) the Chorus addresses Zeus as *anax anactōn*, which (in spite of the Egyptian setting) conveyed a Persian flavor to Greeks. So in later Stoic usage, Zeus becomes "great king of kings."[104] At Deut 10:17 (cf. Ps 136:2–3, Dan 2:47) Yahweh is "God of gods and Lord of lords"; this presumably reflects Assyrian or Babylonian usage, although Medo-Persian is not quite excluded.[105] The literal meaning, "a God reigning over other gods," is confirmed by Ps 95:3 "a great King above all gods."[106] It is Hellenistic that 2 Macc 13:4 calls the God of Israel "King of kings."[107] The usages of the Apocalypse, the *Hymn of the Soul*, and R. 'Aqiba above have an implicit subversive component: the authority of God is superior to all political authority, and the divine court, although modeled on the Parthian, is far above it. Even today, the Anglican liturgy addresses God in modified British court terms, "thy divine majesty"; audiences must stand for Handel's *Hallelujah Chorus* on "king of kings and lord of lords"! The Scillitan martyr of 180 CE audaciously raises God above both empires in confessing him as *domnum meum, imperatorem regum et omnium gentium,* "my Lord, Emperor of kings and of all peoples."[108]

IMPERIAL MODES OF REPRESSION

Assyria has justifiably had a bad name for "frightfulness," Hitler's *Schrecklichkeit.*[109] Persia and Rome are sometimes given credit for mitigating it. But, as with the Allied victors in World War II, their route to take over its sway lay through mass killings. When Darius took Babylon, he crucified three thousand citizens (Herodotus 3.151.1). Cyrus the younger was praised (Xenophon *Anab.* 1.9.13) for making highways safe for Hellene and barbarian by lopping off hands and feet and gouging out eyes of criminals. When Crassus defeated Spartacus in 71 BCE, six thousand captives were strung up all along the road from Capua to Rome (Appian *Civil Wars* 1.120). When Rome in the same year took Carthage and Corinth, it found sanctions for imperial control ready at hand: conscription, tattooing and flogging, crucifixion. In the opposite sense to what the poet intended, *Graecia capta ferum uictorem cepit,* "Captured Greece took her fierce victor captive" (Horace *Epist.* 1.1.156).

Conscription ("angareia"). Conscription of ships and animals is first attested in Middle Comedy;[110] then in Ptolemaic Egypt,[111] Roman law,[112] and Talmudic law.[113] There is a summary in Ste. Croix's enormous history of ancient class struggle.[114] The thing is surely Persian and the word (unattested) chancery Aramaic.[115] Under Rome, the same word is used in Herodotus' sense of road service, but now under compulsion. The ex-slave Epictetus says, "You should treat your whole body as if it were a laden donkey; . . . then if there is conscription (*angareia*) and a soldier lays hold of it, let it go" (Arrian *Epict.* 4.1.79). Matthew 5:41 attests conscription by distance: "If anyone forces you to go one mile, go with him two miles." At Mark 15:21 // Matt 27:32 some parties conscript one Simon of Cyrene. In both Gospel passages, the Vulgate and the Palestinian Syriac merely transliterate the Greek.

Tattooing, flogging. C. P. Jones, in a notable article,[116] maintains that Greek (and Latin) *stigma* means "tattoo," not "brand"; certainly the verb *stizō* means "prick," so that on a previous view its use for "brand" would be metaphorical. I accept his conclusions and translate accordingly. Religious and decorative tattooing were exotic. Penal tattooing was a Persian innovation in Greece: Xerxes tattooed the Thebans taken at Thermopylae with the "royal *stigmata*"—as earlier he did symbolically the Hellespont (Herodotus 7.233.2, 7.35.1)! The Athenians, quick studies, tattooed Samian captives with their owl, and the Samians in turn Athenians with their trireme.[117] The Syracusans tattooed Athenians with their horse (Plutarch

Nic. 29). A *stigmatias* was a male or female runaway slave caught and tattooed.[118] Such a tattoo was normally of three letters, for example, FVR, meaning "thief."[119] The Romans saw it as an act of "writing."[120] The mark of the Beast (Rev 13:16) on forehead or right hand is then primarily a mark of ownership; here also it is of three letters, interpreted as numbers. In a Jewish community of Persian Egypt, the owner's name was marked on the right hand of a slave.[121] A soldier was in a status close to slavery, and a captured deserter also was tattooed (Aeschines *Emb.* 79). During the Roman proscriptions, masters (who feared a recurrence of slave revolts) treasured the memory of "a tattooed slave who saved the master that had tattooed him" (Dio Cassius 47.10.4).

The meaning of *stigma* is extended to the permanent scars from flogging, as in "one tattooed (*stizomenos*) by the rod" (Aristophanes *Wasps* 1296). When Paul says, "I carry the marks (*stigmata*) of Jesus branded on my body" (Gal 6:17), he surely means that he had been flogged by Jews and Gentiles (2 Cor 11:24–25, Acts 16:23) just as Jesus had been—hardly that he had been made a slave to Christ by religious tattooing. The Franciscan understanding of the *stigmata* continues the same line. Jewish Aramaic reveals its underclass status by having *two* foreign words for "flogging," one from each empire. Ezra 9:26 in a descending scale of penalties, "death, flogging, confiscation, imprisonment," for the second has *šršw*; that the LXX translation *paideia* is correct is shown by Egyptian Aramaic, where *srwšyt'* is a punishment for slaves.[122] The word is Iranian: it appears in the Avesta in the phrase *yo ništayeiti kǝrǝtǝ̄e sraošyǝm*, "who orders the execution of punishment."[123]

Roman practice was found different and abhorrent enough that *flagellum* was taken into Palestinian Aramaic in a vulgar form *pargol;* and so in the Greek of John 2:15 *phragellion*. The whip is used on Jesus (Matt 27:26 with a participle), where the Syriac restores the vulgar noun, "scourged him with a whip (*pargol*)." The Passion narrative is echoed in a Rabbinic dialogue with a Jewish martyr: "Why are you getting a hundred lashes (*pargol*)? Because I performed the ceremony of the Lulab."[124]

Crucifixion.

Hengel's compilation of the classical materials needs little supplement. The Babylonian text of Darius' Behistun inscription (cited above) follows the language of the Assyrian kings. Thus Tiglath-Pileser III and his successors use *zaqīpu*, "stake"; Ashurnasirpal regularly says *ana GIŠ zi-qi-pi uzaqqip*, "I staked [him] on a stake."[125] The whole spectrum of humiliations inflicted on the bodies of the captured, living or dead, by the Assyrians[126] is reflected in the last books of the *Iliad*; somehow the word got around.

Plato thinks that Homeric Troy both feared Assyria and relied on it "as we now fear the Great King" (*Laws* 685c). But with Homer, what in the Assyrian reprisals is "national propaganda, to intimidate potential enemies of the king, is turned to the expression of the final horror of the death of noble warriors, and to the last extremity of passionate heroic hatred."[127]

The essence of the punishment is *deterrence through public humiliation.* Prometheus must be "*taught* to accept the tyranny of Zeus" (Aeschylus *PV* 10–11); the psalmist says "all who see me mock at me" (Ps 22:7); opponents say, "If we let him go on thus, every one will believe in him" (John 11:48). The *Digest* lays it down that "infamous bandits" (*famosos latrones*) are to be crucified (*furca figendos*) on the spot,

> so that others may be *deterred* by the sight from similar crimes, and so that the punishment carried out in the very place where they committed murders may be a *solace* to the relatives of those killed.[128]

Crucifixion was the main sanction of the Persian empire, especially on those of high rank.[129] Lampon proposes that Pausanias avenge his uncle's crucifixion by crucifying Mardonius (Herodotus 9.78), and we saw how Herodotus ends his tale by Greeks taking over the punishment. Glaucon presumes that the just man will be "scourged, racked, bound, have his eyes burned out and in the end be impaled" (Plato *Rep.* 361e). Clement of Alexandria applies Plato's text to Jesus.[130]

Crucifixion was standard procedure in the Hellenistic empires, particularly the Seleucid.[131] The Maccabees saw themselves as Hellenistic monarchs, and Alexander Jannaeus crucified eight hundred captives while drinking and reclining with his concubines.[132] Carthage made a specialty of crucifying its own defeated generals as well as captured enemy ones.[133] Thereby Carthage continued Assyrian and Persian practice, evidently mediated by the Phoenician cities, which owed their independence and wealth to their inland neighbors. Phoenicia alone could supply various luxury goods as well as "the enormous quantities of iron required by the Assyrian 'war machine.' "[134] Hannibal the great crucified a false guide in Italy *ad reliquorum terrorem* (Livy 22.13.9), as Voltaire said "pour encourager les autres." Thus the example of Carthage was closest at hand for Rome. Rome had an archaic version of the penalty in the old formula of execution *arbori infelici suspendito* "hang him from a barren tree";[135] this may be Etruscan and itself Oriental in view of Deut 21:22, "hang him on a tree." Still the Roman ruling class had more solidarity than the Carthaginian, and as a result the punishment was transformed from one of nobles to one of slaves.

The birds and beasts. Prometheus is fed on by an eagle; the psalmist is encircled by dogs. Each has fallen victim to the old curse,[136] "Your dead body shall be food for all birds of the air, and for the beasts of the earth" (Deut 28:26). It is frequent as a taunt in Homer: twice the birds are specified as vultures, *gypes*, with a phonetic resemblance to Hebrew '*ōp*, "birds."[137] Midianite leaders are named for carrion eaters (Judg 7:25), Oreb "Crow" and Zeeb "Wolf." The creatures are variously specified as crows and wolves; vulture and crow, dogs and wolves; crows (Prov 30:17; Lucian *Timon* 8; Catullus 108.4–6). Sherlock Holmes says of the convict Selden's body on the moor, "We cannot leave it here to the foxes and ravens." Hence Jesus' mordant prophecy, "Wherever the body is, there the eagles will be gathered together" (Matt 24:28 // Luke 17:37).[138] Ancient Near Eastern art is fond of vultures on corpses.[139] The theme almost bypasses Greek art[140] but resurfaces in an Etruscan vase.[141] The Greek sophist Gorgias called vultures "living tombs," *gypes empsychoi taphoi* ("Longinus" *On the Sublime* 3.2). Vermeule outrageously observes:

> Where carnivorous animals and birds had been made the agents for the cleaning of the dead, they prevented pollution, first physically, then spiritually. They assisted the natural cycle of birth and death in an economical style, and were in a sense allies of those who kept order, the gods.[142]

The ancient world found this fate bad enough for a corpse;[143] further, a crucified one like Prometheus may be eaten while alive. An inscribed verse epigram from Caria of about 100 BCE, speaking in the name of the dead man, tells us that a slave killed him, "but my fellow citizens hung up *alive* to the beasts and birds the one that treated me so."[144] So in Latin we read *non pasces in cruce coruos*, "you will not [like others] feed crows on the cross" (Horace *Epist.* 1.16.48; cf. Petronius 58.2).

The female companion. The exposed corpse may have a female companion who keeps off the carrion eaters "day and night": Rizpah for the bodies of her sons (2 Sam 21:10); Aphrodite for Hector's body (*Iliad* 23.185–86). There is some risk, for the imperial power that crucifies the man also prostitutes the woman, as we saw with Jannaeus: "Women are ravished in Zion. . . . Princes are hung up by their hands" (Lam 5:11–12). Pheretima, queen of Cyrene, even more barbarously crucified the men of Barca and nailed their wives' breasts to the city wall (Herodotus 4.202). Elsewhere[145] I note that each of the rebel-victims has a prostituted female companion. Prometheus has Io, Zeus' concubine; the Servant of Yahweh has the "captive daughter of Zion" (Isa 52:2), who has been sold into slavery, that is, prostitution (Isa 50:1); Jesus has the Magdalen from whom seven demons had gone out (Luke 8:2), naturally identified with the prostitute of Luke 7:36–50. At John 19:25, the Magdalen is replaced by Jesus' mother, another Rizpah; early representations of the Crucifixion show John and the Virgin on the left, the three other women at the right.

CONCLUSION

The demand of Socialist theology for a Promethean Christ has been realized pictorially by the Mexican muralist José Clemente Orozco in three exemplars of manhood.[146] In the Prometheus of Pomona (1930), the Titan, cramped under a Gothic arch, brings down fire from heaven; in a side panel, Zeus, Hera, and Io. The Christ of Dartmouth (1932–34) is shown frontally as Vitruvian man, with left hand raised before a rubbish heap of weapons, a broken Ionic column, and a Buddha. In his right hand he holds an axe with which he has just chopped down his cross behind him. His feet are still skeletal; the resurrection body in lurid reds and blues is emerging from his split thighs. Nearby, ferocious vultures are on another rubbish heap of Western culture. As a ten-year-old I saw the artist at work, and it is alleged that I appear as one of the blond schoolchildren in the New England panel. The Man of Fire of Guadalajara (1938–39) stands overhead in the cupola of the Hospicio Cabañas as if seen from below, beside three prostrate blue figures. He is naked; his arms, legs, and head are burning.

The unity of suffering and exaltation in all three figures is very marked, as in John's double theme of Christ being "lifted up" both on the cross and in the Ascension. Elsewhere[147] I have discussed the symbolism of Yahweh with his axe: destroying presumptuous empires (Isa 10:15) as they previously took an axe against the forest of Lebanon; turning the Roman *fasces* against collaborators (Matt 3:10 // Luke 3:9). Today, in a decade that must undo the damage done by the axe to the planet's rain forests, the axe has become as ambivalent a symbol as fire, the supposed monopoly of the Mazdaean Achaemenids, brought down by Prometheus. Orozco's greatness appears in his transferring the real complexity of Aeschylus' Prometheus to the axe-bearing Christ. Evidently the Man of Fire of Guadalajara has also brought down fire from heaven—it is hoped, not in vengeance (Luke 9:54), nor as insupportable nuclear power, but as the "refiner's fire" of Mal 3:2. "I came to cast fire upon the earth; and would that it were already kindled!" (Luke 12:49).[148]

10 Debt Easement in Israelite History and Tradition

Marvin L. Chaney

This brief essay is scant compass to discuss even one of the several forms of debt easement evidenced in the Hebrew Bible. Detailed analyses have been and could again be devoted to prohibitions of interest on survival loans to the poor, protection and manumission of debt-slaves, forgiveness of debts, restoration to the debtor of real estate subjected to foreclosure or articles taken in pledge, and various regulations designed to protect debtors from humiliation or loss of the artifacts necessary to daily life.[1] The specifics of that literature—both primary and secondary—are only partially related to the discussion that follows, however.

Rather, I want to address one basic question: Why were extensive traditions of debt easement included and even featured in the Hebrew Bible, when the literary "collages" that preserved them are the obvious work of elites whose vested interests as a class would appear to be jeopardized by such easements?

To treat this issue in a *Festschrift* honoring Norman Gottwald is appropriate for at least three reasons. First, my interest in the subject was first piqued in the process of writing a formal response to one of his many erudite papers.[2] Not the least of Professor Gottwald's enormous contributions is his ability to provoke new questions and to suggest fruitful categories and methods for their investigation.

Second, Gottwald himself has done much to lay a firm foundation for reassessing traditions of debt easement in the Hebrew Bible. Of particular significance is his placement of the discussion of debt in the biblical world into the context of a twofold system of surplus extraction.[3] State taxation in kind, in labor, and later in coin, narrowed peasants' economic margins substantially. State policies simultaneously eroded the risk-spreading mechanisms characteristic of traditional village agriculture by pressing for intensive and specialized cultivation of a few preferred crops. Such agriculture in Palestine was also subject to the vicissitudes of periodic drought, pestilence, blight, war, and other disasters. Coupled with the curtailment of risk spreading, the size and consistency of state exactions insured that small producers would be forced to seek frequent survival loans from those privileged with economic surplus by the workings of the state. Debt instruments were thus the means of a second and escalating round of surplus extraction in the political economies of Israel and Judah.[4]

Third, although Gottwald is justly famous for sharpening scholarly focus upon such realities of social stratification, his work provides an additional rubric of great utility for addressing the question posed in this essay. That analytical category recognizes that agrarian societies are not only starkly stratified vertically, but also segmented into factions horizontally, particularly at the elite level.[5] In biblical Palestine, this phenomenon of factionalized elites was intensified by both internal topography and international geopolitical location.

Topographically, Palestine was broken into a number of cantons, each with its own variations in the natural environment, and hence in the means of subsistence. Within the larger genus of agrarian societies, those characterized by such balkanization are particularly prone to factionalized elites. Once an agrarian state was in place, each region provided its own rival(s) for the positions of power and privilege within that state. Biblical examples are too frequent and well known to require rehearsal here.

The larger geopolitical environment, moreover, reinforced this topographical proclivity for factionalized elites. Biblical Palestine was ringed by societies more populous and powerful than itself. A significant role for these superpowers in the political economies of Palestine did not begin with their defeat and exile of the national leaders of Israel and Judah. Long before they were able to dominate these states outright, they never ceased meddling in the affairs of their smaller neighbors, who occupied the land bridge where superpower interests met and clashed. Under such circumstances, Egyptian, Mesopotamian, and other foreign diplomats sought influence with various factions of the Israelite and Judahite elites. The latter, just as obviously, sought to strengthen their own hands domestically through powerful international connections, while at the same time retaining as much autonomy as possible from their foreign allies. Specific alignments were as intrinsically unstable as the generic dynamic was constant over extended periods.[6]

In understanding those portions of biblical tradition and history that involve debt instruments, attention to these dynamics of factionalized elites can add an important diachronic dimension to what is often a largely synchronic class analysis. According to most scholars who discuss causation at all, biblical traditions such as those prohibiting interest on survival loans to the poor and granting various other easements and protections to debtors find their fountainhead in the communitarian values of premonarchic Israel, values that then survived and persisted with tenacity in later, state-dominated periods and traditions.[7] But what were the mechanisms of this tenacious persistence, and how may one account for its literary and historical particulars?

An analysis that integrates the realities of class conflict with those of elite segmentation and conflict allows a fuller answer to that question. The ultimate source of traditions such as that stipulating interest-free survival loans is likely to be found in the agrarian village, where mutual assistance loans without interest to one's village neighbors are widely attested.[8] Within the village, such conventions were a means of risk spreading, a form of "insurance policy." Faced with the state and the exactions of those who controlled it, however, Israelite village courts probably sought to broaden this customary law to cover the survival loans that villagers were forced to seek beyond the village, preponderantly from the urban elites who benefited from the surpluses extracted by the state. The appeal of such legal traditions to debt-ridden peasants in all times and places is obvious. So, too, is the general incentive for the elites, who controlled the state's legal apparatus above the village level,[9] to subvert and override such traditions. Yet within the Hebrew Bible, as noted above, these traditions are preserved in several books and literary strata, each of which, in its final form, is demonstrably the work of one or another elite. A focus upon patterns of stratification alone cannot explain why.

Several lines of evidence and reasoning, on the other hand, suggest that conflicts between and among factionalized elites played a frequent role in the official embrace of such measures of debt easement. A faction that was out of power or seeking to consolidate power recently acquired, gained two advantages from espousing—at least temporarily—various forms of debt easement. First, against the faction currently or recently in power, it thereby gained sympathy and support from elements of the peasantry, who teetered perennially on the brink of economic ruin because of the dynamics of political economy discussed above. Second, because members of the faction most recently in power were the primary beneficiaries, not only of state taxation, but also of the secondary cycle of surplus extraction accomplished by debt instruments, any easement of the terms or effects of indebtedness served to diminish that faction's economic base and power. Once the "reform" faction gained and consolidated power, however, programs of debt easement tended to be honored more in official rhetoric than in actual practice.

Evidence from various areas and periods of the ancient world confirms a prominent role for political elites in the promulgation of documents of debt easement. None of this evidence is more striking than the *mīšarum* materials from the Old Babylonian period in Mesopotamia and their probable relationship to the cuneiform "law codes."[10] A *mīšarum* or "justice" involved the king's proclamation of an edict or decree that variously canceled debts, suspended taxes, released debt-slaves, returned land seized by creditors, and remitted other economic burdens. Although the *mīšarum* texts proper are restricted to the Old Babylonian period, they almost certainly continue practices that go back to the kingdoms of Isin and Larsa and are adumbrated already in the "reforms" of Urukagina.[11] They are also closely related to texts ranging from the Old Akkadian to Late Babylonian periods that witness an *andurāru*, a "remission of (commercial) debts," a "manumission (of private slaves)," or "the canceling of services illegally imposed on free persons."[12] Though some of the later of these texts may refer to actions of private individuals and not to royal decrees,[13] the king's proclamation of a "release" of some kind clearly lies at the heart of this whole cluster of evidence from Mesopotamia.

Beyond this centrality of the royal initiative, several other aspects of the debt easement reflected in these cuneiform documents deserve emphasis. Although the remissions were usually inclusive of various "ethnic" or "national" groups, they were otherwise characteristically partial, often giving special consideration to certain classes or districts. The majority of the documents that witness these easements, in fact, concern practical attempts by creditors to insure that the "release" did not apply to their particular cases. *Mīšarum*-acts customarily occurred at the outset of a king's reign, but monarchs whose tenure on the throne spanned decades often proclaimed "releases" in subsequent years as well. Although some scholars have argued that these enactments were spaced at regular intervals, the current evidence establishes no such pattern, but rather tells against it.[14]

Finally, one must ask what motivated Mesopotamian kings to issue such proclamations of debt easement. The answer almost universally given is that these "releases" addressed crises wherein the accumulated burden of indebtedness, particularly among the lower classes, threatened economic, social, and political order. The rulers' intent, then, was not to transform fundamentally the structure of a heavily stratified society, but to mitigate the most extreme imbalances and restore economic equilibrium and viability.[15]

Although few would doubt that these kings acted out of a practical concern for order and a workable economy, closer scrutiny suggests an admixture of other motivations as well. The literary contexts of these documents demonstrate, for instance, that debt remissions, however partial, were given the most positive "spin" possible by those responsible for the king's public image. Royal apologia wasted no effort in presenting the monarch as the enactor of justice, the vindicator of the vulnerable and oppressed.[16] When the ruler was so viewed by his subjects, his grasp on the reins of governance was strengthened. The need to foster that royal image and the political consensus it nurtured was never greater than when a new king began to reign. Monarchs of considerable longevity on the throne, moreover, probably found it necessary to refurbish both image and consensus from time to time. At least such motives coincide perfectly with the timing of the Old Babylonian proclamations of *mīšarum*.

D. O. Edzard both confirms the scholarly consensus regarding the purpose of these proclamations and supplements it:

> The king's intervention in the country's economy, annulling private debts and rescinding certain taxes (both are temporary and not permanent measures), has a twofold aim: to prevent the collapse of the economy under too great a weight of private indebtedness (the normal interest rate for barley was 33 1/3%, for silver 20%); and to prevent excessive accumulation of private wealth in too few hands.[17]

The second aim deduced by Edzard from the evidence can be nuanced in light of the theoretical perspective of this essay. *Mīšarum*-acts were partial in their application, and kings controlled to a considerable extent the legal apparatus that determined how and to whom the decrees applied. Is it not plausible to suggest, therefore, that one purpose of the "releases" was to enable kings to weaken potential rivals who were wealthy and powerful?

The timing of the edicts also favors such a purpose. At the beginning of a new king's reign, he had need (1) to ameliorate economic abuses severe enough to threaten the viability of his state, (2) to project a public image as a just statesman who took good care of his subjects, and (3) to weaken the power of elite factions that threatened his firm hold on power. Skillful proclamation and administration of debt easements could accomplish all three goals simultaneously. Long-lived kings found need to repeat the process for all three reasons at intervals dictated by the vicissitudes of history rather than numerical regularity.

Such an understanding of the evidence obviates Finkelstein's insistence that—despite the irregularity of the evidence—

enactments of this type had to recur *at fairly regular or predictable intervals*. Were this not the case, and had kings been free to announce the *misharum* without warning and at widely disparate intervals, there would have occurred a drying-up of the sources of credit and a virtual paralysis of economic activity every few years[18]

Deuteronomy 15:9–10 and Lev 25:26–27, 50–52 undoubtedly inform Finkelstein's formulation of the issue. But if the royally proclaimed "releases" were administered selectively toward all the purposes articulated above, no general paralysis of economic activity need have occurred—only the economic diminution or ruin of the king's rivals and enemies, actual and suspected.

The world of Greek antiquity also supplies pertinent evidence for the decisive role of political elites in effecting programs of debt easement. Unlike the Mesopotamian data, however, the best-documented Greek example involves, not royal leadership, but the archonship of Solon in Athens in the first decade of the sixth century BCE.[19] By Solon's time, Athens had reached a state of debt crisis. While the wealthy few were becoming wealthier and their estates larger, the small farms of Attica were being mortgaged at a rapid rate. As a result, many of the small proprietors were losing their land, and growing numbers of the landless laborers, the *hektemoroi*, were being sold into slavery (often abroad) because of default on survival loans, or fleeing into exile to avoid this fate. The masses longed for a tyrant to bring relief, and agitated for land redistribution.

A moderate member of the aristocracy, Solon rejected both the role of tyrant the *demos* would gladly have thrust upon him and their demand for redistribution of land. He sought instead to mediate the class strife with a series of debt easements. In 594 BCE he was elected archon with extraordinary legislative powers and began to institute economic reforms, though only for Athenians, of course. He canceled all existing debts and prohibited for the future not merely enslavement for debt, but all forms of mortgages and debts in which the debtor's person was pledged as security.[20] As far as possible, he brought home all Athenian debtors sold into slavery abroad. A limit was fixed on the amount of land a single person could own. Because higher commodity prices abroad were leaving an inadequate food supply for the local population, he forbade the export of agricultural products from Attica, except for olive oil. In an attempt to mold public opinion and forge a political consensus for his moderate approach to economic reform, he wrote and distributed pamphlets. Couched in poetry, according to the canons of the day, some have survived as characteristically Greek exemplars of apologia for particular forms of debt easement and their powerful political exponents.

Solon's reforms came in the midst of great conflict. As a moderate, he pleased few Athenians completely. The rich, who were hit hard, were angry. The poor, who had agitated for more radical reforms, were far from satisfied. Party strife broke out again soon after Solon's archonship, with powerful political leaders dividing between the party of the Coast, that favored his new constitution, and the party of the Plain, that opposed it. The division was not simply along class lines, but was often a function of the particulars of Solon's implementation of his program. Those hurt by specific decisions were opposed, those helped in favor.[21]

Although the evidence is perhaps more diffuse than in the case of either Mesopotamia or Greece, ancient Rome, too, offers significant examples of the close relationship between factional conflict among elites and the promulgation of debt easements. Most of the evidence for debt easements in the earlier Republic appears in the context of the Struggle of the Orders. H. C. Boren characterizes succinctly the dimensions of this struggle most pertinent to our discussion:

> Often, historians have viewed the struggle as a general uprising of the lower classes (the plebeians) against the upper class (the patricians). It was not that simple, however. The leaders of the "struggle" were plebeians, true; but they were from important families. In the later stages of the struggle, often these leaders were aristocratic heads of states that had been absorbed by Rome.[22]

Such leaders depended upon the masses for political support and often espoused economic causes popular with the masses for political reasons. Yet, as P. A. Brunt writes:

> There was no identity of economic interest between the masses and their political leaders, but only an alliance of temporary convenience, which was indispensable to the success of the political demands.[23]

Even the briefest summary of examples can serve to illustrate the important truths articulated by Boren and Brunt.[24]

Early in the fifth century BCE, the patricians were forced to accept plebeian officials, the tribunes. By the middle of the same century, the patricians acceded to another demand of the plebeians—the reduction to writing of the previously unwritten body of law and its public display on the Twelve Tables. Although the Twelve Tables contained some provisions against the maltreatment of debtors, they allowed that the debtor who would not or could not pay was liable to be sold into slavery abroad by his creditor. Nor did the Twelve Tables alter a political economy that insured that small farmers were constantly falling into debt. Then, too, there was the hated contract called *nexum*, whereby the poor worked in bondage to the rich in return for loans, and creditors were empowered to levy execution upon a defaulting debtor without recourse to a court of law. Large parcels of public land remained under the effective control of the patricians. As a result of such circumstances, the decades following the promulgation of the Twelve Tables witnessed intermittent outcries for land distribution and relief of debts.

This agitation came to a head in 367–366 BCE under the leadership of the tribunes Licinius and Sextius. Laws were passed requiring that one consul be plebeian, limiting the amount of public land any single citizen could hold, restricting the sale of debtors to satisfy debts, and easing the terms for repayment of loans. Forty years later, in 326 BCE, *nexum* was abolished.

Although the lower classes—upon whom the burden of debt fell with crushing severity—probably benefited in the short term from these laws, that reality should be viewed in the light of several others. The relief was short-lived, as various reports of the need for moratoria on debt payments or the cancellation of interest due demonstrate. By 287 BCE, the debt problem again rose to such proportions that it led to the appointment of a plebeian named Quintus Hortensius as dictator. The abolition of *nexum* probably involved more the niceties of legal procedure than any great practical relief for this class of debtors.

The real winners in this struggle, on the other hand, were rich and powerful plebeians. It was they who gained continuing access to the higher offices and thence into an enlarged governing oligarchy. The Twelve Tables had banned intermarriage between the orders, but this stricture was set aside in 445 BCE after plebeian agitation. "Evidently there were now plebeians rich enough to entertain social ambitions and patricians ready to gratify them, perhaps in greed for handsome dowries."[25] The ambiguous position of these upper-class plebeians is epitomized by a story that Licinius himself was fined for violating the law limiting the amount of public land any one citizen could hold.

Thus, although the data from Mesopotamia, Greece, and Rome exhibit myriad differences in specifics, they all confirm the pivotal role of conflicting elite factions in the espousal of debt easements as public policy in the ancient world. Informed by these analogies, we can now turn to an all-too-brief review of the biblical traditions of debt easement and the historical contexts of their promulgation.

If this review moves in roughly chronological order, the first materials encountered occur in Exodus 21–23. Although most knowledgeable opinion concurs in granting this "Book of the Covenant" chronological priority, it agrees about little else. The nature, purpose, genre, composition, and date of this legal collection are matters of continuing dispute, as is its relation to the narrative strands of the Tetrateuch. Space prohibits even a cursory discussion of the varying positions[26] and requires instead that the preferred option be explicated briefly in the operative categories of this essay.

That preferred option is provided by R. B. Coote's cogently argued thesis that the laws of Exod 21:1–22:17 (Heb 16) are the culmination and goal of the Elohistic writings.[27] According to Coote, "E" never existed as a separate "strand," but came into existence as a polemical recomposition of "J," designed to legitimate the regime of Jeroboam I in northern Israel after that region's secession from the House of David.

Coote's hypothesis helps to explain the placement of laws regarding the manumission of debt-slaves at the beginning of the "Book of the Covenant" in Exod 21:1–11. Such is not the position one would expect on the basis of other slave laws from the ancient Near East. They tend to be scattered under various rubrics in the latter parts of other legal collections, or left to the end.[28] By placing the laws on debt-slavery first in his promulgation, Jeroboam I emphasized stipulations that in the main other-wise followed legal precedent.[29]

Nor are Jeroboam's purposes in so doing difficult for us to discern from his historical situation. Most villagers in the north had been pushed to the brink by Solomon's economic policies. Debt-slavery was the un-happy result for many.[30] Because Jeroboam had ridden to power on the resultant wave of popular resentment against the Davidids, he needed to signal sensitivity to the plight of the peasant masses. He could ill afford their ire.

But their support alone was an insufficient base upon which to consol-idate his power. The much larger fish in his ocean included the powerful landholding families of the north, the magnates that headed them, and the holy persons and sites that gave them sacral legitimation. Jeroboam needed the support of these as well for his regime, which meant recognizing the magnates' traditional authority, at least in part, while containing their factional rivalries and infighting. Jeroboam's promulgation of law thus sanctioned much of the magnates' historical jurisdiction, but sought to present their authority as derivative from that of his own successionist and Egyptian-sponsored state. The same laws on debt-slavery that signaled concern for impoverished villagers, therefore, also authorized the rights of those who held debt-slaves "legitimately."

The courts of both Jeroboam and the northern magnates whose favor he curried, however, would have been quick to declare "illegitimate" such debt-slave contracts as profited creditors loyal to the House of David. Because the workings of the Solomonic political economy had placed much of the "surplus" to be lent in the hands of those beholden to the Davidids,[31] selective application of Jeroboam's debt easements to creditors oriented to Jerusalem could both disenfranchise his enemies and please his intended constituents—high as well as low.

Elohistic traditions of debt easement shaped in this context almost certainly would have come to the fore again in Jehu's time. To unite various military, landholding, and prophetic factions with a disgruntled peasantry behind a dynasty founded in usurpation and bloodbath, Jehu posed himself as the champion of all those elements against the Omrids, whom he epitomized in Ahab as the "Solomon of the North."

Exodus 22:25–27 (Heb 24–26) occurs in a section almost universally regarded to be a later addition to the "Book of the Covenant." Although the date of its composition may always remain open to quibble, Coote argues plausibly that it reflects Hezekiah's time.[32] If so, this articulation of debt easement fits a socio-historical paradigm by now familiar. Hezekiah sought to reassert the hegemony of a Davidic dynasty whose reputation had been severely tarnished by the depredations of Assyrian imperialism. Certain of the power brokers within the traditional Judahite sphere of influence constituted impediments to Hezekiah's policy. In the territory of the recently fallen state of northern Israel, where Hezekiah sought to extend his power, the foreign elites ensconced by Assyria played a similar role. Meantime, the cost of defending against Assyria or paying tribute to it had once again impoverished the peasants of both regions. Hezekiah's promulgation and selective enforcement of traditional village norms for survival loans would have polished his image among hard-pressed peasants of both areas, while weakening those among their creditors who were his rivals for regional power.

Josiah's "reform"—almost certainly the context for the *promulgation*[33] of Deut 15:1–18; 23:19–20 (Heb 20–21); 24:6, 10–13, 17–18 — shared most of the dynamics just enumerated as characteristic of Hezekiah's time. Rather than recapitulating those elements, a discussion of the functions of debt easement in the Josianic context can concentrate on specific distinctions.

The crumbling of Assyrian power gave Josiah a certain latitude denied Hezekiah. It also freed from Assyrian control descendants of the foreign elites moved into the territory of the fallen northern kingdom as a matter of Assyrian policy. In addition, Josiah inherited a Judahite elite deeply divided. He came to the throne as a child because his father had been assassinated in factional infighting. This grisly event was one of many symptoms that decades of Assyrian imperialism had effaced the prestige of the House of David. Revenues flowing to the royal coffers and the dynastic chapel in Jerusalem had suffered at least as much abridgment as the royal image. When Josiah's assumption of full adult authority coincided with the retreat of Assyrian power, he faced well-ensconced local and regional magnates and their legitimating and revenue-collecting cultic sites as impediments to his policies for rejuvenating centralized monarchic authority. This was especially true in the territory of the former northern kingdom, where Josiah sought to reassert the hegemony of the Davidids after a lapse of three centuries.[34]

All aspects of the Josianic "reform"—nationalism, political and religious centralization; "cleansing" and repair of the Davidic kings' dynastic chapel; extirpation of local, regional, and "foreign" cults and their personnel; territorial expansion; extended court apology; and royal promulgation of law—are to be understood in this context. Legal traditions of debt easement played their part. Once again, a king desiring to consolidate and expand his power at the expense of diverse and entrenched opponents needed to appeal to the debt-ridden peasant farmers who formed the numerical majority of his constituents. Because the dynamics of political economy in the period immediately prior to Josiah had left an increasing proportion of the region's "surpluses" in the hands of magnates and priests opposed to the enhancement of centralized, royal power, these rivals for Josiah's magistracy and tax base would have been the principal creditors. Debt easement administered under the king's jurisdiction thus killed two birds with one stone for Josiah—it weakened rivals and enemies of his reassertion of centralized monarchic authority, while simultaneously wooing most commoners.

Although Jer 34:8–22 is obviously related to Deut 15:1–18, it does not involve a royal promulgation of law about debt easement, as have all the biblical passages previously discussed. Scholars have reached no consensus on this text's complex literary relationship to the laws regarding the manumission of debt-slaves, nor about the various possible motivations for the actions of the masters of such slaves in Zedekiah's time.[35] For purposes of this essay, suffice it to say that Jer 34:8–22 does witness the tendency of several classes of power-holders (cf. v. 19) to manipulate traditions of debt easement in order to serve their changing perceptions of their own vested interests.

Leviticus 25:8–55 is a literarily composite complex of debt easement law. Whether or not the factional conflict occasioning its promulgation involved a royal figure, as did the related texts in Exodus and Deuteronomy, its concerns probably witness a priestly elite disputing jurisdiction over land, peasant production, and cult. A clue to the more specific context for which some version of the Leviticus text was formulated may be found in its inclusion of a feature not known from the stipulations of Exodus or Deuteronomy.[36]

That feature is the addition of the forty-nine- or fifty-year "jubilee" cycle to the seven-year "sabbatical" cycle attested elsewhere.[37] If, as seems likely, the first exiles to return from Babylon to Jerusalem under Shesh-bazzar—a member of the Davidic royal house—left as soon as practically possible after Cyrus' decree in 538 BCE,[38] their arrival in Palestine would have occurred forty-nine years after the destruction of Jerusalem and its temple and the attendant deportation of its political and priestly elites.[39]

Upon their return, these elites and their descendants did not find a power vacuum. The intervening half-century had seen other regional and local magnates and their legitimating cults assume jurisdiction over the lands and cultivators previously tied to Jerusalem. The returnees faced an uphill battle to reclaim fields, peasants, and loyalty to their refounded cult. In this battle of conflicting elites for the hearts and minds of the peasant cultivators, traditions of debt easement would have proved a potent weapon. Forty-nine years was more than enough time for most peasants to become heavily indebted to the magnates exercising power on the scene. The espousal of traditions of debt easement by the returnees would have struck deep resonance in the peasants. If implemented, the remissions would have worked to the hurt of the creditors involved.

Returning members of the exiled priesthood would have had at their disposal an ideological reinforcement for this policy. While in exile, they had developed a version of what is now known as the Priestly Tetrateuch. Its unifying category was the Sabbath. Established by God in creation, this holy seventh day of the week was also the sign of the all-important Mosaic covenant.[40] When the legal content of that covenant already included a "sabbath year" remission, could these masters of religious symbolism have missed the symbolic power of "seven times seven years" between the destruction of their beloved temple and the time of the debt easement that they now sought as part of a larger program to reassert their jurisdiction and to rebuild that temple?

If this must remain speculative, though plausible, a later version of the same conflict between rival elites in postexilic Palestine is the certain context of Neh 5:1–13; 10:31 (Heb 32). Nehemiah represented the interests both of the returnees and of his Persian masters, whose weakening western flank he had been sent to reinforce. The "nobles" and "officials" (Neh 5:7) against whom Nehemiah inveighed were his rivals for regional jurisdiction, who probably also had sympathies and connections with the Athenian-Egyptian axis opposed to Persia.[41] As usual, the peasant majority was caught between. Nehemiah's self-righteous embrace of debt remission was classical apologetic, much in the mold of the Greek tyrants.

Each of these biblical examples cries out for fuller explication. Enough has been said, however, to demonstrate that the traditions of debt easement preserved in the literature of the Hebrew Bible have been shaped by their promulgation in the context of jurisdictional disputes between rival elite factions. Comparative materials from elsewhere in the ancient world confirm this conclusion. Because factionalized elites were a perennial feature of Palestinian history for reasons of both regional topography and larger geopolitical environment, multiple variations on the theme of debt easement are to be expected in biblical literature. Given the political economies in which even the most sincere and well-intentioned of the elite "reformers" was involved, the long-term succor that their policies of debt easement afforded struggling peasants as a class was minimal. Each generation of aspiring elites was motivated to promulgate its own version of debt easement, because each generation of peasants was forced into poverty and debt by the structures of agrarian society. Only the fundamental transformation of those societal structures could address the root problem.

11   *Why Is Anat A Warrior and Hunter?*

Peggy L. Day

Reconstructions of nonbiblical, ancient Near Eastern religions have been particularly vulnerable to the political agendas of biblical exegetes. In order to buoy up claims for the superiority of biblical religion, there has been a marked tendency for biblical scholars to portray nonbiblical religions as more primitive[1] and morally deficient.[2] The attack has been especially virulent on Canaanite religion, the closest and most persistent rival in the Hebrew Bible texts themselves.[3] But describing this tendency to denigrate nonbiblical religions as a probiblical bias is only partially correct, for there is another exegetical agenda interwoven with it. Disproportionally, it is the goddesses and their female cult functionaries and devotees who are made to shoulder the bulk of the blame for alleged moral depravities.[4] When the proverbial bushes are beaten to see what deities lurk therein, "fertility" goddesses emerge from under every green leafy tree. And "fertility," when applied to goddesses and their votaries in mainstream scholarly parlance, has carried the connotation of illicit sexual activity.[5] In addition, the overwhelming propensity for all goddesses to be labeled fertility goddesses reduces them to a single common denominator, thus obscuring their individuality and making them interchangeable, less threatening, and easier to trivialize.[6]

Portrayals of the Ugaritic goddess Anat are no exception. She is typically described as a fertility goddess[7] and given the status of Baal's "consort," a word that can denote partnership outside of marriage. Thus her alleged sexual relationship with him is not quite legitimate. She is further alleged to act like a hooker, both to entice Baal in particular[8] and in her general conduct.[9] Even when described as his sacred bride,[10] this carries overtones of illegitimate sexuality, for it implies cultic enactments of the so-called sacred marriage and ritual defloration outside of wedlock.[11] And, when portrayed as the mother of Baal's offspring,[12] she is made to fulfill her reproductive destiny and thus take her place among all the other goddesses of fertility.

I have discussed elsewhere the Ugaritic texts that typically are purported to support the image of Anat as the fertility deity described above.[13] Very briefly summarized, I find no hard evidence upon which to base this reconstruction.[14] Rather, presuppositions of the political agenda outlined above have been read into the lamentably numerous lacunae proffered by the Ugaritic texts, whereas *hapax legomena* and other cryptic words and episodes have been invested with appropriately supportive meanings.[15] In short, now that we can see them clearly, it is time to divest ourselves of the biases of previous scholarship and take a fresh look at the evidence. Accordingly, I propose a different starting point. In spite of the efforts to make her into a fertility goddess "like all the others," certain well-attested aspects of her activity have belied the complete success of this endeavor: Anat is a warrior and a hunter. This essay will address the apparent paradox of a female deity whose sphere of activity includes two areas—hunting and combat—that were culturally defined as masculine pursuits.

Despite attempts to characterize her as a fertility goddess, Anat's depiction as a warrior is widely acknowledged among scholars and vividly portrayed by the texts themselves. Anat vanquishes both human (*KTU* 1.3 II)[16] and supernatural (1.3 III 35–43) foes, employing typical tools of combat such as the bow (*qšt*, 1.3 II 16) and sword (*ḥrb*, 1.6 II 31). By depicting her prowess in battle, armed with the standard weapons of war, the texts identify her with powerful symbols of masculinity. As Harry Hoffner has shown,[17] the ideal "man's man" in the ancient Near East was a skilled warrior, whose masculinity was symbolized by the regular accoutrements of war. Indeed, women were typified as the antithesis of warriors. In ancient Near Eastern treaties (for example, the treaty between Ashurnirari V and Mati'ilu, *ANET* 532–33), the list of curses sometimes included the threat of turning the soldiers of the treaty violator into women. And in a text relating loyalty oaths taken by Hittite soldiers (*ANET* 353–54), we find the following imprecation against the man who reneges on his pledge:

> Let these oaths change him from a man into a woman! Let them change his troops into women, let them dress them in the fashion of women and put on their heads the *kureššar* headdress! Let them break the bows, arrows (and) weapons in their hands and let them put in their hands distaff and mirror [i.e., symbols of femininity].[18]

On the symbolic level, women and warriors were clearly mutually exclusive categories.

Although Anat's warlike side is generally acknowledged and discussed in the scholarly literature, her association with hunting has received considerably less attention.[19] Again, hunting was culturally defined as a male activity. As Aqhat himself observes, bows and hunting belong exclusively to the male domain (1.17 V 39–40), yet Anat has Aqhat murdered in order to obtain his hunting bow (1.18).[20] She accomplishes the murder by using her accomplice, Yatpan, like an eagle (*nšr*), a bird of prey used by hunters in the ancient Near East.[21] Thus Aqhat, the aspiring hunter, is killed by Anat as if he himself were the quarry. Anat's portrayal as a huntress in the Aqhat series is underscored by two other texts that explicitly depict her pursuit of game. In 1.22 I 11, birds are her prey,[22] and in 1.114 22–23, she leaves El's banquet to go hunting.[23] But Anat's association with hunting is not limited to the predatory role of chasseuse. Crucial to a steady supply of game for the hunter to hunt is the continued increase of the herd. This aspect of Anat's association with the hunt is illustrated in 1.10 and 1.11.[24] In 1.10 Baal has left his house, bow in hand, to go hunting, and Anat follows him to the hunting ground. She provides a cow/cows[25] for Baal to mate with, thus presiding over and ensuring the increase of the herd.[26] In a badly damaged text (1.13),[27] Anat also may be depicted in the capacity of benefactress of animals. The crucial word has been assigned widely divergent meanings,[28] but if *agzrt* (line 29) should be translated "cattle," as Caquot has suggested,[29] then once again we have a reference to Anat facilitating the increase of the herd. Finally, there is the iconographic evidence. Three items dating to the Late Bronze age, found in excavations at Minet el Beida, Ugarit's port, depict an indigenous goddess as "Mistress of Animals" (*potnia thērōn*). This mistress of animals is both a successful huntress[30] and a benefactress.[31] Though not identified by name, I would maintain that her functions indicate that this goddess is Anat, who is clearly the mistress of animals of the Ugaritic texts.

Having demonstrated Anat's associations with the culturally male pursuits of warfare and hunting, we can turn to the question of why this is so. Although scholars generally note her warlike character and activites (and, less frequently, her associations with the hunt), few have attempted to explain why she is active in these culturally masculine spheres. The explanations can be divided into two categories: psychological and "physiological." I will treat each in turn.

Baruch Margalit[32] sees Anat as the patron deity of the warrior aristocracy at Ugarit and understands her as an evil, violent force, a projection of "man's vices and frailties" in general and of "collective Raphaite [i.e., warrior class] fantasies" in particular. This interpretation of Anat rests heavily on Margalit's own peculiar understanding of the Aqhat story as a critique of the warrior class and its values, an interpretation I do not find convincing. In any event, Margalit does not address the question of why a *female* deity supposedly embodies male warrior-class values. Nicolas Wyatt[33] suggests that her warlike character "is essentially the heroic quality of a king (she is nothing less than the *anima* of the king)." This at least pays attention to the fact that she is female, but Wyatt does not develop an argument or present evidence to support his assertion that she is the king's *anima*. Moving on to the "physiological" explanations, Alfred Eaton[34] posited that Anat was originally androgynous. In the course of time, she lost her masculine identity and "came to be thought of as simply feminine—but with overtones of what is normally associated with male activity." Although there is some evidence for the existence of a male deity named 'An,[35] there is no evidence that he and Anat were ever considered to be aspects of a single, androgynous god/dess. Dijkstra and de Moor[36] think that Anat is depicted as androgynous or bisexual in the Ugaritic material itself. They argue that she has a beard and, being androgynous, could not bear children in a normal way. The contention that Anat is portrayed as bearded (1.6 I 3) was challenged by S. E. Loewenstamm,[37] but not to de Moor's satisfaction.[38] Loewenstamm's response[39] included a reference to an article, apparently overlooked by de Moor, by David Marcus.[40] As rallied by Loewenstamm and Marcus, cognate evidence, descriptions of Anat in uncontested texts and visual evidence all argue against Anat having a beard. The contention that Anat could not bear children normally, a twist on an often cited and grossly misinterpreted Egyptian reference to Anat,[41] is a theory peculiar to Dijkstra and de Moor that has no firm basis in the Ugaritic texts.[42]

Rather than positing something that is difficult if not impossible to prove (projection of Raphaite fantasies; king's *anima*; primitive androgyny)[43] or basing arguments on contentious readings and reconstructions, I believe that the question of why Anat is associated with culturally male activities can be answered by taking as a starting point precisely that which both regularly typifies her and marks her as distinctly different from either Asherah or Astarte. This starting point is her most frequent epithet, *btlt*.

Although the meaning of *btlt* cannot be determined solely on the basis of the Ugaritic material, cognate evidence makes it clear that the term refers to an age group, approximately equivalent to the English term "adolescent," but applied specifically to females. It acknowledges the onset of puberty and therefore the potential to bear children; it does not mean virginity per se. This can be illustrated clearly in Akkadian[44] and Hebrew.[45] In the biblical corpus, for example, the term *bĕtûlâ* is twice qualified by the information that the women in question had not "known a man," a well-known expression denoting sexual intercourse (Gen 24:16, Judg 21:12). If *bĕtûlâ* simply meant "virgin," the qualification would be unnecessary. This conclusion is reinforced by an admittedly late text, the book of Esther. In chapter 2, the women whom King Ahasuerus has slept with in his search for a new queen are nevertheless referred to as *bĕtûlôt*. Finally, Joel 1:8 describes a *bĕtûlâ* lamenting for the husband (*ba'al*) of her youth, thus clearly demonstrating that the term *bĕtûlâ* was not restricted to unmarried women. Although I know of no text that explicitly confirms it, I would propose that a woman could be described as a *bĕtûlâ/btlt/batūltu* until the birth of her first child.[46] This hypothesis is attractive for three reasons. First, if entry to the age group is marked by menarche, the potential to bear children, then it is logical to suspect that the point of exit is reached when that potential has been realized.[47] Second, if the termination point is, as I have demonstrated, neither marriage nor first intercourse, the next "normal" change in a female's social status was motherhood.[48] Third, it goes some distance toward explaining a component of Anat's second most frequent epithet, *ybmt limm*. On the theory that *ybmt* is cognate with Hebrew *yĕbāmâ*,[49] the feature that both epithets, often found in parallel construction, would share is the notion of childlessness.[50] Thus the culturally defined "symbolic space" that Anat occupies is the transitional phase between childhood and being fully and demonstrably a woman by virtue of giving birth.[51]

I submit that Anat can engage in male pursuits because she is a *btlt* and therefore not (as defined by her patriarchal culture) fully an adult woman. Adolescence is the time when males and females part ways in terms of their respective and normative social roles. Anat as perpetual *btlt* is suspended, as it were, at this crucial point in time where male and female are becoming differentiated. Using a running movie as an analogy for the progression of life through its various stages, Anat is a frozen frame of a critical transition phase—puberty—during which males and females are in the process of separating both in terms of their reproductive roles as well as their social roles more broadly defined. But Anat never crosses the threshold between puberty and the exclusively female sphere of motherhood.[52] As frozen frame, she is caught in the liminality of adolescence, where male and female are not yet fully distinct. This is expressed mythologically by a "confusion of categories," the absence of a boundary between male and female.[53] As *btlt*, there is no gender boundary to impede her, and so she can move freely into what is normally defined as the male sphere. In short, Anat is a warrior and a hunter precisely because she *is not* the sexually active, reproductive "fertility" goddess that so many scholars have made her out to be.

12 The Evil Eye in the First Testament

The Ecology and Culture of a Pervasive Belief

John H. Elliott

INTRODUCTION

Evil Eye belief and practice is attested throughout the ancient and modern worlds. The phenomenon has been studied extensively by historians, folklorists, and social scientists, but has been virtually ignored by biblical exegetes and theologians. This essay, at the hand of relevant cross-cultural research, summarizes salient features of Evil Eye belief and its ecology, and then examines evidence and features of this belief in the biblical communities, especially in the writings of the First Testament.[1] It aims at clarifying both the common and distinctive contours of biblical Evil Eye belief, the material and cultural conditions in which it assumes plausibility, and its capacity for symbolizing evil, reinforcing traditional values and norms, and serving as an informal mechanism for regulating behavior and social interaction.

Concern over the Evil Eye in the biblical communities is a relatively recent focus of my research and publication. However, the *method* for examining this issue, namely, the combining of traditional exegetical operations with the research, theory, and models of the social sciences, is a subject on which our honoree and I have been working together for the past twenty years. Since our co-organizing of the BASTARDS (Bay Area Seminar for Theology and Related Disciplines) in the late sixties, Gottwald has moved from Berkeley to New York and academic stardom. But I hope that the perspectives and methods that we were then just in the process of formulating look familiar in this piece I offer as a token of *amicitia et admiratio—kein ayin horeh!*

EVIL EYE BELIEF AND BEHAVIOR:
ITS CROSS-CULTURAL OCCURRENCES
AND SALIENT FEATURES

Fear of the notorious "Evil Eye" and precautions taken to avoid or ward off its injurious powers have persisted from ancient to modern times. Although evidence of its presence in the biblical writings is generally obscured in modern translations and ignored in the commentaries, the ancient Israelite, Jewish, and Christian communities formed no exception. From the ancient Near East and the Circum-Mediterranean region, where it is thought to have originated, from the witchcraft culture of Sumer and the Egyptian *Eye of Horus* to the 'ayin hāra' of the Hebrews, the *baskanos* and *ophthalmos ponēros* of the Greek world of Plato, Aristotle, and early Christianity, the *fascinatio* and *invidia* of the Romans and later Church, through medieval Europe, the Arabic *ayin hara* and the Yiddish *ayin horeh*, down to the present (Italian *malocchio, jettatura*; Greek *vaskania, matiasma*; Spanish *mal ojo;* French *mauvais oeil;* German *böser Blick*, etc.), belief in the Evil Eye has spanned the centuries and crossed the globe. A cross-cultural survey of 186 societies has traced this belief to no less than sixty-seven cultures, 36 percent of a total world sample.[2] Accordingly, the phenomenon has been the subject of a vast body of historical, folkloristic, and social-scientific research.[3] Theological investigations of the subject, on the other hand, are nonexistent, and exegetical analyses of its occurrences in the biblical record, few and far between.[4] In what follows, therefore, I will summarize and expand upon my own research on the subject,[5] with particular attention to the Evil Eye texts of the First Testament.

In all sectors of social life, among all classes, and from cradle to grave, the ancients believed, humanity was vulnerable to and needed to take constant precautions against the injurious power of the Evil Eye.[6] Basic to this belief was the conviction that certain individuals, animals, demons, or gods had the power of casting a spell or causing some damaging effect upon every object, animate or inanimate, upon which their glance fell. Through the power of their eye, which could operate involuntarily as well as intentionally, such Evil Eye possessors were thought capable of injuring or destroying life and health, means of sustenance and livelihood, familial honor and personal fortune. Because the eye was considered the window to the heart and the physical channel of one's innermost attitudes and desires,[7] an Evil Eye was regularly linked with the negative moral attitudes of envy and greed; displeasure at another's health, success, or social standing; and stinginess or unwillingness to share one's possessions or bounty with those in need. In social relations, therefore, concern over the

Evil Eye figured prominently in interactions between the "haves" and the "have-nots." An Evil Eye, as we will see in the biblical texts, betrayed, among other things, a heart that was hardened and a hand that was shut to a neighbor in need.

Traces of the belief and of the myriad measures employed to ward off the injurious power of the Evil Eye have been found throughout the Near East and Circum-Mediterranean regions. The evidence ranges from popular incantations to sacred texts, from monuments, mosaics, and art designed to protect public spaces to apotropaic devices and gestures for protecting homes, family members, fields, and graves, from the plethora of incidental literary references to occasional intellectual discussions.

The Evil Eye could strike anywhere and anything; all spaces public and private and all persons and objects of value required protection. Particularly vulnerable, however, were children, domestic residences, fields, animals, places of work, means of sustenance, persons engaged in dining, and individuals involved in personal rites of passage or interaction with strangers. In the basically two-class social system of antiquity consisting of elites and subelites, haves and have-nots, it was the former, those upon whom fortune and favor had fallen, who had to worry about the Evil Eye of all those who resented and envied their prosperity and status. Relative economic disparities of any sort, especially the sudden experience of a "lucky" windfall—the birth of a child, a bountiful harvest, success in business or warfare—were thought to make one vulnerable to the Evil Eye of envious neighbors.

Ubiquitous fear of the Evil Eye entailed constant concern for detecting its potential possessors. Prime candidates included persons with unusual ocular features (e.g., joined eyebrows), those suffering blindness or ocular impairment, those otherwise physically deformed (e.g., humpbacks) or disabled (epileptics), or, more generally, the socially displaced (e.g., widows), the socially deviant (e.g., persons lacking in generosity or virtue), strangers, and enemies.

Methods and devices employed for warding off the Evil Eye were many and varied.[8] Personal protective measures included avoiding eye contact; concealing of women, children, food, and prized possessions from another's stare; the denial of any improvement in one's economic situation; and the wearing of anti–Evil Eye objects (cloth colored red or blue, strings of knots, sacks of herbs such as rue or garlic, jewelry/amulets engraved with eyes or phalluses, small replicas of genitalia [*fascina, ficae*], or crescents [Judg 8:21, 26; Isa 3:18–23], phylacteries and bells/tintinnabula).[9]

Public places, thoroughfares, city walls, and the like[10] were also guarded against the Evil Eye by similar apotropaic devices of grotesque masks (e.g., images of Medusa's head, *gorgoneia*), statues and monuments of enormous *fascina* (as on the island of Delos), or *probaskania* erected scarecrow-fashion in shops and fields (Ep Jer 69). Domestic residences were protected by *fascina* images set in the doorways and thresholds (as at Pompeii and Ostia)[11] or by portal plaques inscribed with anti–Evil Eye incantations.[12]

In personal interactions, manual gestures involving the *digitus infamis* (clenched fist and extended middle finger), the *mano cornuta* (clenched fist with extended second and last fingers) and *mano fica* (clenched fist with thumb inserted between second and third fingers), along with spoken imprecations, were used against suspected Evil Eye possessors, as well as the practice of spitting in their presence (see Paul's comment in Gal 4:14).[13]

To avoid appearing as an Evil Eye possessor oneself, one had to be generous with one's possessions, ready to give to those in need without minimizing or begrudging the gift. Admiring other persons or their property, on the other hand, could suggest envy and an Evil Eye.[14] Accordingly, the ancient Romans, when intent on praising others, prefixed their remark with the expression *praefiscini (dixerim)*, "no fascination/Evil Eye intended." The custom has been retained among Yiddish-speaking Jews in the phrase *kein ayin horeh* ("no Evil Eye intended"). Related to this is a similar custom among Arabs, Italians, and others of accompanying words of praise or admiration with such phrases as *Mashallah* or *Grazia a Dio* ("God be praised"), whereby envy is disavowed and God is credited for the other's blessing.

Specific features of Evil Eye belief and practice, of course, have varied over time and from one geo-cultural area to another. On the whole, however, the sketch above summarizes aspects of the phenomenon attested frequently enough in the sources to provide a reliable model of its consistent contours and characteristics.

THE ENVIRONMENT OF EVIL EYE BELIEF AND BEHAVIOR

The cultures where Evil Eye belief originated and flourished were those of the so-called Circum-Mediterranean, the region embracing the biblical world as well. Classified as "The Peoples of the Book" or "The Peoples of the Plow," these cultures, as characterized by Garrison and Arensberg,[15] involve "complex stratified societies possessed of both milk animals (or nomadic herding populations) and grainfields (or stable peasant agricultural communities)."[16] The "symbiosis of part-cultures (landlord, bureaucrat, agriculturalist, herder, artisan) . . . note the destructive effect of the nomadic herders upon settled village and state societies," and the periodic redistribution of peasant fields typical of these societies created an environment of constant tension and conflict, suspicion and uncertainty.[17]

The notion of the Evil Eye was a symptom of these conditions, tensions, and uncertainties. Among the constellation of features thus characterizing Evil Eye societies are a fragile and unpredictable ecological environment; a precarious crop-and-cattle economy rife with internal social tensions; constant competition and conflict over scarce resources; weak or ineffective centralized means for resolving conflicts, enforcing law, or insuring equitable distribution of resources, thereby resulting in recourse to patron-client arrangements and informal mechanisms of social control; a stratified two-class society of haves and have-nots fostering resentment and envy over economic and social inequities; a perception of "limited good" (according to which all goods and resources existed in finite supply so that one person's gain meant another's loss),[18] reinforcing a competitive ethos and a fear of all rivals; "ocular aggression" as a potent expression of this conflictive cultural world;[19] and a perception of life in general as a continuous struggle for survival endangered by hostile malevolent forces both human and demonic.

The biblical communities shared with their surrounding cultures both the environment and the pattern of beliefs and perceptions[20] typical of Evil Eye societies as presented above. It now remains for us to examine specific articulations of that belief in the biblical writings and its particular nuances.

THE EVIL EYE IN THE BIBLE

References to the Evil Eye recur throughout the First and Second Testaments. In the Hebrew text of the First Testament, the expressions for Evil Eye are *ra' 'ayin* ("Evil-Eyed," Prov 23:6, 28:22), or its verbal equivalent *'ayin* with *r"* (Deut 15:9; 28:54, 56). The Septuagint employs two conventional sets of Greek expressions for the Evil Eye: (1) *ophthalmos ponēreuesthai* (Deut 15:9), *ophthalmos ponēros* (Sir 14:8, 31:13), *ophthalmos ponēros phthoneros* (Sir 14:10), *ophthalmos phthonein* (Tob 4:7, 16), or (2) forms of the *baskanos* word group: *baskainein tǭ ophthalmǭ* (Deut 28:54, 56; Sir 14:6, 8), *baskanos* (Prov 23:6, 28:22; Sir 14:3, 18:18, 37:11), *baskania* (Wis 4:12). The Vulgate likewise employs the standard Latin terminology for the Evil Eye, namely, *oculus malus/nequam* (Sir 14:10, 31:13), *invidere* (Deut 28:54, 56; Prov 28:22; Sir 14:6) or *fascinatio* (Wis 4:12).

The Evil Eye terminology is noteworthy not only for its consistency but also for its implications. From Hebrew to Greek to Latin the constant associations of eye-look-hostility-envy become increasingly explicit. *Baskanos* (*baskainein*, etc.) belongs to a large family of terms of the *bask*-root attested since the fifth century BCE, and denotes an eye and its possessor ("fascinator") who had the power and often the desire to injure the health and well-being of another.[21] This family of Greek terms, in turn, was taken over into Latin as *fascino*, *fascinum*, and *fascinatio*.[22] From *fascinatio*, in turn, derives the English "fascination." Thus, behind the notion of "fascination" lies the ancient concept of the Evil Eye.

The association of the Evil Eye with envy is explicitly stated in the combination of Greek terms in Sir 14:10 and Tob 4:7, 16. The Latin *invidia*, from which the English "envy" derives, and the verb *invidere*, from which *invidia* derives, communicate this same association linguistically. In the Vulgate, *invidere* (*invidus*) is the Latin equivalent of *baskainein* (*baskanos*) for the Hebrew of Deut 28:54, 56 and Prov 23:6, 28:22. *Invidere* (*in* + *videre*, literally "to over-look") means "to look askance at, to look maliciously or spitefully at, to cast an evil eye upon."[23] *Invidia*, in turn, is the envy implicit in this evil glance. Thus, as the Greeks regularly associated envy, *phthonos*, with the Evil Eye and spoke of an *ophthalmos phthoneros*,[24] so the Romans reflected this association in their language through terms uniting the concepts of malevolent stare, envy, and Evil Eye.[25] These associations have perdured in Evil Eye cultures down through modern times.[26]

Within the First Testament we find no less than eleven text segments involving sixteen explicit references to the Evil Eye or to one whose eye is evil, hostile, envious, stingy, or covetous. Several additional implicit traces of Evil Eye belief and practice can be suspected in texts likewise referring to the envy, miserliness, hatred, greed, or covetousness of the eye or heart (e.g., Gen 4:5; 30:1; 37:11; Exod 20:17; 1 Sam 2:32; 18:8–9; Ps 73:3; Prov 23:1; Jer 22:17) or to apotropaic amulets (e.g., Judg 8:21, 26; Isa 3:20) and eyes (Ezek 1:18; cf. Rev 4:8) customarily used against the Evil Eye.[27]

Further traces of the belief in the intertestamental period are found in the First Testament Pseudepigrapha,[28] Philo,[29] and Josephus.[30]

The New Testament attests the persistence of Evil Eye belief within the primitive Christian communities.[31] Four explicit references to the Evil Eye (*ophthalmos poneros*) are attributed to Jesus (Matt 6:22–23 // Luke 11:33–34; Matt 20:15; Mark 7:22). In Paul's letter to the Galatians, the explicit question, "O foolish Galatians, who has injured you with the Evil Eye (*tis hymas ebaskanen*)?" is but one of several indications of the role that Evil Eye accusations played in Paul's encounter with the Galatians.[32]

In the following centuries, Jewish and Christian concern over the Evil Eye and its prevention continued unabated. This is evident from the abundant literary and archaeological evidence including the writings of the Apostolic Fathers (Ign. *Rom.* 3:1, 7:2; *Mart. Pol.* 17:1), the Church Fathers,[33] the literature of the Mishnah and the Talmud and Jewish lore,[34] and the evidence of Evil Eye prevention found in excavated houses, vestibule mosaics, synagogues, churches, and grave sites.[35]

In sum, an abundance of biblical and extrabiblical evidence indicates that ancient Jews and Christians shared with their pagan neighbors the ubiquitous fear of the Evil Eye and constant concern for avoiding or warding off its destructive power. Specific nuances of Evil Eye belief in the biblical literature will become apparent in an examination of some representative texts.

REPRESENTATIVE FIRST TESTAMENT EVIL EYE TEXTS

Among the First Testament texts, Deut 15:7–11 illustrates a number of contextual and conceptual factors associated with biblical Evil Eye belief and will be examined in detail further on. A preliminary look at other biblical references to the Evil Eye, however, will provide a useful conceptual and cultural framework for approaching this text.

A double reference to the Evil Eye occurs in Deut 28:53–57. This passage falls within the concluding section of the book, chaps. 28–34; more specifically within the section, vv. 47–57, elaborating on the divine curses to befall Israel because of its nonobservance of the commandments and its failure to serve the Lord with joyfulness and gladness of heart (28:47). The details of the divine punishment reflect the gruesome experiences of Judah during the neo-Babylonian invasion of 587 in the reign of King Zedekiah (2 Kings 25). Judah will be attacked and besieged by a merciless enemy, stripped of its cattle and food, and its population reduced to want and starvation (28:48–52). The besieged will finally resort to eating their own children (v. 53). In this extreme situation of deprivation, family members will be subject to the depraved power of the Evil Eye.

> The man who is tender among you and very delicate, his eye shall be evil (*tēra' 'ênô*) against his brother, and against the wife of his bosom, and against the remnant of his children whom he has remaining; so that he will not give to any of them of the flesh of his children whom he shall eat, because he has nothing left him, in the siege and in the distress with which your enemy shall distress you in all your towns. The tender and delicate woman among you, who would not venture to set the sole of her foot upon the ground because of delicateness and tenderness, her eye shall be evil (*tēra' 'ênāh*) against the husband of her bosom, and against her son, and against her daughter, and against her afterbirth that comes out from between her feet, and against her children whom she shall bear; for she shall eat them secretly for want of all things, in the siege and in the distress with which your enemy shall distress you in your towns (28:54–57).[36]

Here in the situation of food shortage and the throes of starvation, the extremes of human dispositions and behavior are depicted. Normally tender and delicate fathers and mothers will act with an Evil Eye against each other and other family members, not only by cannibalizing their own children but also in refusing and begrudging a share to their starving households. The text constitutes the most extreme illustration of Evil Eye behavior in all of scripture. In this most desperate of human situations, the most extreme manifestation of evil (as another text will describe the Evil Eye) will be unleashed.

The wisdom literature contains the predominant number of references to the Evil Eye. One passage of Proverbs warns of the danger of eating in the presence of one with an Evil Eye.

> Do not eat the bread of one with the Evil Eye (*ra' 'ayin*); do not desire his delicacies; for he is like one who is inwardly reckoning. "Eat and drink!" he says to you; but his heart is not with you. You will vomit up the morsels which you have eaten, and waste your pleasant words (Prov 23:6–8).[37]

Like Deut 28:54–57 (and Sir 14:10 cited below), the passage indicates that the situation of dining and the sharing/nonsharing of food was regarded as a typical occasion for the operation of the Evil Eye. Here the advice explicates the assumed link of Evil Eye and evil disposition of the *heart* (cf. Deut 15:7–9) as well as the injurious effect of the Evil Eye: vomiting food[38] and wasting pleasant words.

A passage of Sirach on table etiquette (31:12–31) contains a further reference to the Evil Eye and the dining situation. The concern in this case is with the Evil Eye of the guest.

> If you sit at a great man's table, do not be greedy at it (literally "do not open your throat upon it"). Do not say, "There is abundance upon it!" Remember that an Evil Eye is an evil thing (*rā'â 'ayin rā'â*; LXX *kakon ophthalmos ponēros*). God has created nothing more evil than the (Evil) Eye. Therefore it must weep over everything (Sir 31:12–13).[39]

In addition to illustrating the equation of Evil Eye and greed, the passage reckons the Evil Eye as the most evil object of the created order. Consequently, it forever weeps.

Thus, in the ambiguous setting of the meal, dissimulation of genuine hospitality on the part of the host (Prov 23:6–8) and greed at table on the part of the guests (Sir 31:12–13) were considered manifestations of the Evil Eye, that most pernicious of evils, and had negative consequences, both physical and social.

The sharing or nonsharing of food is just one instance of the social exchanges in general associated with the operation of the Evil Eye. Another important area of social interaction where the Evil Eye was feared involved the acquisition of wealth and the refusal to share one's possessions with the needy. This is illustrated by a trio of wisdom texts, the third of which is particularly rich in Evil Eye terms and associated motifs.

> (A man with) an Evil Eye (*ra' 'ayin; anēr baskanos*) hastens after wealth and does not know that want will come to him (Prov 28:22).[40]

> A fool is ungracious and abusive, and the gift of an Evil-Eyed man (*baskanou*) dims (lit. "melts") the eyes (Sir 18:18).[41]

> (3) To him that is small of heart wealth is not fitting, and why should the Evil-Eyed man (*lĕ'îš ra' 'ayin; anthrōpō baskanō*) have gold?[42] (4) Whoever accumulates by depriving himself, accumulates for others; and others will fare sumptuously on his goods. (5) If a man is evil to himself, to whom will he be generous? He will not enjoy his own wealth. (6) No one is more evil than the man who Evil-Eyes himself (*baskainontos heauton*);[43] and the recompense of his evil is in himself; (7) even if he does good, he does it with forgetfulness, and betrays his wickedness in the end. (8) Evil is the man who eyes with the Evil Eye (*ponēros ho baskainōn ophthalmō*)[44] averting his face and disregarding people. (9) The eye of a greedy man is not content with a portion and an Evil Eye (*wĕ'ayin ra'*)[45] withers the soul.[46] (10) An Evil Eye falls enviously on bread (*'ayin ra' 'ayin; ophthalmos ponēros phthoneros*[47]) but it is lacking at his (own) table (Sir 14:3–10).[48]

Parallelismus membrorum indicates the association of the Evil Eye with stinginess (smallness of heart, v. 3), averting one's attention from the need of others (v. 8), greedy discontent with one's portion (v. 9), and the contrast between an Evil Eye possessor's envy of the bread of others and yet its absence on his own table (v. 10). Verses 3–4 illustrate the ancient notion that a wealthy person with an Evil Eye violated the norm of expected generosity toward others. Moreover, vv. 5–6, like other ancient evidence,[49] illustrates the notion that one could also damage oneself with one's own Evil Eye. Refusing or begrudging gifts to others, like enviously coveting their possessions, resulted in self-inflicted wounds to one's social reputation and status and a shriveling up of one's own life (v. 9). Wealth, to be enjoyed in a limited good society, must be shared. To have an Evil Eye and be miserly with one's goods was to lose their enjoyment and the honor such sharing would have earned. Evil Eye belief reinforced this code of honor and generosity in a world of limited good.[50]

Finally, a text from Tobit reiterates the moral implications of biblical Evil Eye belief and its bearing on social relationships and religious obligations.[51] In anticipation of his death (4:3), Tobit offers final words of moral counsel to his son Tobias, summing up his philosophy of life and the moral teaching of the book as a whole (4:1–21). In this summary Tobit twice makes mention of the Evil Eye.

> (5) Remember the Lord our God all your days, my son, and refuse to sin or to transgress his commandments. Live uprightly all the days of your life, and

do not walk in the ways of wrongdoing. (6) For if you do what is true, your ways will prosper through your deeds. (7) Give alms from your possessions to all who live uprightly, and do not begrudge with an Evil Eye (*mē phthonesatō sou ho ophthalmos*) your alms when you give it. Do not turn your face away from any poor man, and the face of God will not be turned away from you. (8) If you have many possessions, give alms from them in abundance; if few, do not be afraid to give according to the little you have. (9) In this way you will be laying up a good treasure for yourself against the day of necessity. (10) For alms delivers from death and keeps you from entering the darkness; (11) and for all who practice it, alms is a good gift in the sight of the Most High. . . . (16) Give of your bread to the hungry, and of your clothing to the naked. From all of your abundance give alms, and do not begrudge with an Evil Eye (*mē phthonesatō sou ho ophthalmos*) your alms when you give it. . . . (18) Seek advice from every wise man, and do not despise any useful counsel. (19) Bless the Lord on every occasion; ask him that your ways may be straight and that all your paths and plans may prosper (Tob 4:5–19).[52]

Religious as well as moral sentiments frame this instruction involving the Evil Eye and its counterpart, generosity. The giving of alms and liberality toward poor coreligionists involves behavior consonant with the divine commandments and redounds in divine blessings (vv. 5–6, 11, 19). An Evil Eye manifested in a begrudging offer of alms is thus contrary to the will of God. To avert one's eye from a poor man's plight, like the begrudging of a gift, is the behavior of an Evil-Eyed person and results in God's averting his gracious face (v. 7). Human lack of generosity hinders the experience of God's generosity. The remark of v. 9 regarding the laying up of good treasure is echoed later in Jesus' remark in the Gospel of Matthew concerning the contrast of good and Evil Eye and laying up treasure in heaven (Matt 6:19–22). The notion of seeking sound counsel (v. 18) recalls the Evil Eye text of Sir 37:7–12.

In this text of Tobit are indications of the economic, social, and moral ramifications of Evil Eye belief within the Jewish tradition: the obligations of the haves toward the have-nots, the need for generosity on the part of the former in a society marked by economic disparity, and the divine disfavor toward the Evil Eye begrudging of alms to the needy. The text thus provides an instructive bridge for a concluding consideration of the Evil Eye and Deut 15:7–11.

DO NOT EVIL-EYE YOUR NEEDY BROTHER (DEUT 15:7–11)

Deuteronomy 15:7–11 is part of a larger text segment (15:1–23) dealing with the year of release and the canceling of debts (vv. 1–6); treatment of the poor, especially in relation to the year of release (vv. 7–11); the release of fellow Israelite slaves after six years of indentured service (vv. 12–18);

and the consecration of unblemished firstling males of herd and flock for sacrifice (vv. 19–23).

Linking vv. 7–11 to vv. 1–6, von Rad notes a consistent compositional pattern in vv. 1–11, 12–18, and 19–23.[53] Each section opens with an older legal maxim that is then commented on and applied to the later and altered economic, political, and social situation presumed in the Deuteronomic Code (ca. the reign of Manasseh, 687–642 BCE). Changes in the situation included a settled urban society with a centralized sanctuary and political structure, a developing latifundialization, increased state taxes, and a resulting economic threat to the rural peasantry. The latter, often obliged in times of reduced harvests to float loans, had to bear the burden of the old sacral ordinance requiring a fallow land each seventh year. In vv. 1–11, this earlier ordinance (Exod 23:10–11), cited in v. 1, is then subjected in v. 2 to a legal interpretation taking into consideration the altered circumstances.[54] Here the "release" is extended to a release of *debts* affecting creditors and creditees alike. Verses 3–11 shift from apodictic command and legal considerations to moral exhortation (von Rad: "preaching") regarding the just treatment of the needy and potential borrowers.[55]

Within this literary and social context, vv. 7–11 exhibit a concern for the Evil Eye in conjunction with the treatment of needy fellow Israelites seeking loans when the year of release is imminent.

> (7) If there is among you a needy person (*'ebyôn*), one of your brothers, in any of your towns within your land which the Lord your God gives you, you shall not harden your heart or shut your hand against your needy brother; (8) but you shall open wide your hand to him, and freely lend him sufficient for his need of that which he wants; (9) Take care that there be no mean thought in your heart and you say, "The seventh year, the year of release is near," and you Evil-Eye (lit. "your eye is evil against" [*wĕrā'â 'ênĕkā*; *kai ponēreusetai ho ophthalmos sou*]) your needy brother and give him nothing, and he cry to the Lord against you and it be sin in you. (10) You shall give to him freely and your heart shall not be evil when you give to him; because for this the Lord your God will bless you in all your work and in all you undertake. (11) For the needy will never be lacking from the land; and for that reason I command you to open wide your hand to your poor and needy brother in your land (Deut 15:7–11).

In regard to the translations, the KJV and JPSV, as usual, render *idem per idem*: "Thine eye be evil against thy poor/needy brother." Other versions attempt to render the assumed sense of the Evil Eye reference.[56] By now, however, it should be apparent from both the terminology and the context that in v. 9 reference is being made to the Evil Eye.

From v. 9 it is clear that the situation of "the seventh year, the year of release" (cf. vv. 1–6) is still in view. With the year of release of debts imminent, a situation of tight credit is envisioned in which creditors would be reluctant to make loans that would soon be canceled. Nevertheless, the hearers are urged to lend freely to the poor kinsman whatever he needs and to give generously (vv. 8, 11b). On the whole, this economic and social situation fits closely the circumstances where Evil Eye suspicion is evoked, as outlined by Garrison and Arensberg.[57] Allusion to the Evil Eye in v. 9 thus comes as no surprise. Moreover, additional aspects of the Evil Eye phenomenon are also present. For one thing, the text reflects the assumed link of heart (vv. 7, 9, 10), including a "hardened" (v. 7) or "evil" heart (v. 10), and an eye that acts evilly (v. 9).[58] Furthermore, as is typical in Evil Eye cultures, the phenomenon of the Evil Eye is invoked here in an another ambiguous situation where legal regulation is lacking and "matters of the heart," attitudes and moral dispositions, are of concern.

The issue at stake is the proper attitude and behavior of potential creditors toward potential borrowers, haves toward have-nots, at a critical but legally unclarified juncture just prior to the commencement of the year of release. Where no recourse to law is possible, appeal to traditional values and beliefs take over, along with regard for the action, judgment, and blessing of the Lord (vv. 7–10). As the Lord God has given (v. 7a), so his people should give (vv. 7b–8). Whereas an Evil Eye toward the needy brother is "sin" (v. 9), the gift of a nongrudging eye and heart earns the Lord's blessing (v. 10). The notion of the Evil Eye is invoked here as elsewhere when the focus is on wealth and the selfish accumulation of goods (Prov 28:22), the miserly refusal to share of one's substance (Deut 28:54–57), and the neglect of the virtue of generosity and the begrudging of gifts and alms (Prov 23:6–8; Sir 14:3–10; 18:18; 37:11; Tob 4:5–19). Here too an Evil Eye is linked with a heart that is hardened to another's need and a hand that is shut to a poor brother in want.

Socially, this warning against an Evil Eye reflects the concern for mutual support and covenantal solidarity in a society plagued by economic disparity, conflict, suspicion of wealth, and a perception of limited good.[59] Morally, exercise of the Evil Eye is identified as "sin" (v. 9), a violation of covenantal obligation and behavior incompatible with the experience of a generous God (vv. 7, 10–11). The principle at stake here is captured by a later word of Sirach: "The bread of the needy is the life of the poor; whoever deprives them of it is a man of blood" (34:21). Or as Tobit, echoing our text, puts it, also in explicit connection with the Evil Eye: "Do not begrudge with an Evil Eye the gift when you make it. Do not turn your face from any poor man, and the face of God will not be turned from you" (4:7).

CONCLUSION

The biblical communities shared with their neighbors a dread of the Evil Eye, a horror of being publicly labeled an Evil Eye possessor/fascinator, and similar stratagems for avoiding or warding off its injurious power. Belief in the Evil Eye in the ancient world formed part of a larger belief system involving concepts of demons, witchcraft, sorcery, and related extraordinary forces and agents affecting the natural and social environment. This worldview constituted a symbolical rendition of the ecological, economic, and social conditions in which the ancients felt themselves exposed and vulnerable. In a precarious natural environment where economic survival for the greater portion of the population was uncertain, where a mixed economy and both economic and social disparity led to persistent competition and conflict over resources perceived as scarce and limited,. where the eye was regarded as linked with the heart and as the channel of its attitudes and dispositions, there ocular aggression and fear of the Evil Eye played a dominant role in human behavior and social interaction.

For the biblical communities, as for their neighbors, Evil Eye belief and practice was no more incompatible with belief in the high gods or in Yahweh than was a fear of witches, sorcerers, or magicians. On the other hand, in contrast to their neighbors, the biblical communities never attributed the Evil Eye to their deity, who could be thought of as "jealous" of that which he possessed but never envious of, or malicious toward, his creatures. The Evil Eye constituted for them a predominantly human trait and moral quality, the very worst of the evils created by God, a constant source of tears. It was an expression of envy, greed, miserliness, and malice that was injurious to others, to the fascinator him/herself, and to the fascinator's relationship with God. In ambiguous occasions unregulated by formal laws or arrangements, concern for the Evil Eye was invoked to promote traditional values such as generosity and the sharing of goods, especially with those in need. For the community defined and bound by the covenant, the Evil Eye symbolized unacceptable social and moral deviance. Avoidance of the Evil Eye, on the other hand, reinforced mutual support and communal cohesion and fostered the values and ideals of covenantal justice.

13 The Deuteronomic Law Code and the Politics of State Centralization

Naomi Steinberg

Deuteronomy 19:1–25:19 appears on first glance to address a wide range of legal issues in ancient Israelite life. Upon closer reading, one discovers that the laws within this section of the Deuteronomic law code regularly concern one basic institution of Israelite society, the family. However, there has been no comprehensive interpretive sociological model that would enable a reader to understand these Deuteronomic legal provisions. This essay will assess these laws and propose the thesis that they gradually functioned to serve the interests of political centralization that began at the time of the inception of the monarchy.

I

Typically, scholars have explored the relationship of Israelite to other ancient Near Eastern laws. For example, Phillips[1] argues that, as a result of the seriousness of adultery in ancient Israel (it is an offense against God), it was treated not as a civil offense but as a crime.[2] Hence, punishment for a wife's behavior in such circumstances was not left to a husband's discretion but instead became a community concern and required the death penalty. Phillips views Deuteronomic thinking on both adultery and seduction as distinct from principles of ancient Near Eastern law, and an innovation in Israelite sexual ethics, because it construes women as legal adults responsible for their actions. For example, in comparison with biblical and cuneiform law, what is original about Deut 22:22, according to Phillips, is that in a case of adultery "both of them are to die."[3] Phillips contends that Deuteronomic legislation on adultery and seduction was designed to settle

161

issues of paternity, and not, as is commonly argued, to protect a husband's or father's property, namely, his women. Concerning the emphasis on paternity, Phillips remarks, "This was of vital importance in a society which did not believe in life after death but rather that a man's personality went on in his children."[4] Phillips, and others who take this evolutionary approach, attempt to locate the biblical legal material on family life in the context of a developing moral consciousness that distinguished ancient Israel from her neighbors. They do this by highlighting one of the distinctive Deuteronomic humanitarian concerns, which Weinfeld and McBride have addressed,[5] namely, extending the scope of the law to include women. Phillips concludes that the death penalty for both the adulterous man and woman reflects the distinct ethical character of Israel's sacral criminal law and distinguishes it from the ancient Near Eastern legal tradition. For Phillips, the unique features of Deuteronomic legislation reflect Israel's particular theological foundation.[6]

In this essay, I will assess the singular qualities of the Deuteronomic legislation on family life by focusing on political concerns, not on moral evolution. I will analyze Deuteronomic laws on family life and sexuality as one arena in which political control is exercised. I am interested in refuting Phillips' argument for the putative uniqueness of Israelite family law in order to demonstrate that from a cross-cultural perspective these legal provisions can be interpreted as part of the politics of state centralization. State centralization altered judicial authority as exemplified in the Book of the Covenant, which is generally regarded as an earlier legal tradition. Using the perspectives of comparative legal studies, I will demonstrate that the change in ancient Israel's judicial administration was aimed at weakening local political boundaries in order to strengthen the authority of the central government under the united monarchy.

II

In order to understand the sociopolitical realities that lie behind the Deuteronomic legislation, we must appropriate the work of social historians who associate laws on marriage, family, and kinship patterns with attempts by politicians to exercise power. Such laws compel subjects to conform to institutionalized authority in a way that other laws (e.g., tax laws) do not. For example, a recent study by Goody[7] traces the connection between the growth of the church in medieval Europe and changing forms of domestic life to a "moment" parallel to the one I presume in ancient Israel for Deut 19:1–25:19. In particular:

> For the Church to grow and survive it had to accumulate property, which meant acquiring control over the way it was passed from one generation to

the next. Since the distribution of property between generations is related to patterns of marriage and the legitimisation of children, the Church had to gain authority over these so that it could influence the strategies of heirship.[8]

Goody's argument that early medieval Christianity benefited by passing legislation that, on the surface, appeared to provide independence for women parallels the sociopolitical dynamics behind the legislation in Deut 19:1–25:19. Changing laws, whether they be to discourage the remarriage of widows or to safeguard inheritance of paternal property by daughters, benefited church interests, because women were more likely than men to bequeath their property to the church. Further, legislation concerning marriage eligibility patterns (thereby altering notions of kinship) provided the church with an alternate source of revenue. If one violated prohibitions on marriage to near kin, one could be absolved of the sin by buying a dispensation from the local priest. Beyond providing revenue, legislation on sexual behavior succeeded in breaking down local autonomy and in establishing religious authority at the expense of lineage relationships. As a result, a woman gained a certain degree of freedom from the authority of her husband or her father as the church took control of family and marriage relationships, though whether women ultimately benefited from this "liberation" is open to question.

Goody provides evidence that suggests that political authority can be exercised through control of family life and sex roles; that is, general laws on sexuality may provide a centralized authority (either church or state) with a means of redirecting individual loyalty from one social institution to another, so that, in the case Goody presented, family allegiance was no longer in competition with the interests of church or state. For ancient Israel, legislation intended to accomplish that same goal may be identified in the Deuteronomic law code.

Only in the legislation of Deuteronomy 19–25 does one find laws where centralized authority is established at the expense of local political boundaries, thereby emphasizing the primary importance of the nuclear family unit. There are many examples of this concern. Besides the legislation concerning adultery considered by Phillips, Deuteronomy stipulates that foreign women who are taken captive in war will be protected from the capriciousness of their Israelite husbands (21:10–14). Moreover, the Deuteronomic law code legislates premarital sex. Deuteronomy 22:28–29 decrees that the man who rapes an unbetrothed woman must marry her.[9] Having done something dishonorable to her once, the new husband may not act in a similar fashion again; he can never attempt to divorce her. These laws establish rights for women in the interest of preserving nuclear family units whose existence depends on the protection of both spouses in the marriage.

The only legislation from ancient Israel on remarriage is found in Deuteronomy. Based on the many conditions specified in Deut 24:1–4, including the specification that a husband may not later remarry his wife, a husband must be serious about his decision to divorce. Another example of concern for the nuclear family unit, the law of Deut 24:5, mandates that the interests of the family be placed before those of the state, as when it exempts a bridegroom from military service for the first year following his marriage. This provision allows the alliance formed by the couple time to strengthen, such that their loyalties will now be to each other rather than to the families from which they originated. Maintenance of social order in ancient Israel, as represented in these laws, appears directly linked to the preservation of the nuclear social unit.

One law aimed at preservation of the nuclear family is worth examining in detail precisely because at first glance it appears to presume an extended family dwelling. This is Deut 25:5–10, the law of Levirate marriage. As stated here, the law appears to have two goals in mind: first, that the property of the dead man be kept within the family (presumably this is the reason that the responsibility the dead husband's brother is to show toward the widow falls only upon brothers who dwell together); second, that the name of the dead be perpetuated through the child born of a union between the widow and her brother-in-law.

The Deuteronomic formulation of this law allows for an element of choice. The brother of the dead man may elect not to fulfill his responsibilities to his dead brother and the widow. In that event, the widow is to make her brother-in-law's decision known to the local elders. She, rather than he, initiates this legal action. The law guarantees that the widow is not dependent upon her brother-in-law's unwillingness to acknowledge his obligations publicly. It protects the woman's interests through the sequence of events stipulated here. The denial of family responsibility by the living brother brings shame upon him, which must be witnessed before the local authorities. If the brother-in-law declines his Levirate duties, the woman informs the elders, who are instructed to quiz the man to determine the veracity of the widow's allegations. Having established that the brother-in-law will not fulfill his obligations toward his sister-in-law, the elders are directed to take legal actions to shame him publicly. The brother-in-law's sandal is pulled off by the widow; she then spits in his face, before renaming him, "The house of him whose sandal was pulled off" (v. 10).

Scholars have regularly understood this law to presume that the wife of the deceased man is legally the property of her husband's family.[10] Yet, the child born from the Levirate union not only allows for the continuance of the dead man's name, it also provides the widow with support in her old age.[11] The law maintains her right to a child, and protects her against her brother-in-law's refusal to redeem his brother's name, by placing authority for control of this family situation in the hands of individuals who administer the law from outside the setting of the nuclear family involved.

As noted above, a reader may get the initial impression that the Deuteronomic formulation of the Levirate law presumes an extended family unit. However, as Lemche notes, "if the custom has any meaning, it is that it points to the existence of nuclear and neolocal families, since it is the nuclear family that is threatened by extinction when the father of the house dies without having left sons behind him. Such a nuclear family simply ceases to be an autonomous unit."[12] Thus Deut 25:5–10 is another law that is concerned with preserving the nuclear unit.

Our survey of Deuteronomy 19–25 indicates that this legislation intends to preserve the nuclear family unit and guarantees that the nuclear family will endure by limiting the power of men and by creating rights for women. This protection is provided not because an individual is a woman; rather, this legal protection is mandated because the woman is defined by Israelite society as an integral member of the family unit. The law presumes that the nuclear family is more important than the individual.

III

Judicial practice in Deuteronomy purportedly safeguards justice for all people. For the nuclear unit, this norm is achieved through laws administered by Israelites outside the immediate family. Legal decisions connected to family problems are taken out of the hands of the individuals directly involved in the family relationship and placed in the hands of an impartial body, the elders, who are responsible for maintaining social stability.[13] If one compares Exod 22:16–17 with Deut 22:28–29, it is clear that what could have been resolved by the *paterfamilias* in Exodus is in Deuteronomy expressed in categorical terms. In fact, the father is not even mentioned in Deut 22:28–29. Such an arrangement for the administration of legal rights qualifies the power of adult males of the nuclear family and supposedly provides legal protection for women and children. The successful transition to a centralized state comes from both using and subverting existing judicial authority structures, in this case the elders.[14]

In comparing the Book of the Covenant to Deuteronomy, Weber remarks on the decline of authority granted to the father in the latter over against the former. He relates these changed social conditions to the rise of the monarchy.[15] The Deuteronomic law code effects a shift in social boundaries away from the kinship structure characteristic in the premonarchic period, in order to reduce local authority, which was seen as threatening to the nascent monarchy. As a result, the cohesiveness of the nuclear family is strengthened and the extended family is weakened; authority on both levels is, in the case of the laws of Deuteronomy, redirected to the control of the elders. The bureaucracy of the state promulgates law, which the local elders are responsible for enforcing over individual family units. The result is that what might formerly have been an *ad hoc* function exercised at the city gate by the elders becomes regularized through the regulation of behavior.[16] This is seen in the case of the law of the rebellious son (Deut 21:18–21) and the law guaranteeing the virginity of the bride (Deut 22:13–21). In effect, then, state centralization does not drastically renovate the organization of village life. In village life, the elders administer justice; with the imposition of monarchy, these individuals continue to regulate local business. In addition, they serve as liaisons to the central authority when necessary. One could argue that the rise of monarchy diminished the political functions of the elders while increasing their judicial role. Elders retain local power despite the monarchic overlay.[17]

A study by Y. A. Cohen that includes monarchic Israel in an attempt to comprehend the relationship between legal systems and the growth of political and economic organization builds on Weber's discussion of the legitimation of authority, and analyzes cross-cultural data from Murdock's "World Ethnographic Sample."[18] Cohen identifies an explicit connection between political control and laws of sexuality. He concludes that, concomitant with the centralization of political authority, a state ruler strives to manipulate allegiance to his government through the use of sexual controls; one mechanism for political control involves control of sexuality. Cohen maintains that the state places primary emphasis on the marital bond through legislation on adultery, incest, and celibacy. This is done in the interest of making the nuclear family—rather than the lineage, which can, but may not, have resided in the same town or village with other lineages—the primary unit in society.

Most relevant for our analysis of the laws in Deuteronomy 19–25 are Cohen's remarks on adultery:

> I interpret laws prescribing capital punishment for adultery as having four principal consequences: (1) the weakening of local corporate groups; (2) the

strengthening of bonds that cannot serve as sources of rebellion; (3) the control of the polity through the encouragement of the conjugal pair's mobility; and (4) the maintenance of social distance between rulers and ruled. Common to the first three is the strengthening of the marital network's boundaries.[19]

Cohen concludes that an emerging and growing state is interested in redirecting individual loyalties in a way that will not conflict with allegiances to the political organization.[20] In a social system where lineage has previously been of primary importance, the local kinship relationship must be subverted, lest individuals unite in rebellion against the state. The possibility for such rebellion is seriously diminished when the strongest personal bond in society is based on the marital unit; the marital bond is strengthened at the expense of the kinship bond. In sum, Cohen interprets legislation regulating sexual behavior as a means of exercising political control in what he labels a "state organization."

For Cohen, state societies are those with centralized authority, stateless societies those with local autonomy, or what Cohen calls "horizontal organization." Chiefdoms are characterized by "multiple power centers; one of their central characteristics is a notable resistance to centralization of authority."[21] Thus, they are segmentary societies.

Cohen discerns a diachronic relation between state development and the sanctions imposed for the violation of adultery laws. Political organization in state societies moves along a continuum from early to late institutionalization of government. In the later stages of state organization, it is no longer necessary to enforce legislation guaranteeing the allegiance of the individual to the central leader. Local autonomy no longer threatens centralized authority.[22]

Potential obstacles to the imposition of state control over local autonomy through the use of control of sexual behavior may, according to Cohen, be overcome by couching the legislation in the language and ideology of local groups. In fact, it is not simply a matter of one group and its interests replacing another, but of a gradual shift that, over time, results in the disappearance of one type of control and its substitution by another.[23] Thus it would be incorrect to argue that, through laws of sexuality, the extended kin group is totally broken down and replaced by the nuclear family unit. The latter was present prior to the new legislation, and the larger kinship structures remain important (e.g., the "father's house"—a term recognized to refer to various social groupings).[24] Nonetheless, laws controlling sexual behavior reduce the emphasis on extended family units and replace it with a focus on the nuclear family.

IV

At this point it is appropriate to integrate Weber's discussion of the legitimation of authority with the work of Cohen and Goody, thereby linking analysis of sociopolitical organization with the regulation of family life. Most biblical scholars are familiar with informal theories of how a national leader might work to channel individual loyalty away from local authorities and toward the national level of government. At the time of the united monarchy, Solomon (961–922 BCE) recast tribal boundaries into fiscal districts in order to focus allegiance away from the tribal level and toward his own state organization (1 Kgs 4:7–19). This destruction of the old tribal boundaries was an attempt to prevent local rebellion through the erosion of kinship connections.[25]

Solomon's redistricting obviously violated tribal organization and raised the ire of many. Regardless of whether or not there is a connection between Solomon and the laws being discussed here, in both situations religion became a means to justify politics. In the case of Solomon, there is an appeal to the theology of Zion as the basis for royal prerogatives; in Deuteronomy the political motivation for the control of sexual behavior is made less offensive than it might otherwise be through the application of religious sanctions (e.g., in Deut 24:4 remarriage is an abomination to God). As a result, in Deuteronomy, laws on family life are understood as God's statement of proper social relationships within the Israelite community. Here one may identify the reciprocal influence of religion and politics.

Promulgation of the laws in Deuteronomy 19–25 may have met with little resistance from women because women appeared to benefit from these laws; power over them is taken out of the hands of their fathers and husbands, who become subordinate to the jurisdiction of the elders. The result of such a shift, ironically, is that women are actually controlled— along with men—in the interest of the politics of state centralization.[26] According to the newer legislation, women could be killed for lack of virginity (Deut 22:13–21) whereas men could not, just as in the issue of complicity of rape, women had to prove themselves in a way that men did not (22:23–27). Thus one may question whether Deuteronomic justice is truly egalitarian in intent, as some have claimed.[27] Women may have gained legal autonomy from their fathers and husbands through the legislation in Deuteronomy 19–25, but they were thrown on the defensive in ways that put them at a social disadvantage vis-à-vis men. These laws, which initially appear to relate to family status and roles, have less to do with gender as such, and more to do with political and social control of individual behavior of the entire "ruled" populace.

In light of comparative social histories, it seems reasonable to conclude that sanctions concerning sexual relations in Deuteronomy 19–25 should be seen as connected to a movement toward centralization, or tightening of control, on the national level. Although women appear less subject to the authority of the *paterfamilias* in the Deuteronomic legislation than in the Book of the Covenant, the former laws encourage nuclear family units and discourage extended family units. Rather, through these laws both men and women appear to be controlled by legal ordinances promulgated outside of the local group. All family issues are controlled to suit the sociopolitical aims of the form of government that replaced the old kinship-based social system.

There is one more point of contact between the comparative data and the biblical evidence. Cohen argues that adultery laws ultimately widen the social distance between the nation's rulers and their subjects. In other words, the laws of sexual behavior for commoners are not binding upon the royal court—despite what Deut 17:14–20 suggests. The ruler is separated from his subject not only in the matter of sexual conduct, but in other social and political realms.[28] The pattern of family dynamics consistently revealed in the Deuteronomic law code exists in obvious contrast to the actions of the Davidic house.

V

Even though this essay is concerned primarily with examining the way in which comparative material can help us understand the relation of family law to state formation in ancient Israel, such perspectives may contribute to the discussion of the Deuteronomic legislation's date of composition. Although many scholars think that Jehoshaphat's reform (873–849 BCE) resulted in a shift in the administration of justice[29] such that professional judges (Deut 16:18) took over responsibilities formerly delegated to elders at the city gate, the analogy between the comparative data and the biblical texts suggests that we consider the inception of the monarchy as the beginning locus for the gradual promulgation of legislation emphasizing the nuclear family. In light of the present uncertainty on the issue of dating the Deuteronomic corpus and the range of dates already posited for this material, this suggestion should not overburden the discussion.

Using comparative social history, this study has argued that in the tenth century Deuteronomy 19–25 would have provided an important means for centralizing the political authority of the king by weakening local political boundaries and strengthening the nuclear family unit. This argument allows us to make sense of the fact that this legislation was promulgated at all: it was intended to reshape and maintain community organization. Laws need not be written down unless the collective disagrees with them and refuses to obey. Laws that are publicly formulated are those that society has failed to internalize. They require promulgation in order to be enforced.[30] In this regard, it is interesting to note that the statutes affecting family life in Deuteronomy 19–25 include sanctions for enforcement (the one noticeable exception is 24:5, which is more an abstraction than a legal decision). Thus it would appear that the Deuteronomic legislation was grounded in an actual sociopolitical reality. The analytical perspectives of comparative studies suggest that this reality began with the centralization of government under the monarchy.[31]

The Theory and Praxis of Biblical Scholarship

14 Revolutions In Reading the Bible

Lee Cormie

> We see our lives in the Bible and the Bible in our lives.
>
> Lay Pastoral Agent
> Popular Christian Community
> San Salvador, El Salvador
> Easter 1989

The worldwide irruptions of poor and oppressed peoples in recent decades—of poor peoples throughout the Third World and in the First World too, of indigenous peoples; of blacks and other peoples of color in societies and a world dominated by whites; of women; of gays and lesbians; and of all the voices speaking on behalf of the earth itself—have revealed once again that people today, indeed all of life as we know it, exist at the juncture of suffering and hope. In the midst of these struggles for the liberation of all the oppressed, for justice, for peace, and for the integrity of creation, many Christians are learning to reread the Bible and are discovering anew its revelatory and inspiring power.

This essay arises at this juncture of suffering and hope. The concerns that inform it cut across theology and social analysis, exegesis and hermeneutics, and it is informed by many different voices.

I have tried to listen to oppressed peoples, whose voices have historically been distorted and silenced, concerning the nature of the social order in which we live—its institutions, structures, and ideologies both nationally and globally—their hopes in this life on earth, and their faiths. I have tried to understand the place in this social order of the upper classes—their fears, hopes, and gods. I have tried to listen to those in the working class and in the so-called middle class too—in particular, whites in the First World like my parents, and men like my father and me and my sons, who are not so obviously "oppressed" yet have never had a voice in ruling circles. I have tried to listen to rereadings of the Bible among groups of poor and oppressed peoples in the Third World, and in North America too. And I have tried to follow the expression of similar sensibilities and concerns among a growing number of scholarly exegetes.

It is clear, however, that efforts like this to listen to the growing number of so many "new" voices confront many obstacles and challenges. In the first place, in comparison to the vast resources mobilized in service of amplifying the voices of the rich and powerful, there are few resources available for promoting these new voices and the dialogues among them.

There are other reasons why the irruptions of these new voices have profoundly complicated every effort to speak authoritatively about any aspect of life on this earth—about the economy, politics, family and community, the church and its mission, the nation and the world, about all of creation and of its Creator. The sheer number of voices, reflecting different social contexts and different racial, ethnic, cultural, linguistic, and religious backgrounds, means that no one can hear all of these new voices equally well. There are few forums for promoting this dialogue. There is no single theory or doctrine that can encompass this rich diversity of experiences and perspectives, and there is no single shared language for communicating among all these different groups.

Clearly, we have discovered again and again in the struggle of each group of poor and oppressed people that no one can speak for all the others, and there can be no last, definitive word in this ongoing dialogue. The Spirit of truth and justice continues to address us in surprising new voices, calling repeatedly for new conversions from old ways of thinking and acting, from old forms of politics and faith.

Yet, in the face of such great obstacles to justice, peace, and the integrity of creation, hope for the future requires avoiding the two extremes of reasserted authoritarianism or pure relativism, political impotence and despair. It requires discernment of some signposts of the Spirit in the midst of this conflict of interpretations that characterizes our world. Thus I offer the following hypothesis concerning points of intersection and convergence in this ongoing dialogue. It concerns the central drama that has been (re)discovered by the movements of poor and oppressed peoples, a drama that both shapes our lives today and lies at the heart of the Bible:

> In a hierarchically organized world, all of life—the economy, politics, family and community, culture, and religion, indeed all of creation—turns on the struggles for liberation of poor and oppressed peoples and those in solidarity with them. In biblical terms, the nature of God, evil and grace, sin and salvation, the Christian community as the people of God—all in the heavens and on earth—are experienced and defined in relation to the sufferings and hopes of the poor and oppressed.

I offer in this essay some reflections on the context in which this insight concerning the central drama of history and salvation has emerged, and on some of its implications for reading the Bible today.

REREADING OUR HISTORY: THE IRRUPTIONS OF THE POOR AND OPPRESSED IN THE WORLD AND IN THE CHURCH

In the 1960s, social scientists and politicians were praising the countries of the West as the most advanced, modern, rational, scientific, productive, affluent, free societies in history—the very epitome of the long history of social evolution and the ideal to which the peoples of the other nations of the world aspired.[1] Indeed, the experts proclaimed, there were no longer any social problems of great significance and no great disagreements about the course of social development; thus, they cheered, we live in a period characterized by the end of ideology. Each of us was affluent, or soon could be by discipline and effort, and therefore free to become and to do whatever "he" wants. The only questions concerned the details of how best to manage advanced society, and these were best left to the experts who alone were trained to deal with them.

Mainstream Christian theologians in North America and Europe shared this spirit of great optimism. In fact, some were so ecstatic that they declared the "death of God" as the last remaining obstacle to this godlike exercise of freedom by modern "man."

Most mainstream Christian thinkers were less ecstatic and radical, but they too were imbued with a deep sense of the unique character of the modern world and of its challenge to "traditional" Christianity and to the ethos of the Bible. This was the period of the widespread triumph of "scientific" exegesis in mainstream Western theology, as biblical scholars, equipped with the latest and most sophisticated intellectual categories and theories, wrestled with the existential meaning of Jesus of Nazareth for the modern world, which, in their eyes, was so different. They saw their task as demythologizing the Bible in order to make sense for modern "man" of the good news that Jesus announced.

However, no sooner had the end of ideology been triumphantly declared than long marginalized and silenced voices erupted, breaking into the discourses from which they had so long been excluded and pressuring for changes that go to the roots in all the allegedly separate domains of life—economic, political, social, familial, psychological, technological, cultural, and religious.

In many respects, these irruptions have constituted the most significant political development since the establishment by United States elites and their allies of the framework for global development at the end of World War II.[2] These movements and the thinkers associated with them have revolutionized our social theories and analyses, and have transformed the debates and struggles over social order and the meaning of life within it. They have transformed our politics, involving a far broader range of people, movements, and organizations in debates and struggles with the experts and managers over the policies of every institution. Indeed, they have transformed the character and scope of politics itself, making clear that these debates and decisions involve far more than narrowly economic or social considerations, but the very texture of life and the possibilities for the future.

Of course, in the late 1970s and early 1980s the defenders of the reigning order, which is experienced as disorder by the majority of the world's peoples and by the earth itself, succeeded in reestablishing their agenda with the administrations of Reagan and Bush in the United States, the Thatcher governments in England, the Mulroney governments in Canada, and elsewhere. It was increasingly clear by the end of the 1980s, that they have done so only at the cost of policies that are fueling the fires of economic, social, political, and ecological crisis. There is a growing sense that hope for the future depends on radically different responses to the issues raised by the popular movements, responses that require radically transformed relations of authority and power involving the active participation of the historically marginalized in defining the problems, in envisioning alternatives, and in choosing among them.

These irruptions also constitute the most important religious development. They have radically challenged our images of God, our spiritualities and ethics, and our visions of the mission of the church in this world. And they have changed the way we read the Bible.

There have been at least two distinct strands of these theological and exegetical irruptions—popular and academic—and both are important.

In the context of the then current black power movement and against the background of the long history of struggle against slavery and racism, black pastors and theologians in the United States rediscovered the liberating dimension of the gospel.[3] Existing scholarly resources for this task were meager and of limited help.[4] In fact, the first wave of black theology was quickly criticized by many blacks for relying on standard academic insights and perspectives and ignoring the rich tradition of popular black culture and religion, which did not find expression in academic—and therefore largely white and professional middle class—discourse.[5] This tradition had often been interpreted as promoting passivity and submission, a vain seeking of liberation after death while accepting oppression in this world; indeed, under slavery, biblical texts served as a major tool of pro-slavery ideology. But as soon as the discourse, with the subtleties and subterfuges inevitably made necessary in a racist social order, was properly reread from below, from the experience and frames of reference of oppressed black people, it became clear that this tradition was full of powerful and liberating messages.

This shifting appreciation of the black religious tradition contributed to a shifting appreciation of the Bible. In particular, these insights called into question the claims of academic exegesis to lead to the most reliable and adequate interpretation of the biblical message. Indeed, it became clear that though black people had been fundamentally shaped by the Bible, their interpreting had not been primarily a matter of academic scholarship. On the contrary, blacks had historically been deprived of the opportunity to learn to read and write. They learned about the Bible through stories and sermons in which they heard biblical expressions of their predicament, such as slavery in Egypt, invasions by foreign empires, deportations into captivity, and the bedevilment by the principalities and powers of the age. As Clarice Martin has pointed out, "Black slaves were always distrustful of their masters' interpretation of the Bible, and preached the Christian Gospel in terms of their own experience."[6]

In other words, reverence for the Bible as the revealed Word of God grew out of the "experiential sympathy" that black people discovered with so much of the Bible, an interpretation that was distinct from the standard biblical interpretation in the dominant white churches and among biblical scholars.[7] This gap was still evident in the 1960s, when black theology emerged in more scholarly forms in North America.

There has been a parallel development in Latin America. The first scholarly publications in the late 1960s depended on existing exegetical resources for establishing the biblical foundations for a theology of liberation, centering all of theology on the notions of oppression, injustice, and the hope for liberation. As is well known, this development focused especially on the account of the Exodus as the liberation of the slaves from Egypt.[8]

In conjunction with the notion that poor and oppressed people should be active participants—subjects—in their own liberation, this meager exegetical foundation helped to open the door to an amazing development— the widespread use of the Bible by poor people themselves in basic Christian communities. In sharp contrast to the great difficulties that scholars had in crossing the great chasm they saw between "modern" experience and culture and that of biblical peoples, the Christians in these communities quickly discovered their lives in the Bible and the Bible in their lives, as some lay pastoral agents in El Salvador told me in a conversation after Mass on Easter Sunday in 1989.[9] In other words, in a way that took them far beyond current biblical scholarship,[10] they discovered the immediacy and the relevatory and inspirational power of the Bible in their lives today.[11] So many biblical stories sounded familiar, like the stories of their own lives. It is easy to recognize the main actors and central dynamics of a drama that does not appear to them to have changed so much in two thousand years.[12]

More recently, some biblical scholars, influenced by the experiences and sensibilities of poor and oppressed peoples and their allies in Latin America and elsewhere in the Third World, have affirmed these connections in scholarly terms.[13]

Developments in feminist exegesis have been more complicated and ambiguous. The problem here is that women's equality in particular, as it is understood today, is not a prominent concern in biblical texts. On the contrary, there are many texts that support the subordination of women. Most of the major actors in the Bible are men; indeed, God is often imaged as a father, and the definitive revelation of this God in the Christian scriptures is the "Son" of God.[14]

These ambiguities and contradictions have contributed to undermining the authority of the Bible for many feminists. Some have felt compelled to reject it entirely, as an inherently patriarchal text hostile to any notion of women's equality with men, and with it all of Christianity. Others, however, have discovered in the Bible a variety of affirmations of the dignity and integrity of women in their struggles against exploitation and oppression. These glimpses of a different stance toward women have made them question patriarchal readings of the Bible by contemporary exegetes, preachers, and church officials.

These glimpses of a different stance toward women have also made many feminists question the process by which the biblical traditions themselves were developed and canonized. They question the institutionalization of modern exegesis in the church and in the university. I will return to these issues below; here I want to note only that the Bible is being read in a liberating way in some groups of oppressed women,[15] and that these readings confirm scholarly conclusions concerning the positive significance of some texts for women. Moreover, these feminist rereadings of the Bible, although critical of patriarchal tendencies within the Bible itself and of the way so many biblical texts are used to bless the continuing subordination of women, permit the affirmation by some feminists of the Bible's continuing, if qualified, authority in the Christian community.[16] These developments have contributed to a significant convergence with shifting attitudes toward the Bible among other groups of oppressed peoples and the scholars identified with them.

These developments in exegesis among scholars working in solidarity with oppressed groups have contributed to the growing recognition of the inadequacies of the reigning frameworks for scholarly exegesis—its professional middle-class, white, male bias, which has resulted in highly distorted, "spiritualized" interpretations of biblical religion, cut off from the concrete struggles of poor and oppressed peoples for the fullness of life, as it was imagined in their time, against all the religious, political, economic, and military forces arrayed against them.[17] Thus, for academic, theological, and political reasons, these kinds of scholars are increasingly insisting on the necessity, for understanding biblical texts, of reconstructing the social context in as much concrete social, political, economic, military, cultural, and technological detail as possible.[18]

In the search for alternative approaches to reading the Bible, these scholars are uncovering at the heart of the Bible the same dynamic of oppression and liberation so visible in the world today, and they are making clear the relevance of the Bible for poor and oppressed peoples today.[19]

In various ways, these kinds of studies represent the scholarly expression in the broader struggles over the soul of the church and its mission. These struggles in the church and the academy are important expressions of the struggles over the future of the world. To the surprise of many, perhaps to liberal and radical intellectuals most of all, progressive or leftist forces in the church have become important actors in these struggles in many countries around the world, especially in the United States and Canada, in many Latin American countries, in South Africa, and in the Philippines.

These struggles have changed much in the last twenty-five years. As we approach the twenty-first century, there are many signs of hope: in the tearing down of the Berlin Wall, in the release of Nelson Mandela from prison, in the partial return to democracy in Chile, in the irruptions of the voices of all the long-silenced and marginalized oppressed.

But there are also many signs of increasing suffering in the world: in the so-called debt crisis that is causing a massive hemorrhage of capital from the Third World, resulting in the suffering and deaths of tens of millions and widespread social crises; in the increasing devastation of the environment, which threatens all of life as we know it, in the growing homelessness, alienation, drug addiction, and violence in the shadows of the greatest concentrations of wealth the world has ever witnessed.

In this context, reading the Bible has never been more important.

THEOLOGY: THE CENTRALITY IN THIS LIFE
ON EARTH OF THE DRAMA OF SUFFERING
AND HOPE, CRUCIFIXION AND RESURRECTION

Over against the previously dominant approaches to biblical faith that stressed its purely "religious" or "spiritual" character, and its devotion to concerns with life beyond this one, we are learning to recognize that biblical faith always concerned the most mundane matters of everyday life, the ways in which groups of people organized their lives together on this earth, and the course of history. Specifically, the Bible continually returns to the notion that, in a hierarchically organized society, poor and oppressed peoples *should* hope for liberation—for a new, just social order on this earth. They should hope for liberation and the fullness of life because God promises it. Indeed, the very nature of God, the authors of the biblical texts concluded again and again, concerns the coming of this reign of God on earth.

I can illustrate this claim by reference to only a few studies.

Gottwald's extraordinary *The Tribes of Yahweh* powerfully grounds these claims in a convincing reconstruction of the origins of Israelite religion.[20] Building on and expanding Mendenhall's suggestion, he developed a reconstruction of the origins of Israel that posited a "Moses group" that left Egypt and gradually entered into alliance with various Canaanite underclass groups, who together revolted against the Canaanite city-states and established a tribal federation of rough equality. In this interpretation, then, Israelite faith in Yahweh evolved as a symbolic expression of the struggle for liberation.

In other words, Israelite religion concerned the emergence of the hopes and commitments of the various components of what came to be the Israelite confederation of tribes, It encompassed (1) their "faith" in the possibility of this egalitarian confederacy, in spite of the enormous power of the Pharaoh and his allies in the Canaanite city-states, and (2) their commitment to solidarity, in spite of the endless sources of disagreement and conflict among the members of this motley alliance in a continually shifting and intensely conflictual environment. In theological terms, we can say that Yahweh was revealed in the course of these struggles as the God concerned above all with the oppressed—the bad who promised their liberation in spite of all obstacles.[21] The hope, faith, and commitment to solidarity that came to make up the core of Israelite religion were central and irreducible dimensions of these historic struggles.[22]

There can be no doubt that this faith and experience infused the subsequent generations of Hebrews and early Christians, and the development of the traditions and texts that finally came to make up the Bible.

But Israelite history did not stand still, nor did Israelite faith. As we have learned from the experience of struggle in our own time, there are many factors that complicate the articulation of faith and hope in changing historical circumstances. This is so because the articulation of what can be hoped for and of what must be resisted—of liberation and oppression—changes; also, the articulation of the ground for this hope and of the nature and meaning of solidarity changes.

Technological developments, like the development of lined cisterns or of the use of iron in making farm implements and weapons, significantly changed the possibilities for organizing and managing everyday life. Plagues devastated whole populations, radically changing the whole social fabric. Changing forms of social order, in response to internal developments or to changes imposed by external forces, also transformed the experience of everyday life, of privilege and deprivation, of wealth and poverty, and posed anew all the questions concerning the nature of community and the meaning of this life on earth. After the development of the monarchy in Israel, for example, it is not surprising that, in a world of monarchies, the hope for liberation came to be articulated in terms of a king who would deliver the people from foreign oppressors. Some, however, like Amos, apparently held out a more radical vision of egalitarian Israel without a king at all.[23]

The encounter with empires, as the victor or more frequently as the victim, radically changed the experience of everyday life and the horizons of what could be dreamed for. In particular, the emergence of the powerful Philistines on the outskirts of Canaan signaled the closure of the historical space for the Israelite experiment in egalitarianism, as did successive empires, which, in addition to dictating slave labor, crushing taxes, and political subservience, powerfully influenced popular understandings of what was possible and impossible, reasonable and unreasonable, realistic and utopian. In subsequent Israelite history, there are many stories of similar threats from the outside, conquests, and defeats. Indeed, later Jeremiah even interpreted conquest by a foreign empire as the vehicle of Yahweh's deliverance from oppression. What a long way the people had come from simple belief in the immediate possibility of creating a life free from oppression and domination, which came to characterize the emerging movement in Canaan![24]

In the midst of these changing internal and external circumstances, the very nature of the actors in this drama of salvation also changed. The experience and categories of *tribe, family, clan, people, race, culture, nation, empire,* and *world* are all social constructs with an extraordinary variety of manifestations that change with changing social circumstances. (We are learning in our own time, from the point of view of language and social order, that *nature* is a social construct too, which humankind's pollution, nuclear weapons, and capacity for genetic manipulation are now rapidly destroying, in possibly apocalyptic ways, with fatal implications for all of life as we know it.) Because biblical faith emerged as the expression of a "people" and their hope for liberation, its expression was always bound up with particular expressions of race and ethnicity—of a "we" and of all the "others." Not surprisingly, different texts reflect in different ways the frequent historical ambiguities of this process as the social infrastructure of group identity was eroded and transformed, cutting across racial, ethnic, tribal, and/or national lines, a process reflecting at times clear traces of imperialistic tendencies. [25]

Similarly, there remained ambiguities and contradictions concerning gender. Feminists have wondered whether women fared well in the early Israelite revolution, for example. There are good reasons for concluding that they did. [26] But it is also clear that the later development of the monarchy involved the reassertion of patriarchal ideology and forms of social organization, resulting in the intensification of the oppression of women in particular, along with that of the lower classes as a whole. In general, every form of tribal, racial, ethnic, and/or national identity involved a particular configuration of class and gender differentiation, as well as of attitudes and policies toward "outsiders," with direct impact on the historical possibilities for the fullness of life for each and for all.

In all of this messy historical process, exposure to different cultural traditions and the accumulation of the "tradition" itself transformed the array of resources in terms of which people could think about themselves, others, and their experience. Similarly, the development and institutionalization of "authoritative" interpretations of past expressions of the tradition changed the nature of this interpretive process, of authority in this process, and of the struggle within the community over the tradition's legacy to them and its implications for the future.

The complex and contradictory character of this historical process of the development of a people, of their tradition, of the process of interpretation and of authority is revealed in the Bible itself. The Bible gives ample testimony of the many ways in which established authorities, in their devotion to their own riches and power, and to the gods that symbolize this way of life, can use the tradition, including parts of the Bible, against the people. The Bible shows clearly that no image, no symbol, no doctrine is "sacred," that is, above being used in the interests of exploitation and oppression. [27] This lesson has been amply reinforced by the uses of the Bible in our own time to legitimate exploitation and oppression against blacks in South Africa, against women, against those of other faiths, against gays and lesbians, against workers, against indigenous peoples, against the poor.

But it is also clear that the Bible is not simply relativistic and fatalistic about this ongoing struggle over authoritative interpretations of the tradition and its legacy. The story of Exodus, as the foundational event for the subsequent Israelite and Christian traditions, remained central, and with it reference to the hope of poor and oppressed peoples for liberation, faith in the God who promises it, and solidarity of and with the poor and oppressed in the face of all obstacles. The "option for the poor and oppressed" reflected in this event served as a signpost of the Spirit in history. But this point of reference did not automatically remove all the ambiguities and questions concerning how concretely to live in particular times and places, for it is also a simple fact that the forms of this option and of the faith flowing from it, and in significant respects its content, inevitably changed.[28]

As we learn to appreciate the wide variety of historical contexts and experiences and the different challenges confronting each historical community, we are also learning to recognize the absolute irreducibility of theological questions concerning hope and faith and commitment, and the necessity in each new historical context for each community to face these questions anew.

How do people in a particular time and place envision the fullness of life on this earth? How do they understand suffering? What dare an oppressed people hope for in the face of particular forms of crushing authority and power? Are not resignation and despair or individualistically striving to take advantage of whatever few opportunities are available more "reasonable" responses than hope for the liberation of all the oppressed? How can the suffering of the oppressed be explained? Is it their fault, or fate, or God's will? Is the hope for liberation purely a dream of some distant eschaton, or is it experienced as already present in some powerful yet mysterious way in the midst of suffering? How is it possible to live in fidelity to the Spirit of Life in a world where the forces of death are so powerful? Is suffering and death for affirming one's dignity and that of the oppressed the last word, or do those who die somehow live on? In view of the power of evil, what kind of God grounds this hope and solidarity?

Faith and hope did not stand still, and at times hopelessness seemed the only reasonable option. The Bible gives much testimony to the difficulties of the task of keeping hope alive in apparently hopeless situations, perhaps above all, in the book of Job.[29] The Christian scriptures give much evidence that the first century was such a period.

The structuring of Palestinian life by Jewish elites in collusion with Roman elites may have served these elites and the upper classes generally. Certainly, they enjoyed great wealth, status, and power. But the control of the land concentrated in the hands of a few, the massive burden of taxes to support royal and priestly building projects and the military, and the systematic use of terror to crush every expression of the dignity and rights of the poor majority, including widespread torture and crucifixions—all these resulted in widespread poverty and the corresponding psychosomatic syndromes, like blindness, alienation, depression, and despair, giving embodied expression to a life-destroying social (dis)order. No aspect of life escaped the effects of this kind of social order.[30]

In such a context, any expression of hope for liberation seems inevitably irrational. Yet we know of many messiahs announcing different versions of the good news of liberation.[31] Jesus was like them in many respects, although he seems to have had a more realistic sense about the actual historical possibilities for liberation in his own time; at least, his apparent resistance to military options seems more realistic in retrospect, in view of what happened to the rebellion of 67–70 CE so brutally crushed by the Romans. Nevertheless, in the eyes of the Roman and Jewish elites, his announcement of the good news of the coming reign of God promised radical disorder, and they colluded in arresting, condemning, torturing, and executing him as a threat to the existing "order" in all its dimensions— political, economic, religious.

For his followers, of course, Jesus' fate shockingly, radically undermined the hope for the fullness of life that he had announced and that they had already experienced in some mysterious and partial way in the vital community that formed around him. History was not ripe for liberation. Oppression and execution seemed so clearly to have the last word, as they had so many times before for those struggling for dignity and liberation. In this sense, the fate of Jesus was significant, not because it was so unique, but because it was so typical of those who affirm the dignity and hope of the historically marginalized and those who are in solidarity with them in hierarchically organized societies.

The power of the story of Jesus, however, is that suffering, torture, and death did not have the last word in this struggle for liberation, that mysteriously he lived on in the community, striving to witness to the good news of the reign of God on this earth.

In their efforts to articulate the meaning of this mysterious confirmation of the hope for life of poor and oppressed people, and of all those in solidarity with them, in the midst of the experience of overwhelming suffering and death, the early Christians came to affirm that Jesus was God incarnated on earth. No more radical theological affirmation is imaginable, for it meant that the very nature of God is connected to the struggles of poor and oppressed peoples for liberation, and that God too suffers in their suffering.[32]

This affirmation mysteriously transformed the cross from a symbol of the defeats and deaths experienced daily in countless ways by the poor and oppressed in every hierarchical social order into a symbol of hope for the fullness of life on this earth. As I heard in El Salvador, we live every day the *via crucis* in our country. Yet the deaths of our martyrs are signs of hope for us, for they are showing us how to live.[33] These dead martyrs do tangibly live on in the people, empowering them in their struggles for life.

The early Christians groped in many directions for ways to interpret the power of Jesus in their lives; they struggled to understand what this faith and hope meant concretely for the organization of their lives and their communities, in the midst of deep exploitation, oppression, and repression—and outright war.

Some interpreted Jesus' witness and words in ways that permitted accommodating themselves and their communities in various ways to the imperial order, in terms of the treatment of slaves, or women, or Gentiles, or in terms of the relations between the poor and the rich. Others, however, as Schüssler Fiorenza has insisted, interpreted "Jesus' *praxis* and *vision* of the *basileia*" as "the mediation of God's future into the structures and experiences of his own time and people."[34] They struggled to continue this vision in their own lives, even at the cost of continued conflict with the reigning authorities, as their only hope for the fullness of life on this earth, even unto death.

HERMENEUTICS:
THE PRIVILEGE OF THE OPPRESSED

There is a temptation to portray the Bible as if it speaks unequivocally, definitively, and with a single voice concerning the nature of God, the good news of salvation, and its implications for the lives of individuals and communities. Presenting the biblical message, "God's revelation," in this way seems to reinforce its authority—and the authority of its interpreters—within the community of believers today.

But simple, naive, "fundamentalist," or "orthodox" views of the story of the developing biblical faith reflected in the passages of the Bible betray the testimony of the Bible itself. At the core of the Bible are insights concerning the nature, in theological terms, of the revelatory process itself. Again and again the Bible confronts us with the often ambiguous, frequently contradictory and conflictual, process of how to interpret the tradition and its relevance in the present context. And, as momentous as the outcome of this process of interpretation is—all on earth and in the heavens is portrayed as depending on it—there is no escaping it.

Yet, in addition to the requirement of openness to the truth in all its forms and from whatever source in changing historical contexts, the Bible does offer another criterion for guiding this process of interpretation—the hermeneutical privilege of the oppressed.[35] In hierarchically organized societies, some voices by definition speak louder and with more "authority" than do others—the voices of affluent, powerful, and influential elites. Elites have a near monopoly on the resources for speaking, for writing (and in our day for researching and broadcasting), and indeed for defining the criteria for authoritative ("inspired," or congruent with the "tradition," or "infallible," or "scientific") pronouncements.

In the modern context, it is quite appropriate to speak of the manufacturing or production of traditions, a process managed by elites in their efforts to manage society as a whole in their interests, drawing heavily on techniques developed in the production, advertising, and sale of commodities.[36]

Long ago, ancient elites learned to manage tradition and authority in their interests.[37] We can see examples of the effects of this kind of conscious manipulation of the "tradition" and "authority" in the Bible, for example, in the reconstruction evident in the Pentateuch of the identity of Israel and its tradition by a group of priests in the postexilic period—a reconstruction that centered around the restored Temple and its rituals managed by the priests.[38]

In the Bible, though, this kind of elite construction and interpretation of the tradition is not the only voice or the most important one. Again and again, the Bible includes texts that refer to poor and oppressed peoples' experience of God, to their articulation of the character of this life on earth, to their hopes for the future. It is abundantly clear that elites can interpret any doctrine in support of their continued domination. The Bible offers abundant testimony to the inevitable clash, in a hierarchically ordered world, in reading the tradition, the signs of the times, and the character of the hope that the faithful are called to in each context. In the end, however, the Spirit of God speaks most clearly through the lowly, as in Jesus.

What can be read as broad biblical support for the hermeneutical privilege of the oppressed is confirmed by common sense: What possibility can there be of truly understanding the character of life in a particular society, the problems besetting it, and the hope for the future apart from addressing the experience of the great majority who are so often marginalized and silenced? What hope can there be of understanding this experience apart from listening to their voices? And what hope can there be for changing the world if they do not have a voice in making the policy decisions that are shaping, or misshaping, the future?

Certainly, this insight has been abundantly confirmed in our own day through the challenging and radical insights flowing from the movements of historically oppressed and marginalized peoples in our own society and around the world. No one, not even professional middle-class or rich and powerful people, can understand their lives, or prospects, or those of society as a whole apart from listening to these voices. Clearly, the hope for progressive change—in corporate and governmental policies, and in other institutions including the churches—requires radically opening up the discernment and decision-making process, making space for the active participation of the historically marginalized.

In this light, it becomes clear again that interpreting the truth of the tradition depends likewise on the voices of the oppressed. Indeed, the struggle over defining the core of the past tradition, the canon, is at the very heart of the struggle over social order in the present. This struggle is itself evident within the Bible. We have only to recall that Jesus was a Jew calling on the Jewish tradition in announcing the coming of the reign of God in his time, and that Jewish religious elites, promoting a radically different reading of their tradition, collaborated in condemning and executing him. The same story has been repeated throughout the history of Christianity and is being repeated today.

For these reasons, because of the necessity for each community to reread the Bible and the tradition in the light of its own experience and the challenges to justice and peace and the integrity of creation, biblical scholars like Schüssler Fiorenza are rethinking not only the interpretation of particular biblical texts, but the authority of the Bible itself. She proposes thinking of the Bible not as an archetype, "an ideal form that establishes a binding timeless pattern or principle," but as a prototype that is not binding or timeless but is "critically open to its own transformation." Indeed, I am suggesting that this understanding of biblical authority is evident within the Bible itself, in the ways in which each community wrestled in its own context with the tradition.[39]

This insight has been echoed by other liberation theologians. For example, the Latin American biblical scholar Carlos Mesters has made a similar suggestion: "The Bible is not the one and only history of salvation; it is a kind of 'model experience' [or 'prototype' in Schüssler Fiorenza's terms]. Every single people has *its own* history of salvation." And thus, Mesters observes, in the popular Christian communities of Latin America, "the common people are putting the Bible in its proper place, the place where God intended it to be. They are putting it in second place. Life takes first place!"[40]

EXEGESIS: CHALLENGES TO CONVERSION

In the recent history of the various liberation struggles, we have learned once again that the defining of "tradition" and of any other kind of authority is inevitably caught up in the struggles over social order. In particular, a growing number of studies confirm that elites have mobilized enormous resources in the production of tradition or, more accurately, versions of traditions—religious and secular, including scientific—that support their way of life. Both the institutional churches and the secular universities—dependent as they are on donations and project funding from wealthy individuals and corporations, as well as more recently consulting firms, research institutes, advertising agencies, and the media—have been profoundly shaped by this agenda.

Against the background of the academic and established church home for scholarly exegesis, the experience in recent years of rereading the Bible in groups struggling for liberation has resulted in a wide range of radical challenges to biblical scholars concerning the concepts, theoretical frameworks, and methods employed in reading the Bible, as numerous scholars have pointed out.[41] Moreover, the disciplinary divisions of labor characteristic of the modern university have come to be seen as a fundamental part of the problem, inhibiting efforts to understand how the realities referred to under the heading of "economics" are related to those labeled "religious," "political," "social," "cultural," "psychic," and so forth. These divisions, and the paradigms reigning in the various disciplines—especially in the social sciences in universities and in policy-making circles in think tanks, corporations, and government offices—clearly inhibit more integrated readings of the signs of the times today, and reading the Bible.

Moreover, as suggested above, the irruptions of the oppressed also involve the fundamental question of who reads the Bible today, of whose voices are heard in articulating the meaning of the text. This question has posed another series of fundamental challenges to the institutionalization of exegesis, indeed to every discipline and to the organization of the university as a whole.

As, for example, the feminist and black movements have made clear in North America, modern science and the secular university had been organized to the exclusion of the voices of the "others," of people of color and of women. Their struggles for liberation have involved many battles to gain entrance to the halls of learning—as graduate students, professors, and members of professional associations—and to have their experiences, interests, concerns, and points of view taken seriously. Much progress was made in these battles over the last twenty-five years, though recently there have been serious setbacks, in black studies in American universities in general, and for women in Catholic seminaries around the world.

There is another dimension of this struggle that so far has received less attention but is equally important. The academic division of labor is a class division between professional middle-class specialists (and those above them in the social order) on the one hand and the great majority of poor and working people on the other. In other words, the voices of the majority are systematically screened out of elite academic discourse; in the mainstream churches and the academy, the reading of the Bible has been taken over by elites. As Mesters describes it in his popular little parable, the house of the people, the Bible, was gradually taken over by the scholars, and its windows and doors were closed to the people.[42]

But as we have seen above, in the Bible itself and in our own experience there are many fundamental reasons why these voices must be included. They are absolutely necessary both in reading the signs of the times today and in reading the Bible. This is not a matter merely of unsophisticated ("unschooled"), more popular expression of what scholars have already concluded. Rather, it is a matter of their primary input concerning the nature and extent of suffering and oppression in our world, the nature of hope, the meaning of solidarity, and the character of faith. It is a matter, we Christians could say, of the voice of the Spirit of Truth, of the creation, of the prophets, and of Jesus in our world today.

Indeed, this challenge to incorporate the voices of poor and marginalized peoples has erupted within the movements for liberation themselves. For example, Schüssler Fiorenza has pointed out that feminist analyses and strategies generally have not taken their political measure, standpoint, and strategy with the women at the bottom of the totem pole of patriarchal oppression. Instead, "Euro-American feminist discourse has tended to take its measure from an idealized version of the Man of Reason, the sovereign subject of history, culture, and religion," that is, to reflect professional middle-class sensibilities.[43]

Black theologians have confronted the same challenges. As Cone has acknowledged, "Despite our black militant rhetoric, we wanted a piece of the capitalistic American pie. . . . Furthermore, when some of us got a little piece of that pie, we quickly lost our radicalism and became 'big-time' executives and seminary professors."[44] In this connection, he has also confessed that "black theology learned the patriarchal bad habits of its [male] progenitors."[45]

In other words, these scholars are testifying in terms of their own experience, the hermeneutical privilege of the poor and oppressed presents a challenge not only to the dominant ways of thinking, of producing knowledge and knowledge elites. It also presents a challenge to every movement and organization, even to those of oppressed and marginalized groups, that can so easily develop internal hierarchies of speaking and power reflecting the hierarchies, logic, and modes of rationality of the larger society.

In the theological terms of the Salvadoran Jon Sobrino, then, the poor within the church are "the hermeneutical principle for a primary concrete expression of important Christian concepts and realities."[46] Accordingly, the doing of exegesis, and of theology and social analysis too, must be transformed so that it escapes the captivity of academic life defined by professional middle-class culture and sensibilities, in ways that fundamentally incorporate ongoing dialogue with the great majority of historically marginalized peoples and with the historically marginalized concern for the earth itself.[47]

Opening the dialogue to include the voices of more and more of the world's poor and oppressed does not automatically solve all our problems of interpretation, for poor and oppressed peoples do not speak with a single voice, and they do not always say the same thing. Indeed, at times they have been in conflict with one another, both within particular constituencies and across them. This diversity and this conflict have inevitably complicated their speaking and the response to them by others.[48]

At times, then, the result of the challenges to reread our society or the Bible from the perspective of so many different constituencies—Third World poor, blacks, women, Hispanics, gays and lesbians, the biosphere, and so forth—seems only to be increasing fragmentation as it confirms the validity of reading from each particular point of view and the relativization of all interpretations.[49] This path of increasing fragmentation is endless, involving not only the deconstruction of every other perspective from each point of view, but also the fragmentation of the self as each discovers multiple and conflicting selves, needs, desires, hopes, and perspectives within, as Paul testified in terms of the law (Rom 7:14–25).

Certainly, this pluralism of points of view and the obvious conflicts among these constituencies have contributed powerfully to confusion, to difficulties in understanding and responding to particular "others" and even more so to the many "others," to conflict, and to the capacity of elites to maintain the status quo in spite of widespread opposition and pressures for substantial changes in elite policies, in the functioning of major institutions, and in the structural principles informing the ongoing reproduction of social "order."[50]

Yet, in the midst of this fragmentation of old identities and the social constituencies reflected in them, there are many signs of the seeds of new, more inclusive identities. The key here is not widespread agreement on religious, economic, or political "dogma," or on theory. Rather, it is concrete solidarity of and with all the oppressed, including solidarity with the earth. In other words, the very process of responding to the criticisms of new voices among the oppressed testifies to the increasingly widely shared, foundational commitment to the ongoing reading and rereading of the signs of the times, and the Bible, in dialogue with all the oppressed, and to reconstructing personal and group identities as a fruit of this process, in active solidarity in the struggles to witness concretely to the transformation of the heavens and the earth.

This process resonates deeply with the witness of the Bible. As Schüssler Fiorenza has insisted, "Christian identity grounded by the reading of the Bible must in ever-new readings be deconstructed and reconstructed in terms of a global praxis of liberation."[51] In other words, from the point of view of the Bible, we can recognize this ongoing process, in individuals and communities, of ever-new deconstruction and reconstruction of identity and solidarity, hope, and faith, from the point of view of the poor and oppressed, as an organic dimension of the process of revelation in response to the Spirit.

CONCLUSION

Against liberal declarations about the inevitability of progress and the certainty of science, we have rediscovered the fact that faiths and hopes and solidarities—and gods—are real, material, historical forces shaping the world. Thus the key questions concern not simply faith and hope or their absence in a "secular" world, but which kind of faith and hope, and devotion to which gods.

The intellectual debates about these questions are endless. We are constantly encountering new insights and new angles, new analyses and new theories, from which to view issues. And, in light of the irruptions within the last twenty-five years and of the multiplication of standpoints, the appearance of orthodoxy in theology and biblical studies (and in the social sciences) has given way to a bewildering profusion of perspectives.

At this level, it is clear that there can never be any closure. The endless manipulation of images, symbols, words, and phrases by the advertising industry powerfully reinforces the perception that no interpretation is any better than any other or counts in any concrete way.

From the point of view of the historically privileged, this endless profusion of interpretations is, perhaps, entertaining if also bewildering. From the point of view of poor and oppressed peoples, however, the reality is massively, destructively different, because concrete decisions are being made every day by elites—in corporations and other major institutions, governments, and international bodies such as the International Monetary Fund—that presume closure on the whole range of important questions and certain points of view and perspectives on the key issues. These decisions have life and death implications for the poor and oppressed, for the future of life on this earth, and thus, ultimately, for all. But the experiences of poor and oppressed peoples and of those in solidarity with them, their perspectives, and their voices are overwhelmingly excluded in this process. So, from this point of view, the debates are not open and endless. There is effective, material closure in these debates in terms of issues, perspectives, judgments, and participants every time such a decision is made.

In this concrete historical process, choices are inevitable. And, in the context of a hierarchically organized social order, now genuinely global in many respects, choosing sides for or against the poor and oppressed, and for or against the earth itself, is also inevitable. (As has often been pointed out, in this context of profound social conflict, failing to take stands on historic issues functions as a form of support for elite perspectives and options, whether or not individuals are aware of it, even when their values and commitments would lead them in other directions.) In making such choices, the forms of faith and hope that inspire us are revealed, and so are the gods we worship.

For us Christians, the Bible clearly defines the point of reference in making such choices. As Pixley has pointed out, "It is because other so-called gods do not right the wrongs of this world that they expose themselves as not gods."[52] Thus, in the spirit of the parable of the last judgment (Matt 25:31–46), we are challenged to confirm that the truth of the Bible and of hope for the future—for poor and oppressed peoples especially and ultimately for all, indeed, for all of life as we know it on this earth—is finally discovered and witnessed to in what we do concretely with the resources and spaces at our disposal in our own historical context.

The deepest challenge, then, to every reading of the Bible, and of the God revealed there, concerns its capacity to inspire concrete action in solidarity with all the oppressed, including the earth, and the redefinition of our identities, our communities, and our organizations in terms of this orientation. As Cone has insisted, "The acid test of any theological truth is found in whether it aids victims in their struggle to overcome their victimization."[53] This test is itself derived from the Bible.[54]

Otherwise, any theological claim, any interpretation of the Bible, any social analysis, any form of authority, is simply an instrument of oppression, an expression of faith in idols. In our own time, as in biblical times, the cost of devotion to these idols, which promise life, riches, and happiness, is suffering and death—for the poor and oppressed majorities in the first place, but ultimately for all, and for the earth itself.

Thus in our own time, as the apostle Paul said in his time, "The whole creation has been groaning in travail together until now" (Rom 8:22). And the Spirit of Truth, Justice, Peace, and all of creation is speaking through the voices of the poor and oppressed.

15 Unresolved Issues in the Early History of Israel

Toward a Synthesis of Archaeological and Textual Reconstructions

William G. Dever

I find it ironic that, at the very moment when my colleagues in biblical studies are belatedly discovering the "new archaeology," I, an unsuited cleric, am rediscovering hermeneutics. For me, the essential issue in the dialogue between archaeologists and biblical historians is epistemological:[1] How can we know anything with certainty about early Israel, whatever our sources?

It is clear from many recent works that after a century's scholarly efforts we are at an impasse in writing the premonarchic history of ancient Israel. The crucial issue for biblical historians has always been the nature of the source materials in the Hebrew Bible, until recently thought to be virtually our only witness. But I shall argue that in the last few years the "archaeological revolution" predicted by William Foxwell Albright, after many false starts, has finally begun to gain real momentum with the extensive application of the powerful tools of the "new archaeology"; and that a series of recent discoveries now forces upon us a radical rethinking of *all* previous explanatory models for understanding the emergence of Israel. Furthermore, if we are to undertake a serious dialogue between the mature disciplines of Syro-Palestinian archaeology and biblical history (which some of us have been advocating for nearly twenty years),[2] then it is self-evident that the fundamental problems of Israelite historiography must now be completely rephrased. Indeed, the task is already being undertaken, as we shall see presently. And no one is more in the forefront than Norman K. Gottwald, a colleague of rare courage, to whom I am honored to dedicate this essay.

Two questions are inescapable, however we begin: (1) To what extent do strictly archaeological data, as distinguished from the rare written remains, provide raw materials for writing history, in this case specifically the early history of Israel? In my opinion, biblical historians have not adequately addressed this issue. (2) Is it now possible, and desirable, to write a "secular history of ancient Palestine"; and for early Israel may this not take precedence? Or does the best solution lie in a composite history, combining many approaches and sources of data?

THE BIBLE AS HISTORY: CURRENT VIEWS

In evaluating the Bible as a source of history, the archaeologist can only reinforce the consensus already achieved by a century or more of critical biblical scholarship. It appears that the historical reconstruction enshrined in the Hebrew Bible in its present form (especially in Dtr) is late; highly selective in what it includes; elitist in perspective; and, in its final redaction, propagandistic in nature throughout.[3] In short, the basic framework of "theocratic history" in the Hebrew Bible makes it extremely difficult, some would say impossible, to reconstruct a more factual account of ancient Israel's existence, even though the tradition may preserve genuinely historical information here and there. Can archaeology, on the other hand, enable us to get at "the history behind the history"? Can we not at least achieve an outline of what may have actually transpired, which gave rise to the Sacred History?

This brings us directly to the fundamental problems: (1) What *is* "history"? and (2) What constitutes *adequate* history writing? A renewed and long-overdue emphasis on these theoretical issues is seen in a number of recent biblical studies.[4] What strikes me about all these treatments, however, even the most sanguine, is their salutary but rather naive assumptions concerning the potential of "archaeology as a science" on the one hand, and on the other hand their almost total disregard of the actual progress and results of modern, or the "new," archaeology. Having hailed a revolutionary tool for rewriting biblical history, these and other biblical scholars either use archaeology in desultory fashion, or in most cases simply discard it altogether. One cannot, of course, fault biblical scholars for being only "amateur" archaeologists, if at all. But it is legitimate, I think, to expect that such scholars—insofar as they are historians and not theologians—avail themselves of the latest data and of expert, professional guidance from archaeological specialists. It is a mark of the parochial nature of much of current biblical scholarship that the call for interdisciplinary cooperation—for a true dialogue between the two disciplines, the "two kinds of histories"—comes almost exclusively today from a handful of archaeologists.[5] I acknowledge, of course, that many Syro-Palestinian archaeologists today are overly specialized, often uninterested in the biblical connection, similarly unversed in historiography, and above all, derelict in their responsibility to publish their data.

Before we turn to the possibilities of a more integrated approach, however, we may pause to reflect once again on the biases and limitations of the biblical materials, as well as those of our own approach. In the light of modern critical scrutiny, the biases of the biblical writers are abundantly clear. The question concerns *our* biases—specifically those of the male liberal Protestant thinkers who have largely shaped modern scholarship, both biblical-historical and archaeological. Although not biblicists or pietists (and certainly not fundamentalists), most of us seem uncritically, perhaps even unconsciously, to have appropriated the overriding theocratic framework of the biblical writers themselves.[6] Nevertheless, if modern biblical historians come to share such a theological agenda, that is, a programmatic and frankly partisan approach, the bias may limit and perhaps ultimately frustrate our attempts to write a more adequate history of ancient Israel. I believe that it is not hopelessly naive to ask, What *really* happened in history? Otherwise, we must be content simply to retell the biblical "story," as James Barr eloquently terms it, to paraphrase the writers of the Hebrew Bible.[7]

Here I can only suggest two strategies. The first would be to undertake much more probing into what we may call "the sociology of knowledge" so as to help free both biblical historians and archaeologists from some extremely misleading presuppositions as well as dangerous illusions. Second, it might be useful to distinguish several *kinds* of history, and especially of history writing. Even though English possesses no such nuances, German, for instance, does.[8] Thus one might characterize "ascending levels" of history, such as *Story, Historie,* and *Geschichte.* Let us look at each briefly.

Geschichte is history *writing*—the creative, interpretive synthesis, a distinctly modern literary genre. This sort of history is an intellectual construct, in Huizinga's sense; or what Krister Stendahl has called the attempt to answer the question: "What *do* the events described by the biblical writers mean?"[9] This could be thought of as the province of systematic theology and of hermeneutics, as well as of intellectual, political, and socioeconomic history.

Story, the next earlier and most primitive form of history *making,* comprises legend, saga, oral tradition, and especially myth, which despite a certain obvious fictive character may contain genuinely factual, historical material. This would represent an attempt to answer Stendahl's other question: "What *did* the purported events mean?" Much of Israelite historiography obviously and necessarily operates at this level; that is, as "tradition," handing down both facts and interpretation in a subtle, self-conscious, and often surprisingly sophisticated manner. It is at this level that literary-critical scholarship must also operate, including philology, exegesis, *Religionsgeschichte*, and more modern approaches such as those of the socio-anthropological school.[10]

Yet behind these quests, and fundamental to them, I would argue, there lies a deeper level of inquiry, or *Historie*. This gets at the question that Stendahl and other biblical scholars, preoccupied as they are with literary criticism (which tends to result not in history per se, but simply in the history of the literature *about* biblical life and times), often seem loath to ask: "What really happened?"[11] Here we must begin with factual, contemporary eyewitness accounts, annalistic data, and, I would add, not only written materials, but also artifactual remains (see below on nonepigraphic data as "mute"). These are the raw data, the real "stuff of history." Such material is always fragmentary and difficult to interpret, but it is neither as rare nor as intractable as most biblical historians seem to believe. And today, the "new archaeology" is increasing our store of such data exponentially, as I hope to show. Neither historians nor archaeologists can go back to the naive nineteenth-century positivist notion that modern literary-critical methods would ultimately enable us to speak confidently of *wie es eigentlich gewesen war*, as von Ranke and others thought. But I think that we can, at last, begin to sift circumstantial from direct evidence, to get at aspects of historiography, rather than romance, to recover events-in-context rather than simply ideology.[12]

ARCHAEOLOGY AND HISTORY: PRELIMINARY METHODOLOGICAL CONSIDERATIONS

We turn now from history to archaeology. One of the limitations on using archaeology in history writing is the typical biblical historian's somewhat naive overvaluation of texts and the concomitant denigration of nontextual data. Thus, for instance, Max Miller, even with considerable archaeological experience, can declare: "Occasionally the artifactual remains witness to specific events. . . . But these events remain anonymous unless interpreted in the light of written records." Or again: "Non-written, artifactual evidence . . . is silent by nature, is not particularly useful in dealing with specific historical questions." And on our specific topics, the early Israelite settlement in Canaan, Miller states that "the archaeological evidence is ambiguous, or essentially neutral, on the subject."[13] I submit that archaeological data are *not* mute; but some historians may be hard of hearing. It is a truism in archaeological epistemology that we hear answers only in response to those questions that we are prepared to ask. Thus both biblical historians and archaeologists, in phrasing the question of Israelite origins solely in terms of "conquest" or "nomadic infiltration" models, have been asking the wrong questions—or at least unproductive questions. The "new archaeology" revolutionizes the whole discussion by substituting a new agenda (below), and also by demanding a new interaction between textual and archaeological data.

Having claimed so much for archaeology, I must, of course, defend that claim. Elsewhere I have written extensively on the potential of the "new archaeology," and with special reference to the Israelite settlement, so here I will be brief and specific.[14]

In what ways may archaeological data take precedence over biblical (and other ancient) texts? First, archaeological data, as Albright and others long ago correctly pointed out, constitute an "external" and thus independent witness, in contrast to the texts' demonstrably "internal" witness. The long-lost evidence brought to light by archaeology is completely independent of the religious community and its perspectives. It is not only earlier, and thus often closer to the original events than the biblical texts, but it is also "neutral" with respect to the often-reworked tradition. Artifacts, when found *in situ*, or capable of being placed in a reconstructible natural and cultural context, may be regarded as "frozen in time." Thus they have not been subjected to reformulation in the literary process, or socially conditioned by the ongoing community's experience, "filtered," as it were, through biblical spectacles. Archaeological discoveries are at the outset raw, uninterpreted data. Even though, like texts, they will be subject later to our manipulation, initially they possess an intrinsic concreteness, an empirical quality that we acknowledge in calling these data *realia*. They may have a "historicality" that texts do not always have. The notion of some of our colleagues that texts provide objective evidence, whereas artifacts are vulnerable to subjective interpretation, strikes me as incredibly naive. The fact is that one category of information no more constitutes *realia* than the other; both texts and artifacts are *symbolic* expressions, encoded messages about the past. And both require cautious and similar interpretation before they can become true "data," meaningful in context. Here is where the epistemological dilemma comes into sharp focus.[15]

The Hebrew Bible, in contrast to archaeological artifacts, is what I have suggested may properly be termed "a *curated* artifact." That is, it was not long-lost and then rediscovered as a pristine relic, but rather was continually preserved and reused in changing contexts, constantly reworked by both the Jewish and Christian communities. If we take seriously either a doctrine of progressive revelation (in any form) or the insights of modern canonical criticism, we must begin by recognizing this secondary use of the Hebrew Bible, which, although legitimate, in many instances vitiates its usefulness as a "primary source" for writing the history of ancient Israel.[16]

Second, archaeological data possess the advantage of not having been deliberately selected and preserved, as the biblical texts obviously were. Of course, there have been selective processes, both cultural and environmental, at work in forming the archaeological record.[17] But I would argue that the way we develop research design, excavate, and record today can factor these processes into our interpretation far better than we can compensate for the biblical writers' selectivity, which has usually expunged discordant data in the oral and written tradition, so that it is lost forever. Specifically, I would argue that archaeological data, by virtue of their very "anonymity" and random occurrence, provide a populist view that may offer a vastly different, and sometimes more accurate, picture than that yielded by the elite perspective of the biblical texts. The latter stem largely from royalist and priestly circles and give us a portrait mainly of great individuals and public events—"political history" again, history written "from the top down." Elsewhere I have argued that archaeology is much more conducive to the study of socioeconomic history than the biblical texts—especially with the *longue durée* model of Braudel and other historians of the *annales* school, from whom we could learn a great deal.[18]

Third, the archaeological data produced by today's ecological and multi-disciplinary approach are infinitely more rich and varied, more dynamic in nature, than the fixed data in the biblical texts could possibly be. In theory, the archaeological record is limited only by our imagination and enterprise in exploiting it, by the questions we can conceive of asking the data. Thus, where the Bible, with its view of history *sub specie aeternitatis*, is understandably silent, archaeological discoveries can nonetheless fill the lacunae in our knowledge of ancient Israel by illuminating the whole gamut of material culture and daily life. This would include not only pottery and building remains (which we have concentrated on rather myopically), but, far more significant, environmental considerations; settlement types and patterns; subsistence; technology; demography; socioeconomic structure; art, symbolism, and aesthetics; and even such matters as political structure, ideology, and religion, which are usually but mistakenly thought to be the exclusive province of textual studies (see below and Figure 1). Let me drive this point home by saying that henceforth the motto for all of us ought to be the dictum of Norman Gottwald: "Only as the full *materiality* of ancient Israel is more securely grasped will we be able to make proper sense of its *spirituality*."[19] Archaeologists cannot be caricatured as economic determinists or cultural materialists simply because they define their inquiry in terms of "the science of material culture." It is true that archaeologists and anthropologists today highlight the importance of material factors, but they also stress the role of culture. It is worth remembering that even Marx included ideology and religion in the discussion of his basic "modes of production."[20]

Finally, archaeological data are much more informative on context than the biblical texts, with their isolated perspective, can be. Again, Albright, Wright, and others correctly emphasized archaeology's unique contribution to historical studies in reconstructing the original context, the sociocultural background, of the Bible. Only archaeology is capable of resurrecting the long-lost peoples and places of the ancient Near Eastern world, the larger context within which the events claimed by the biblical writers happened and the biblical tradition took shape. Archaeology reconstructs the stage on which the "drama of redemption," as well as the secular history of ancient Israel, was enacted. It fleshes out the plot—renders it dramatically alive and arresting—by painting the backdrops, supplementing the tantalizing libretto in the Hebrew Bible with all the other actors in the story. Archaeology "humanizes" the Bible, and therefore makes it more credible, by illustrating unforgettably that the story is about real people, in a real time and place and circumstance—people like us.

Not only is the original context provided by archaeology essential, so is the longer context of settlement history. Here Coote and Whitelam's recent book *The Emergence of Israel in Historical Perspective* represents for biblical scholars a bold departure. It sees the appearance of Israel on the scene as but one episode in the long, turbulent *Siedlungsgeschichte* of Palestine, from prehistoric to Turkish times. That is the larger context that we archaeologists have been envisioning for some time. Yet good as it is, this would have been an even better work had its authors collaborated with specialists in Palestinian archaeology, who could have helped to interpret the often unpublished and exceedingly difficult data more fully. What Coote and Whitelam conceive as settlement history is what I have recently described as perhaps archaeology's most important contribution—"the ecology of social change." When this sort of context is analyzed over very long time spans, based on studies of both environmental stimulus and historical response, the result is *Kulturgeschichte*, or cultural evolution in the proper sense, that is, in a multilinear and *truly* historical framework. Thus the "new archaeology" is not "ahistorical," as some claim, but in fact aspires to history painted on an even broader canvas.[21]

PROLEGOMENON TO THE STUDY
OF ISRAELITE ORIGINS

The renewed discussion of the question of "Israelite origins" goes back a number of years, as seen in the works of a number of biblical scholars.[22] On the archaeological side, interest has been galvanized by a number of excavations of hill country Iron I sites, and in particular by the extensive surveys of younger Israeli archaeologists in the West Bank in the territories of Ephraim and Manasseh.[23]

Early attempts to call attention to the new data on the Israelite settlement were made by Callaway, Dever, and Stager; and a full synthesis of the material has now appeared in English in Israel Finkelstein's exceedingly important new work *The Archaeology of the Israelite Settlement*.[24] Few biblical historians are yet cognizant of the data, however, some of it available nearly twenty years ago, although the beginnings of a dialogue may be seen in the papers and responses at one session of the First International Congress on Biblical Archaeology in Jerusalem in April of 1984.[25] Not only are crucial questions of early biblical history involved, but also fundamental methodological issues for both biblical and archaeological research. Indeed, I have argued that the "archaeological revolution" predicted by Albright has at last come to focus in this fledgling discussion of the past half-decade or so. The full implications of this for either traditional-style or a possible "new biblical archaeology" have not, however, been grasped as yet by anyone, it seems.[26]

As a prolegomenon to the coming discussion, I would like to suggest that archaeologically and historically speaking, two issues must be central: (1) the proper assessment of the continuity/discontinuity at the transition from the Late Bronze Age to the early Iron I period in terms of the basic categories of material culture, and thus of the supposed emergence of "Israelites" from Canaanite society; and (2) a rigorous evaluation of the material correlates of individual and social behavior that might enable us to identify "Israelite ethnicity" in strictly archaeological terms, which could then be related to the Merneptah Stele, biblical texts, and other literary sources. These are hardly revolutionary suggestions, for many observers today sense that the above are indeed the pivotal questions. The issues must be made explicit, however; and, even more crucial, there needs to be elaborated an acceptable and agreed-upon methodology that will allow us to move beyond unfounded assertions and nostalgic longings for certainty—especially as questions of "faith and history" are involved.

Cultural Continuity

On the question of cultural continuity from Late Bronze into early Iron I, there has now emerged, after considerable confusion, a near consensus, especially on ceramic developments. The older models of an "Israelite" conquest ca. 1225–1175 BCE inevitably produced an overemphasis on a cultural break. With the gradual abandonment of that model in the light of more recent archaeological evidence, however, scholars have come to appreciate the fact that Late Bronze ceramic traditions continue through the twelfth and even well into the eleventh century BCE. In fact, it is now possible to hold that whereas the "Iron Age" may have emerged as a discrete archaeological phase by the mid–late twelfth century BCE, a distinctive, characteristic "Israelite" ceramic repertoire is not discernible until the tenth century BCE, that is, contemporary with the emergence of an Israelite state.[27]

To illustrate how far and how fast scholarly opinion has evolved, Finkelstein's 1983 Hebrew dissertation claimed that the twelfth-century BCE 'Izbet Ṣarṭah pottery was novel, and moreover, that it indicated an eastern (or Transjordanian) origin for the Iron I settlers. In the publication of the revised work in English, as well as in his synthesis of the hill country Iron I villages, both in 1988, Finkelstein has given up these views altogether. He properly points out, as I had in 1987, that the 'Izbet Ṣarṭah Iron I pottery is strongly in the Late Bronze Canaanite tradition. Indeed, it is virtually identical to the local twelfth/eleventh-century BCE pottery at nearby Gezer, which is certainly *not* an "Israelite" site, as both archaeological data and biblical tradition attest. Now Fritz and Kompinski have underlined this ceramic continuity on the basis of Tel Masos. Callaway stresses the same continuity at 'Ai and Radannah, as does Mazar at Giloh. The general Late Bronze–Iron I ceramic continuity of Canaan has meanwhile been documented in detail by Wood and by Dever and colleagues.[28] Thus it is no exaggeration to say that a consensus on the part of ceramic experts has now been reached. Henceforth all biblical scholars and historians who deal with this horizon must start with this fundamental datum: ceramically there is little "new" to distinguish the Iron I villagers/newcomers—"Israelites" or not—not even the much-debated collar-rim storejar. Virtually all early Iron I ceramic changes (except, obviously, the Philistine bichrome wares) are normal and even predictable developments out of the thirteenth-century Late Bronze repertoire. Furthermore, the pottery of the hill country, Negev, and Lower Galilee villages is not markedly different in type or frequency from that of urban "late Canaanite" sites like Aphek, Gezer, Lachish, or even Megiddo and Beth-shan in the north in the twelfth century BCE. Those distinctions that are evident can easily be explained by the differences in social organization and subsistence, that is, the expected variables between the pottery repertoire of urban and rural settlements.[29]

It is a fundamental axiom of archaeology that ceramic developments are among our most sensitive criteria for discerning cultural changes, but we must also look at other aspects of the material culture. Using a modified "systems theory" approach that is now widespread, I would suggest the following categories (not necessarily in the order of importance): (1) settlement types and distribution; (2) subsistence and economy; (3) technology; (4) architecture; (5) demography and social structure; (6) political organization; and (7) art, ideology, and religion (see below and Figure 1). Some of these elements have now been analyzed by a number of archaeologists recently, notably by Stager.[30] His assessments of such criteria as iron technology, plastered cisterns and stone-lined silos, and hillside terrace farming, demonstrating that these are not necessarily Iron I innovations, is in my opinion definitive. Yet Stager seems to assume that these elements define "Israelite" ethnicity. He is much more successful in analyzing the module of the early Iron I courtyard and four-room house, as well as their typical arrangement in the small, open hill country villages we have noted above. He suggests that these "facts on the ground" can be connected directly and in detail with reminiscences of early Israelite tribal society in such later sources as Joshua-Judges-Samuel. Stager's conclusion—that the biblical tradition is faithfully reflected in the new archaeological evidence—is still to be proven, although he admittedly makes a strong case.

I would hold, rather, that the key to Iron I "innovations" is the successful change of these and other elements of Late Bronze Age Canaanite society and material culture to the highland frontier. The result was an agrarian economy (and probably also a distinctive social structure) that was ideally suited to the challenge of successfully settling the hill country. Thus there emerged what we might call (to paraphrase Marx, Sahlins, and others) an "Israelite mode of production," a phenomenon that deserves much more consideration.[31] Archaeological survey has demonstrated beyond doubt that just such a large-scale settlement did take place at the end of Late Bronze and the beginning of Iron I, primarily in central Palestine. Whether the newcomers can be identified as our "Israelites," on the other hand, is much more difficult to establish. That brings us to the second issue, the problem of "ethnicity" in the archaeological record.

Ethnicity

By "ethnicity" I mean, with most ethnographers and social anthropologists, simply "peoplehood." Whatever model we may adopt in assessing the archaeological evidence for "Israelite ethnicity," we must begin by assuming that no matter what else early Israel was (or later thought itself to be), it was also a minority ethnic group in a multiethnic society in Iron

I Canaan. By "ethnic group" we mean, at minimum, a social group that (1) is biologically self-perpetuating; (2) shares a fundamental, uniform set of cultural values, including language; (3) constitutes a partly independent "interaction sphere"; (4) has a membership that defines itself, as well as being defined by others, as a category distinct from other categories of the same order; and (5) perpetuates its sense of separate identity both by developing rules for maintaining "ethnic boundaries," as well as for participating in interethnic social encounters. It is especially important to note certain ways in which ethnic groups typically originate, maintain themselves, and assimilate or otherwise change. The origins of ethnic groups, however, are difficult, often impossible to ascertain, even where we have historical documentation; but we can point to some reasons for both the existence and the persistence of such groups, as well as documenting their collective self-consciousness.[32]

Such a subjective and ideological phenomenon is, however, extremely difficult (many would say impossible) to identify from material remains alone, without the aid of texts. Historians often thus declare that archaeology is "mute" (see above). I would insist, however, that given enough data, archaeologists with today's sophisticated methods are capable of distinguishing a short-term cultural change marked by a consistent and homogenous group of material culture traits. When they can do so, they are entitled to characterize the social agents of that change as (in all likelihood) an "ethnic group." Obviously, they cannot supply a label, like "Israelite" or "Philistine," without textual evidence, but the discrete cultural group is no less real for that. I believe, however, that we now do have sufficient evidence to label the cultural complex of the early Iron I highland villages discussed above as "Israelite," if only as a heuristic device. If so, then instead of debating the label, we ought to be testing this notion against the archaeological record, in keeping with the whole thrust of modern, multidisciplinary archaeology. International teams, using compatible methods and identical research designs, should deliberately select and excavate, side by side, representative twelfth-century BCE type-sites that on external grounds could be expected to be, respectively, "Canaanite," "Israelite," and "Philistine." The results might prove dramatic. In any case, such a strategy would certainly be more productive than further debate about earlier models that almost everyone now regards as obsolete.

Nevertheless, much more research will be required before we can effectively isolate "Israelite origins" archaeologically. I would suggest, however, one line of argument that has apparently not been pursued, namely, the convergence between continuity of material culture *and* textual tradition. All authorities would agree, I think, that the tenth-century BCE

material culture west of the Jordan from northern Galilee to the northern
Negev, excluding only perhaps the southern or Philistine coast, reflects a
people and state that by the time of the monarchy called itself "Israel."
Such an entity may be legitimately designated "Israel" by us, on the
ground that "ethnicity" is simply the consensus of what people think and
say about themselves; and furthermore on the witness of the well-known
"Victory Stela" of Merneptah (see below). I am aware that many biblical
scholars are skeptical whether we can know what the content of the term
"Israel" was in the early period.[33] Or they may hold that the later biblical
tradition has projected back upon the earlier periods a cultural unity that
does not conform to the social reality. Our uncertainty due to the precise
meaning of the term does not, however, alter the fact that an "Israel" did
emerge by the tenth century BCE. Furthermore, the people of later Israel
and Judah felt themselves to be, and rightly so, the authentic heirs of a self-
conscious ethnic tradition, expressed both in literary sources, biblical and
extrabiblical, as well as in what we term the Iron II/Israelite material
culture.

Now it follows from the above that if we can trace this "Israelite"
complex continuously back from the well-documented tenth century BCE,
through the eleventh and into the early twelfth (or even late thirteenth)
century BCE, we may in good faith label the early highland villages of Iron
I as "Israelite," or perhaps better "Proto-Israelite." This would, of course,
be the "Israel" of the Merneptah Stele ca. 1207 BCE, an external and
contemporary witness (without which I admit that I would have a great
deal of hesitation in using the term so early). This entity would also
approximate Boling's "Earliest Israel" (although I definitely am not as
sanguine as he about *any* Israelite presence in Transjordan).[34] We cannot at
this moment, however, penetrate much further into pre-Israelite,
much less ultimate, origins, except to say that all the current archaeological evidence points to an indigenous derivation from Canaan itself,
not Transjordan or Egypt, dating well back into the Canaanite Late
Bronze Age.

When did these "dispossessed Canaanites" (to use Gottwald's term,
though not necessarily his model) become "Israelites"? It is so far impossible to say with certainty, but I think that we can nevertheless recognize
their emergence in the historical (i.e., in this instance, archaeological)
record as an ethnic group, one that was already distinctive in many ways,
by the midtwelfth century BCE or so at the latest. To put it another way: if
the early highland settlers in Iron I were not "Israelites" in the same sense
as those of the later biblical tradition (which, of course, produced the
literary sources we have), they were nevertheless their progenitors.

Such an ethnic identification may stand up to further scrutiny, and I predict that it will, although some might not recognize this as much of an accomplishment. Archaeologically, however, it would represent the most significant advance that so-called biblical archaeology has ever made in correlating artifacts with the biblical texts. If that statement makes me a "biblical archaeologist," so be it.

WHAT WE CAN AND CANNOT KNOW ABOUT EARLY ISRAEL FROM TEXTS AND ARTIFACTS

It may be instructive, by way of concluding this essay, yet pointing the way for future research, to compare what we might wish to know, and indeed actually *can* now know, from both the study of textual and artifactual remains. In the interest of efficiency, let us summarize the basic data in chart form (Table 1).

Our chart should make several points quite clear. First, as expected, there are a number of convergences between the two classes of data—a welcome reassurance that the two approaches to history writing are compatible. Second, perhaps more significant, however, are the many discrepancies, if not outright contradictions, between what is revealed by strictly textual remains and archaeological remains. Nor do the rather strikingly different portraits diverge only in minor details: they have implications for such basic questions as the origins and the very character of ancient Israel. Inevitably, some will feel faced with a dilemma: *Which* history? Third, in the comparison, archaeology seems to come off considerably better in that its picture is much broader in perspective, more detailed, richer in particular as socioeconomic history. And with archaeology only in its infancy today, this approach would seem to promise much more in the future. Finally, however, it appears that both approaches are required to yield an account that is comprehensive, balanced, and ultimately more persuasive as a reflection of the complex reality that we seek to apprehend. Only in the correlation of texts and artifacts—each supplementing and correcting the partial view of the other—are we likely to find a truly satisfying portrait of early Israel, one that does full justice to both its materiality and its spirituality.

Category	Biblical Texts Alone	Archaeological Data
1. Historical-cultural outline; date, origins	Unified invasion from Egypt, via Transjordan, ca. 1450 BCE. "Yahwists," some nomads. Canaanites, then Philistines, completely vanquished.	Socioeconomic and cultural change ca. 1250–1150 BCE. Indigenous; no Egyptian or Transjordanian influence. Canaanite culture continues; all Philistine along coast. .
2. Cultural level	Impoverished, unsophisticated. Scant data on material culture. →	Impoverished, unsophisticated. Material culture well illuminated.
3. Settlement type and pattern	Scant data, but urban and rural throughout Palestine implied.	Abundant data; mostly small rural villages, confined to hill country, Lower Galilee, Negev.
4. Ecological	Little interest or evidence. Implied mostly rural, agrarian setting.	Critical factor, abundant data. Subsistence farming; some stockbreeding; no urban sites.
5. Subsistence; economy, trade	Agrarian, but scant data. → Iron technology significant.	Primarily agrarian, reconstructible. Little iron; but terraces, cisterns, silos, etc., more important.
	Little Canaanite contact.	Considerable Canaanite contact.
	Isolated from larger setting. →	Isolated from larger setting.
6. Demography, ethnicity	Perhaps 2 million population. Radically new "Israelites."	Maximum population 100,000. Largely indigenous population; "Israelites" only via Merneptah stele.
	Multiethnic overall. Language and script "Hebrew." →	Multiethnic overall. Language and script "Old Canaanite."
7. Social structure	Scant data, but implies → "egalitarian," family and clan-based.	Considerable data; can reconstruct a nonstratified society, largely segmented.
8. Political organization	Tribal, decentralized, yet → "tribal league" throughout Palestine.	Perhaps tribal; undeveloped, entirely local.
9. Ideology, art, religion	"Yahwism" unique, developed. Primary factor in cult development.	Virtually no cult recognizable. Socioeconomic factors mainly.
	Little art of any kind.	Little evidence of art.

Table 1. Comparisons of current data from two sources, developed according to simple systems-theory approach. Arrows indicate strong or moderate convergencies.

16 New Constructs in Social World Studies

James W. Flanagan

INTRODUCTION

In his book *The Overview Effect*, Frank White documents the change in human consciousness that has been caused by space exploration and the space movement. The experience of orbiting the earth and viewing it from the moon has transformed astronauts, cosmonauts, and earthbound observers alike. The thesis is that those who have orbited the globe are consciously and unconsciously impressed by its seamlessness and massiveness, whereas those who have gone farther to enjoy extraorbital and lunar missions speak additionally and mystically of "no frames and no boundaries."[1]

The two groups differ markedly in their perceptions of scale. For the twenty-four people who have traveled to the moon's orbit and the twelve who have walked on its surface, those who have escaped the earth's systems and watched its orb grow smaller and smaller as it drew away, feelings approach imponderability. Earth is diminutive and increasingly insignificant, whereas the awesome grandeur of the entire universe that serves as its backdrop is overpowering. The emptiness of vast space takes precedence and begins to be absorbed as a realized human experience.

These experiences, the thesis continues, transform human consciousness, impress upon humans their personal universality and mortality, and reshape the proportionality attributed to microcosmic, cosmic, and macrocosmic phenomena. Knowledge and emotion combine within orbiters and observers alike to mark a new stage in the evolution of human society and human self-understanding. New perspectives on problems of life are

209

gained, so that when permanent space settlement—the logical next step in the evolutionary process—is accomplished, then politics, religion, social relations, psychology, and science will be transformed.

White's opinions stand within a long intellectual tradition that relates technology to the most profound human experiences and expressions. In a broad sense, such arguments extend from the classical period down to the modern, and they include studies that treat writing, literacy, and the printing press as technologies affecting human consciousness.[2] Bolter's *Turing's Man* is perhaps the most "popular" statement today. It argues the case for "defining technologies" most forcefully. A defining technology, in Bolter's study the computer, is one that "break[s] out of the corner of human affairs . . . that it was built to occupy, to contribute instead to a general redefinition of certain basic relationships: the relationship of science to technology, of knowledge to technical power, and, in the broadest sense, of mankind [*sic*] to the world of nature."[3] On these criteria, the introduction and application of iron working in ancient Israel has been identified as a defining technology that symbolized and effected the formation of a people and their traditions.[4]

This abbreviated list points to a direction that scholarship on ancient societies, including biblical societies, is moving. In this essay I presume to suggest that the work of Norman K. Gottwald has been instrumental in setting us on that course. His attempt to detach Israel's history from its biblical anchor and to connect it to a set of sociopolitical paradigms from outside the Bible and, I would suggest, from outside religion as well, does not entail a step toward space technology, but the effort does set biblical studies free to explore new options and paradigms. Beyond Gottwald, I argue for the importance of the new orientation toward technology-based studies on antiquity, and I point out several changes in building research designs that may assist in the current metamorphosis within our discipline(s). With gratitude and humility, I dedicate these comments to Norman Gottwald, a person of great moral and intellectual integrity, and compassionate scholar and friend.

FOUNDATIONS OF SOCIAL WORLD STUDIES

Since the 1960s, Gottwald's contributions to humanities-based and social-scientific studies on biblical religion have included social world studies on biblical antiquity. In the 1970s, a research group that he cochaired within several learned associations became the forum for experimenting with innovative approaches to the mental, social, and ecological worlds of ancient Israel. His monumental *The Tribes of Yahweh*[5] drove an intellectual and historical wedge between Israel's period of Judges and the so-called

United Monarchy. With it, he laid to rest once and for all any hope of finding a historical base for the myth of Israelite conquest that had dominated biblical scholarship down to his time.

It is important to note both the results for the history of a biblical period and the change in research designs that social world studies such as Gottwald's inaugurated. In the first instance, a great deal of sociopolitical and religious "stuff" began to seep out from eleventh- and tenth-century BCE data once the well-established categories of conquest and amphictyony on the one end, and kingship and centralization on the other end, of the state formation process had been pried apart. For generations, scholars had assumed that a religious judge-type tribalism had been succeeded directly and immediately by monarchy in ancient Israel. Once Gottwald examined biblical history under the high intensity light of Marxist and materialist social and political theory, traces of longer, more complicated, and less idealistic religio-political strategies became visible.[6]

It would be too restrictive to measure the consequences of Gottwald's breakthroughs by their effect upon a single period of history, group of scholars, or branch of scholarship. Nevertheless, his interest in the origins of Israel, state formation, and political transformation were sustained publicly in a second research group, the Sociology of the Monarchy Seminar, of which he was a member. It was there more than elsewhere, perhaps, that collaborative American social world studies on biblical antiquity were nurtured toward maturity, and attention was turned toward research designs.

The openness to adjusting historical presuppositions and restructuring research designs may prove to be a longer-lasting contribution than the details of either Gottwald's own approach or his specific interpretations. For this essay, three fundamental shifts in approach are especially important.

First, Gottwald's use of Marxism forced recognition that aspects of Israel's state formation process could be likened to similar processes in other societies, including modern polities. Second, he insisted that material and ecological phenomena interacted positively with religious, cultural, and ideological domains in order to produce the distinctive life that was Israel's. Stated in Godelier's words, this is the realization that "human beings, in contrast to other social animals, do not just live in a society, they *produce society in order to live.*"[7] Third, he realized on the one hand that hypotheses about historical events "behind" the biblical story must come from outside the Bible itself, and on the other hand that the biblical story in its arrangement and details must itself be viewed as a historical hypothesis rather than as evidence for testing a hypothesis.

These contributions, especially the third, provide a basis for the new orientation toward technology mentioned in the opening paragraphs above. The metamorphosis proceeds on two levels. First is the new content and subject matter—like the "stuff" mentioned above—that becomes available and is drawn into treatments of biblical antiquity once old paradigms and approaches are superseded. The second is that of method and discipline, that is, the need for new approaches.

It is easy to enlist a weak simile that likens social world studies to White's analysis of the space movement. The ability to view one's home planet from beyond the force of its gravity is the way that social world critics insist the Bible must be used when examining biblical history, that is, from afar, away from its seductive power, and against the backdrop of its universe. In this sense, the space movement and its technologies make real for the first time a powerful physical image that legitimates the hermeneutical principle by demonstrating that from another lifeless planet, humans can really view human realities with new fullness and as observers only. Biblical research is hardly lifeless and sterile or conducted from the stratosphere; but like any truly ground-breaking intellectual endeavor, it is conducted from the lonely silence of one's abilities and beliefs even when they are at odds with the world about. Like the spaceship earth, the paradoxical insignificance and importance of the Bible are both feared and revered.

Thus, on a superficial level, the movement into weightless space symbolizes the free-floating, anchorless openness that accompanies the first testing of a historical biblical hypothesis. Whether attached by Marxist theory or any other faith-less fetter, the move away from the security of biblically based assumptions as the starting point in a research design is sure to leave the twentieth-century biblical historian vulnerable and awestruck. And yet, those steps must be taken if biblical reality and history are to be seen in new lights and perspectives. To borrow again, it is the logical next step in the evolution of historical consciousness.

There is a substantial difference between arguing that the experiencing of new technologies shapes the views of modern observers, as White[8] insisted, and saying that the past both was shaped by such experiences and can be known because of them and through models based on them. McNutt has documented an instance of ancient technology's having such an effect on ancient consciousness, religion, and the structure of traditions and texts.[9] Other cases, as well as the relationship between past and knowledge of the past, are currently under investigation within the Constructs of Ancient History and Religion Group sponsored by three learned societies.[10] These studies are less romantic and more substantive than my analogy implies, for behind them lies a quest for a new common ground shared by science and technology on the one hand and religion on the other.

The meaning of this comparison, as well as the subjects of comparison, also deserves investigation. A great deal of confusion prevails, principally because the popular mind—and at times scientists and technologists— harbors a naive view of religion and its academic study. As a result, the comparison is often drawn between intellectual, scholarly research on the one hand and modern belief and practice of religion on the other. Searching for similarities and differences across this line is interesting and personally and spiritually rewarding, but it does little to advance scholarship in the field of ancient religion.

The religion pole in the comparison may be more clearly and accurately understood if, instead of "religion," the claim is written to contain distinctions similar to those implied by "science and technology." Although it is not for us to dictate to our colleagues what science and technology are or what professionals in those fields do, for our purposes here it is appropriate to suggest that technologies apply scientific knowledge and lead to further scientific discoveries, and that the knowledge of both incorporates both a discipline or disciplines and the subject matters under investigation. There are three or more levels of meaning encoded in "science and technology."

Analogously, religion and its study comprise at least three levels of inquiry. In the case of ancient religion, these include (1) the meanings, beliefs, and practices of the past that we call religion and seek to understand; (2) the manifestations and traces of those religions that survive in the historical record (concretely, these often result from "applying" the religion in ways that leave behind texts and artifacts that can be examined as bases for hypotheses about the ancient religions—these are the humanists' and social scientists' "laboratory samples"); and (3) approaches, methods, and disciplines used in doing the research. Therefore, scholars of religion also have unknown knowledge, indications and applications of that knowledge in the past, and disciplines for examining the historical traces in order to gain fuller knowledge about the unknowns.

Describing the fields in this manner does not resolve all the differences by any means, but insisting that there are distinctions on each side of the equation allows us to maintain a classical distinction that has prevailed since Schleiermacher, and, like the difference between science and its many applications, localizes the meaning sought in historical religious studies where it belongs, that is, "beyond" the sources and data that are available for formal inquiry in studies on religion. Beyond one set in the equation are "scientific" phenomena; beyond the other is human meaning, belief, and aspiration.

The common quest is for unknowns *qua* unknown. Constructs research hypothesizes that in order to understand the peculiarities of Yahwist history, as the ancients did or did not, we must pull into the research swirl all that can be known about its past from the humanities, all that has been learned about social and cultural processes and postures from the social sciences, and all that can be learned about the internal and external relationships of systems from science and technology. From the technology we borrow especially models, metaphors, and insights into the creating and functioning of complex systems, including those that humans have invented but do not know or understand.

I hypothesize that the unknowns and approaches to them in the harder disciplines will be important because they can teach us about complexity and mysteriousness, and thus about religion and approaches to studying religion. Whether it is Yahwist Israel's history, a stealth bomber, a spacecraft, or a computer chip, no single person understands or knows the reality being created or explicated. That is the lesson of modern technology. Learning it can teach us to live and work with intangibles that lie beyond sense perception and human understanding.

I mean exactly that in modern technology, as in recreating ancient religious history, no human being can know the reality, object, or implement under investigation in all its complexity. The entity, all its internal and external relationships and each of its parts comprised as a single reality, is too complex for one to know. Human consciousness may struggle up this slope of understanding, but the learning curve is too steep. The ropes of protection are consensus, consensuality, and consensibility that philosophers of science have identified as the hallmarks of scientific inquiry and knowledge.[11]

To be concrete: technologists and, perhaps more so, scientists deal constantly with realities that are unknowable and unattainable. They work with entities that presumably have purpose in transcendental spheres whose very existence can only be hypothesized. They formulate hypotheses and test again and again, at times with no success or with successes that are often followed by failures. In such instances, only their solitary convictions inspire them to continue, but personal confidence without approval of knowledgeable peers carries no weight, and, formally speaking, the knowledge they generate does not exist until it is accepted and used by the professional community.[12]

How such scientists and technologists seek, attain, or project knowledge of unknown entities, I suggest, can illuminate religious historians' quest for the biblical past, both in terms of the nature of the past, that is, of "pastness," and the way that knowledge of the past is transmitted and gained. It is there that science and religion, technology and social world studies intersect and interact.

MODELS AND ANALOGY

Applying technology-based models to human history implies, on first glance, a reductionism that is sure to displease some in biblical studies.[13] Justification for the venture, however, can be sought beyond the disciplines and studies cited above, in fields as diverse as the arts and philosophy of science. From the latter, both the problem and the solution can be seen to pertain to the role of models.

> By definition, a model is not a complete and faithful rendering of reality. It is no more than an analogy or *metaphor*. It implies a structure of logical and mathematical relations that has many similarities with what it purports to explain, but cannot be fully identified with it. The wise theorist does not assert or attempt to prove the necessary validity of his [*sic*] model; this is to be discovered by further experience. . . . At its conception, a model is no more than a guide to thought, or a framework for a mathematical interpretation of inexplicable phenomena.[14]

Therefore, the reductionism, if it exists, results from the need to comprehend complexity and obscurity simultaneously.

Elsewhere, in the arts, the emergence of science and technology in the nineteenth and twentieth centuries can be shown to have had a direct impact on cubism, "flat art," and other forms of modern art.[15] The same can be inferred from music, especially from works of composers such as György Ligeti, whose experiments with "micropolyphony" represent an attempt to draw the timelessness of post-Newtonian space-time physics into a medium that historically depends fundamentally on an ability to measure time.

The massiveness of the relationship in terms of both the magnitude of the technological symbol and the impact of the technology on consciousness has been demonstrated in Miriam Levin's work on the Eiffel Tower's role in France as a people and nation.[16] Both the structure and its representations in poster art via print technology, Levin argues, were used to fuse the social and cultural bonds of a nation in ways that cut across economy, class, regionalism, and education. In sum, a nation's self-understanding and self-determination were nurtured by the power of technology symbolized by the Eiffel Tower and its images.

One might argue that this iron, pinnacled arch, built as a triumphal entry to a world exposition, constitutes an epiphany, a spatial moment, as it were, in the history of France, but a vernacular expression that by itself and through its print manifestations affirms the existence of a new state. For foreigners who visit and stand in awe, it is a window onto the past and into the mind of another people. It speaks to observer as lecturer speaks to audience. For the French people themselves, it is their voice singing proudly of their ability to combine French sensibility for fineness and individuating art with French technology and industry that give physical strength and national unity. The tower's spire stands alongside France's gothic cathedrals as an expression of a peoples' deep religiosity and a sign of their belief in transcendence. Once again, eyes are raised and spirits moved to think beyond immanence, beyond time, and beyond space, and to seek means for surviving and excelling.

I do not pretend to enjoy either breadth or depth of knowledge in these fields, but the concatenation of voices raised across a wide disciplinary spectrum stretching from art to technology bespeaks a need for biblical scholarship to remain abreast and lead the search for alternate ways of understanding the past.

A first step is to adopt an attitude toward the past and research on the past that is comparable to the attitude philosophers of science describe scientists and technologists as having toward their research.[17] Although practitioners of the hard sciences do not hold a monopoly on such feelings, the attitude does require, first, an admission that the past is allusive and at times incapable of being firmly grasped, and second, that our "knowledge" of it does not depend on the accuracy of our interpretation as much as on its acceptance by competent peers. The former raises epistemological questions; the latter restates the need for consensus mentioned above.

NEW CONSTRUCTS OF SOCIAL WORLD STUDIES

Before proceeding, it will be useful to illustrate the progress within social world studies that has brought the field to this point.[18]

In order to understand recent research, it is helpful to envisage several motions that are oriented along two axes. The orientations are arranged first at right angles like the x and y axes in a diagram or graph, and then like a twisting double helix whose separate "strands" become increasingly entwined. Let the axes stand for synchronic and diachronic relationships. Diachronic, that is, change over time, and synchronic, that is, the functional relationships of one aspect of life to another, are interactive. In the first illustration, horizontal and vertical axes intersect, but movement along one orientation does not affect the other. Applied to historical studies, the comparative method, or functionalists' interpretations, activates only the synchronic path. Events, personalities, or domains are investigated only in a single period; to view change over time, similar studies must be done period by period before these are linked diachronically.

This was the structure of the research program in Gottwald's *The Tribes of Yahweh*. There was no progressive interacting or twisting of the two axes. Diachronic and synchronic studies proceeded separately. Synchronic relationships were laid out in planes, and later the planes were examined diachronically. Marxist concepts of political processes eventually provided the integrating structure for relating the two axes.

In contrast, my article on chieftaincy and Frick's book on state formation gave pride of place to diachronic change.[19] We "traced" the stages of political development with little attention to synchronic analyses. In retrospect, I see that Frick and I had quite different interests that overlapped to a great extent because of the integrating metaphor, chieftaincy. Both of us used cultural evolutionary models almost exclusively and matched, somewhat woodenly, the stages found there with information from ancient Israel, I citing the literature and Frick the archaeology. The studies were useful, but they became quickly dated in the fast-developing subdiscipline of social world studies.

The first real effort to integrate diachronic and synchronic analyses, and therefore to expose interactive diachronic and synchronic relationships in Israel, was a volume by Coote and Whitelam.[20] The change in the relationship is somewhat like a change toward a twisting double helix. In this volume, the double helix began to twist. Although the authors generalized to the extreme in order to describe the big sweep of Yahwist history in Braudelian fashion and framing, the two axes interacted and intersected constantly in Israel as they moved together in a trajectory toward statehood. The mental image was like a computer screen, a graphic, that was rotated or extended before our eyes. We could see the movement and sense its meaning, but we had difficulty describing it. Centralization emerged because of the combined pressures back and forth along synchronic axes and forward along the diachronic line.

Although my book[21] was not written in order to go beyond earlier studies, it did attempt to address the issue of synchronic and diachronic interaction. The others had moved toward integration and holism by including ever more data, theories, and models. But, it seemed to me, they lacked a model and metaphor for the integration itself. To put it another way, more was known about synchronic relationships and about diachronic processes, and we knew more clearly that changes in one affected the other. We could understand how relational entities were being transformed interactively in ancient Israel, but we had not described the way that all the relationships between and among the realities related to each other. We were dealing with very complex systems. We knew that synchrony and diachrony were integrated, but we could not express this in a term that suited the specific reality, that is, the relating of entities compounded by the relating of relationships. The complexity of the problem increased when we recognized that literary information, archaeological information, and comparative sociological information each have different ontological statuses and yet interrelated across status lines, sometimes positively, sometimes negatively. Separating the domains led me to create analytical models that divided actors' perspectives from observers', and notional information from actional.

Technology in the form of holography and holograms offered a way to think and talk about the complex interacting of synchronic and diachronic axes, about information from differing and competing domains, and about viewers interacting with their subject matters, and to do it all simultaneously. In its richness, holography was ritual stood still. Or again, it was like MRI, Magnetic Resonating Imagery (= Nuclear Magnetic Resonance), a CAT scan process that lets one see inward three-dimension images and motion simultaneously. The axes of socioreligious development no longer extended only along separate planes.

When we stop to think about it, the difference between the two axes we are discussing is similar to differences between space and time. In conventional Near Eastern and biblical studies, contemporary languages, institutions, and civilizations are compared synchronically from culture to culture across the geographical spatial expanse of the Near East. Development over time at first is not an issue. First concern is for the samples, where they are (their space) and the fact that they are contemporary. Every precaution is taken to collect samples that are contemporary and to pinpoint their location.

Shortly afterward (in practice simultaneously), development of the samples within each culture and among them all diachronically is traced according to typologies. Here, spatial matters recede and temporal concerns come to the fore. A successful "reconstruction" depends on balancing and integrating both realities that represent the axes of space and time.

But this is the Cartesian grid that holography, like much of modern science and technology, moves away from. In the near future, it is hoped, a new epistemological base derived from those fields will help us understand more fully the way in which religious traditions evolve and devolve, blossom and wither, when a complex set of factors exert pressure on religion as it moves along the arrow of time.

REFERENTIAL REALISM VERSUS TRUTH REALISM

Situating, somewhat retrospectively, the use of holography within the development of social world studies serves to link those studies with the science and technology introduced above. Rom Harré has addressed the nature of scientific knowledge and rejects what he calls "truth realism," that is, the assumption that a hypothesis is true or false because it conforms or fails to conform to reality beyond itself. To demand that scientific concepts must conform directly to their referents is too rigid a description for science. Instead, he separates scientific knowledge into three interacting levels, each with its own kind of science: Realm 1: the *perceptual* level where science describes objects of common experience. This is the level of direct observation and experimentation. Realm 2: the *possible* level where science describes objects of possible experience. This is the level of theoretical abstractions. Technical devices such as microscopes and telescopes are used to reach this realm. Realm 3: the *transcendent* level where science purports to describe objects beyond all possible experience. This is the level of advanced physics, tendencies, powers, liabilities, and so forth. Social structures belong to this realm.[22] Religion can be treated as belonging there as well.

Each of these requires its own kind of processing. Again, there are three kinds, but they do not correspond exactly to the three realms. Generally they are divided into Theory 1: theories pertaining to observable phenomena; Theory 2: iconic theories; and Theory 3: mathematical theories.

Perhaps more important for us than the complexities of the levels of information and meaning, and the approaches to them, is Harré's insistence on "referential realism," which stands over against truth realism. According to this view, hypotheses are not true or false, but adequate or inadequate. Moreover, they function not to identify in themselves the truth of a reality, but to frame or bracket, as it were, a set of data. A hypothesis allows a researcher to establish an analytical model, to lift a set of data out of its field so that it, the relationships in it, and the relationships between it and its field can be examined. This, I contend, is what we do in our studies on ancient history and religion.

Viewing our task this way begins to move us beyond the Cartesian concepts of space and time.

> The manifolds so far considered are discrete grids of actual existents. But the exigencies of human life and scientific practice require acts of reference beyond the current reach of those observable locations and moments that are marked

by real things and events. Space and time are extensions of the grid of locations and moments, both "outwards" to infinity and "inwards" to the infinitesimal. As human constructions our ideas of these extended grids are clearly the result of cognitive rather than empirical activities. What then is the ontological status of the manifolds which the concepts of space and time might be taken to denote? And how do the special and general theories of relativity affect this simple picture?[23]

At this point, Harré does not answer; but eventually, when he speaks of his Realm 3, the level of reality that cannot be seen or known, he points to physics and to David Bohm.

It is the conservative metaphysical predilections of physicists that push the ontology and bring space-time with them as a referential grid which is to make location possible. Could there be a metaphysics for Realm 3 that was not particulate, and so did not smuggle in an isomorphism between the referential grids of the three epistemic realms? Few thoroughgoing alternatives have been seriously canvassed. David Bohm's . . . "implicate order" is a bold but so far isolated attempt.[24]

The relevance of Bohm's study is documented by his reviewer.

In Bohm's view . . . [s]cientific laws and theories are abstractions and idealizations that hold true only to a certain degree of approximation within limited domains. Scientific progress is not identified with convergence toward an absolute truth, but consists in the proposal of new theories, often based on radically new conceptual frameworks, which reveal the limitations of older theories, suggest new kinds of experiment and establish new criteria of relevance.[25]

Accordingly, Bohm applies the whole/part characteristics of holography analogously to the relationship between human unconsciousness and consciousness, the latter being an explicate manifestation of the former's implicate order.[26]

SPACE AND TIME AND SPACE-TIME

In *David's Social Drama*, I contended that ancient historians' concern for details and emphasis on creating a whole picture by adding more and more detail to our historical mosaics has caused us to ignore or forget the whole image of the past. Similarly, scholars of religions in their reconstructions of major traditions, institutions, and processes of the past have proceeded on assumptions of the validity of a space and time Cartesian grid. Under the influence of historical and source criticism, the history of religion school, and the referential truthfulness of texts, religious scholarship has presumed to recreate the past and to locate persons and events in real-life fashion on that stage.

For a host of reasons, that confidence has collapsed and the methods that supported it are believed to be exhausted. This has led many to abandon completely their interest in history, as well as the attempt to understand change over time in antiquity. It has left others continuing their quests with a shrinking corpus of data and fragmented and fragile theories and methods.

Social world studies, as we call them in biblical research, and now construct studies, offer fresh ways of looking at the past. The technology of holography and holograms, and other technologies, make it possible to create valid research designs and find suitable categories and metaphors for expressing our thoughts and views of the past. I stress as an aside that they are views *of* the past and not views *from* the past. The hypotheses that are created by borrowing from technology in order to discover the mesoforms that are betwixt and between our sources are mesoforms themselves.

Here I borrow a category adopted from Herbert Spencer by Joseph Needham and passed on by J. T. Fraser, one that on the surface may not seem to fit exactly with the cognitive entities outlined earlier. Not everyone accepts the fact that time is merely a cognitive entity. Some argue straight-forwardly for a material status of time and that species of time, like other entities, have evolved. One of those people is Fraser, former professor of physics and founder of the International Society for the Study of Time.

Needham developed the theme of hierarchical integrative levels of nature, that is, of successive levels of organization, of successive forms of order along a scale of complexity.[27] Such levels are distinct, stable, and bear a hierarchical nested relationship to each other so that, along the evolutionary trajectory, each successive stage adds to and subsumes the levels beneath it. Fraser, in fact, speaks of six levels, and hypothesizes that each has its own kind of time. Between the levels, however, each scholar argues that the assumption of integrative, stable levels demands a corollary, namely, the existence of mesoforms. These are structures and functions that fall between integrative levels, require a special language, and are rare and unstable. They have their own form and their own time. Because of their rarity and instability, they have left no trace in the evolutionary record, but their existence can be hypothesized and defended.

It is not my intention to make such a defense. Rather, I adopt the concept of mesoforms, transformed perhaps, as a category for understand-ing holographic history. Compared to paintings, statues, photos, and other material-based metaphors, holograms are unstable images. They move and shift before our eyes as we change our perspectives. There is a now-you-see-it, now-you-don't quality in all holograms because of the need for an illuminating beam and the narrow parallax that restricts the angle of viewing to approximately forty-five degrees, but it is especially the case when more than one image is encoded on the same plate.

My thesis, therefore, that goes beyond that presented in *David's Social Drama*, is that the views of the past that we construct on the basis of information from texts and tells are mesoforms that exist between our sources, our so-called disciplines, and the individuals, institutions, and worlds of the past. They also exist between space and time and between the several different kinds of time that are appropriate to texts and tells respectively. They are mesoformic holograms, as it were, that are reconstituted between (or among) the integrative levels of information that are used in constructs scholarship.

Furthermore, although Fraser may be correct in identifying six integrative levels along the arrow of time, holograms, that is, the views of the past that we create or constitute, are mesoforms that not only stand between but also integrate categories of space and time in a manner similar to the category space-time. The issue is obviously much more complicated than can be portrayed here, but it is time to point toward a direction of research that is being explored in constructs studies.

Applications are easily found. As Binford and others have argued, archaeologists do not dig up time or the past. Their sites are modern. They exist now, in the present, so that if time is relevant at all, archaeologists dig the present and in the present, or more accurately, the excavation is "now." Moreover, the categories of excavation are all spatial. Areas are so many meters long and wide, artifacts are so many meters deep, pottery is so many centimeters thick, and so on. The temporal information that is applied to the spatial information, therefore, must come from some other source. It is true that there is a general assumption that deeper probably means earlier, but that assumption is an erroneous pit that must be avoided until it has been tested.

Radiocarbon and thermoluminesce dating, flint and ceramic typologies, and other standards are used in conjunction with stratigraphy in order to establish relative dates of excavated materials. In the past, texts have been used to date sites from historical, literate periods, but the relationship between these sources is seriously challenged today and in every instance must be tested on a case by case basis. Because information that is taken from external indicators of chronology and absolute dates is not spatial but temporal, historians draw their sense of time from those indicators and, in turn, integrate it with spatial information gained from stratigraphy and other excavation techniques.

CONCLUSION

The integration of spatial and temporal information in a referential hypothesis produces a mesoform that exists in neither source. The image is a cognitive construct created in the same way that cognitive categories of past and future are assigned in respect to a succession of "nows," the only time that can give those categories meaning.[28] Tells and texts, like the face of an aging friend, contain the hints of a former identity, but the limited information in each separately or together is not the entire picture. When a religious historian recognizes a time that correlates the archaeological record with biblical assertions, for instance, then the recognition is in the researcher's mind and hypothesis, and not in either source. New or temporary epiphanies and insights, spatial moments as it were, stand among the disciplines but are centered in none. They are constructs that are mesoforms and hypotheses that, in turn, allow us to lift new combinations of information out of several fields simultaneously. By linking those fields in hypotheses, we are able to catch a glimpse of the mesoforms of the past. They are rare and unstable "moments." In those moments, I contend, we discover the meanings of past life that otherwise would elude us. Thus we are not simply heirs of the religious or historical past. We are its creators as well as its custodians. That is true of religion, it is true of the Bible, it is true of archaeology, and I suspect it is true generally.

17 Sociological Criticism and Its Relation to Political and Social Hermeneutics

With a Special Look at Biblical Hermeneutics in South African Liberation Theology

Frank S. Frick

In a paper that Norman Gottwald and I coauthored in 1975 as coconveners of a new SBL program unit, "Consultation on the Social World of Ancient Israel," we sought (1) to identify emerging (and reemerging) types of sociological study of the Hebrew scriptures in relation to other forms of biblical study, and (2) to explore the potentialities and implications of sociological method for the understanding of biblical Israel. In that paper, we said:

> Among Old Testament scholars there is a reawakening of interest in the social dimensions of ancient Israel and the beginnings of a determined effort to use sociological methods to supplement the more familiar methods of literary, historical, and theological study of the Old Testament.
>
> This interest has been fueled in part by factors external to the discipline, such as the worldwide impact of social ferment and revolution on the life and thought of the churches, and the expansion and refinement of method in the social sciences.[1]

Among the signs of reawakening interest in sociological study of the Hebrew scriptures are the organizational expressions it has taken among American scholars in the last fifteen years. Our first consultation in 1975 was followed by the formation of a group on the "Social World of Ancient Israel," cosponsored by the SBL and the AAR, and chaired again by Gottwald and me. After that group had run its term, another group was formed, this time a seminar with a more defined membership and agenda. Its focus was "The Sociology of the Monarchy in Ancient Israel"; it was cochaired by James Flanagan and me, and cosponsored by the SBL and

ASOR, with ASOR sponsorship arising out of our concern to be in touch with those working with the material remains of ancient Israel. This seminar had its final session at the 1987 annual meeting.

Since 1987, three new groups have emerged, giving continuing expression to the expanding interest in the application of methods and theories from the social sciences to the criticism of the Hebrew scriptures. Flanagan and Jo Ann Hackett now cochair a group on "Constructs of Ancient History and Religion," which is specifically concerned with interdisciplinary, synthetic matters. Philip Davies and John Halligan cochair a group on the "Sociology of the Second Temple." At the 1990 annual meeting, a new section, which I chair, on "The Social Sciences and the Interpretation of the Hebrew Scriptures," convened. This new section offers both junior and senior scholars a forum for the presentation of exploratory papers dealing with sociological criticism. Because by SBL's own definitions of program units a section is established to reflect major continuing areas of academic interests, the approval of this new section is the society's recognition that sociological criticism has an established place in the discipline.

THE PLACE AND ROLE
OF SOCIOLOGICAL CRITICISM

Accompanying this recognition, however, have been questions concerning what sociological criticism *is* or *ought* to be. Such queries are both descriptive and normative. On the one hand, descriptive, sociologically informed analyses of the world of ancient Israel are now more persuasive than they were fifteen years ago. This is because, at least in part, they are more sophisticated, both at the historical and theoretical levels, and because younger scholars are emerging who have had solid academic preparation in the social sciences throughout the course of their higher education, rather than having to "retrofit" as many senior scholars in the field have had to do.

Other developments in the field, however, have led to normative questions about what the role of sociological criticism ought to be in relation to other prevailing paradigms of biblical criticism, and what its proper function in the development of a normative social hermeneutics ought to be. I concur with Robert Morgan when he says:

> Enlarging the historical perspective and sharpening historical observation with help from the social sciences is by now accepted in principle, whatever skepticism remains about its successful application. But to assess this approach by its historical results alone would be to ignore other dimensions present in modern interpretation of religiously significant texts.[2]

In the same period in which sociological criticism has reemerged and consolidated its position, other developments in biblical studies have undermined some of its results when it is viewed simply as an extension of the historical-critical paradigm. In her recent SBL presidential address, Elisabeth Schüssler Fiorenza said:

> In the past fifteen years biblical studies has adopted insights and methods derived from literary studies and philosophical hermeneutics [and, I would add, from the social sciences]; but it has, to a great extent, refused to relinquish its rhetorical stance of value-free objectivism and scientific methodism.[3]

From one perspective, sociological biblical criticism *is* simply an extension of the historical-critical method, with different reference points. Gottwald's own definition of sociological exegesis supports this:

> Sociological exegesis tries to situate a biblical book or subsection in its proper social setting—taking into account the literary and historical relations between the parts and the whole. It further attempts to illuminate the text according to its explicit or implied social referents, in a manner similar to historical-critical method's clarification of the political and religious reference points of text.[4]

Questions about the nature and function of sociological criticism have come into sharp focus around the issue of the relation between sociological criticism and some newer forms of literary criticism. For some, literary criticism and sociological criticism cannot peacefully coexist; either one or the other must prevail, or the two must operate in separate domains with no reference to or contribution from the other. Other developments in literary theory, however, both along deconstructionist and Althusserian Marxist lines suggest paths along which literary-social interaction might proceed. Again, it is Gottwald who envisions a comprehensive approach to the Hebrew scriptures that does justice to and harmonizes literary and sociological methods. He maintains that even though different dimensions of biblical texts imply their own methods of interpretation, the literary, social, and theological perspectives require one another for the interpretation of the fullness of the text:

> In the critical practices associated with the other three coordinates are disclosed the simultaneous expressions of human beings who lived in communities of a certain social character and who wrote their thoughts and feelings in texts of certain types and who found meaning in their life together through religious categories of a specific sort. These literary, social and theological "worlds" that we split for analysis were inhabited by real people for whom those worlds were dimensions of their lived experience and shared meanings. The three coordinates that we are trying to bring together coexisted in their collective lives and interpreting minds, filtered through linguistic and cultural socialization processes.[5]

In order to advance the discussion, it is necessary to distinguish between ways that social-scientific methods and theories have enlarged the historical methods on the one hand, and the hermeneutical dimensions of a sociological approach on the other. Again, I think that Morgan is correct when he sees Gottwald as one who is explicitly developing a sociological hermeneutics, though still working within the historical paradigm.[6] Gottwald has been disturbed by the fact that biblical scholarship, on the one hand, has pursued its interests insulated by the demands of "scientific" academic interests from contemporary social, religious, and political issues, and that the contemporary social, religious, and political scene, on the other hand, has been left untouched by the results of biblical scholarship. He has led the call for a more constructive engagement between biblical scholarship and real-world concerns. Even his "descriptive" sociological biblical scholarship, certainly his *The Tribes of Yahweh*,[7] has a normative stratum just beneath a thin historical top layer. This normative thrust begins with a call for biblical scholars to be in touch with their own social location, their own context. Again, it is Schüssler Fiorenza who speaks of an emergent paradigm in biblical studies:

> The literary-hermeneutical paradigm seems presently in the process of decentering into a . . . paradigm that inaugurates a rhetorical-ethical turn. This . . . paradigm relies on the analytical and practical tradition of rhetoric in order to insist on the public-political responsibility of biblical scholarship.[8]

In contrast to formalist literary criticism, this rhetorical-ethical paradigm insists that *context* is as important as *text*. What we see depends on where we stand. One's social location or rhetorical context determines how one sees the world, constructs reality, and interprets biblical texts. The positivistic paradigm of biblical scholarship continues to suppose that through disinterested and dispassionate "scientific" exegetical methods, biblical critics can step out of their own context and study history "on its own terms," free of any hindrances stemming from their contemporary environment. But, as Schüssler Fiorenza says:

> The reluctance of the discipline to reflect on its sociopolitical location cannot simply be attributed to the repression of biblical scholarship by organized religion. It is as much due to its ethos of scientist positivism and professed value-neutrality. Scientist epistemologies covertly advocate an apolitical reality without assuming responsibility for their political assumptions and interests.[9]

SOCIOLOGICAL CRITICISM AND SOCIAL LOCATION

Sociological criticism, understood in this fuller sense, can not only enlarge our understanding of the past; it can, and *should*, serve us as biblical scholars by making us conscious of our own locations and interests. Such a turn to the subject also can "soften" both history and some social science (especially cultural anthropology), and bring them closer to literary theory than the older positivistic approach would have ever allowed. A social scientific approach can strengthen the links between past and present, which both history and literature tend to weaken by their emphasis on one or the other. Certainly, the time has arrived when the sociopolitical location of the interpreter must become the subject of critical scrutiny *together with* the social location of the text. In what follows I do not advocate a kind of criticism that would read biblical texts in the light of certain values that are related to political beliefs and actions. All criticism does this. The idea that there are "nonpolitical" forms of criticism is a part of the objectivist myth that only serves to further some political uses of biblical literature all the more effectively, while filtering out others. "The difference between a "political" and a "nonpolitical" criticism, as Terry Eagleton has put it, "is just the difference between the prime minister and the monarch: the latter furthers certain political ends by pretending not to, while the former makes no bones about it."[10]

LIBERATIONIST HERMENEUTICS

The issues of the social location of the interpreter and of political criticism have been addressed most explicitly in recent years by two groups of scholars—feminist and liberationist biblical critics. Feminist and liberation hermeneutics are certainly interested in the social settings out of which scripture arose, but they are not content just to explore that context as an end in itself. They are equally, if not more, concerned about the social setting in which the text is received and the implications of this dynamic for the contemporary claims of scriptural authority.

It is my conviction that the bonding of this perspectival stance of feminists and liberationists with social world studies can provide us with a research framework not only for integrating historical, archaeological, sociological, literary, and theological approaches as perspectival readings of texts, but also for raising ethical-political and religious-theological questions as constitutive of the interpretive process. It can help us divest ourselves of a view of texts as data and evidence for historical reality, and instead see texts as perspectives on social worlds and symbolic universes. Differing interpretations of such texts are neither right nor wrong, but different ways of reading and constructing historical meaning in the biblical text. One's own experience and perspective as interpreter not only can enter into the hermeneutical process but should do so in order to make one's context as interpreter visible, and capable of critical interaction with other perspectives. Again, in the words of Schüssler Fiorenza:

> Not detached value-neutrality but an explicit articulation of one's rhetorical
> strategies, interested perspectives, ethical criteria, theoretical frameworks,

religious presuppositions and sociopolitical locations for critical public discussions are appropriate in such a . . . paradigm of biblical scholarship.[11]

There have been a number of recent efforts to integrate a class reading or political hermeneutic with social scientific analysis. These studies, unlike those that simply continue the historical-critical task using the tools of structural-functionalism or interpretive sociology, point, however tentatively, toward a real theoretical break with the traditions of liberal biblical scholarship, and the elaboration of the theoretical conditions for the fusion of historical materialism, that is, the scientific study of the structure and development of human social formations, with the traditions of faith.

In what follows, I will examine such efforts that have arisen in the particular sociopolitical context of South Africa, and the work of one South African biblical scholar, Itumeleng J. Mosala, of the University of Cape Town, in particular.

BIBLICAL HERMENEUTICS AND
BLACK THEOLOGY IN SOUTH AFRICA

It is a curious coincidence that what has been called "black theology" first emerged in South Africa at about the same time as sociological biblical studies was reemerging in the United States. This South African black theology, because of its great concern for liberation, can accurately be described as a subset of liberation theology, even though black theologians in South Africa were not, initially, directly influenced by Latin American liberation theologians. The term *black theology* in South Africa was borrowed from North American black theologians, in particular from James Cone. John de Gruchy observes that the earliest articulation of black theology under that title was the work of Cone, whose first book on the subject appeared in 1969.[12] The major point borrowed from Cone was his insistence that the content of the Christian gospel is liberation. As Louise Kretzschmar insists, however, it is not valid to argue that Cone's liberation emphasis was simply imposed on South Africa. Rather, its espousal by black theologians is a consequence of their conviction that it is pertinent to *their* context and *their* desire for liberation."[13] South African black theology accepts liberation as the hermeneutical key that unlocks the meaning of the scriptures. In so doing, it combines the situational emphasis of Cone (i.e., the belief that blacks need to be liberated from their situation of exploitation) with that of Latin American liberation theology, which, with some reservations, regards the primacy of liberation praxis as the solution to the hermeneutical problem. The result is a preferential sensitivity to the oppressed, a sense of solidarity with them, plus a commitment to action—hence the centrality of praxis and the relegation of theology to the place of being a reflection on praxis.

The fundamental methodological problem of a biblical hermeneutics of liberation for black biblical theologians in South Africa is defining the relation between two "norms": the authority of scripture and the authority of one's own experience of being oppressed. There are three ways in which liberation theologians in South Africa relate scripture to experience. One way is to choose and cite particular biblical passages against one's oppressors. If no effective passages can be found, they are discovered through etymology or allegory. In this way, if one so desires (and many in South Africa do), one can claim to be Calvinist, operating under the pretext of *sola scriptura*.

A second way is to start from biblical models and then remodel them according to the needs of one's own experience of being oppressed. This method operates on the premise that all truth, including biblical truth, is only true for one's own situation, that is, when it is contextualized. Whether this way can be Calvinist too, or not, is a question of interpretation.

Third, the oppressed can also move beyond the Bible, to experience within themselves God's solidarity with their inner and outer struggles, in a way for which the Bible can provide no proof because of the uniqueness of the present oppressive structures. "One's consciousness is one's theology," is the presupposition for this way of thinking. This method may have difficulties in being convincingly Calvinistic.

This problem of conflicting norms in the use of scripture by South African liberation theologians brings me to the consideration of the work of Mosala. I choose to focus on his work, because in my estimation he, more than any other black South African biblical scholar, is both thoroughly informed by the most recent social critical biblical scholarship from Europe and North America, *and* fleshes out a South African contextual hermeneutic. One of the many surprises of my first trip to South Africa, in 1988, was to see papers that had been presented to our Sociology of the Monarchy Seminar on the reading list for Mosala's courses at the University of Cape Town. It was also Mosala who introduced me to apartheid in the black townships of Cape Town.

Mosala, in a radical and sweeping *tour de force*, goes straight for the jugular in his analysis of the practice of biblical hermeneutics in the context of apartheid, with its unique form of oppression under which people of color in South Africa have suffered, not just since the official beginnings of apartheid in 1948, but under British administration as well, a situation whose roots go all the way back to the arrival of the first Dutch settlers in

1652. Mosala begins by criticizing those hermeneutical schemes of black theologians in South Africa that give priority to the Bible as "The Word of God," including even Archbishop Desmond Tutu and the Reverend Allan Boesak. He criticizes Boesak for his contention that liberation theology is true to the "age-old gospel," and he calls the claims made by Boesak and others about the status of the Bible as "Word of God" a "theoretical tragedy."

According to Mosala, any hermeneutics that begins with a belief in the Bible as the "Word of God" is anti-black working class and anti-black women and merely "bourgeois exegesis applied to the working class situation."[14] What Mosala advocates is a new exegetical starting point, one provided by the sociopolitical and economic world of the black working class and peasantry, which he maintains "constitutes the only valid hermeneutical starting point for a Black Theology of liberation."[15]

Mosala has correctly seen the logical flaw in the use of the Bible in conventional liberation theology. He is absolutely on target when he says that one simply cannot have it both ways: one cannot begin with the situation or context of the readers *and*, at the same time, begin with the Bible as the Word of God. The attempt to embrace both starting points is traced back to Cone, whose scheme of biblical hermeneutics, according to Mosala, has been uncritically reproduced in South Africa, without sufficient attention to the South African context. For Mosala, the insistence on the Bible as the Word of God must be seen for what it is:

> . . . an ideological maneuver whereby ruling class interests evident in the Bible are converted into a faith that transcends social, political, racial, sexual, and economic divisions. In this way the Bible becomes an ahistorical, interclassist document.[16]

Furthermore, such a starting point presupposes a hermeneutical epistemology for which truth *by definition* is neither historical, cultural, nor economic. To start with the category "Word of God" is to cloak the real nature of liberation in the Bible, because it presumes that liberation exists everywhere and unproblematically in the Bible.

Mosala speaks positively, however, of the work of Cornel West, who, unlike Cone and others, does *not* interpret the black experience with the "Word of God" as the starting point, but advocates interpreting the Bible in the light of the black experience. Like Cone, West insists on there being a biblical truth according to which God sides with the oppressed in their struggle for liberation. This, Mosala maintains, is true so far as it goes. But as any hermeneutics that derives from the crucible of class struggle will attest, the biblical truth that God sides with the oppressed is only one of the biblical truths. The other truth is that the struggle between Yahweh and Baal is not simply one pitting *religious* beliefs and practices against one another, but a struggle between the God of the Israelite landless peasants and subdued slaves, and the God of the Israelite royal, noble, landlord, and priestly classes.[17]

For Mosala, the key word in biblical hermeneutics is the word *struggle*. Notice its predominance in the following paragraph, which lays out his conception of an adequate hermeneutic:

> The real reason that the dominant groups in society are able to claim to be grounded in the best traditions of Christianity and at the same time to be part of the structures and societal processes that alienate and impoverish others is that that accommodation happened in the biblical texts themselves. Thus to overlook that internal biblical contradiction is to be in danger of uncritically . . . transmitting such *struggle*-ridden texts as part of the unproblematical Word of God. There is a trajectory of *struggle* that runs through all biblical texts, and a recognition of this fact means that it is no longer accurate to speak of . . . the Word of God unproblematically and in absolute terms. Both the Word of God and the gospel are such hotly contested terrains of *struggle* that one cannot speak in an absolutizing way of being alienated from the gospel. What one can do is take sides in a *struggle* that is not confirmed by the whole of the Bible, . . . but is rather encoded in the text as a *struggle* representing different positions and groups in the society behind the text. That provokes different appropriations of those texts, depending on one's class, gender, culture, race, or ideological position and attitude.[18]

The emphasis on struggle leads to two explicit moves in a materialist hermeneutical scheme. As his or her first move, the biblical interpreter must first *decode* the biblical text, which has *encoded* the struggles between different positions and groups in the society that lies behind the biblical text. In the second move, the biblical interpreter must take sides in the struggle. According to Mosala, "It is not enough to be existentially committed to the struggles of the oppressed and exploited people. One must also effect a theoretical break with the assumptions and perspectives of the dominant discourse of a stratified society."[19]

The category of social struggle as a basic category for biblical hermeneutics necessitates some historical-critical starting points for exegesis. Questions emanating from this approach for Mosala are, among others: What historical point is reflected by the discursive practice a text represents? What are the social, cultural, class, gender, and racial issues at work in this text? What is the ideological-spiritual agenda of the text, that is, how does the text itself seek to be understood?[20] For Mosala, a materialist biblical hermeneutics of liberation, which sees the Bible as the product, record, and site of class struggles, provides the necessary tools for decoding the text.

Mosala's materialist hermeneutical method has three distinct steps. The first of these is what he calls the critical appreciation of the history and culture of the hermeneuticians. To arrive at such an appreciation, Mosala uses the concept of modes of production, a vital area of Marxist theory. Mosala divides the black struggle in South Africa into epochs that are characterized by the dominance of a particular mode of production as the fundamental feature of a social formation. He sees three successive stages of this struggle in South Africa: the communal, the tributary, and the capitalist stages. Mosala periodizes the black struggle in order to appropriate it as a biblical hermeneutical factor for liberation. The communal, tributary, colonial, and modern capitalist modes of production represent the struggle contexts that inform the contemporary discourses of the black struggle. The class and ideological choices made vis-à-vis these contexts determine the specific hermeneutical tools for reading and using the Bible.

The second step in the process is the delineation of the historical and cultural struggles of the biblical communities. Here, Mosala uses the mode of production, together with class forces and dominant ideology, to get at the material conditions of the communities behind the biblical text. At this point he is also interested in the ideological conditions of the text, specifically, with the class origins and interests of the text.

The third step of the process confronts the signified expressions of the cultural struggles of the biblical communities in the texts.

Let us now examine Mosala's three steps in turn, focusing on the three key concepts of the *mode of production, ideology*, and *class struggle*. Clearly, the key concept in a materialist approach is the concept of the mode of production, the combination of the forces and relations of production. Mosala begins by periodizing the black struggle in South Africa in terms of three successive modes of production. Although Mosala admits that these three modes of production may coexist, he prefers to see these modes as successors of one another. This use of the rather traditional schema of various modes of production as so many historical "stages" has been criticized by many, not least because it encourages typologizing. Fredric Jameson is foremost among such critics:

> Every social formation or historically existing society has in fact consisted in the overlay and structural coexistence of several modes of production all at once, including vestiges and survivals of older modes of production, now relegated to structurally dependent positions within the new, as well as anticipatory tendencies that are potentially inconsistent with the existing system but have not yet generated an autonomous space of their own.[21]

For Mosala, however, the way a society produces and reproduces its life is fundamentally conditioned by its mode of production, seen typologically:

> The legal, religious, political and philosophical spheres of society develop on the basis of the mode of production and refer back to it. Any approach, therefore, that seeks to employ a materialist method must inquire into (1) the nature of the mode of production; (2) the constellation of classes necessitated by that mode; and (3) the nature of ideological manifestations arising out of and referring back to that mode of production.[22]

Thus, in his first step, in which he is concerned with the critical appreciation of the history and culture of the hermeneutician, Mosala holds that it is necessary to discern both the material conditions of the biblical reader (understood in terms of the mode of production, classes, and dominant ideology) *and* the ideological conditions of the biblical reader (understood in terms of the class origins and commitments of the reader).

In my estimation, any attempt to construct a materialist hermeneutic, such as Mosala's, must necessarily confront objections to traditional Marxist models of interpretation raised by the influential school of so-called structural Marxism, based on the work of the French Marxist theorist Louis Althusser. These objections have been forcefully set forth by Jameson. One striking and fundamental difference between Althusser and traditional Marxism is the modification of the traditional Marxist theory of levels. The vulgar Marxist theory of levels included the conception of base or infrastructure (the economic, or mode of production) and superstructure (culture, ideology, legal system, and political superstructure). This conception of levels either conceived or perpetuated the impression of the "ultimately determining instance" or mode of production as the narrowly economic—that is, as one level within the social system that "determines" the others. The Althusserian conception of mode of production identifies this concept with the structure as a whole. For Althusser, then, the more narrowly economic—the forces of production, the labor process, technical development, or relations of production, such as the functional interrelation of social classes—is, however privileged, not identical with the mode of production as a whole, which assigns this narrowly "economic" level its particular function and efficiency as it does all the others.[23]

Mosala appears to use the concept of ideological superstructure in the traditional Marxist way, in that ideology is not in the first place a set of doctrines, but rather signifies the way people live out their roles in class-society. Ideology consists of the values, ideas, and images that bind persons to their social functions and so obstruct a true knowledge of society as a whole. This Marxist conception of ideology sheds light on both the second and third steps in Mosala's materialist hermeneutic of liberation, in which he seeks to explicate the relationship of ideology and biblical literature. There have been, of course, various ways of viewing this relationship. One way is to equate the two—to say that literature *is* ideology, that biblical literature merely reflects on the ideologies of its time, while being imprisoned by them. This position, however, has been unable to explain how so much biblical literature actually challenges the ideological assumptions of its time. On the other end of the spectrum there is the view, espoused by many biblical scholars, that because so much of biblical literature seems to challenge the ideology it confronts, it is defined de facto as a counterideological cultural expression.

Mosala's position on this relationship reflects Althusserian Marxism, particularly as it is reflected in the work of Eagleton. Eagleton, following Althusser, argues that literature cannot be reduced to ideology: it has, rather, a particular *relationship* to it. Ideology, understood in this way, signifies the imaginary ways in which persons experience the real world, which is, of course, the kind of experience literature gives us too. Literature, however, does more than just passively reflect that experience. Literature is held within ideology, but also manages to distance itself from it. In so doing, literature does not enable us to *know* the truth that ideology conceals, because for Althusser "knowledge" in the strict sense means *scientific* knowledge. Although *science* gives us *conceptual knowledge* of a situation; *literature* gives us the *experience* of that situation, which is equivalent to ideology.[24] Because ideology has structure, it can be the object of scientific analysis; and because literary texts belong to ideology, they too can be the object of such scientific analysis.

Mosala's method thus seeks to interpret biblical literature in terms of the ideological structure of which it is a part. At the same time, he recognizes that literature can transform ideology by searching out the principle that both ties the literature to ideology and distances it from it, what Mosala calls "the signified expressions of the cultural struggles of the biblical communities."

Finally, let us look at Mosala's use of class as a fundamental hermeneutical factor in the biblical text, as indeed in the communities behind the text and those appropriating the text presently.

Why does Mosala choose to focus on the theory of social class as the key to his biblical hermeneutic? Perhaps he does so because, as Emmanuel Terray has suggested, the concept of class is what one could call a "totalizing" concept: one must refer to all aspects of social reality in order to define it. Class is, as it were, the place where the various dimensions of social life—economic, political, ideological—intersect. In other words, within the field of social relations, class is the product of the conjoined action of different structures—economic, political, ideological—the combination of which constitutes a determinate mode of production and social formation.[25] To define a class one must begin, as Mosala does, not only with the mode of production, but also with the social formation of which it is a part. Not only the economic infrastructure, but also the political and ideological superstructures, must be taken into account. Indeed, a class is the product of the combined action of all these structures. This point cannot be stressed too much. By confining oneself to the economic base alone, one will only grasp what Marx calls classes "in themselves," characterized by their function within the mode of production, their position at one end or other of a relation of exploitation. But even when it is a case of an exploited class, a class "in itself" is not necessarily simultaneously a class "for itself," conscious of itself and capable of collective decision and action. To be sure, where there is exploitation there is always some form of revolt and struggle, but such struggles may remain fragmented, temporary, and defensive. In such situations, the class does not constitute a genuine historical force liable actively to determine the course of events. What we want to know next are the conditions and circumstances in which a class "in itself" becomes and remains a class "for itself." This transformation will vary with the mode of production. Such variations are not arbitrary; they are a function of the nature of the relations of production basic to the mode of production in question. In other words, the specific way in which surplus is created, drawn off, and allocated—the specific form the relation of exploitation assumes—determines not only the nature of the classes present, but also their ability to organize themselves and act as classes, the forms and intensity of confrontation between them, and the possible outcome of such confrontation.

Some of Mosala's definitive assumptions of traditional Marxism on the mode of production may well be too restrictive or even erroneous when applied to precapitalist societies in general, and to ancient Israel specifically. For example, to emphasize interclass conflict as a force of social change, and to hold as axiomatic that history is in the last instance determined by the mode of production, can impede rather than advance our understanding of complex precapitalist societies.

My anthropological colleague Elizabeth Brumfiel observes that Aztec history, like the history of ancient Israel, was filled with conflict, but much of this conflict cut across class divisions: noble was set against noble, commoner against commoner. The success of the Aztec state can actually be attributed to the absence of class solidarity among either nobles or commoners. Within the nobility, the Aztecs commonly sacrificed the well-being of some elites to others, playing favorites in the provincial domains under their control. Less is known about the fortunes of commoners under Aztec rule, but the common soldiers of the Aztec armies show real zest for pillaging the towns and fields of their enemies, nobles and commoners alike. And litigation between commoners over land boundaries was a common feature of native life.

Of course, there are incidents in both Aztec and Israelite history that smack of class conflict, and every aspect of life was affected in some way by the underlying class structure. But Brumfiel observes that Aztec history is primarily a record of intraclass competition and factionalism. It provides convincing evidence that those who labor in the same way also compete for the same resources and that intraclass competition for the same limited benefits can overwhelm the bonds of class solidarity.[26]

In the Epilogue to his *Biblical Hermeneutics and Black Theology in South Africa*, Mosala concludes:

> In a society divided by class, race, and gender, there must certainly be a plurality of biblical hermeneutics. These expressions of hermeneutics function to reproduce or to rationalize or to transform the socioeconomic and political status quo. South Africa is probably the best, though not the only, modern example of a country in which the ruling political group has consciously developed a biblical hermeneutics that reproduces and sustains its ideological and political interests. The theoretical tragedy in South Africa has been that black theologians, in opposing the theology of the dominant white groups, have appealed to the same hermeneutical framework in order to demonstrate a contrary truth. . . . The Bible is the product, the record, the site, and the weapon of class, cultural, gender, and racial struggles. And a biblical hermeneutics of liberation that does not take this fact seriously can only falter in its project to emancipate the poor and the exploited of the world. Once more, the simple truth rings out that the poor and exploited must liberate the Bible so that the Bible may liberate them.[27]

Amandla! Ngawethu!

18 Feminism and "Mode of Production" in Ancient Israel

Search for a Method

David Jobling

> I must create a system, or be enslaved by another man's.
>
> William Blake

INTRODUCTION

As several contributions to this volume illustrate, the search for methodological integration has become a powerful and exciting force in biblical studies[1]—not with the expectation that we will reach a consensus and solve all our problems, but under the ethical imperative not to let our discipline continue as an aggregate of bits and pieces, with practitioners of different approaches agreeing, within a comfortable ideology of pluralism, to a standoff. Commanding particular attention is the relationship between literary and social-scientific methods. Norman Gottwald, at the beginning of his introduction to the Hebrew Bible, identified these as the most important emerging "paradigms" and raised the question of their integration.[2]

In this debate, however, women's voices have not been prominent, and there is perhaps some ambiguity in feminist biblical scholarship over the issue of methodological integration. On the one hand, it is committed to the overcoming of disciplinary boundaries that it did not make and under which it has suffered.[3] On the other hand, there is a perceived link between the impulse to create systems and male dominance, for systems have often been created for political purposes of exclusion. So far as I know, the only feminist work carried out on the Hebrew Bible in the framework of a specific proposal for methodological integration is that of Mieke Bal, based on the distribution among subjects of speaking, focalizing, and acting, which is unusual also in that it comes from the literary, as opposed to the social-scientific side.[4] Bal insists that the best defense against an

239

oppressive system is the working out of a countersystem, and that we need to respond to the exclusionary "coherences" in biblical studies with "countercoherences."[5]

It is dangerous, it seems to me, to go on pursuing the debate over methodological integration in the traditional framework of white, male scholarship, however well-intentioned, at a distance from the claims of feminism (and analogous claims from other directions). It is the purpose of this essay, therefore, to bring the integrative framework most favored, and most explored, by our honoree—the Marxist concept of "mode of production"—into critical relationship with some works of feminist biblical scholarship in which the interdisciplinary impulse is at work. I will use as a focus the question of the impact on women's lives of Israel's transition to monarchy.

After presenting, and critiquing from a feminist perspective, the relevant aspects of the mode of production approach, I will turn to detailed consideration of two feminist works that raise the issue of interdisciplinary method in very different ways. Carol Meyers, in *Discovering Eve*,[6] employs a basically social-scientific method; she offers a social description of early Israel, and of women's places within it, making use of archaeology and comparative ethnology. But she also includes two chapters of literary reading of Genesis 2–3. Mieke Bal, in *Death and Dissymmetry*, offers a literary reading of Judges closely attuned to the social sciences, especially anthropology. But her social-scientific notions of ancient Israel are very unfashionable, with much input from psychology, but little from archaeology.

Neither of these two book-length works, though they provide the best basis for methodological discussion, is focused directly on the transition to monarchy. Meyers' focus is on the premonarchic period, the transition being covered in an epilogue. Bal shows little interest in the monarchy, and indeed hardly tries to locate historically the (nonetheless decidedly historical!) process that she sees as generating Judges; but I suggest that this process, a transition from one form of marital organization to another, invites an interpretation that links it to the transition to monarchy. Hence I shall draw supplementarily on two article-length works, by Naomi Steinberg and Regina Schwartz, which make the transition to monarchy central, and which methodologically are closely aligned to Meyers and Bal respectively.[7]

MODE OF PRODUCTION

Having already, in *The Tribes of Yahweh* and *The Hebrew Bible*, made significant use of the concept "mode of production," Gottwald concluded the latter book with a very important (and insufficiently noticed) method-ological statement,[8] and followed this up with an oft-quoted but still unpublished paper in which he traced the dominant modes of production through the whole of biblical history.[9] To use his own definition, a mode of production is

> a combination of the material forces of production, including human physical and mental powers, and the social relations of production, which specifies the way that producers and nonproducers organize society's work and appropriate the labor product.[10]

Of special importance in Gottwald's use of this theory is his insistence on analyzing literary production as an integral part of general production in Israel; specifically, it is part of the production of ideology, which stands in a complex but analyzable relationship with material production and the (re)production of social forms.[11] It is in line with this insistence that he has recently made a point of intervening, from his social-scientific base, in the debate over literary approaches to the Bible.[12]

In early, and still in orthodox, Marxism, every society must necessarily follow a "unilinear" sequence of modes of production: primitive com-mune, classical society, feudal society, bourgeois society [capitalism], socialist society.[13] But Marx himself (though inconsistently) posited an "Asiatic" mode, to take account of societies (notably large empires from ancient to modern times) that the orthodox sequence failed to account for.[14] Gottwald takes up this mode, under the preferable name of "tribu-tary," describing it as follows:

> The primary producers were legally free cultivators who were in use-posses-sion of their land and tools but who were tributary to a state in the forms of tax (= rent) in kind and labor conscription. The exploiting class was composed of state officials and client groups dependent on state favor or sponsorship.[15]

He posits Israel's transition to monarchy as a shift in mode of production, specifically from a "communitarian" to a "(native) tributary" mode,[16] and it is these two, therefore, that I will consider in the following discussion.

Mode of production in premonarchic Israel. There are major problems with the "communitarian," or "primitive commune," mode, both in its tradi-tional formulation and in relation to Israel. As classically presented by Engels,[17] this mode is very much tied up with evolutionary notions of primitive human development, especially a preagrarian stage characterized by *Mutterrecht* (matrilineal and matriarchal organization). Although such a notion has appealed to some feminists, it seems to have no relevance for an early Israel, which was basically agrarian and certainly not "primitive" (emerging, as Gottwald thinks, from the tributary systems of Egypt and Canaan by a deliberate "retribalization").[18] But a major step forward may lie in Marshall Sahlins' proposal of a "familial mode of production" characteristic of tribal societies.[19] Accepting the Marxist concept of mode of production, he presents a global analysis of a mode under which the production base is the family household, but in which status and access to power is, however, subject to relations of production in the form of "counteracting institutions such as kinship, or chieftainship."[20] This, of course, represents a major modification of any traditional Marxist scheme, but our data now go far beyond what Marx and Engels had at their disposal. In our present context, Sahlins' proposal offers a twofold advantage. First, it has real potential, which the "primitive commune" never offered, for treating premonarchic Israel as a "mode of production." Second, the questions from the side of women's studies can hardly continue to be neglected when the focus is on the family household; as he says: "Families are *constituted* for production primarily by the sexual division of labor."[21]

Mode of production in monarchic Israel. There is an extensive literature on the Asiatic/tributary mode of production,[22] but views of the systemic location of women in it are conspicuous by their near-absence. This is in part a result of the ambiguity over the Asiatic mode. Though he had himself contributed to the development of its theory, Engels ignored it in his treatment of women and the family.[23] The only significant points I have found are the following. Based mainly on study of early Chinese society, Wittfogel correlates the shift from primitive commune to the Asiatic mode with shifts (1) from mother- to father-right (a "patriarchal system of kinship"), (2) from extensive (female-dominated) to intensive (male-dominated) agriculture, and (3) from communal to individual ownership. The move to the small family with strong patriarchal control (the Confucian ideal) is strongly favored by the emerging state.[24] He further takes up the issue of polygamy in the Asiatic system: it is not a universal but a class phenomenon, a status symbol. In the extreme case of the ruling house, this leads to the phenomenon of the harem. Such accumulation of women, for sexual purposes, but also for "women's work" like textile production and food preparation, must be seen as systemic; in one society arguably close to the stage of development of early monarchic Israel, Wittfogel quotes a figure of 5 percent of all the women in the population being concentrated under the personal control of the ruler.[25]

Important as these few issues undoubtedly are, it is fair to say that existing literature on mode of production, to which women have scarcely been contributors,[26] issues scant invitation to feminism in general, or to feminist analysis of Israel's transition to monarchy in particular. The systems have tended to be defined in terms of men's work and activities, those of women being ancillary. The familial mode of production holds promise, but very much more is needed on the systemic roles of women in the tributary mode.

FROM SOCIAL-SCIENTIFIC TO LITERARY

Carol Meyers' methodological preamble, in *Discovering Eve*, to a description of the lives of women in premonarchic Israel begins with a critique of assumptions that have governed scholarship up to now. First, our approach has been too much defined by the Bible and the settings in which it has been studied. The biblical text is inevitably our primary resource, but it comes from a time so much later than that of the world it purports to depict that input from other directions, wherever it is available, needs to be used to the full. But biblical research has tended to be done in religious settings that have not been welcoming to interdisciplinary method. The potential contribution of archaeology has not been realized because "biblical archaeology" has been too defined by the scope and the concerns of the text, and comparative ethnology has hardly been exploited at all.

Second, the biblical text enshrines male bias, and the interpretive tradition we inherit has typically gone even beyond the text in this respect. Feminists have begun to name and counteract this bias. But they have not, for the most part, exploited the social sciences in an adequate way, and have tended to replace one set of anachronisms with another. The term *patriarchy* is used loosely, out of its anthropological context. Twentieth-century assumptions and concerns are illegitimately projected into the past, as when large family size is taken necessarily to indicate the oppression of women. The social sciences themselves are only beginning to respond to feminist questioning by developing more subtle approaches. Analyses of power based on a dualistic model of public versus private arenas may fail to notice extensive, systemic, but nonovert female power. A " 'myth' of male control" may be "superimposed on a . . . functional nonhierarchy,"[27] in which women's domination of informal interaction fully counteracts formal disadvantage, and men's and women's *experience* is of mutual dependence. This is especially the case in societies that are heavily domestic oriented. Male dominance has proved to be an elusive concept in anthropological research; Meyers notes Whyte's "surprising" finding that no "*pattern* of universal dominance" can be found cross-culturally—only discrete areas where women's relative status must be measured case by case.[28] The question must always be asked, How did women *experience* what seems to us oppression?

Most of Meyers' book deals with the evidence from the new archaeology and from comparative ethnology for building a picture of premonarchic Israel and women's roles in it. She largely accepts Gottwald's
account of "liberated Israel," and concludes that women to a considerable
extent shared in the liberation, enjoying a substantial degree of equality.

Premonarchic Israel was an intensive agriculture society, but one
further defined by its pioneering situation, in which agriculture required
the opening up of new and difficult land. Although comparative studies
tend to correlate intensive agriculture with a diminished status for women,
the pioneer location counteracts this.[29] Division of labor does not entail
any undervaluing of women's work, because a marginal society depends
critically on the labor of everyone. In ancient Israel, Meyers sees forest
clearing, cistern cutting, and terrace building as likely exclusively male
activities,[30] but women's work in such areas as food production and
processing, or textile work, as no less important and valued. Most misleading of all would be to take family size as an indicator of oppression,
because there was an urgent need for rapid population growth.[31]

Israel's basic productive unit was the household, which was quasi-
independent within tribe and clan, and was the most immediate context
for individual activity.[32] Meyers notes[33] that only domestic, not public,
buildings are found in Israelite Iron Age settlements, and that fortifications
are extremely rare. She surmises that the compound of two or three linked
conjugal units, widely unearthed by archaeologists, is the biblical *bêt 'āb*,
and housed a kin-group.[34] Almost all subsistence needs could be supplied
within such a unit,[35] where women would perform a variety of pivotal
tasks, such as cooking (which entails control over the assignment of limited
food resources) and textile crafts, the socialization and education of children, the adjudication of family and marriage law, family-based religion
(cf. the ubiquitous female figurines), music and dance.[36]

The value of this stress on the household is to disarm typologies based
on the relative value of public and private spheres of activity. The admitted
male domination of most public arenas becomes less significant if the
balance in Israel was toward the private rather than the public. Women's
informal "power" counterbalances male "authority."[37]

Meyers' picture of the change wrought by the transition to monarchy
is two-sided. In the epilogue,[38] she sees male dominance in Israel as the
legacy of the monarchic period, and offers cross-cultural evidence on how
females lose status with state formation. Centralization, based on exclusively male hierarchical structures, forces peasants into wage labor, leads
to a decline in household-based economy, and jeopardizes old kinship
structures. One consequence of this process is the appearance of a nonpro-

ductive type of urban woman. But elsewhere she suggests, again with cross-cultural evidence, that the changes will have had little impact on the day-to-day life of those women—the great majority—who lived in villages.[39]

At an early stage of her analysis, Meyers dismisses the concept of mode of production, with reference to Engels, as outmodedly evolutionary.[40] Although this is understandable, it perhaps throws out the baby with the bathwater, for closer attention to the Marxist discussion would have been helpful in places. For example, when she assumes growing private property in monarchic times, she shows no awareness of the unimportance of private property in the tributary mode.[41] More generally, the anthropological literature upon which she draws itself suffers from the lack of a mode of production framework, tending to be divided between typologies stressing forces of production and ones stressing relationships of production; in other words, she is able to refer to studies that correlate the role of women on the one hand with level of sociopolitical development (rule by elders, chieftains, kings, etc.), on the other with productive technologies (hunting and gathering, horticulture, pastoralism, agriculture), but rarely both at once. In fact, Meyers accepts the term "mode of production" in Sahlins' "familial" form, even referring to her own equivalent proposal as "the household mode of production."[42] Indeed her analysis constitutes, to my mind, a major step in the application of Sahlins to Israel. I wonder, though, if she does not make the household *too* dominant, to the weakening of other levels, such as communal production, or Israel's political unity. Even if it was the center, so that the terms "familial" and "household" are apt ones to characterize the entire system, Israel consisted of more than households. As Sahlins says, " 'Familial mode of production' is not synonymous with 'familial production,' " and again, "The organization of authority . . . stands against the organization of production."[43] It is not that Meyers neglects these other levels, but she does not deal adequately with their systemic impact on the household.[44]

Naomi Steinberg provides support for the view that women tended to lose legal status as a result of the coming of monarchy, and suggests that this trend would not leave village women unaffected.[45] Her thesis is that Israel's monarchy sought to bolster up the nuclear family at the expense of larger social units (kinship groups). This they did by legislation, some of which is to be found in Deuteronomy 19–25, in which family law is central. Steinberg produces cross-cultural evidence, notably from medieval Europe,[46] that state systems, as part of their program of political centralization, seek to bolster the nuclear family, which poses no political threat, while suppressing larger social groupings, which might become alternative centers of political power. The sharp point that Steinberg makes, in feminist perspective, is that the laws in question are precisely ones that have often been regarded as prowoman.[47] Paradoxically, the status of the nuclear family is bolstered by taking power away from "heads of families" (i.e., *bêt 'ābôt*); the authority traditionally exercised by the *paterfamilias* is handed over to an extrafamilial judiciary (elders). Steinberg refers to the state's "both using and subverting existing . . . structures."[48] The effect is that both women and men are under tighter control. Finally, she notes that such laws widen the distance between ruling and ruled groups; the ruling groups are much less subject to them in practice. As particularly this last point indicates, Steinberg's conceptual framework is, though she does not use the term, very compatible with the mode of production approach.[49]

Roughly in the middle of her socio-historic treatment, Meyers turns her attention to the reading of a text, Genesis 2–3, with one chapter on the text as a whole, and another on 3:16. She reads this text "as a reflection of the particular conditions of highland life," which she has been describing.[50] She accepts many of the points made by Phyllis Trible in her classic treatment,[51] such as that the term *'ādām* is generic, not gender specific, and that no subordination is implied in the term "helper" (2:18, 20).[52] Meyers' extended treatment of 3:16, than which "perhaps no single verse of scripture is more troublesome, from a feminist perspective,"[53] issues in a translation of the first couplet:

> I will greatly increase your toil and your pregnancies;
> (Along) with travail shall you beget children,[54]

which exactly reflects her view of the highland woman's contributing to her group both by a full share of work and by numerous pregnancies. Read in its historical setting, therefore, and in a framework that is certainly not without tragic dimensions for *both* sexes (life *is* hard!), J's view of female existence is as positive as possible.

Meyers' literary treatment is problematic at several levels. It is not to my purpose here to dwell on specific literary techniques,[55] or even on the text's general meaning.[56] I have two main issues. First, Meyers uses the Genesis text to support views already developed on extratextual grounds, ascribing to it a primarily referential function. Second, if a contrast is to be established between premonarchic and monarchic Israel, this text (and J as a whole) is on all kinds of grounds likely to lie on the monarchic side. I see no reason to question the usual view that J is ideologically related to royal Jerusalem. The Eden tradition has known royal connections (Ezekiel 28), including the very idea of a garden (cf. the Persian royal "paradise").[57]

And Meyers herself links Genesis 3 to "the speculative type of wisdom" that is usually thought to flourish under royal patronage.[58] Nor can I get myself to believe that such a story—one that sees Yahweh as granting them such a second-best existence—would have developed among Gottwald's early Israelites. What is lacking here, in terms of mode of production, is a theory of *literary* production. A reading of any text needs to propose a model for its production, distribution, and consumption (including its preservation—*re*production—under circumstances different from those of its composition).

FROM LITERARY TO SOCIAL-SCIENTIFIC

What Mieke Bal is about, in *Death and Dissymmetry*, is at first sight so different from our discussion to this point that my use of it needs some justification. Bal aims, through a new reading of the book of Judges, to critique the entire structure of biblical studies as now constituted. The dominant approach to Judges, she claims, privileges history over anthropology, the public over the private domain (which implies men's affairs over women's), and, at the deepest level, culture over nature and change over continuity. Over against the imposed "coherence" of this consensus, Bal sets out to delineate a "countercoherence," the most basic aspect of which is that the conflict that shapes the book is at the level of domestic, not national, politics; a conflict, namely, between "virilocal" and "patrilocal" marriage (respectively, the wife moving to the husband's house and the husband moving to the father-in-law's house; I shall return shortly to the terminology). She pays particular attention to the story traditionally called "the Levite's concubine" (chap. 19); this is itself polemical, because the "coherence" has privileged the "judges" part of the book, chaps. 2–16, reducing chaps. 17–21 to the status of an appendix.

To argue her case, Bal draws upon the most varied areas, not only literary criticism (narratology and speech-act theory prominently), but also film-theory, anthropology, psychoanalysis, and others. This is to demonstrate further the thesis stated in *Murder and Difference*, that women's studies not only are inherently interdisciplinary, but offer the most consistently interdisciplinary approach in current intellectual life.[59] She advocates a practice that sits uneasily on the boundary of biblical studies as currently established, trying to be a voice both from within and from without.[60]

For Bal, the text of Judges evokes a historical process out of which, we may therefore hypothesize, the text itself was generated. It is a historical process to which the lives of women are central, "a social revolution that concerns the institution of marriage, hence, the relations between men and women, sexuality, procreation, and kinship."[61] It is the shift in Israel from what traditional anthropology calls "matrilocal" to "patrilocal" marriage. Bal's first move, as the great analyst of "focalization" in narrative, is to redefine these terms because they focalize inappropriately, implying the point of view of the child of a marriage, who lives in the native place of either its father or its mother. Bal's usage, "patrilocal" and "virilocal" (exactly reversing the meaning of "patrilocal"), makes the woman the focalizer—does she reside in her father's or her husband's house? The literary shape of the book and the extremity of the domestic violence it depicts are best accounted for on the hypothesis that this, rather than anything overtly "political," was the historical process that generated it. For the domestic *is* the political.

But why do I choose to link this historical process with the transition to monarchy? Bal has barely anything to say about monarchy,[62] but I would point to various clues in the text of Judges. The book closely anticipates the arrival of monarchy, and its closing chapters, so key for Bal, are under the sign of "there was no king in Israel." Israel's unhappy first step in monarchy happens around characters, Gideon and Abimelech, who are also much implicated in Bal's treatment of marriage.[63] Further support can be derived from Steinberg's suggestion that the monarchy enacted legislation in behalf of the nuclear, as against the extended, family.[64]

But because Bal is not clear on this issue, it is useful to be able to turn to the work of Regina Schwartz,[65] which one may read almost as a sequel to *Death and Dissymmetry*, carrying a similar agenda forward into the books that follow Judges. The powerful compulsion that biblical scholarship feels to present Israel's history, including the transition to monarchy, as a smooth development she sees as a legacy of its origin in a Germany that needed to view its nationhood in just the same way.[66] The biblical narrative, she claims (though not without being aware of how her own assumptions may be at work), is more compatible with Foucault's view of history as "rupture." The transition to monarchy is presented as a series of ruptures, cuttings, rendings; and references to Israel's becoming "like the nations" indicate nostalgia for what it was before.[67] To a remarkable extent, the transition is processed literarily through sexual scenes. As in the exchange systems discussed by Lévi-Strauss, because sexual rights over women confer political power, so can that power be expressed in terms of sexual rights over women: Absalom's taking of David's harem is a claim to power.[68]

But Schwartz concentrates on David and three of his wives: Abigail, Michal, and Bathsheba. Each is married to someone else,[69] so that there is a male as well as a female victim—Nabal, Paltiel, Uriah—over whom

David gains power; two die, the other goes grieving home. The three episodes form a series, the consequences in each case underlining the stories' being paradigms of political power. In the case of Abigail, no apparent guilt falls on David, and at least one child ensues (2 Sam 3:3). His guilt in the Michal episode is not stressed, but Michal is childless, whereas his extreme guilt over Bathsheba leads to the death of her child. And there is play also on political and sexual "folly." At the start of the series, Nabal (whose name means "fool") denies David's power—"Who is David?" (1 Sam 25:10). But at its end, the text seems to suggest, David becomes himself a *nabal* (because in the scene immediately following the Bathsheba story, Amnon is precisely so characterized for a similar act [2 Sam 13:13]).[70] This last sequence, it seems, rather than merely signaling another shift in power relations, calls monarchy as such in question. David's adultery is set off against Uriah's faithfulness to God in following traditional ways (including sexual customs), and Tamar's characterization of rape as something "not done in Israel" signals nostalgia for these (imagined) premonarchic sexual arrangements.[71]

Viewed as a proposal for methodological integration, Bal's treatment raises, at first sight, severe problems. She wishes "to contribute something new" to biblical studies "on *its* own terms," and her concern for the "sociocultural background" of Judges is explicit.[72] But she attempts to deal with the history of early Israel without regard for the archaeological literature or for current models (notably those of Gottwald and his associates). To point to a background of "nomadism" for early Israel, or to reach back to Morgenstern as an authority on its kinship arrangements,[73] is to locate herself so far outside of current debate as to risk being ignored not only on these issues, but also on others where her potential contribution is immense.

Once this major complaint has been registered, however, there is much more to be said, and I would suggest that social-scientific researchers cannot afford to ignore such work even on their own ground. The findings of Bal and Schwartz are, in the first instance, the results of *literary* analysis, but of a kind that, because of its intense concern with the historicity of the text, cannot fail to compass historical and social-scientific concerns, and often highlights these in startling new ways. Bal's anthropology of *beena* marriage, or of nomadism, may be liable to critique, but who has thought to bring the anthropology of sacrifice so heavily to bear on Judges?[74] This is, however, an anthropology that enjoys no privileged autonomy in Bal's radically interdisciplinary framework; its findings are to be looked at and challenged from the perspective of other disciplines, notably psychology.[75] Even the redefining of "patrilocal" invites anthropologists to ask the question of whose point of view their terminology enshrines. To take a specific issue, can we, in view of the mass of sections of Judges that Bal has been able to analyze in matrilocal terms, go on simply assuming that early Israel's kinship was "patri-" across the board?[76] Her literary findings demand social-scientific accounting.

Though neither Bal nor Schwartz makes reference to "mode of production" or offers a specific theory of literary production for the texts they read, their whole theoretical background brings them close to the assumptions of such an approach. Reading the Bible as a site of *our* ideological struggles inevitably exposes the ideological struggles of which it is itself a product.[77]

It is a commonplace of Marxist theory that the transition from one mode of production to another is fired by systemic contradictions in the old mode (rather than by accidental historical causes). Israel's transition to monarchy is almost always explained as first of all a response to an external threat (Philistine aggression), though Gottwald has begun seriously to explore the internal contradiction option.[78] But if, as Bal and Schwartz insist, the sexual and the political are not separate spheres, a contradiction within the marriage customs of early Israel may be part of a constellation of causes of a shift in mode of production. "Indeed, the political chaos may even be the consequence of the social revolution."[79] Israel gets a king because its men resent the relative equality of women! Such a possibility, which does not occur to the authors of social-scientific models,[80] emerges in a quite direct way out of literary treatments such as those of Bal and Schwartz. May it be that we are dealing here with an issue, the relatedness of the contradictions within two parts of a system, which *only* literature can adequately process? The question implies just the sort of theory of literary production on which Marxism insists, a theory that Gottwald has adumbrated.[81]

CONCLUSION

The concept of mode of production was proposed in an attempt to create a system of the utmost comprehensiveness, to account for human sociopolitical history in its entirety (and, of course, not only to understand history, but to change it). On account of the particulars of its own historicity, though, this system has become exclusionary in its turn. It has been deficient in its treatment of women's issues, but there is no intrinsic necessity for it to continue so. It has not always been sophisticated in its treatment of literature and the arts, but shows signs of becoming more so, and it has the major advantage of having always insisted that these are integral parts of human production, rather than epiphenomena. I believe that it has the vibrancy to continue as an important matrix for debate about the Bible, if it opens itself to the claims it has excluded.

Social-scientific research on ancient Israel has made enormous recent gains and has become prolific in generating integrative proposals for the future of biblical studies. Its enormous potential for feminist input is beginning to be exploited in work like that of Meyers and Steinberg.[82] By far its major deficiency, in my view, is its lack of access to sophisticated views of literature. With the notable exception of Gottwald, none of the social-scientific treatments I have mentioned—even ones that aspire to include the study of biblical literature in their integrative schemes—makes reference to a single important (nonbiblical) literary theorist.

Literary research on the Hebrew Bible has produced paradoxical results, from the perspective of the need for methodological integration. In my view, literary criticism has recently become the strongest and most comprehensive discipline, theoretically, among the humanities and social sciences, and this is due as much as anything to the massive impact of feminist criticism. But "the Bible as literature" has often been "a critical escape"[83] rather than an impulse to methodological debate; even its many feminist practitioners have been slow to draw on the resources of feminist literary criticism in general. And it has tended to be out of touch with social-scientific biblical research.

The bottom line is that we see now a convergence, from different biblical subdisciplines, on the need for methodological integration and mutual critique, with critical input from groups whom earlier "integrations" were designed to exclude. It is this trend that makes biblical studies today so intensely exciting. In establishing it, few have played so notable a role as Norman Gottwald.[84]

19   *Interpretation*

Reading, Abduction, Metaphor

Bruce J. Malina

Since the appearance of Gottwald's *The Tribes of Yahweh* ten years ago, the practitioners of the social-scientific criticism[1] of the New Testament have likewise become quite self-conscious and self-critical in their labors. Most have gotten beyond the subjective/objective dichotomy generally used to assess the procedures and results of scholarship. They are sensitive to the realization that interpretations invariably involve implicit theoretical models rooted in the social structures of interpreters.[2] Further, they have moved beyond the academic prima-donna-hood or the enduring mentor-student roles characteristic of the guild since its European structure was imported. Instead, collaboration and team effort are the rule.[3] And the point of the whole exegetical task is, once again, enjoyment, play, creativity, and insight supported by one's colleagues.[4] As Csikszentmihalyi[5] has indicated, the proper response to such an approach is "I feel so enthusiastic about," "I find it enjoyable to discover that," "Isn't it surprising that?"

WHAT IS BIBLICAL INTERPRETATION? OR "THANKS, NORM, FOR THE SCENARIOS OF ANCIENT ISRAEL"

Social science criticism of the Bible is essentially concerned with biblical interpretation, that is, finding out what some ancient author said and meant to say to his (rarely: her) initial audience. The focus here is on persons envisioned in scenarios—notably those spoken of in texts, yet including the authors and first hearers of those texts. Biblical interpretation consists in an interpreter's diligent application of those mental functions

253

that serve to select, shape, and adapt some set of real-world environments that might match the scenarios depicted in texts.[6] The reason for this is that biblical interpretation is rooted in reading, and reading entails the reader's bringing a set of scenarios about the world—internal, external and experiential—and allowing an author to rearrange those scenarios by means of textual communication.

The act of reading further involves the same two assumptions posited by the social sciences in general—that human beings mean and that this meaning can be understood by others (whether translation is possible is quite another question).[7] Interpretive understanding involves making sense out of what people say and do (said and did). The problem is how to perceive the sense people want to impart. If sense-making behavior can generally be said to reside in mutually shared patterns, then the problem is how to discern and understand such patterns.

In other words, there is essentially only one approach to the Bible, and that approach is rooted in sense perception and a reader's socialization. One must be trained to hear sounds (not noise) or read patterns (not squiggles). What occurs as one reads or hears depends largely on the reader's and/or listener's interests.[8] For every text, whether written or spoken, evokes what can never be put into a text by any writer or speaker, and this is the commonsense, socially shared, understanding of the reader.[9] It is precisely and specifically that which can never be put into a text by any author that exercises the skill and discipline of the alien interpreter, scholarly and nonscholarly. Interpretation is in fact supplying what is lacking in a text so that the text might mean something. Authors normally rely upon the commonsense, socially maintained understandings that they share with their audiences. Yet, for both professional and nonprofessional biblical interpretation, one might ask, From where does the reader derive his or her sense or understanding held in common with the author? Must the reader have this sense "in common" with the author? With whom does the reader converse?

Rabinow has noted: "But conversation, between individuals or cultures, is only possible within contexts shaped and constrained by historical, cultural and political relations and the only partially discursive social practices that constitute them."[10] It is precisely the historical, cultural, and political relations along with discursive social practices that constitute, in large measure, the social system of a group. Thought, for example, including philosophical ideas, is likewise a historically locatable set of social practices. It is the social system that constitutes common sense.

Because no author can fully control the reader's commonsense understanding of how the world works, no text can provide for a cognitive "uchronia" (a time frame embracing all time, much as "utopia" embraces all places). A reader's response to any text is in fact initially this common-sense understanding of how the world works, brought to the text to allow for some interaction. The goal of the social-scientific approach is to outfit the contemporary reader with scenarios that befit the alien texts that he or she seeks to understand. Scenarios are evoked in a reader's mind by means of words serving as signifiers. The original signifiers of the original authors obviously could call up the whole and full set of signifieds that constituted the social system of the first audiences. However, when the text is removed from its native social system and placed into the hands of readers who no longer share the signifieds available to the author and original audience, the signifiers are set free to be attached to whatever a reader seeks to attach them to. This separation of signifiers from the original social system of signifieds points to the text taking on the new life its later non-native readers wish to attribute to it.[11]

Social science interpretations of the New Testament are obviously addressed to a limited audience interested in reading about alien persons and their noncontemporary mode of life. As a rule, they are not directed to persons interested in learning to live a first-century, Mediterranean mode of life. Yet there are those who would seek direct contemporary relevance from such interpretations, although they do not specify the quality of that relevance. Furthermore, biblical scholars adopt one of two ultimate stances. The one involves the scholarly reader as interpreter; the reader wants to understand what the author says and means. Some would take this stage a step further and play the historian; the reader wants to tell a story on the basis of what she or he reads, yet the story nearly always has contemporary relevance.[12] The result, then, is four major categories of scholars.[13] Obviously, the scholarship of the Synoptics and John belongs under "irrelevant history," as would any non-U.S. story.

	Relevant	Nonrelevant
Textual Interpretation	Scriptural exegesis; ancients as moderns in faith body	social-scientific exegesis
Storytelling	Church history; Israeli history; ancients as moderns	irrelevant history

What is there to test the validity of the social scenarios reconstructed by interpreters? The consensual common sense of scholars? We know that "those domains that cannot be analyzed or refuted, and yet are directly central to hierarchy, should not be regarded as innocent or irrelevant. We

know that one of the most common tactics of an elite group is to refuse to
discuss—to label as vulgar or uninteresting—issues that are uncomfortable
for them."[14] We also know that to inquire into the quality or range of
structures and patterns of various types of writing in themselves is to
question the social structures realized by these modes of writings! These
structures mediate what Rabinow calls "the politics of interpretation in the
academy, . . . the conditions under which people are hired, given tenure,
published, awarded grants and feted."[15] Do these observations point to
why social-scientific criticism has so few adherents among scholars, male
and female, in Euro-American institutions?

CIRCULAR ARGUMENTS AND ABDUCTION, OR "THANKS, NORM, FOR SHARING YOUR HUNCHES WITH US"

The main criticisms against the use of the social sciences in biblical
interpretation have taken the form of "psychobabble" and "ontogurgle."
Psychobabble tells us of the psychological state of the critic: "I fear that,"
"There is danger that," "Unconvincing," and the like. Some psychobab-
blers project their feelings on social science models, labeling them with the
nasty name "cookie cutters." Ontogurgle, on the other hand, looks to the
ontological truth claims affirmed or dismissed by users of social science
methods. For the "unconvinced" and their "cookie cutter" perceptions, I
consider circular argument and abduction. For those who know our use
of certain cross-cultural models is "naive," "backward," and downright
"wrong," I consider the metaphoric nature of curiosity and fear
preferences.

Circular arguments. Social-scientific method begins with some problem
known only to the interpreter and his or her friends. The problem usually
arises from some new information relative to life in the Eastern Mediterranean. The question is, Did such behavior exist in the first century (e.g.,
concern for the Evil Eye, magical practices, lying and deception, modes of
child caring)? Do the persons described in the Bible give witness to it? To
deal with this problem, a model or scenario is postulated, based on the
actual behavior of real people.[16] Passages, that is, segments of texts, are
then cited to embody the model or scenario—to serve as illustrations of
some scenario or features of a scenario under development. In this respect,
such text-segments are not unlike segments of buildings found by archaeological excavation. When one finds a room in the location of the traditional women's quarters, it is not considered specious to say that women
and men were kept apart in Greek or Mediterranean society. The same
holds for the women's quarters pointed out in museum presentations of

bedouin tents. Rather, the model of gender separation serves to explain the floor plan of the building or tent in question, which in turn sheds light on the model of gender separation. In effect, the text-segments, like the floor plan of an ancient ruin or a recent tent, are samples, recording and reporting behavior that relates to the scenario in question. In effect, the scenario serves to help imagine what is going on in the description provided by the sample, and the sample serves to clarify further the dimensions of the scenario. The argument is circular. But it seems that is the way humans proceed in some thought processes:

> Experience with modern systems for processing information has taught us that such circles need not be vicious. Minsky and Papert (1972) remark in this connection that it is quite common in computer programs—and presumably in thought processes—for two different procedures to use each other as subprocedures. When the system is forming a percept, object-forming procedures can call on shape-recognizing procedures as subprocedures; when it pays attention to shape, shape-recognizing procedures can call on object-forming procedures as subprocedures. The assumption that one set of procedures must in every case precede the other imposes a rigid and unnecessary constraint on the complexity of our hypotheses about object perception.[17]

A similar argument emerges from cybernetic systems:

> With the advent of cybernetics we now have a theory of adaptive machines, which modify their design constraints depending on the other three sets of conditions.[18] This is a step from machines that execute to machines that also control—from dumb to intelligent machines.
>
> The internal dynamic of any machine replays for subsystems the general theme: other subsystems constitute the situation of each subsystem and the performance of each subsystem is analyzed and evaluated in the same terms as the performance of the whole machine.
>
> Increasingly biologists have been employing, more or less consciously, the metaphor "machine" in the analysis of living systems as well as in the design of prosthetic subsystems and simulacra. In psychology the use of the metaphor has been equally widespread, though largely unconscious or denied.[19]

Examples of such a procedure in psychology or in the area of intelligence analysis entail "postulating the disposition of particularly constrained personalities to differential performances in specified situations."[20]

The perception of a "circular argument" or "vicious circle" requires the critic to espouse a linear approach to thinking in which the return to origin is viewed as unaffected by what happened while the argument was developing. It is as though an initial equilibrium goes to disequilibrium and returns to the identical equilibrium. The fact is, a disturbed equilibrium is never the same when it is restored. Something new and different is inevitably involved.

Of course it may be objected that we are back inevitably to the hoary "free will vs. determinism" riddle, which, like "nurture vs. nature," remains a major philosophic conundrum. The most acceptable modern position is that this is an operationally meaningless dichotomy; that reality lies somewhere between these poles, depending upon the circumstances and the participants.[21]

Historians wishing to argue for or against some scenario ask for validation or verification in the form of a passage describing the behavior. Yet the existence of such a passage does not really validate anything yet. The passage in question surely serves to witness to the existence of some value, assessment, behavior, or structure. Yet to interpret the value, assessment, behavior, or structure in question, one must still provide a scenario. Unless one takes the effort to develop cross-cultural, comparative scenarios, the witnesses can only be heard in terms of one's own operative presuppositions and the scenarios that provide those presuppositions.

Induction. Usually, underlying the general critique of using models based on contemporary Mediterranean behavior for antiquity is the historian's suspicion of some anachronistic and ethnocentric model afoot. We are asked instead to adhere to the historical-critical method and its "inductive" path. The inductive models in question, however, always remain implicit and beyond discussion.[22] Such induction is quite questionable and has to evoke suspicion, because without some explicit control, what is perceived by the historian must necessarily be similar to the historian's present experience. The outcome has to be inductively built models that are eminently relevant to and suspiciously like the historian's present experience.[23] I think what needs to be proved is that induction *in vacuo* is possible. If historians are not aware of their own culture's value preferences, of their own culture's values relative to self, others, nature, time, space, gods, how can historians keep these out of their inductions? Nineteenth-century historians had the same sources as twentieth-century historians, and nineteenth-century historians too insisted they were proceeding inductively. But the picture of antiquity that they developed using such induction turned out to be so much like their nineteenth-century contemporaries, their problems and their concerns.

On the other hand, if people actually behave and think in a certain way today, and there is no indication of radical cultural change in their history, then they surely could have behaved and thought quite similarly in the past as well. Such an assumption is far more secure for a given historical scenario than one based on possibility. Starting with actual, customary behavior in a localized time and place makes for better quality history than using untestable scenarios or inductively constructed scenarios of the possible. These latter are very often simply not testable or verifiable. One must simply give loyalty to and trust the imagination (i.e., authority) of some historian, who develops the scenario for his or her own purposes. If there is no evidence in the world of human experience available on the planet today that people actually behave the way some historian claims they do, naturally there is every reason to doubt what the historian claims. That a given historian's models might be valuable conceptually, as ideas, is good. They fulfill the requirements of the possible. For the possible is simply what is conceivable in a given culture, what does not contain inherent contradictions in ideas perceivable within a given society. The problem with conceptual models of the possible is that such models do not account for bumblebees. Historians often believe they are in pursuit of the unique in a given time and place. It is conceivable that certain behaviors are structurally totally and entirely unique. Yet without a background of similarity or commonality, the unique could not be perceived at all.

Reasons for accepting a hypothetical reconstruction would be the extent to which available data fill out the reconstruction in question. Most historians are concerned only with analyzing reasons for accepting a hypothetical reconstruction. They begin with the reconstruction as given. They omit the vital question as to how the hypothetical reconstructions are "caught" in the first place.

In this regard, parallel to the case of the normal circular argument, there is that of the normal oscillating method, a sort of spiraling circular deductive induction and inductive deduction by means of which hypothetical reconstructions are developed. Here I refer to Peirce's abduction. Scheff calls abduction a "kind of shuttling back and forth between deductive and inductive methods."[24] Fann explains:

> Peirce wished to show that reasoning *towards* a hypothesis is of a different kind than reasoning *from* a hypothesis. He realized that the former "has usually been considered either as not reasoning at all, or as a species of Induction." But, he said: "I don't think the adoption of a hypothesis on probation can properly be called induction; and yet it is reasoning."[25]

Reilly, in turn, notes:

> In opposition to Hume, Peirce emphasizes that our knowledge is not derived from experience alone. In fact "every item of science came originally from conjecture, which has only been pruned down by experience. . . . The entire matter of our works of solid science consists of conjectures checked by experience."[26]

Abduction is reasoning that begins with data and moves toward hypothesis with the introduction of a new idea. It is reasoning toward a hypothesis; it deals with how a hypothesis is adopted on probation, with reasons for suggesting a hypothesis in the first place. There are reasons for suggesting a hypothesis initially as a plausible type of hypothesis. The verification process makes known the approximation to reality of the suggested hypothesis. In turn, the hypothesis may render the observed facts necessary, or at least highly probable. Abduction then entails drawing up a hypothesis by explaining a curious circumstance by supposing it to be a case of a general rule. In the process, facts not capable of direct observation are inferred.[27]

> The scientific explanation suggested by abduction has two characteristics that must be pointed out now (along with others that will be dealt with later): 1.) an explanatory hypothesis renders the observed facts necessary or highly probable; 2.) an explanatory hypothesis deals with facts which are different from the facts to be explained, and are frequently not capable of being directly observed.[28]

For hypotheses are of three types: factually not observed but observable, factually not observable (history), and factually and theoretically not observable. A hypothesis would be explained by supposing that it was a case of a certain general rule, and thereupon adopting that supposition. This sort of inference is called "making a hypothesis." When we adopt a certain hypothesis, it is not solely because it will explain the observed facts, but also because the contrary hypothesis would probably lead to results contrary to those observed.[29]

Such abduction is behind choosing the traditional peoples of the Circum-Mediterranean as source of scenarios for New Testament interpretation, rather than the Circum-Baltic or the imagination of the historian of ideas. And circular argumentation is what fleshes out the scenario to allow for intelligible, historically sensitive reading.

THE BASES FOR INTERPRETATION, OR "THANKS, NORM, FOR STICKING WITH THE PRAGMATIC AND PRACTICAL ASPECTS OF LIFE"

There are those who are suspicious of the social-scientific approach to biblical interpretation because, they say, it lacks a philosophical basis. Should one look for the ontological bases of the present social-scientific approach to biblical interpretation, perhaps the best guide available is Bernard Lee.[30] He describes the foundation of the empirical approach at work here as the combination "of several traditions that are quite congenial to one another:

> —empiricism in the Jamesian and Whiteheadian senses, as further elaborated by William Dean and others to attend diligently to its historicist temper;

—the metaphorical tradition that insists upon the imaged and analogical ways we perceive, feel, know and communicate;
—and the hermeneutical tradition that recommends highly disciplined conversation as an image not only of interpreted experience, but of world-making."[31]

It is ways of perception, feeling, knowing, and communicating that often escape the attention of critics of social science approaches to the Bible. Richard Jung has recently argued that there are fundamentally four main metaphors of an individual living being employed to conceptualize life: mind, organism, machine, and template.[32]

Briefly, the metaphor of mind, for example, refers to the perception that human beings are essentially *like* mental beings, spiritual beings, that true humanity is located in the "soul"; thus the self, the "I," is immaterial. The metaphor of organism looks to human beings as essentially *like* biological organisms, with true humanity located in human life rooted in a living, organic, biological entity; thus the self, the "I," is a living organism. The metaphor of machine would see human beings as essentially *like* systems of energy, with true humanity located in homeostatic systems countering entropy perhaps largely by producing meaningful performances; thus the self, the "I," is an energy system. The metaphor of template refers to the perception that human beings assess what they are *like* essentially in terms of their relationship to other persons and/or in their situation within some institution; the "I" is the sum of its social roles.

Not only do these distinct metaphors conceptualize life in general, and human being in particular, they serve as basis for theoretical formulations and discourses about life. In fact, the four are merely (but powerfully) different matrixes for expressing different, necessary, and complementary epistemic attitudes. With an eye to the accompanying table, consider each in turn.

With the first metaphor, mind or soul, all phenomena of life can be treated as *dicta/scripta*, constituting texts to be interpreted (a meaningful configuration of language). The situated individual is conceived as a mind acting in a situation. The aggregate system is conceived as a sociological system that includes political and economic systems as well. The individual is a psychological system; the group is a sociopsychological system. The relation of the individual system and its situation is action, activity: meaning is assigned to this action as expression of the *intention* of the individual's mind. The main preoccupation urged upon members of society is with the innermost nature of human being. The main symbols of this preoccupation are the psyche or soul along with intellect and will, and the preferred philosophical approach is rationalism. Preferred academic disciplines—that is, sets of questions best answered—include theol-

PARADIGMATIC DISTINCTIONS	All of Life Is	Nature of Persons	Nature of Society	Nature of Reality	Philosophical Base	Basis of Behavior	Answers to Cause Type
Paradigm of Mind	A Text to be Interpreted	Psychological	Sociological	Mental with Objective Foundation	Rationalism	Reasons Free Choice	What? Why?=End? Material/Final: Configurations of Meaning
	(INTENTIONALITY)	(THEORY)					
Paradigm of Body	Behavior to be Observed in an Environment	Physiological	Ecological	Objective	Determinism	Causes	What? Why?=End? Material/Final: Configurations of Behaving Energy
	(POTENTIALITY)	(GENETIC CODE)					
Paradigm of Machine	Work to be Performed	Mechanical	Civilizational	Factual	Pragmatism	Forces and Factors	How? Why?=How? Efficient: Working Machines
	(DISPOSABILITY)	(BLUEPRINT)					
Paradigm of Configuration	Comportment to be Evaluated as to Fit in Game/Play	Enculturational (Roles, Position in Game, e.g.)	Cultural	Social with Objective Foundation	Relationalism	Symbols & Motives	Why?=Why? Formal: Role-Playing
	(APPROPRIATENESS)	(CULTURAL SCRIPT)					

ogy, philosophy, psychology, sociology, political science, economics. This metaphor answers especially to the question: "What?" What there is consists of configurations of meanings. Here "Why?" means end or goal— final cause, the reason or purpose for which something exists. This type of knowledge is Hellenistic, rooted in nature (nature here means those purposes that obviously exist apart from human ones), based on a desire to conform, to act in a certain way. The main orientation is final outcome as known in the mind of the artisan, that is, intentionality.

With the second metaphor, body, all phenomena of life can be treated as *acta/gesta*, that is, behavior to be observed. Such behavior is a configuration of energy exchanges with the environment. The situated individual is conceived as an organism living in an environment. The aggregate system is conceived as ecological system (= thermic web, i.e., temperature and food chain). The individual is a physiological system; the group is an eco-organismic system. The relation of the individual system and its situation is behavior: energy is assigned to this behavior as expression of the *potential* of the individual organism. The main preoccupation urged upon members of society is with the nature of living systems. The main symbol of this preoccupation is determinism, and the preferred philosophical approach is determinism. Preferred academic disciplines—sets of questions best answered—include biology, ethology, sociobiology, ecology, medicine. This metaphor answers especially to the question "What?" What there is consists of configurations of "behaving energy," that is, energy purposefully expending itself. Here "Why?" means end or goal—final cause. "Why?" refers to the reason or purpose for which something exists, excluding human ones, for nature is presumed to display an array of entities characterized by energy expended with a view to realizing some purpose. This knowledge is equally Hellenistic, with a focus on nonhuman nature, revitalized in the Renaissance.

With the third metaphor, machine, all phenomena of life can be treated as *facta*, that is, a piece of work done. Work means a configuration of energy exchanges by a particular system of external constraints. The situated individual is conceived as a machine (system of external constraints) at work. The aggregate system is conceived as civilization. The individual is a mechanical system; the group is a technologically productive system. The relation of the individual system and its situation is performance: energy is assigned to this performance as expression of the *disposition* of the individual machine (system of constraints). The main preoccupation urged upon members of society is with effectiveness. The main symbol of this preoccupation is concern for efficient performance, and the preferred philosophical approach is pragmatism. Preferred academic disciplines—

sets of questions best answered—include engineering, agronomy, medicine, domestication/behavior modification, cybernetics. In education, the phrase "behavior modification" describes the situation in which one person elicits a specific response from another. The first person acts as a control system for another person, and this other person is seen to act as an executing system from which the control system elicits specific performances. This metaphor answers especially to the question "How?" Answers to how consist of explanations of performance, working machines. Here "Why?" means how, that is, efficient cause, the reason by means of which something is produced, how to realize something. This is the orientation of technology; change is the process by means of which a producer produces a product.

With the fourth metaphor, template, all phenomena of life can be treated as *ficta*, that is, configurations of roles, statuses, and the like, in niches, to be evaluated as to fit. The template is a shaped cast, like a plaster cast. Whatever is put in the cast or template gets its shape from the surrounding and supporting walls. Thus Jung defines template as the meaning or form of an entity arising from the characteristics of its context. The situated individual is conceived as a configuration or system of internalized constraints, comporting itself. Here a configuration is an entity formed by and deriving from the characteristics of its context. The constraints internalized by the individual are the social system and the roles occupied in its distinctive networks. The aggregate system is conceived as culture. The individual is a configuration or cast system formed by context; the group is a cultural system. The relation of the individual system and its situation is comportment: adequacy is assigned to this comportment as expression of the *fit/adaptation* of the individual configuration. This individual configuration derives from the template formed by context. The main preoccupation urged upon members of society is with appropriate comportment, a sort of harmony that may be discordant at times. The main symbol of this preoccupation is concern for adequacy or fittingness, and the preferred philosophical approach is relationalism. Preferred academic disciplines—sets of questions best answered—include ritual and ceremonial study, symbolic analysis, culture as meaning system, as value system, and the like. What is analyzed is comportment, conduct, demeanor, air, bearing, and deportment in terms of statuses institutionalized by custom. This metaphor answers especially to the question "Why?" Answers to why consist of explanations of roles deriving from an entity's formation. Here "Why?" means why, that is, formal cause, essence, that which makes something to be what it is; the formative context shapes the role entity's play. This is knowledge based on curiosity and wonder as well as fear and anxiety.

Jung's point is that the ultimate reality of a living system is simply not directly knowable. According to the socially available options and our epistemic purposes, the kind of curiosity or fear that impels us, we choose an appropriate discourse to conceptualize and explain phenomena.

Not a few persons employ these metaphors as though they described actual reality.[33] The models are confused with the far richer real world objects and experiences they are meant to help clarify. The question is not, ontically, which discourse is true, but rather epistemically, which is appropriate to a particular concern. Each discourse is also semantically closed with respect to the others; hence it is senseless to argue from any determination made in one discourse against a determination made in another. Dichotomies consisting of focal metaphors of one closed system over against those of another—for example, body-soul, mind-matter—are vacuous.

When the metaphors take on ontological reality, the results are fascinating for a number of reasons. Jung[34] specifies these reasons in seven theses:

> *Thesis 1:* ". . . each metaphor is a basis of a coherent and distinct system of discourse, capable of conceptualizing most, if not all phenomena characteristic of life. The systems are mutually conceptually exclusive, in that an intrusion of terms from one system of discourse into another leads to conceptual confusion with severe theoretical consequences."
>
> *Thesis 2:* ". . . while the four metaphors seem to be contradictory if treated as an ontological statement about the nature of living systems, and thus the opposition of any two of them gives rise to an unsolvable paradox, the paradoxes are dissolved when each metaphor is treated as a different matrix for expressing different epistemic attitudes."
>
> *Thesis 3:* ". . . each metaphor does indeed reflect a different type of curiosity about living systems, and thus gives rise to a different system of discourse appropriate to a specific kind of epistemic concern. While each is valid and irreplaceable as a vehicle for a given epistemic attitude, all four are necessary for the conceptualization and explanation of all the phenomena of life that give rise to different types of legitimate curiosity."
>
> *Thesis 4:* ". . . each metaphor (and the theoretical formulation and type of discourse based on it) is complementary in the strict sense to each of the three other metaphors, theoretical formulations and types of discourse."
>
> *Thesis 5:* ". . . while employing a particular metaphor, an ontological commitment to its reality is psychologically inescapable, since the interpretation of experience occasioned by its employment gives rise to a compelling sense of empirical validation. During the period of such epistemic engagement, the three other metaphors appear as ontologically imaginary."
>
> *Thesis 6:* ". . . a different interpretation of life arises depending on the order in which the different metaphors are employed."

Thesis 7: ". . . in view of the previous theses, the task of the theory of life is not the reduction of the phenomena to any single metaphor, but the development of all into formal theories, and ultimately the development of a theory of transformations enabling us to move in an orderly fashion from one type of theory or discourse to any of the others."

CONCLUSION

The social-scientific approach to biblical interpretation today is rooted in a theory of reading best characterized as a scenario model. Further, the use of models, especially models from the Mediterranean region, requires circular reasoning with the use of abduction to form hypotheses about the relations and the behavior of the persons described in the texts. Finally, although such models might espouse one or another metaphor to explain human existence in first-century Palestine, they do not claim ontological status. They offer us, at varying degrees of abstraction, more or less adequate and fitting windows on the world of biblical authors and their audiences.

20 Bible and Liberation in South Africa in the 1980s

Toward an Antipopulist Reading of the Bible

Itumeleng J. Mosala

At the conclusion of my recent book, I pleaded for the need to "liberate the Bible so that the Bible may liberate [us]."[1] In South Africa, the impotence of the Bible in the process of liberating oppressed and exploited communities has increased as the decade of the 1980s drew to a close. Ironically, it was the mode of the centrality of the churches' and Christians' participation in social and political issues, rather than their inactivity, that accounted for this impoverishing of the Bible's role in the struggle for human liberation in South Africa. This essay seeks to explore the reasons why this happens and to propose a way out of this dilemma.

Norman Gottwald's work has revolutionized the study of the Bible at two very crucial levels. First, it has exploded the myth that biblical studies is an ideologically neutral activity. Serious biblical scholarship no longer admits the view that there is any approach to the Bible, academic or devotional, that has no political implications. The question is not whether one's scholarship has a political agenda; the question is, *Which* political agenda is inscribed in one's scholarship.

Second, Gottwald's approach to the study of the Bible has an abiding significance at the level of practical politics. By its seriousness as a theoretically well-grounded scholarship, his work exposes the sterility of purely existential immersion in social affairs on the part of biblically inspired persons. Nowhere is chairman Mao Tse-tung's call for the unity of theory and practice more relevant than in the biblical hermeneutics of liberation.

Theologies of liberation have undoubtedly invaded the world of theological studies irreversibly. They have not, however, dealt a death blow to

267

the ideological dynamics of dominant bourgeois Western male theology and the church that draws sustenance from this theology. In particular, they have been weak at the crucial point of the politics of how the Bible is read by different social classes, gender populations, races, and cultural groups.

The primary concern of my own biblical scholarship has thus been to indicate that although liberation theology, and in my situation black theology, has laudably espoused the liberation project of the poor and oppressed in the world, it has nevertheless operated with the hermeneutical assumptions of the dominant bourgeois biblical scholarship. I submit that this enslavement to dominant ideology does not make for liberation of the oppressed.

Recent developments in South Africa in the area of politics and of the church have confirmed my contention about the poverty of the biblical "readings" that draw their tools of struggle from the oppressive culture and ideology themselves. I will argue here that the reason Christian activists are experiencing a sense of paralysis has to do with the poverty of the biblical analysis underlying the resistance politics of the churches and of Christians in South Africa.

It is an open secret that since the unbanning by the apartheid regime on February 2, 1990, of the major political movements,[2] the churches and Christian activists have run out of things to do or say. The poverty of thought that characterizes their present silence was already evident in the populist tendencies of the Kairos Document.[3] By 1990, a debilitating anxiety seems to have come to grip theologians of the struggle whose basis of involvement had been only a sweeping political populism, and not an autonomous, though socially and politically grounded, theological praxis.

In July 1990, the Institute of Contextual Theology (ICT) held its Annual General Meeting in Marian hill, near Durban. This institute is the most politically active religious infrastructure outside of the South African Council of Churches. Its political credentials, broadly speaking, in the struggle against apartheid are internationally known and cannot be questioned. After the meeting, ICT published a report. The repeated complaints not only of its director, but also of many delegates, confirm the crisis of populist Christianity based on purely existentialist readings and applications of the Bible. They illustrate what became of a theology of liberation (in this case contextual theology) once the reactionary government forces of F. W. de Klerk had co-opted the populist idiom for their own brand of reform. The following quotations from the report illustrate the point. In the Foreword:

Now, however, the situation has changed. Liberation movements and other popular organisations have been unbanned. Nelson Mandela and other leaders have been released. Exiles are beginning to return. The Church finds itself challenged again. And it asks itself the question: What is our role now?

At its Annual General Meeting, the Institute for Contextual Theology (ICT) chose to focus its deliberations on the theme: The Role of Christians in the Present Political Crisis in South Africa. From the outset . . . the point was made that the urgency of this question is all the more acute in view of a tendency now among Christians and churches to stand back from the political situation and return to the sanctuary.[4]

"Return to the sanctuary" is presumably a veiled reference to Archbishop Desmond Tutu's statement that he will return to his proper role as a priest now that the political organizations have been unbanned. What this attack on the archbishop's position fails to grasp is that his perspective is perfectly commensurate with the biblical hermeneutics of his theology.[5]

The keynote speaker at the conference, the Reverend Dr. Beyers Naude, a longtime activist churchman against apartheid, continued in his address to reflect not only the sense of emptiness on the part of the churches, but also a lack of awareness of the source of this sudden missionlessness, namely, populist biblical readings for a populist politics of resistance.[6]

A biblical exegetical approach based purely on theological affirmations has long been a feature of South African theology. The advent of theologies of resistance, even in South Africa, has not altered the fundamental presuppositions of our biblical scholarship. The problems now being experienced by "contextual" theologians are not novel.

A historic National Conference of Churches held recently in Rustenburg, Transvaal, continued to labor under the same kind of hermeneutical assumptions that had underpinned a white theology of colonial enslavement, even as this conference sought to identify politically with perspectives of social change. Many years of sustained biblical scholarship have had no effect on such political populism, as is exhibited in a crucial part of the *Rustenburg Declaration*:

> The practice and the defence of apartheid as though it were biblical and theologically legitimated is an act of disobedience to God, a denial of the Gospel of Jesus Christ and a sin against our unity in the Holy Spirit.[7]

This way of articulating the liberatory discourses of the Bible does not do the cause of human liberation today real good. Although it expresses well the intentions of Christian communities committed to the liberation of oppressed peoples in the world, it does not liberate the real power of the liberatory messages of the Bible. That power resides in the choices that underscore the importance of struggle as the motor of history, and as the medium for interpreting what theologians have called the will of God in the world. For oppressed and exploited peoples, that discernment must of necessity happen in the context of struggles between classes, between races, between genders, and between generations.

The point is that there must be a way for those engaged in the struggle for human emancipation to express the intentions of the statement quoted above in a manner that reflects a critical, analytical, and liberatory reading of the Bible. The unliberating prejudices of the Bible must be exposed by a critical and liberatory hermeneutics of the Bible. A liberatory appropriation of the Bible is not the same thing as populist co-optation of the Bible in the name of the liberation struggle. Such a co-optation not only fails to liberate the Bible, it also does not free those for whose liberation the Bible is claimed to exist.

What is more, populist readings of the Bible lead to clumsy theology. The Rustenburg National Conference of Churches is led by such a populist reading to a clumsy statement of confession by those who benefited and continue to benefit from apartheid in South Africa, much to the excitement of the contextual theologians to whose biblical hermeneutics we must return shortly. In another significant part of the Confession section, the *Declaration* states:

> Some of us actively misused the Bible to justify apartheid, leading many to believe that it had the sanction of God. Later, we insisted that its motives were good even though its effects were evil. Our slowness to denounce apartheid as sin encouraged the Government to retain it.[8]

The difficulty is that this well-intentioned but theoretically misguided method of appropriating the Bible leaves victims of oppression and exploitation in the world undefended from parts of the Bible, such as the conquest texts, that have been the basis of their colonial enslavement. The preachers, theologians, and ministers of the Dutch Reformed Churches, the English-speaking churches, and the black churches of South Africa are unlikely to have returned from the Rustenburg Conference proclaiming an altered view of the origins of the undeniably imperialist and colonial strain in the conquest texts of the Hebrew Bible.

The *Rustenburg Declaration* isolates justice, church and state, peace, violence, and spirituality-mission-evangelism as key areas of affirmation that define the churches' role in the process of transformation in South Africa. On the key issue of peace it states:

> In both Old and New Testaments God's Peace or Shalom speaks of a comprehensive wholeness and rightness in all relationships, including those between

God and His people, between human and human and between humans and creation. In South Africa Peace and Shalom are shattered, not only by personal but also by social and structural sin. The consequences are devastating: racial alienation, mistrust, humiliation, exploitation of humans and the environment, privation of basic needs, denial of self worth. Perhaps most devastating has been the emergence of a social climate in which violence and death rather than co-operation and life have become the norm.[9]

This is an excellent theological affirmation. It is, however, one that cannot be more than a platitude for those who see in the Bible oppressors similar to those who pulverize their lives today. The real challenge of a biblical hermeneutics of liberation is to restore such an affirmation to a respectable position in the way in which oppressed and poor people read the Bible. My contention is that an antipopulist approach to the texts of the Bible is necessary if the potency of the Bible as a weapon of struggle for oppressed and exploited people is to be restored.

The tragedy, of course, is that those who rightly uphold the theological position represented by the above quotation cannot, if pressed, explain why it is that those who violate the theological principles of this affirmation can still claim to worship the God of the same Bible from which this splendid statement comes. What is more, they cannot tell why it is that such a theological position as the one they derive from this biblical affirmation has not and evidently cannot become the weapon of struggle in the hands of colonized and exploited black working-class masses.

Toward the end of a powerful review article on Michael Lipton's book, *Why Poor People Stay Poor: A Study of Urban Bias in World Development*, T. J. Byres makes this point about populism:

> The voice of populism, indeed: what Lenin called "a sentimental supra-class point of view" . . . is the rock upon which, for example, India's community development programme and Tanzania's *ujaama* programme foundered. Populism, when put into practice, can only be a blind alley. As an ideology, however, it continues to carry a powerful charge.[10]

In this review, Byres makes a biting critique of neo-populism. He points out that in relation to the underdevelopment of the Third World, populism typically abhors the poverty of the "people" and denounces macrosystems as the source of evil. It idealizes microsystems and nostalgically reimports old preindustrial forms in the place of what it regards as the indifference of the industrial culture. It nevertheless does not really disapprove of the benefits of the present forms of production, exchange, and distribution.

The seductive yet fundamental political impotence of neo-populism has been succinctly described by Cornel West:

> It represents an oppositional yet nostalgic form of radical plebeian humanism which is anti-bourgeois yet not anti-capitalist. To put it crudely, populists

tend to want modern liberal capitalist democracy without impersonal forms of bureaucracy, centralized modes of economic and political power, and alienating kinds of cultural practices in pluralistic urban centers.[11]

The "progressive" Christian movement in South Africa has certainly wandered into a blind alley. The apparent culprit? The political events of 1990, themselves dictated largely by an equally populist co-optation of this movement's slogans, metaphors, and indeed political practice by the de Klerk regime. The evidence from activist "contextual" theologians is unequivocal:

> In preparation for the way forward we need to identify a number of shocks for Christians. To give only a few examples: The South African Communist Party will be launched as a legal political party on 29 July. This follows shortly on the June 16 commemoration services. For the first time in many years these well attended services were a purely secular affair. This was in stark contrast to the past 14 years. Church services are half empty since the unbanning of people's organisations.[12]

"Contextual theologians" in South Africa never had their own theological reasons for being political. Politics made it necessary for theology to be involved in the struggle; theology did not have a politics of struggle demanding the participation of Christians. The upshot of this situation is that when politics (or shall we say, more accurately, politicians) no longer requires the support of theologians, the theologians are left with no internal reasons for being political.

Gonzalo Arroyo has exposed a sociology of theology and of the church that accounts for their contradictory behavior under different sociopolitical situations. His study was an analysis of the church in Chile before, during, and after the military coup of September 11, 1973. The central hypothesis of his study of events in Chile in that period:

> *Institutionalized churches and religions are integral parts of the overall socio-economic system; insofar as the latter system alters its political structures, the former tend to adapt themselves to the new circumstances.*[13]

This is a crucial proposition for understanding not only the churches and religion, but above all the origins, history, purposes, and nature of the Bible.

According to Arroyo, the churches in Chile supported ideologically contradictory social forces, depending on which one was in power. At one point class interest, at another populist opportunism dictated which ideological garb the churches decked themselves with.

In addition to its grand totalizing perspectives, populism is characterized by its mystical faith in the mass of the people, its lack of historical particularity, and its supraclass tendencies. For this reason, it takes something as momentous as a military coup, or an apparent turnabout in dominant politics such as the apartheid regime is displaying in South Africa, to create the necessary crisis for it. In this regard, Arroyo concludes his study with a perspective to which the hermeneutics of "contextual theology" in South Africa would do well to open itself:

> In conclusion, I would say that the coup has not been without consequences for Christians and the churches. It has brought them into a crisis, forcing them to take a stand and to make political choices that are irrevocable in the accelerated flow of history. Over and above their personal involvement in the revolutionary struggle, the political task of socialist Christians is to be found primarily in the domain of ideology. This task will be made easier for them, since a "third alternative" between fascism and revolution becomes more and more impossible every day for the popular masses and politicized Christians. The reformism of Christian social doctrine, of men like Frei and Tomic, has been laid to rest by the machine guns and bayonets of the military junta. That much is clear at least. Socialist Christians in Latin America now have that much to their advantage in the struggle that lies ahead. The question now is whether they can carry on this struggle within the institutional Church or whether they will be forced to carry it on outside the Church.[14]

If the primary political task of Christians is in the domain of ideology, then ideological universality in reading the Bible will not do for South African Christians, who must overthrow not only a political system that is evil, but also human members of classes who benefit by it and read the Bible from the point of view of those who must continue to benefit by it.

History does tend to reduce the choices facing those who are too timid to make decisive moves one way or the other. The folly of dictators helps, particularly through their more violent methods, to make the task of wishy-washy liberal Christians easier by creating stark choices. The violence of the apartheid system since Soweto 1976 has had a similar effect on the response of the church. The reformism of Christian social doctrine was in a sense laid to rest by the machine guns and bayonets of those in power who shot and maimed schoolchildren. South African theologians must remember, however, that in order for the Bible to be of any use in such a situation, the words of Anthony Mansueto are of abiding significance for us: "Existential or religious commitment to social revolution will not substitute for scientific analysis of the valence of a tradition in class struggle."[15] For this reason the populism—based obviously on a genuine existential or religious commitment to social revolution, or at least the eradication of apartheid—that is inherent in the call for a postexilic theology to replace the present paralysis must be avoided. There are better and more rewarding ways of reading the Bible. I refer here to the call expressed by the *ICT Report* in the following way:

Hasn't the time come for ICT to develop a *post exilic theology?* The release of
Mandela calls to some extent for this. In the booklet on his release we said:
The release from captivity in Babylon was the fulfillment of God's promise
but it was also a sign of hope and a challenge to the people to rebuild the
nation of Israel. . . . While the release of Mandela is filled with promise, it
also spells the need for a long and arduous struggle to bring about the
structures necessary for a non-racial democratic society. Now is not the time
for people to sit back and leave it to our leaders to do the talking. Everyone
needs to get involved in building democratic structures.[15]

Postexilic theology will not liberate black people in South Africa from
white settler capitalist oppression and exploitation. It may bring about a
black government, just as it brought a Jewish government in Judah after
the Babylonian exile. But the liberation of the people of Yahweh is another
matter. Postexilic theology amounts to no more than a form of populist
biblical sloganeering. It says nothing about the God of whom Norman
Gottwald wrote in *The Tribes of Yahweh.* In order to recover that God, the
Bible must be read differently, taking into account class, racial, gender,
cultural, and political issues in our analysis of its texts.

21 Mark's Gospel in the Inner City

John J. Vincent

SOCIOPOLITICAL AS LOCATION AND VOCATION

The sociopolitical interpretation of scripture has become unquestionably the most significant development in biblical studies in our time. To this has probably no other made a greater contribution than Norman Gottwald.

Yet another aspect of that remarkable personality is to me even more noteworthy—that biblical scholarship's outstanding originator and theoretician, in asserting the power of social, economic, and political influence in the time of scripture, has given himself to teaching, research, and fellow laboring alongside workers in the seminary, which as much as anywhere has committed itself to the city. From my own short colleagueship with Bill Webber at New York Theological Seminary (NYTS) in the stormy days of 1970, right up to a decade of part-time work until recently, my experience is that NYTS has maintained a firm commitment to the inner city and to the social, economic, and political realities of inner-city people. It is here that Norman Gottwald has chosen to labor—surely not despite his academic work and convictions, but because of them.

The question now arises: What does it mean for the interpretation of scripture to "work at the Word" in the context of contemporary urban existence? What does it mean to read the stories of Israel's attempts to discover political liberation, or ethnic recognition, or internal justice, or wholeness for all, from among and alongside those who live contemporary history with similar agenda?

No task is of greater importance than to apply the rigor of sociohistorical disciplines now among the contemporary hearers and doers of

275

the Word, as we have learned to apply them to the creators of the Word itself. Put bluntly—does not the still-persisting, educated, suburban, and sophisticated captivity of the Word mean that a fundamental dissonance is set up, if those who attempt today to study the Word stand diametrically opposed, in the corresponding social, economic, and political positions of our day, to those who originally created the stories and the records, among whom the "acts of God" took place, and within whose contexts and concerns the very truths and assumptions that we today distill and use for other purposes originally came to birth?

It was because I found in colleagues like Bill Webber, Norman Gott-wald, and Richard Snyder a deep commitment to urban issues that I sought to link our own work at the Urban Theology Unit (UTU) in Sheffield with theirs. We had set up the UTU in 1970 with a variety of ambitious intentions, most naively stated in our first prospectus of 1973:

> A Community of Study, of Reflection and Prophecy, of
>   Commitment and Creation,
> where Christians and non-Christians, men and women, young
>   and old, of all churches and none, theologians, sociologists,
>   workers, ministers, housewives, teachers, social workers,
>   searchers . . .
>
> Have the chance to live and work together in inner city
>   neighbourhood houses,
> beside deprivation and celebration, racism and demolition . . .
>
> Beginning at the bottom, researching issues and problems,
>   taking sides with people, struggling with politics, hammering
>   out new possibilities, incarnating alternatives . . .
>
> Through studying theories and policies, reading theologies and
>   scriptures,
> building vocations and communities, creating models, getting
>   action from theology, theology from action . . .
>
> As a part of humanity,
> in the name of Jesus Christ,
> for the sake of the city,
> present and future,
> all over the world.[1]

My own journey had taken me through New Testament studies to urban mission and eventually into urban theology. Early, I became convinced that discipleship rather than belief was the essence of Christianity. In 1954–55, I pursued this prejudice in a year at Drew Theological

Seminary (Madison, NJ) and wrote my conclusions.[2] Oscar Cullmann visited Drew, and I got to Basel for a year, where I worked on discipleship, mainly in Mark's Gospel.[3]

Three conclusions followed my enthusiasm. First, that you could not really get a doctorate out of discipleship without yourself being prepared to go in for it. Second, that the way of the disciple could only be carried out in a practical commitment of a specific and alternative kind. I remember saying to myself that "I need to find a place where gospel things might happen." It was not that I would be the originator of gospel things, but that I would be part of them. The third conclusion followed from this: The nearest place to being where Jesus was in his own lifetime was to put myself in one of the great cities. So being a disciple for me meant being a city missioner. My institutional creations twenty years ago followed. Because the inner city was being deserted by the Christians, I helped form the Sheffield Inner City Ecumenical Mission. And as no one knew how to be a theologian there, I started UTU.

So, I want to know not simply what places in the gospel can help me with my place and vocation in the city, but even more, what disciplines and vocations, practice and spirituality, I now as an inner-city person need to be open to in order that the gospel may happen around me; that is, in order that I can also fulfill my vocation as a New Testament student and a theologian in my vocation, in the inner city.

For a start, then, I need to dig as deep as possible into situation, location, place.

THE GOSPEL IN PLACE

The recognition of the importance of location in the biblical traditions owes much to Norman Gottwald's work.[4] Walter Brueggemann's *The Land*[5] is a good summary of the theological significance of specific locations in biblical studies. Doctrine arose because it was the conclusion of conviction and experience concerning divine action that took place in specific times, people, and, perhaps above all, places. Recently, G. R. Lilburne has emphasized the way that place relates to the nature of divine action and human response.[6]

The importance of place is clear in the Markan accounts of Jesus. Jesus proclaimed the kingdom in the economic situation of Galilee, which was no rural, pastoral scene. In fact, it was very much a cosmopolitan area in which successive influxes of foreigners had only in the first century BCE been joined by Israelites. The 350,000 population still had only about 100,000 Jews, and many slaves.

Trade practices, evidence from coins, and recent excavations in the Galilean towns of Tiberius, Capernaum, Sepphoris, Bethsaida-Julias, and Kafar Hananiah reveal a developed Hellenistic ethos. The evidence suggests "reciprocal rather than strictly exploitative trade networks between some small villages and urban centres such as Sepphoris." Galilee had "a sophisticated, urban influenced ethos."[7]

Such a developed urban-style economy produced a variety of people who could be called poor. Peasant farmers with small plots of land were gradually having to sell their land to pay debts or taxes—taxes to Rome, taxes to the Temple. Meantime, large estates were owned by wealthy merchants, either Jews living in Jerusalem or Gentiles living outside Palestine. Thus the typical house owner lived a life of marginal security, heavily dependent upon outside persons and forces. To this was added the indignity and vulnerability of being a subject people, people who were aliens in their own land, facing occupying armies.

Mark is saying: Jesus, coming from a place like this, and with friends and disciples belonging to places like this, living alongside and dealing with issues like these, having friends and enemies among people like these—this Jesus is the one indicated to be Lord of all nations and Messiah of God's chosen people. By being in one place, at one time, with a very specific dialect, lifestyle, culture, parentage, status, and race, Jesus was as cramped and limited by his place as we are: yet this is the one God chooses.[8] And that may immediately say both that all persons cramped and limited by their place—such as all readers!—have a way in; and also that people from places nearest to Jesus' have an easier, or perhaps better, more comprehensible, way in.

What do these insights mean today when applied to contemporary readers and scholars? Fundamentally different things happen when biblical studies are appropriated in specific geographical contexts, let alone social, political, and historical ones. A recent volume of essays contains a chapter by Sean Freyne, a New Testament scholar, appropriating Jesus' commitment to Galilee in the light of the author's own origins in the west of Ireland county of Mayo.[9] Countless volumes have addressed the question of the nature of Christianity from the context of middle-class, Midwest, small-town, educated, and enlightened America. Gottwald devastatingly comments: "Our current social site favors utter amnesia and mindlessness toward critical thought and action."[10] Or as José Cardenas Pallares asks, "Are we modern-day interpreters of the Bible on Jesus' wavelength? Has our sociological condition any affinity with his?"[11]

WHO CAN HEAR IT?

This being so, we may expect that the Gospels were communicated initially to people who could make sense of them. They were, we might say, efforts to communicate the story of Jesus from one place to another, and especially from one audience to another. Recent audience criticism attempts to bring the sociocultural and historical situation of the first readers into attention. Herman Waetjen looks at Mark's Gospel by way of "sociological theory, cultural anthropological insights and reader-response criticism."[12] Obviously we do not know the first audiences of the scriptural writings any more than, in most cases, we know the writers. The text itself has to be pressed for evidence, or at least suggestions, for both items. Waetjen argues that Mark's first readers are "among lower-class strata of Roman-occupied Syria."[13] Others still locate the readers in Rome. But their sociocultural position and status seems to be "among lower-class strata," by increasingly common consent.

It is a small but necessary step from the imaginative reconstruction necessary in first-century "audience criticism" to applying the critique of audience criticism to twentieth-century readers.

That is to say, if it is an obvious part of New Testament inquiry to ask questions about the first audiences, we also need to ask questions about contemporary audiences.

A personal recollection may make the point. From 1978 to 1983, I taught courses in the summer school of the Doctor of Ministry program of Drew Theological Seminary. Each year, I taught a course on urban theology and one on discipleship in Mark's Gospel. In the course on urban theology, my repeated experience was that although it was salutary as well as enlightening for largely suburban or small-town ministers from various parts of the United States to be exposed to the writings of urban theologians, the thing they most valued was to apply the Gospel study and the disciplines of situational, social, and structural analysis to their own contexts. And they attempted to do so. But something different happened to both the theological analysis and the situation analysis when they were being used by people in places radically alternative to the inner city, where the methods had been developed by myself and others.

I looked upon the class more than once and said, after I had heard where each had come from, "I'm not sure that reading the Gospel of Mark is a good idea for you all."

I would argue this way. There has to be some kind of initial and natural rapport between people reading a Gospel, and the Gospel itself.

Now, we already know—or think we know—something about the people and situations for whom and for which the different Gospels were written. Of course, this could be itself mistaken. The Gospel writers could be writing things they knew were diametrically opposed to what the readers were already committed to. There are plenty of scholarly books to argue that. But we can guess that the way the Gospel writers put the story painted pictures that were coherent with certain dominant assumptions, commitments, and lifestyles—and that the writers were in fact aware of where their readers were and what their commitments were.

So, now, look at the Gospels we have got. Each was written from one context of people and places to another context of people and places. Luke is setting forth a Jesus (remember the old textbooks?) who is sympathetic to the poor, to women, to prayer, to the Spirit. That kind of Jesus could be worked with by people in largely middle-class churches with some cultural mixing, who were well aware of the need for generosity by the wealthy, but also were able to welcome a largely pastoral model of salvation ministered through healing, forgiveness, lifestyle change, and radical generosity. Matthew sets forth a Jesus who is the recapitulation and radical reembodiment of the old Torah, which Jesus reincorporates, cleanses, and restates in alternative ways. Such a Jesus made sense to Christians eager to affirm themselves as the true inheritors of the Torah tradition, which yet radically replaced the contemporary reductionist Judaism in favor of a new dispensation, by supporting a new "family" and "household" of God, committed to radical discipleship.

Mark sets out a Jesus who is acclaimed *Kurios*—Lord for Gentiles— and *Messias*—Christ for Jews—on the basis of his healing and miracle-working power, his proclamation of a present kingdom, and his calling disciples into repeating his own radically renunciatory lifestyle. Such a Jesus is obviously comparable to would-be messianic leaders in Galilee and achieves a like following among the disinherited and excluded, whether they be in Syria or in Rome.

So, we need to know, what kind of people in what situations now might expect to resonate with the people for whom the Gospel in particular was written in the first place? Only when some "resonance," some "fusion of horizons"[14] has taken place, can the necessary dialogue and "work on the Word" take place.

For communication of good news takes place between a minister of the good news—the Gospel writer—and the recipient of it—the reader or audience. The reader or audience identifies with the message insofar as it seems to be relevant to them. But a message is "relevant" if it is perceived to be dealing with the customary questions of people within a certain context. The message is heard to be answering questions already being asked within the context of the people. The context decisively influences the hearing. Indeed, it would be worthwhile to evaluate the social, political, cultural, and historical contexts within which each of the Gospels has been especially heard, just as historical-traditional study has traced the historical contexts in which individual texts have been used.[15] Christopher Rowland and Mark Corner put the matter strongly, in the sense of warning of the dangers of "eisegesis":

> A prime task of the exegete is to watch the way in which the biblical material is being and has been *used*. There is more than meets the eye in the way in which we are wont to read and use the Scriptures. We should accept the inevitable eisegesis (i.e., reading into texts, whether consciously or not, our own social and political preferences) which is an unavoidable part of the complex process of finding meaning in texts—what we call exegesis. By recognizing this process at work we will enable one another to be aware of the various kinds of eisegesis which we practise in all their subtlety and sophistication. We will thereby seek to lay bare the various human interests which may be at work in the maintaining of particular theological or political positions of individuals and groups. That is going to necessitate that we take seriously the patient analysis of the particularity of each situation and of whose interests are being served by various interpretations.[16]

But, positively, what kind of people would today be asking the kind of questions (because they are in the place they are, and because they are the kind of people they are) that the Gospel writers wrote to? Obviously, if we are occupied with questions from our own contexts and our own commitments, which are grossly dissimilar to those the Gospel writers wrote from or to, then we are likely to get answers to questions we are not asking, and no answers to the questions we are asking. But then, if we are occupied with questions from our own contexts and commitments, which seem similar to those of the Gospels, does this not give us a "hermeneutical advantage" similar to that which the poor as such are claimed to have by the liberation theologians?

Thus it becomes a matter of evangelistic common sense or hermeneutical appropriateness that we in biblical studies work as much with the contemporary contexts of people as we do with the biblical contexts of writers and audiences.

How is that done?

FINDING OUR PLACE IN THE TEXT

The more I have studied the Gospel of Mark, and the longer I have lived and worked in the inner city, the more I feel that the two have "a fusion of horizons." It is not simply that my vocation as theologian lands me in the inner city with an already conceived gospel. It is that the inner city seems to be playing to me elements of the gospel that I would not have noticed, or would have denied, had I not been there.

The inner city therefore becomes for me an interpretative medium for the gospel. This happens at a number of different levels.

First, there is the level of rational analysis. At this level, I analyze elements in the Markan picture of life in Jesus' Galilee, and elements from the contemporary inner city. In one analysis of this, I expressed it thus:

1. Galilee was a land run by aliens. Most of the great landowners did not live in the villages. They came in from outside. They hired others to do their dirty work. Like the man who owned the vineyard in the parable of Mark 12:1–9, they were absentee landlords.

So, we in the inner city are owned by outsiders. There's no money here. No investment. Actually, there's no work either. The industrialists took their money and ran, some of them long ago, some of them in the 1970s and 1980s.

2. Galilee was the place where the rich passed through. Over the hill, the great trade route carried spices and oils and gold from the east. They had their own supporting facilities at Tiberias. But Galilee itself was only the backdrop for their labours.

So, we in the inner city can walk down the hill and look into the brightly coloured stores, with goods from all over the world. But we do not buy many of them. They are bought by the people in the suburbs, whose automobile trade route races through our community.

3. Galilee had large estates, factories of the earth, which grew abundant produce—figs, olives, grapes, corn. But the locals were kept in poverty. They hung around the market place, on the off chance that they could get a day's work—as in the parable of Matt 20:1–7.

So, we in the inner city wait for the crumbs to fall from the rich people's tables. There is little work that we ourselves can do. The planners have flattened the old workshops, levelled the old gardens, and put useless surrounds of green grass to confirm our idleness.

4. Galilee was an enemy-occupied country, with an active local resistance movement. It needed resolute and firm government. It was not safe to have many of the occupying army actually living there. But when there was trouble, they came in and took firm reprisals. So, in 67 CE, the Roman soldiers marched in to punish the people of Jaffa, and reduced it to rubble, as they had done to Sepphoris when Judas ben Hezekiah set up his revolt in 4 CE.

So, the inner city today is a "no-go" area for police at times. Some of us riot out of frustration, alienation and cynicism. And they come in with their armoured cars, riot shields, helmets and truncheons. They would bring in the army if necessary.

5. Galilee was a "marked" country. It was the north, and its north-country people had strong north-country accents. The language they spoke was a crude "pigeon-Aramaic," scarcely comprehensible to southerners from Jerusalem and Judea.

So, inner city people and people from the north are "marked" people. Sometimes we have different colour skins. Usually, we have different accents. You can always tell.

6. Galilee was a powerless province that produced a firm independence. The religious authorities coming up from Jerusalem might have the power. But the locals had their own religion, and hailed their own prophets. A strongly insular, isolated consciousness resulted. People had to snatch at anything they could, and visitors were "ripped off" for whatever they might bring. They became emotionally hard. Things will not change—so grab whatever you can.

So, inner city people become hard. We take whatever we can from whoever comes. We've been taught to wait. And we get into trouble because we do not always say thank you.[17]

I would argue that this kind of analysis is tolerably faithful to what we know of Galilee. It is certainly faithful to what I know of the contemporary city.

Second, there is the level of personal perception. It seems to me that the stories of Jesus in the context of Galilee could have happened, or sometimes could now happen, in the context of the contemporary inner city. They feel "at home" in the inner city.

In 1989, I worked with a number of friends in our inner-city mission on a BBC broadcast program on "Jesus in the Inner City." One of those who spoke, Amy Richinson, now nearly 80, has lived all her life in Pitsmoor, one of our areas. She declared:

When I hear Jesus, as I do through the Gospel, then it seems to me that He's very much talking not only to the people of the inner city, but about the people of the inner city. That means He's speaking to the other areas of the city about those who we've learned to say are the ones who are at the bottom.[18]

I believe that this instinctive sense of identification through personal perception is an important part of biblical study. It is instinctive rather than rational. The historical, theological, and mythological implications of this kind of instinctive empathy with pieces of scripture has been well explored by feminist theologians. They now need to be explored by inner-city theologians.

Third, there is the level of active discipleship. Many people in the past decade or so have identified a call to Christian obedience with a call to be a disciple in the inner city. This is a phenomenon of the churches in the United States and in most European countries. Not only young people feel that the call to radical discipleship and Christian vocation has to be followed by finding places and communities at the bottom of society. The Gospel passages relating to following, giving up all, moving from one's original place, finding new relatives, having things in common, and being servants one to another achieve a contemporary existence through the life and experiences of such people, who identify such calls with moving into Christian communities in inner-city areas.

In Britain, the phenomenon of Christian inner-city incomers has become sustained by an alternative theology and is, I believe, the locus now of an emerging distinctive British liberation theology.[19]

In these ways, I have experienced the inner city and its Christian communities as places where elements of the Gospel, especially Mark, and especially the Markan discipleship tradition, have been appropriated and have become real. Once one has "found one's place" as location, then one "finds one's place" in the text. And once one has found one's place in the text, then the text comes back and illuminates the location.

Obviously, I do not imply that *only* in the inner city does this happen. My purpose is to reflect on what is happening, not to exclude what might happen elsewhere. Indeed, I recall the work of Neill Hamilton, a Drew contemporary enthusiast for Mark, who designed, especially for contemporary Americans, using the model of Markan discipleship and apocalyptic, guidelines for public and private piety amidst the extremisms of modern apostasy.[20] But my witness is to a particular part of the scriptural text that has become alive in my context.

Location, however, is obviously not the only "way in." We have learned that, with or without empathy through location, we also need empathy through experience. We have to find ourselves in the text.

FINDING OURSELVES IN THE TEXT

How do I find myself in the text?

The method we customarily use is the method of "snap-studies-spin-off." By "snap" we mean an imaginative identification with a biblical story, situation, or person. The term is based on a card game in which piles of cards are set side by side and players shout "Snap!" when the same card is placed on one pile as is already on another.

John D. Davies and I describe the method as follows:[21] first, we use our imagination to see connections between the situation in the Gospel and our own situation (snaps); then we think objectively about the meaning of the text (studies); then we move toward the future and discover the decisions that are suggested for our future work, in the light of our study (spin-offs). (See diagram on the following page.)

The method itself is, of course, not unlike methods of identifying-imagining-deciding, or moving from identification to discovery to reformulation, found elsewhere. It is not unlike the liberation theology method

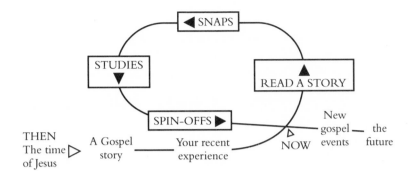

of seeing–judging–acting. The first crucial difference lies in what we call "making snaps" or "making identification." It is to answer the question, "When have I seen something or someone or some happening that is like this?"

When we first developed the method, in the early 1970s, three of us were involved—Alan Dale, the author of *Winding Quest* and *New World*, two biblical translations widely used; John Davies of Selly Oak, Birmingham, now bishop of Shrewsbury; and myself. I well remember a crucial debate among us as to the order of the three parts. Alan Dale felt that studies should come first. You could not identify with a story until you had first discerned its true meaning within its own context. But John Davies recalled that people with urgent questions (he had worked in South Africa) went straight for the story. And I recalled how so often, by the time I had "explained" a passage, everyone in a group or a congregation was totally silenced and afraid to open their mouths! So we said, Let's try to ensure that people at least feel they can "find themselves" in part of the story. So, bring your "snaps" first. There will be plenty of time later to exclude them, or bits of them, as we delve into the original context of the biblical story. But at least you will have got into the text.

The second crucial difference in our method is the third element—the "spin-off." While experimenting with the method, I found myself in the summer of 1974 lecturing at a summer school at St. Paul School of Theology in Kansas City. And who should be there but Walter Wink. Wink's method[22] seemed then, as it does now, to be so totally right at the point of initial "getting into the text," but so totally wrong at the point of its result. Wink's first stage is, like ours, to use memory, experience, acting, imagination, or whatever, to get into the passage with one's whole life and history. Wink's second stage, again like ours, is to study the environs of the passage, what the resonances of it were at the time, and where it stands in relation to other passages. But Wink's third stage is to drive the passage inward, as a tool for psychological self-understanding or group understanding. However, we think the third stage should be to drive the passage into practice, discover its spin-offs, not simply in the area of personal wholeness, but rather in terms of gospel action in the world and the community.

That is, the result of Bible study must cohere with the original purpose of biblical narrative. Biblical narrative stands as the "midpoint" between the prime gospel action and the gospel action today. The biblical text is the interpretative medium between the original action of Jesus and the present action of Jesus people in the contemporary world. The spin-off has to have some coherence with the originating action. The purpose of biblical study must be something like, "If this story describes and legitimates that particular action of Jesus or gospel people, what particular action of myself and my people might take place that could be described in a similar way?" Or, as my colleague Ed Kessler asks regarding parables, "If this parable was used to explain or justify that action of Jesus, what action that we might do today might need this story to explain or justify it?"[23]

The notion of "antecedents" is another method we use. My own experience of it has been in work with the Doctor of Ministry program of NYTS. UTU functioned as an "outpost" for the NYTS doctoral program for British ministers, with periodic visits from Richard Snyder, the dean of the program, and Norman Gottwald. The contributions of Norman Gottwald constantly made me reflect, if this passage or this story originated in this or that situation, and functioned within the tradition in this or that particular way, what does this have to say to people today seeking to be in line with biblically recorded happenings?

Or, as I simplified it, it was to ask the question "When and how in scripture have people similar to us, in situations similar to ours, acted faithfully to the God revealing himself?" "What revelations came to people in this or that circumstance who were seeking faithfulness through their action and commitment?" So, we today in seeking antecedents are seeking

> Who and Where and When and How
> Did people like us,
> In locations similar to ours,
> At similar times and situations to ours,
> Become and identify and act
> Faithful responses?

The quest has led us into various ploys at UTU. Both in the Doctor of Ministry program of NYTS, and now in a Master of Ministry degree, accredited by Sheffield University, the context of the questions about antecedents is that of practical ministry. Here, one begins to expose an obvious but crucial circular element in ministry. The particular scriptures being used by preachers and congregations already determine the shape, content, and effect of the biblical message that is heard. And the particular contexts of preachers and congregations determine the questions that are taken to the biblical material, and thus the answers being heard.

So, we seek to set up a living dialogue or provocation or dialectic between the elements of the biblical tradition and the elements of the contemporary ministry situation. Situational, social, and structural analysis is needed of the ministry situation, but also similar analysis at the biblical end. What economic, social, cultural, and political factors are really at work in the context? That is the question for both ministry situation and Bible. To work at both together and in turn is part of the search that leads to the discovery of antecedents.

In other courses, we try other ploys. We have a small group who spend a year with us at UTU, doing our Diploma in Theology and Mission.[24] The group consists of postexperience and usually postgraduate men and women seeking a year of reflection or stock taking, or else seeking new vocational moves; plus several, often from overseas, on a sabbatical or on specific study. The course includes Bible, theology, urban studies, community studies, spirituality, and vocation. We designed it primarily for those like ourselves, preparing or resourcing for work in the urban scene.

Part of it has to do with getting ourselves and our participants to find themselves in the biblical story and to discover which parts of the biblical story are finding them. So, we try to get them to reflect on what dominant biblical or Christian notions they have so far in life been influenced by. Then we say, "Who are your people? Who are the people you can empathize with in the Old Testament, then in the New Testament, and in Christian history, and in contemporary history?" "Who are the people in Mark's Gospel whose actions or attitudes provoke or invite you? Can you help yourself forward in terms of your personal search for vocation or mission or community by putting yourself alongside friends and kindred spirits in the tradition?" We then get as deep as we can into the identification and see where it leads. It is, we find, not the end of the process of discovering vocation, mission, or community. But it is a good place to begin to take on board the riches of the tradition and to begin to do some serious Bible study at the same time as personal formation. The methods are very much "correspondence of relationships," rather than "correspondence of terms," in the categories of Clodovis Boff.[25]

INNER CITY AS GOSPEL ENCOUNTER

The inner city as context for biblical study, especially of Mark's Gospel, not only leads to empathy with the text and enlightenment regarding biblical realities. It also leads to conversion. It leads to people saying to themselves: Now that I see what battles these people got into, what people they stood beside, what way-out and mysterious arguments they used, what enemies they identified and opposed, and what rewards of being moved in home, work, friends, and future they received—I cannot be in empathy or in common understanding with them and continue to be a person whose battles are solely for myself, who stands only beside people who stand beside me, whose arguments are rational and crystal clear, whose enemies are simply those who oppose what I want to do, and whose anticipated rewards are simply that I will be protected in the home, work, friends, and future I have secured for myself.

Why the inner city? Could not such encounters with gospel realities and the strange wholeness of Mark's Jesus take place anywhere? Do I have to move my body before my mind is moved or my soul is cleansed?

Well, no, of course. As Jesus said, with God all things are possible. But he apparently said that in the midst of avoiding the question of his disciples as to whether the rich could enter the kingdom of God (Mark 10:37–47).

But my witness has to be that, in my experience, a discovery of Jesus in the Gospels that does not go hand in hand with a discovery of discipleship simply leads people into greater self-deceiving sophistication. The present reality is that the churches use the Jesus story merely as a way whereby people dig deeper into strange stories and become more and more enlightened about biblical history, worldviews, relationships, and literature. The end of all this biblical enlightenment is that people either become philosophical pursuers of their own private lives or else become teachers of others in it. The sharp end of the discipleship call is allowed to make its mark only at the edges of life—in relations with friends or in concern for the Third World, or in church activities, or in personal attitudes or value differences. But the enormous questions about Who I am, Where I put myself, Beside whom I live, For what I suffer, Who people identify me with—these questions are set aside. Discipleship has been domesticated into nothing.

Positively, the discovery of discipleship in the inner city simply opens up different worlds. We need the inner city in the church today. We in the inner city need far more of the resources of biblical scholarship—I mean the biblical scholars and the biblical people. We do not need them as theological advisers, as visitors, as consultants, or as reporters. We need them as sojourners, brothers and sisters, people being converted, people putting their own lives on the line. Then from the bottom with us there will arise the new spirituality the churches look for, which will be spirituality from alongside the poor, spirituality out of commitment and meditation on Christ-likeness in terms of discipleship. The inner city is the nearest place for the human being in our time to experiment with the next stage of the globe's development. The Village in the City is an ecological possibility; the village in the prairie is only one more rape of the environment.[26] Justice, peace, and the integrity of creation must be manifest in the inner city to be credible anywhere and can be prophetic for postindustrial society there.

Above all, even if it cannot and should not be the abiding place of all of us captivated by the biblical dramas and visions, it can be the place where the gospel as invitation to radical alternatives is kept before the churches. In 1989–90, I had the unexpected honor of being president of the British Methodist Church and carried my barrow-load of inner-city goodies around the country. I planned days and half days with politicians, university people, and community leaders on the theme "Britain in the 90's." I became convinced that we needed a constant campaign like it, but through people coming to the inner city, not our going to them. Those who have tried taking the message *from* the inner city will share my conviction that such endeavors have limited value. But could the churches use the inner-city churches as retreat centers, as discovery centers, as spirituality centers, as *metanoia* centers, as hermitages and monasteries and seminaries? I wrote:

We need a four-point policy in dealing with the personal implications of our situation. None of them is easy. Each of them needs much work.

1. Provide experiences in which people have their ideological presuppositions challenged by entering into radically alternative ways of life in radically alternative contexts. Thus we develop International Youth Exchanges, Inner City or Urban Priority Area Volunteer Schemes, Alternative Religious Communities and Cooperative workshare enterprises. Conversion is possible. But conversion comes through involvement in alternative experiences over specific and prolonged periods of time—not through bright ideas entertained in the mind.

2. Pursue rigorous gospel analysis tools from the viewpoint of the base of society. There are also socio-economic analytical tools which can be used. Marxist tools have helped people to see economic factors as important. But racism and sexism have not yielded to Marxist analysis, and even classism has persisted in so-called communist countries. What we call in UTU, "Situation Analysis," "Social Analysis" and "Structural Analysis," need to be applied constantly, but bearing the distinctive Christian values, methods and insights.

3. Apply the lessons learned from the poor in dealing with the powers of society. Learn and enable with the poor, but then learn how to translate these

learnings into ways of effectively opposing the actual centres of power. It is no use thinking the solutions will be found in suburbia or the city, in isolation. But the lessons and methods learned among the poor have to be applied there. This is the way that the middle class who "make an option for the poor" need to return to convert their friends, after learning from the poor.

4. Expect the development of those who are at present marginalised to be different from the ways in which development takes place for those at the centres of educational and financial powers in the society. Thus, for a time, there will be "ghettos" of self-conscious, self-protecting life among those on the margins. This is a necessary step towards self-development which is authentic to the groups in question, and is not merely a late "jumping on the band-wagon" of the straight society's derelict values and standards.[27]

CONCLUSION

Such, then, are some experiences in working with the gospel, especially the Gospel of Mark, in the inner city. The experiences related have been mainly from my work in teaching, as it seems to me that biblical scholarship needs to begin to reflect on the implications of doing biblical work in contemporary contexts. Other stories need now to be heard—of gospel "projects" in our area, of gospel "snaps" in our communities.[28] Our experience mirrors that of liberation theologians and base Christian communities elsewhere:

> The text becomes a catalyst in the exploration of pressing contemporary issues relevant to the community; it offers a language so that the voice of the voiceless may be heard. There is an immediacy in the way in which the text is used because resonances are found with the experiences set out in the stories of biblical characters which seem remote from the world of affluent Europe and North America.[29]

The Writings of Norman K. Gottwald

BOOKS

Studies in the Book of Lamentations (SBT, 1st ser. 14; London: SCM, 1954, rev. ed. 1962).

A Light to the Nations: An Introduction to the Old Testament (New York: Harper & Row, 1959).

All the Kingdoms of the Earth: Israelite Prophecy and International Relations in the Ancient Near East (New York: Harper & Row, 1964).

The Church Unbound: A Human Church for a Human World (Philadelphia: Lippincott, 1967).

The Tribes of Yahweh: A Sociology of the Religion of Liberated Israel, 1250–1050 B.C.E. (Maryknoll, NY: Orbis, 1979, repr. with corrections, 1981). Translated into Portuguese and Spanish.

Editor, *The Bible and Liberation: Political and Social Hermeneutics* (Maryknoll, NY: Orbis, 1983).

The Hebrew Bible: A Socio-Literary Introduction (Philadelphia: Fortress, 1985, corr. 2nd printing, 1987). Translated into Portuguese and Korean; Spanish translation in process.

Proclamation 4: Aids for Interpreting the Lessons of the Church Year, Series A: Pentecost 3 (Minneapolis: Augsburg-Fortress, 1989).

ARTICLES AND ESSAYS

"Studia Biblica XXX: Lamentations," *Int* 9 (1955) 320–38.

"The Bible and Authority," *Foundations* 1 (1958) 16–27.

"Immanuel as the Prophet's Son," *VT* 8 (1958) 36–47.

"The Biblical Basis of Worship," *Harvard Divinity School Bulletin* 15 (1960) 1–6.

"The Prophets of Israel and International Relations in the Ancient Near East," *Christian News from Israel* 12/3 (Oct. 1961) 20–24.

"Some Strategies of Nonviolence," *Worldview* 4 (1961) 3–7.

"Whither Old Testament Studies?" *Andover Newton Quarterly* 1 (1961) 1–10.

"Moral and Strategic Reflections on the Nuclear Dilemma," *Christianity and Crisis* 21 (Jan. 8, 1962) 239–42.

"Prophetic Faith and Contemporary International Relations," *Biblical Realism Confronts the Nation* (ed. P. Peachey; Nyack, NY: Fellowship Publications, 1963) 68–87.

"Recent Biblical Theologies: IX. Walter Eichrodt's 'Theology of the Old Testament,' " *The Expository Times* 74 (1963) 209–12.

" 'Holy War' in Deuteronomy: Analysis and Critique," *Review and Expositor* 61 (1964) 296–310.

"A Sleep of Prisoners. Nuclear Deterrence: Dilemma of Religious Conscience," *Worldview* 7 (November 1964) 5–7.

"The Messianic Hope," *Jews and Christians: Preparation for Dialogue* (ed. G. A. Knight; Philadelphia: Westminster, 1965) 66–77.

"Walter Eichrodt's 'Theology of the Old Testament,' " *Contemporary Old Testament Theologians* (ed. R. Laurin; Philadelphia: Judson, 1970) 53–80.

"Domain Assumptions and Societal Models in the Study of Premonarchic Israel" (VTSup, Edinburgh Congress Volume, 1974) 89–100.

"Were the Early Israelites Pastoral Nomads?" *Rhetorical Criticism: Essays in Honor of James Muilenburg* (ed. J. Jackson and M. Kessler; Pittsburgh: Pickwick, 1974) 223–55 = *The Proceedings of the Sixth World Congress of Jewish Studies* (Jerusalem, 1977) 1.165–89.

"The Social World of Ancient Israel," *SBLSP* (1975) 1.165–78 (with Frank S. Frick).

"Are Biblical and U.S. Societies Comparable?" *Radical Religion* 3 (1976) 17–24.

"Biblical Theology or Biblical Sociology? On Affirming and Defining the 'Uniqueness' of Israel," *The Bible and Liberation: Political and Social Hermeneutics* (ed. N. K. Gottwald and A. C. Wire; Berkeley, CA: Community for Religious Research and Education, 1976) 42–57.

"Early Israel and 'The Asiatic Mode of Production' in Canaan," *SBLSP* (1976) 145–54.

"The Impact of Ancient Israel on Our Social World," *Theology Digest* 25 (1977) 335–46 = *Currents in Theology and Mission* 6 (1979) 84–93.

"A Biblical Sociologist Looks at Early Israel: Were the Early Israelites Pastoral Nomads?" *BARev* 4 (1978) 2–7.

"The Hypothesis of the Revolutionary Origins of Ancient Israel: A Response to A. J. Hauser and T. L. Thompson," *JSOT* 7 (1978) 37–52.

"Sociological Method in the Study of Ancient Israel," *Encounter with the Text: Form and History in the Hebrew Bible* (ed. M. J. Buss; Missoula, MT: Scholars Press/ Philadelphia: Fortress, 1979) 69–81.

"Early Israelite Society Revisited: Message to the Twentieth Century. An Interview with Jock Brown," *Sequoia* 1 (June-July 1980) 3–4.

" 'Church and State' in Ancient Israel: Example or Caution in Our Age?" (pamphlet, Department of Religion Lecture Series; Gainesville: University of Florida, 1981).

"Problems and Promises in the Comparative Analysis of Religious Phenomena," *Semeia* 21 (1982) 103–12.

"Sociological Criticism of the Old Testament," *The Christian Century* (April 21, 1982) 474–77.

"Bibliography on the Social Scientific Study of the Old Testament," *American Baptist Quarterly* 2 (1983) 168–84.

"Early Israel and the Canaanite Socioeconomic System," *Palestine in Transition: The Emergence of Ancient Israel* (ed. D. N. Freedman and D. F. Graf; The Social World of Biblical Antiquity, 2; Sheffield: Almond, 1983) 25–37.

"Sociological Method in Biblical Research and Contemporary Peace Studies," *American Baptist Quarterly* 2 (1983) 142–56.

"The Theological Task After *The Tribes of Yahweh*," *The Bible and Liberation* (ed. N. K. Gottwald; Maryknoll, NY: Orbis, 1983) 190–200.

"Two Models for the Origins of Ancient Israel: Social Revolution or Frontier Development," *The Quest for the Kingdom of God: Studies in Honor of George E. Mendenhall* (ed. H. B. Huffmon *et al.*; Winona Lake, IN: Eisenbrauns, 1983) 5–24.

"Tragedy and Comedy in the Latter Prophets," *Semeia* 32 (1984) 83–96.

"The Biblical Mandate for Eco-Justice Action," *For Creation's Sake: Preaching, Ecology and Justice* (ed. D. Hessel; Philadelphia: Geneva, 1985) 32–44.

"The Israelite Settlement as a Social Revolutionary Movement," *Biblical Archaeology Today: Proceedings of the International Congress on Biblical Archaeology, Jerusalem, April 1984* (Jerusalem: Israel Exploration Society, 1985) 34–46.

"Social Matrix and Canonical Shape," *Theology Today* 42 (1985) 307–21 = *The Best in Theology* (ed. P. Fromer; Carol Stream, IL: Christianity Today) 1.59–73.

"From Biblical Economics to Modern Economies: A Bridge Over Troubled Waters," *Churches in Struggle: Liberation Theologies and Social Change in North America* (ed. W. K. Tabb; New York: Monthly Review, 1986) 138–48.

Excerpts from *Studies in the Book of Lamentations, A Light to the Nations* (above), and *The Interpreter's Dictionary of the Bible* (below) repr. in *The Hebrew Bible and Literary Criticism* (ed. A. Preminger and E. L. Greenstein; New York: Ungar, 1986).

"New Perspective on the Hebrew Bible: An Interview with Norman K. Gottwald," *New York Theological Seminary Bulletin* (Winter 1986) 2–3, 8.

"The Participation of Free Agrarians in the Introduction of Monarchy to Ancient Israel: An Application of H. A. Landsberger's Framework for the Analysis of Peasant Movements," *Semeia* 37 (1986) 77–106.

"Sozialgeschichtliche Präzision in der biblischen Verankerung der Befreiungstheologie," *Wer ist unser Gott? Beiträge zu einer Befreiungstheologie im Kontext der "ersten" Welt* (ed. L. and W. Schottroff; Munich: Kaiser, 1986) 88–107.

"Religious Conversion and the Societal Origins of Ancient Israel," *Perspectives in Religious Studies* 15 (1988) 49–65.

"The Exodus as Event and Process: A Test Case in the Biblical Grounding of Liberation Theology," *The Future of Liberation Theology: Essays in Honor of Gustavo Gutiérrez* (ed. M. H. Ellis and O. Maduro; Maryknoll, NY: Orbis, 1989) 250–60.

"Israel's Emergence in Canaan—BR Interviews Norman Gottwald," *Bible Review* 5 (October 1989) 26–34.

"Literary Criticism of the Hebrew Bible: Retrospect and Prospect," *The Bucknell Review* 37/2 (1990) 27–44.

"A Socioliterary Approach," *Approaches to Teaching the Hebrew Bible as Literature in Translation* (ed. B. N. Olshen and Y. S. Feldman; New York: Modern Language Association, 1990) 59–64.

"Biblical Views on 'Church-State' Relations and Their Influence on Existing Political Ideologies" (report volume of the Consultation on Christian Community in a Changing Society, November 1990; Geneva: World Alliance of Reformed Churches, forthcoming).

"Framing Biblical Interpretation at New York Theological Seminary: A Student Self-Inventory on Biblical Hermeneutics," *Reading from This Place: Social Location and Biblical Interpretation* (ed. F. F. Segovia and M. A. Tolbert; Philadelphia: Westminster/John Knox, forthcoming).

"From Tribal Existence to Empire: The Socio-Historical Context for the Rise of the Hebrew Prophets," *God and Capitalism: A Prophetic Critique of Market Society* (ed. J. M. Thomas; Madison, WI: AR Editions, forthcoming).

"Historical Material Models of the Origins of Israel in the Light of Recent Palestinian Archaeology," *New Perspectives on the Emergence of Israel in Canaan* (Archaeology and Biblical Studies 2; ed. W. G. Dever; Atlanta: Scholars Press, forthcoming).

"Social Class and Ideology in Isaiah 40–55: An Eagletonian Reading," *Semeia* (forthcoming).

"Values and Economic Structures," *Religion, the Economy and Social Justice* (ed. M. Zweig; Philadelphia: Temple University Press, forthcoming).

CONTRIBUTIONS TO DICTIONARIES, ENCYCLOPEDIAS, AND COMMENTARIES

"Lamentations, Book of," "Poetry, Hebrew," and "Song of Songs," *The Interpreter's Dictionary of the Bible* (Nashville: Abingdon, 1962).

"Amorites," "Blessing of Jacob," "Nomadism," and "Samuel, Books of," *Encyclopaedia Judaica* (Jerusalem and New York: Israel Program for Scientific Translations, 1971).

"The Law Codes of Israel" (article), "The Book of Deuteronomy" (commentary), *The Interpreter's One-Volume Commentary on the Bible* (Nashville: Abingdon, 1971).

"Israel, Social and Economic Development of," "Nomadism," and "War, Holy," *The Interpreter's Dictionary of the Bible: Supplementary Volume* (Nashville: Abingdon, 1976).

"Chronicles," "Daniel," "Ezra and Nehemiah," "Job," "Maccabees," and "Psalms," *The Academic American Encyclopedia* (Amsterdam and New York: Arete, 1980).

"Lamentations" (introduction and commentary), *Harper's Bible Commentary* (San Francisco: Harper & Row, 1988).

"Sociology of Ancient Israel," *The Anchor Bible Dictionary* (Garden City, NY: Doubleday, forthcoming).

SELECTED BOOK REVIEWS

B. W. Anderson and W. Harrelson (ed.), *Israel's Prophetic Heritage: Essays in Honor of James Muilenburg, JBL* 81 (1962) 300–301.

S. Sandmel, *The Hebrew Scriptures: An Introduction to Their Literature and Religious Ideas, JBL* 82 (1963) 441–43.

B. Albrektson, *Studies in the Text and Theology of the Book of Lamentations, JBL* 83 (1964) 204–207.

G. Fohrer, *Theologische Grundstrukturen des Alten Testaments, JBL* 93 (1974) 594–96.

D. R. Hillers, *Lamentations* (AB), *JAAR* 43 (1975) 311–13.

"John Bright's New Revision of *A History of Israel*," *BARev* 8 (1982) 56–61.

H. Maccoby, *The Sacred Executioner: Human Sacrifice and the Legacy of Guilt, The New York Times Book Review* (Dec. 18, 1983).

I. M. Zeitlin, *Ancient Judaism: Biblical Criticism from Max Weber to the Present*, *Religion* 16 (1986) 383–400.

W. Brueggemann, *David's Truth in Israel's Imagination and Memory*, *Biblica* 68 (1987) 408–11.

M. D. Meeks, *God the Economist: The Doctrine of God and Political Economy*, *Christianity and Crisis* 50 (May 14, 1990) 150–54.

J. W. Flanagan, *David's Social Drama: A Hologram of Israel's Early Iron Age*, *Bible Review* (forthcoming).

Notes

PREFACE

1. N. K. Gottwald, *The Tribes of Yahweh: A Sociology of the Religion of Liberated Israel, 1250–1050 B.C.E.* (Maryknoll, NY: Orbis, 1979).
2. Ibid., 10.
3. Ibid., 5.
4. W. Brueggemann, "*The Tribes of Yahweh:* An Essay Review," *JAAR* 48 (1980) 443.
5. "Early Israelite Society Revisited: Message to the Twentieth Century. An Interview with Jock Brown," *Sequoia* 1 (June-July 1980) 4.
6. J. J. Vincent, "Mark's Gospel in the Inner City," see pp. 275–90.
7. N. K. Gottwald, *The Hebrew Bible: A Socio-Literary Introduction* (Philadelphia: Fortress, 1985).
8. Ibid., 31 (cf. the whole of pp. 29–34).
9. Ibid., 20.

CHAPTER 1: PSALMS 9–10

1. N. K. Gottwald, "Social Matrix and Canonical Shape," *Theology Today* 42 (1985) 307–21.
2. D. Jobling ("Sociological and Literary Approaches to the Bible: How Shall the Twain Meet?" *JSOT* 38 [1987] 85–93) has seen that Gottwald's crucial contribution is not his "peasant revolt" hypothesis, but the methodological revolution he has articulated and modeled.
3. See Gottwald's own comments on the acrostic form in *Studies in the Book of Lamentations* (SBT 14; Chicago: Allenson, 1954) 23–32. On the disorder of the acrostic sequence, see H.-J. Kraus, *Psalms 1–59: A Commentary* (Minneapolis: Augsburg, 1988) 192. On a consideration of some of the specific problems, see J. Leveen, "A Note on Psalm 10:17–18," *JBL* 67 (1948) 149–50, and "Psalm X: A Reconstruction," *JTS* 45 (1944) 16–21.
4. See the useful summary on form by A. A. Anderson, *The Book of Psalms I* (New Century Bible; Greenwood, SC: Attic, 1972) 104–106. See also H. Junker "Unité, Composition et Genre Littéraire des Psaumes IX et X," *RB* 60 (1953) 161–69; and W. Beyerlin, "Die *tôdâ* der Heilsvergegenwärtigung in den Klageliedern des Einzelnen," *ZAW* 79 (1967) 208–24. In what follows, it will be clear that questions of form are not

adequate for an understanding of the movement of the psalm. No doubt, the psalm moves from thanks to complaint. Our interpretation, however, must move beyond form to "voice" and to "interest."

5. On the capacity and power of a poem or narrative to give voice to those who have no other voice, see J. A. Engelbert, "Introduction," *And We Sold the Rain* (ed. R. Santos; New York: Four Walls Eight Windows, 1988) ix–xxiii, esp. xx. See also more generally J. O. Perry (ed.), *Voices of Emergency* (London: Sangam, 1983), and A. Brink, *Writing in a State of Siege: Essays on Politics and Literature* (New York: Summit, 1983).

6. "I will give thanks, I will tell, I will be glad, I will exult, I will sing."

7. "I will recount, I will rejoice." The verb *spr* is used both in the initial statement and in the reprise.

8. "You have done [my justice], you sat, you rebuked, you destroyed, you blotted out, you rooted out." The verbal uses are "declarative" and refer to actual, concrete interventions. See C. Westermann, *The Praise of God in the Psalms* (Richmond: John Knox, 1965) 102–108 and *passim*, and F. Crüsemann, *Studien zur Formgeschichte von Hymnus und Danklied in Israel* (WMANT 32; Neukirchen-Vluyn: Neukirchener Verlag, 1969).

9. Thus, for example, the petition to "blot out" in Ps 109:13–15 would seem to request judicial action. It is important for the governing metaphors of the psalm that the act of nullification need not be warlike violence, but can be the power of a severe court verdict. On the juridical metaphor in psalm 109, see Brueggemann, "Psalm 109: Three Times 'Steadfast Love,' " *Word and World* 5 (1985) 144–54.

10. On the connection between justice and power, see K. W. Whitelam, *The Just King: Monarchical Judicial Authority in Ancient Israel* (JSOTSup 12; Sheffield: JSOT, 1979). Characteristically, the exploited in Israel appeal to the court of Yahweh when lesser courts fail. Note that the prophets regularly inveigh against rigged courts. It is the circumstance of rigged human courts that makes appeal to the court of Yahweh a socially poignant act of rhetoric.

11. C. Westermann, "Struktur und Geschichte der Klage im Alten Testament," *Forschung am alten Testament* (TBü 24; Munich: Kaiser, 1964) 269–95. In the speech of complaint, the speaker seeks to "triangle" with God against the third party of the triangle, the enemy. On the pervasiveness of "triangling," see M. Bowen, *Family Therapy in Clinical Practice* (New York: Aronson, 1978) 373–76 and *passim*, and, less directly, E. H. Friedman, *Generation to Generation: Family Process in Church and Synagogue* (New York: Guilford, 1985) 35–39, 75–78, and *passim*.

12. See the review of the problem by S. J. L. Croft, *The Identity of the Individual in the Psalms* (JSOTSup 44; Sheffield: Sheffield Academic Press, 1987) 15–48. Croft is surely correct to speak of an "empty metaphor" (71) in the psalms, so that it is not possible to trace any evolutionary development in the content of the various terms for "enemy" or for "poor."

13. The structure of "cry-save" is characteristic in Israel's faith, as is reflected in the psalms of complaint, in the initiation of the Exodus narrative (Exod 2:23–25), and in Songs of Thanksgiving like Psalm 107. Both the cry of Israel and the deeds of Yahweh belong to the remembering of God, and it is that twofold remembering that moves God to act in the present. H. J. Boecker (*Redeformen des israelitischen Rechtslebens im Alten Testament* [WMANT 14; Neukirchen-Vluyn: Neukirchener Verlag, 1964] 94–111) has shown that the capacity of Yahweh to remember has a juridical meaning consistent with the juridical metaphor elsewhere in the psalm. See also B. S. Childs, *Memory and Tradition in Israel* (SBT 37; Chicago: Alec R. Allenson, 1962) 31–41.

14. Thus, for example, in Nicaragua the old alliance among the Samozans reappears at the leadership of the "Contras," and in the Philippines the allies of Marcos retain control of the military. The social forces with disproportionate power find various ways in which

to organize and name their exploitative power. Thus the elimination of an instrument of abuse does not eliminate the powers that propel that abuse.

15. On the anticipatory function of the song of thanksgiving, see Beyerlin, "Die *tôdâ* der Heilsvergegenwärtigung," esp. 209–10. The purpose of such a song of thanksgiving is to foster and enact the expectation that present trouble will be resolved into well-being, as was past trouble.

16. It is remarkable that P. Kennedy, *The Rise and Fall of Great Nations*, analyzes recent nation-states in the same categories. His thesis is that nations overstep their rightful claim to natural resources based on territory and populations. He draws the conclusion that in the present time, the United States has overstepped its rightful share and is now having to withdraw from that overextension. Psalms 9–10 describe a situation in which the powerful have claimed excessive portions of life for themselves. On the painful and direct cost of yielding such disproportion, see K. Newman, *Falling from Grace: The Experience of Downward Mobility in the American Middle Class* (Glencoe, IL: Free Press, 1988).

17. On the strategy of such quotation, see H. W. Wolff, "Das Zitat im Prophetenspruch," *Gesammelte Studien zum Alten Testament* (TBü 22; Munich: Kaiser, 1964) 36–129, and R. Gordis, *Poets, Prophets, and Sages* (Bloomington: Indiana University Press, 1971) 104–59. The inclination to quote one's adversary fits well in a juridical context in which the witness of the adversary is then refuted. The accused one is left responsible for what he has allegedly said.

18. Leveen, "Psalm X: A Reconstruction," 17, suggests that the text be adjusted to show that the statement is indeed a direct quote. See also Gordis, *Poets, Prophets and Sages*, 121.

19. The interplay of quoted speech and counterspeech emphasizes the social, political power of speech. As Yahweh can nullify speech, so also in human relationships, the powerful can silence the speech of the weak. Notice in the speeches of Elihu (Job 32–37) how crucial is the power of speech. On the social power of speech, see M. F. Belenky *et al.*, *Women's Ways of Knowing* (New York: Basic Books, 1986) with its accent on "listening" and "voice."

20. The term "be moved" (*mwṭ, niphal*) is characteristically used in contexts of pious obedience and devoted trust (cf. Ps 15:5, 16:8, 21:7, 30:7, 62:7, 112:6, Prov 10:30). The term is used arrogantly here to claim guaranteed well-being, but without the obedience or trust that is characteristically a condition of such assurance. Thus the quote mocks, or offers a caricature of, conventional use.

21. S. Mowinckel (*Psalmenstudien I: Åwän und die individuellen Klagepsälmen* [2nd ed.; Amsterdam: Schippers, 1961]) has given the classic treatment to the "evil-doers," suggesting they are the ones who work magic. I suggest that Mowinckel's classic treatment does not sufficiently take into account the social power wielded by the "evil-doers." It is not necessary to appeal to "magic," but simply to notice how the powerful control the social discourse of the community, that is, define the terms of social communication, and thereby manipulate social power and shape social relations to their own advantage. Those who protest against the "evil-doers" may be those who have "no voice," because the speech has all been usurped.

22. G. E. Lenski (*Power and Privilege: A Theory of Social Stratification* [Chapel Hill, NC: University of North Carolina Press, 1984]), an important influence on Gottwald, has shown how raw material power inevitably depends on the power of ideology, and not sheer force, for the establishment and maintenance of legitimate poetic portrayal. On the control of social *ideology* by the powerful in the interest of their *property*, see M. D. Meeks, *God the Economist: The Doctrine of God and Political Economy* (Philadelphia: Augsburg Fortress, 1989) 202 and *passim*. Note the use he makes of the work of C. Froman, *The Two American Political Systems: Society, Economics, and Politics* (Englewood Cliffs, NJ: Prentice-Hall, 1984).

23. On the crucial power to define, see T. Morrison, *Beloved* (New York: Knopf, 1987) 190. "Clever, but school teacher beat him anyway to show him that definitions belonged to the definers—not the defined." More programmatically, Karl Marx concluded, "The ruling ideas of each age have ever been the ideas of its ruling class" (D. McLellan, *The Thought of Karl Marx* [London: Macmillan, 1971] 46). J. Gaventa (*Power and Powerlessness: Quiescence and Rebellion in an Appalachian Valley* [Urbana, IL: University of Illinois Press, 1980]) has reviewed a dramatic case in which control of the categories of communication and perception forecloses all social possibilities.

24. On the battle for imagination, see A. N. Wilder, *Jesus' Parables and the War of Myths: Essays on Imagination in the Scripture* (Philadelphia: Fortress, 1982).

25. On the power and responsibility of fictive words, story and poem, see Engelbert, "Introduction," xiii–ix. She writes:

    Occasionally this amputation of history, coupled with a rigid censorship, was successful in colonizing the imagination. . . . Against the powerful ideologies imposing themselves in the isthmus, the ancient strategies of the embattled storyteller—parable and allegory, parody and satire, fable and fantastic tale—were in colonial times, as now, invaluable arms in the struggle to ransom the abducted past, to delineate and to denounce a repressive present).

26. See the works cited in nn. 5 and 25. For a more programmatic treatment of the power of imagination to create an alternative, see G. Green, *Imagining God: Theology and the Religious Imagination* (San Francisco: Harper & Row, 1989). Green does not pursue the subversive element of imagination, but his stress on "as" as the "copulative of imagination" suggests that subversive poetry and narrative see the world differently, and not "as" the dominant culture proposes.

27. To be sure, Yahweh is mentioned in 10:3, but only with the verb *n's*, that is, only in order to be mocked. There is no genuine acknowledgment of Yahweh in the alleged quote of the wicked.

28. It is worth noting that in the poem of Job, which deals with issues very much like our psalms, the entire discussion of Job and his friends never mentions Yahweh, but only "God." It is only in 38:1 that Yahweh now speaks. It is the intrusion and voice of this specific God that shatters the argument. Whereas the earlier discussion tended to eliminate Yahweh, in fact it is the voice of Yahweh that nullifies the earlier discussion. On the attempt to eliminate Yahweh (as the wicked have done in Psalm 10), see M. Tsevat, *The Meaning of the Book of Job and Other Biblical Studies* (New York: KTAV, 1980) 35–37. See also A. Neher, *The Exile of the Word* (Philadelphia: Jewish Publication Society, 1981) 27–30.

29. Morrison, *Beloved*, is a clear example of the way in which fictive writing can effect the redefinition of power relationships. Clearly, the novel functions so that as the central character herself arrives at a self, the implied reader at the same time is moved toward a liberated self. In the narrative, the "defined" seizes the power of definition (cf. n. 23).

30. On the dialectic of "function," see N. K. Gottwald, *The Tribes of Yahweh: A Sociology of the Religion of Liberated Israel, 1250–1050 B.C.E.* (Maryknoll, NY: Orbis, 1979) 608–21. The characterization of Yahwism as "the function of socio-political equality" has obviously caused much trouble for Gottwald. The matter needs to be carefully nuanced, but Gottwald's argument is in any case important, more important than his facile critics allow.

31. See M. J. Buss, "The Study of Forms," *Old Testament Form Criticism* (ed. J. H. Hayes; San Antonio: Trinity University Press, 1974) 31–56. It has been especially Erhard Gerstenberger who has paid attention to the sociology of the psalms.

32. See Gottwald, *The Tribes of Yahweh*, 883–916, and "The Theological Task after *The Tribes of Yahweh*," *The Bible and Liberation* (ed. N. K. Gottwald; Maryknoll, NY: Orbis, 1983) 190–200. Gottwald has clearly moved on methodologically in the meantime. No doubt the debate will continue concerning whether such a dialectical notion of "func-

tion" is a workable articulation for theology. My own impression is that our theological work operates in this way, either above the table or beneath it. We have no choice but to let our theology function in relation to socioeconomic reality and power. To deny this linkage is to engage in self-deception. It is to imagine that when we interpret we can preclude "advocacy."

CHAPTER 2: WHAT'S SO STRANGE ABOUT THE STRANGE WOMAN

1. In addition to the commentaries, see G. Boström, *Proverbiastudien: Die Weisheit und das fremde Weib in Sprüche 1–9* (Lund: Gleerup, 1935); P. Humbert, "La femme étrangère du Livre des Proverbes," *Revue des études sémitiques* 6 (1937) 40–64; "Les adjectifs 'zar' et 'nokri' et la femme étrangère," *Mélanges syriens offerts à M. René Dussaud* I (Bibliothèque Archéologique et Historique, tome 30; Paris: Librairie Orientalisk Paul Guethner, 1939) 259–66; L. A. Snijders, "The Meaning of *zar* in the Old Testament," *OTS* 10 (1954) 1–154; J. N. Aletti, "Séduction et Parole en Proverbes I-IX," *VT* 27 (1977) 129–44; C. Camp, *Wisdom and the Feminine in the Book of Proverbs* (Bible and Literature, 11; Sheffield: Almond, 1985); G. Yee, " 'I Have Perfumed My Bed with Myrrh': The Foreign Woman ('*iššâ zārâ*) in Proverbs 1–9," *JSOT* 43 (1989) 53–68; J. Blenkinsopp, "The Woman Wisdom and Creation in Proverbs 1–9" (unpublished paper, delivered at the SBL, Anaheim, CA, 1989). I thank Prof. Blenkinsopp for providing me with a copy of this paper.
2. *Zār*: 2 Kgs 19:24; Isa 1:7; 25:2, 5; 61:5; Jer 5:19; 30:8; 51:51; Ezek 7:21; 11:9; 28:7; 28:10; 30:12; 31:12; Hos 7:9; Obad 11; Joel 4:17; Job 15:19; Lam 5:2. *Nkr*: Gen 17:12, 27; Exod 2:22; 12:43; 18:3; Lev 22:25; Deut 14:21; 15:3; 17:15; 23:21; 29:21; Judg 19:12; 2 Sam 15:19; 22:45, 46; 1 Kgs 8:41, 43; 11:1, 8; Isa 2:6; 28:21; 56:3, 6; 60:10; 61:5; 62:8; Ezek 44:7, 9; Obad 11; Zeph 1:8; Ps 18:45, 46; 137:4; 144:7, 11; Ruth 2:10; Lam 5:2; 2 Chr 6:32, 33; Ezra 10:2, 10, 11, 14, 17, 18, 44; Neh 9:2; 13:26, 27, 30.
3. *Zār*: Lev 22:10, 12, 13; Deut 25:5; 1 Kgs 3:18; Jer 3:13; Ezek 16:32; Hos 5:7; Ps 69:9; 109:11; Job 19:13, 15, 17. *Nkr*: Gen 31:15; Exod 21:8; Ps 69:9; Prov 23:27; 27:2; Job 19:15; Qoh 6:2. Because adultery and harlotry—that is, sexual activity outside the prescribed familial boundaries—are sometimes used as symbols for religious faithlessness, this meaning of *zār/nkr* overlaps at points with the connotation "outside the covenant" noted below.
4. *Zār* only: Exod 29:33; 30:9, 33; Lev 10:1; 22:10, 12, 13; Num 1:51; 3:4, 10, 38; 17:5; 18:4, 7; 26:61. Because the priests are often conceptualized as of one family ("the sons of Aaron"), the connotation of *zār* as "nonpriest" is at points a subset of the connotation "not of one's own family."
5. *Zār*: Deut 32:16; Isa 1:4; 17:10; 28:21; 43:12; Ezek 14:5; Hos 8:12; Ps 44:21; 58:4; 78:30; 81:10; Job 19:27. *Nkr*: Gen 35:2, 4; Deut 31:16; 32:12; Josh 24:20, 23; Judg 10:16; 1 Sam 7:3; Jer 2:21; 5:19; 8:19; Mal 2:11; Ps 81:10; Dan 11:39; 2 Chr 14:2; 33:15.
6. Camp, *Wisdom and the Feminine*, 112–20, 265–71.
7. Ibid., 119; cf. Snijders, Aletti, and, more recently, Yee, for similar opinions. Boström, and McKane (*Proverbs: A New Approach* [Philadelphia: Westminster, 1970]), on the other hand, have emphasized the woman's status as a foreigner, whereas Newsom sees a movement between these ascriptions ("Woman and the Discourse of Patriarchal Wisdom: A Study of Proverbs 1–9," *Gender and Difference in Ancient Israel* [ed. P. L. Day; Minneapolis: Fortress, 1989] 142–60).
8. Blenkinsopp, "The Woman Wisdom." The quotations in this paragraph and the next are from this as yet unpublished paper.
9. P. A. Bird, " 'To Play the Harlot': An Inquiry into an Old Testament Metaphor," *Gender and Difference in Ancient Israel* (ed. P. L. Day; Minneapolis: Fortress, 1989) 75–94.
10. That is, religious faithlessness came to be understood, by virtue of a dying metaphor, to be an almost literal referent of the language of sexual deviance. Cf. Camp, *Wisdom and the Feminine*, 265–71, and L. Archer, "The 'Evil Women' in Apocryphal and

Pseudepigraphical Writings," *Proceedings of the Ninth World Congress of Jewish Studies, August 4–12, 1985. Division A: The Period of the Bible* (Jerusalem: World Union of Jewish Studies, 1986) 239–46.

11. It is worth noting, for example, that, although the vocabulary in Mal 2:10–15, which clearly does refer to exogamy and foreign worship, is very similar to that of Prov 2:16–17, the prophet's concern is with a god (*'ēl nēkār*), not with a goddess, and does not allude to ritual sex.

12. K. van der Toorn, "Female Prostitution in Payment of Vows in Ancient Israel," *JBL* 108 (1989) 193–205.

13. Ibid., 194–97. Van der Toorn suggests that vow making is particularly a form of female devotion. That women make vows is clear; whether they do so more frequently than do men remains unproven, but neither his argument nor mine depends on this point.

14. Ibid., 197–201, for a recent review of literature.

15. C. H. Toy, *A Critical and Exegetical Commentary on the Book of Proverbs* (ICC; Edinburgh: T. & T. Clark) 151.

16. This interpretation of the passage removes much, if not all, of the burden long carried by the tense of the poor verb *šillamtî*. Because the ultimate fulfillment of the "peace offering" vow involves two days of feasting, it seems clear that this process is not yet in every sense complete at the time the woman accosts the young man. It is possible that she has already offered her sacrifice (though the lack of a verb in v. 14a leaves the phrase temporally ambiguous) and that the moment of the sacrifice constituted a technical completion, thus making appropriate a translation of the perfect verb in v. 14b with the English past tense. On the other hand, the "today" (*hayyôm*) of v. 14b may refer to the 24-hour period beginning that night (cf. 7:9) and ending the following evening, in which case the act of sacrifice has yet to take place and a translation of *šillamtî* with modal force (so Boström and van der Toorn) is appropriate. In any case, all we need to know for our purposes is that sometime "today" the act has been or will be complete; hence my choice of the present tense, "fulfill," rendered with the force of a perfect verb.

17. In Blenkinsopp's view, the warning in Prov 5:10 that "strangers (*zārim*) will take their fill of your wealth and your labors will go to the house of an alien (*bêt nokrî*)," which immediately precedes the reference to ruin in the *qāhāl wĕ'ēdâ*, is a further indication that the *'iššâ zārâ* is a foreign woman (cf. the actions taken by Ezra against men with foreign wives). The Hebrew Bible also shows evidence, however, for the *zār* as one who is outside of one's family household (see n. 3). Thus, the beneficiaries of the young man's profanation of the cult could as well be construed as other members of the community to whom his goods would be distributed when he is "cut off." Our interpretation of chapter 5 should perhaps be guided, however, primarily by the poem on marital fidelity in vv. 15–19. In this case, the crime is adultery, but the punishment—loss of status and property to fellow citizens who are nonetheless *zār* with respect to one's patrimony—is still the same.

18. It is in interpreting passages like Deut 23:18 that van der Toorn's argument, in my view, runs astray. He sees this verse as evidence that "among Israelites, the custom of paying vows by means of prostitution was a known phenomenon" (200). I have offered here what seems to me a far more natural interpretation, namely, that prostitutes sometimes made vows and then attempted to pay them with the proverbial wages of sin.

19. Recent studies on sex and cultic impurity include G. J. Wenham, "Why Does Sexual Intercourse Defile (Lev 15:18)?" *ZAW* 95 (1983) 432–34, and J. Milgrom, "Rationale for Cultic Law: The Case of Impurity," *Thinking Biblical Law* (ed. D. Patrick; *Semeia* 45 [1989] 103–109). For a functionalist approach to sociosexual deviance, see T. Frymer-Kensky, "Law and Philosophy: The Case of Sex in the Bible," *Semeia* 45 (1989) 89–102.

20. For an analysis of symbolic modalities related to the human experience of evil, see P. Ricoeur, *The Symbolism of Evil* (Boston: Beacon, 1967), esp. 18.

21. Snijders, "The Meaning of *zar*," 127.
22. This view of our sage as a post-Ezra, priestly Torah-scholar can be supported by at least three other pieces of evidence, which this essay does not allow space to elaborate. First, the urban setting of the poems in Proverbs 1–9 seems to presuppose the existence of a walled Jerusalem, as does the imagery of the harlot, who is a phenomenon of urbanization and some degree of excess wealth (cf. Bird, " 'To Play the Harlot,' " 78). Second, Patrick Skehan's work on the structure of Proverbs ("Wisdom's House," *Studies in Israelite Poetry and Wisdom* [CBQMS 1; Washington: Catholic Biblical Association of America, 1971] 27–45), which shows it to be a literary representation of the Temple structure in 1 Kings 6, may well indicate the same kind of reflection on the written word as that of the allusions to cultic law in Prov 7:14. Third, an analysis by Al Wolters of the woman of worth poem in Prov 31:10–31 indicates the presence of a Hebrew-Greek word-play, thus suggesting a date post-Alexander, at least for this poem ("*Ṣôpiyyâ* [Prov 31:27] as Hymnic Particle and Play on *Sophia*," *JBL* 104 [1985] 577–87).
23. See Camp, *Wisdom and the Feminine*, 71–75, for a fuller elaboration of the theory of metaphor applied here.
24. The one questionable text is Neh 10:30 (Heb 31), which uses the full reciprocal formula: "give our daughters/take their daughters." Toni Craven, in oral communication, has suggested that Nehemiah's policies were in general more egalitarian and inclusive of women as members of the people than were Ezra's (cf., e.g., Neh 5:1–13), a possibility that deserves further exploration.
25. Van der Toorn raises the interesting possibility that a (quite secular!) prostitution service was run by temple personnel for the purpose of enhancing temple revenues ("Female Prostitution," 202–204). Similarly, Bird finds that Hos 4:11–14 suggests "that prostitutes found the rural sanctuaries an attractive place to do business, quite possibly by agreement with the priests" (" 'To Play the Harlot,' " 88). Both scholars caution against taking evidence for such activities as sign of authorized sexual ritual.
26. With respect to gender, then, Malachi makes literal and univocal what had been tensive and disturbing. In Hosea 2 and 4, in Num 25:1 (the story of Baal-Peor), and in Isaiah 57, the authors waver in their depiction of Israel's faithlessness between the image of the wanton female and language about lustful men. Bird (75) notes the special incongruity of Num 25:1: "While Israel dwelt at Shittim the people began to play the harlot with the daughters of Moab."
27. So B. Glazier-McDonald, "Intermarriage, Divorce, and the *Bat-'ēl Nēkār*: Insights into Mal 2:10–16," *JBL* 106 (1987) 603–11.
28. The choice of alternative words for "companion" (*ḥăbertĕkā* in Mal 2:14 and *'allûp* in Prov 2:17) can be explained by the needs of alliteration and assonance. See Camp, *Wisdom and the Feminine*, 319, n. 5.
29. Cf. Snijders, "The Meaning of *zar*," 68, 78, 88–104, and C. J. H. Wright, "The Israelite Household and the Decalogue: The Social Background and Significance of Some Commandments," *Tyndale Bulletin* 30 (1979) 101–24.
30. Bird's analysis of Gomer reveals that the various modes of sexual deviance are interrelated in a similar manner in the prophetic text: Gomer is not a professional prostitute, but rather a wanton woman; only gradually does the context move us to understand her as an adulteress.
31. Bird, " 'To Play the Harlot,' " 79; S. Niditch, "The Wronged Woman Righted: An Analysis of Genesis 38," *HTR* 72 (1979) 147.
32. The point is reaffirmed in Prov 6:26 by the negative comparison between the *'iššâ zônâ*, who may be had for a loaf of bread, and an *'ēšet 'îš*, who "stalks a man's very life."
33. That such "memories" of the dastardly foreign female were held in high regard by members of the wisdom tradition is evident in the fact that Ben Sira's hymn to the ancestors contains allusions both to Phinehas's mighty deed against Cozbi, the daughter of Midian who married an Israelite at Baal-Peor (Numbers 25; Sir 44:23–25), and to the

demise of Solomon, who gave women (here, no longer even qualified as "foreign") dominion over his body (1 Kings 11; Sir 47:19).

34. Cf. Newsom's analysis of the intergenerational aspects of Proverbs' discourse, "Woman and the Discourse of Patriarchal Wisdom."

35. The relationship of the figure of the strange man in Proverbs to the strange woman is the subject of a study currently in progress by this author.

36. Prov 5:3; 6:24; 7:21; cf. 2:16, and for the strange man, 6:2.

37. Other references include Isa 61:5; Jer 5:19; Obad 11; Ps 69:9; 81:10; Job 19:15; Lam 5:2.

38. Cf. Prov 23:33, where drunkenness is said to cause one's eyes to see zārôt, presumably an abstraction ("strange things"), but in a grammatical form that could be construed "strange women."

39. McKane, Proverbs, 287–88.

CHAPTER 3: PSALM 139

1. Taking Psalms 9–10 as one composition and the lack of ldwd with Psalm 33 in the Hebrew text at face value.

2. Psalms 70 and 71 may represent a single composition.

3. In both these cases, the textual attestation is quite ambiguous.

4. In some cases, venerable English expressions have conveniently lost their seventeenth-century edge and have not been replaced in translations of these psalms.

5. The following is a sampling of treatments as the plea of an innocent person: S. Mowinckel, The Psalms in Israel's Worship (2 vols.; Nashville: Abingdon, 1962) 1.24, 2.75, 131–32; G. Fohrer, Introduction to the Old Testament (Nashville: Abingdon, 1968) 292; H.-J. Kraus, Psalms 60–150: A Commentary (Minneapolis: Augsburg, 1989) 512 (but then modified with additional considerations); B. W. Anderson, Out of the Depths: The Psalms Speak for Us Today (Philadelphia: Westminster, 1970) 61–62, 169, 177 (with hesitation: "wisdom psalm?"); L. C. Allen, Psalms 101–150 (Waco, TX: Word Books, 1983) 257–58, 260–63, excellent discussion, with reference to previous literature; P. D. Miller, Interpreting the Psalms (Philadelphia: Fortress, 1986) 144–53, with theological commentary. Norman Gottwald's discussion of the Psalms in The Hebrew Bible: A Socio-Literary Introduction (Philadelphia: Fortress, 1985) is exemplary; the argument here, however, is that Psalm 139 should be classed not as a "wisdom and law" psalm (532), but as an "anonymous individual lament" (527–28).

6. The New American Bible (New York: Kenedy & Sons, 1970) 849. Obviously, not all study resources take this approach, but it represents a propensity with this psalm. Contrast the comments in The New Oxford Annotated Bible (New York: Oxford University Press, 1973) 761–62: "Prayer for deliverance from personal enemies (a lament). . . . An appeal to the Lord . . . to demonstrate the psalmist's innocence and to save him. . . . Prayer for vindication and deliverance."

7. Cult and jurisdiction were inseparable in the biblical world. This connection obviates the discussion in the commentaries on the "religious" character of Psalm 139 in particular.

CHAPTER 4: "TO HER MOTHER'S HOUSE"

1. N. K. Gottwald, The Tribes of Yahweh: A Sociology of the Religion of Liberated Israel, 1250–1050 B.C.E. (Maryknoll, NY: Orbis, 1979).

2. See especially his comments in The Tribes of Yahweh, 695, 700, and n. 628.

3. A notable exception is E. F. Campbell, Ruth (AB 7; Garden City, NY: Doubleday, 1975) 64–65.

4. Dealing with these biases involves what E. Schüssler Fiorenza calls a hermeneutics of suspicion; see her Bread Not Stone (Boston: Beacon, 1984) 16.

5. See my discussion of this bias in Discovering Eve: Ancient Israelite Women in Context (New York: Oxford University Press, 1988) 11–12.

6. An excellent example of a study uncovering such bias is Jane Barr's "The Vulgate Genesis and St. Jerome's Attitude to Women," *Studia Patristica* 18 (1982) 268–73.
7. E.g., the fact that Hannah herself offers a sacrifice is explicit in the MT. Yet 4QSam[a] and the LXX deny her the agency of sacrifice; and modern commentators, assuming that women had little or no cultic role, value the versions over the MT. See my analysis of this incident in "The Hannah Narrative in Feminist Perspective," forthcoming in the D. W. Young *Festschrift* (Winona Lake, IN: Eisenbrauns).
8. Schüssler Fiorenza's challenge to discover "a feminist coin" in a sweep of biblical tradition involves coupling a hermeneutics of remembrance with one of suspicion; *Bread Not Stone*, 19–20.
9. Gottwald, *The Tribes of Yahweh*, 288–90; cf. R. R. Wilson, "The Family," *Harper's Bible Dictionary* (San Francisco: Harper & Row, 1985) 302.
10. See D. L. Smith, *The Religion of the Landless: The Social Context of the Babylonian Exile* (Bloomington, IN: Meyer Stone, 1989) 93–126.
11. See Meyers, *Discovering Eve*, 128–38, for a discussion of the biblical terminology and of the sociological understanding of what is meant by a "family household."
12. I. J. Gelb, "Approaches to the Study of Ancient Society," *JAOS* 81 (1967) 1–7.
13. See Meyers, *Discovering Eve*, 142–64, for a summary of various household functions. The size of the household has been much debated. As a residential and social unit, the usual estimates have been much too high. See L. E. Stager, "The Family in Ancient Israel," *BASOR* 260 (1985) 17–23, for a more realistic appraisal that takes into account archaeological and ethnographic data.
14. See E. Boserup, *Women's Role in Economic Development* (London: Allen and Unwin, 1970) 140, and the discussion in Meyers, *Discovering Eve*, 165–73.
15. See Meyers, *Discovering Eve*, 174–81.
16. Schüssler Fiorenza's understanding of the relationship between androcentric texts and historical reality in *In Memory of Her* (New York: Crossroad, 1985) is eloquent and relevant: "Androcentric texts and linguistic reality constructions must not be mistaken as trustworthy evidence of human culture, history, and religion. The text *may* be the message, but the message is not coterminous with human reality and history" (p. 29; see Part I of her book for a general discussion of the text-reality issue).
17. See, e.g., G. von Rad, *Genesis* (OTL; rev. ed.; Philadelphia: Westminster, 1972) 257; B. Vawter, *On Genesis: A New Reading* (Garden City, NY: Doubleday, 1977) 272; and J. Skinner, *Genesis* (ICC; 2nd ed.; Edinburgh: T & T Clark, 1930) 344.
18. So E. A. Speiser, *Genesis* (AB 1; Garden City, NY: Doubleday, 1964) 181–82.
19. So W. M. Roth, "The Wooing of Rebekah: A Tradition-Critical Study of Genesis 24," *CBQ* 34 (1972) 177–87.
20. G. W. Coats, *Genesis: With an Introduction to Narrative Literature* (FOTL 1; Grand Rapids, MI: Eerdmans, 1983) 167.
21. Coats, *Genesis*, 170; and Roth, "The Wooing of Rebekah."
22. S. Terrien (*Till the Heart Sings: A Biblical Theology of Manhood and Womanhood* [Philadelphia: Fortress, 1985] 31) notes the great admiration the story has elicited and claims that few novellas can rival or excel the Rebekah story, "not even that of Ulysses discovering Nausicäa in the Odyssey."
23. See N. M. Sarna, *Genesis* (The JPS Torah Commentary; Philadelphia: Jewish Publication Society, 1989) 161.
24. Sarna, *Genesis*; see especially his treatment of 32:17.
25. Speiser, *Genesis*, 182, asserts that Isaac "can scarcely be described as a memorable personality in his own right" and is important only as a genealogical link.
26. Ibid.
27. On its genre, see Campbell, *Ruth*, 3–10. For another, very detailed perspective on genre, see J. Sasson, *Ruth: A New Translation with a Philological Commentary and a Formalist-Folklorist Interpretation* (Baltimore: Johns Hopkins University Press, 1979) 197–221. As a

short story, Ruth, like the Rebekah chapter discussed above, has many of the same features as the Joseph story; cf. *inter alia* O. Eissfeldt, *The Old Testament: An Introduction* (New York: Harper & Row, 1965) 38.

28. So P. Trible, *God and the Rhetoric of Sexuality* (Philadelphia: Fortress, 1978) 166–99. Somewhat less generous in claiming positive female traditions in the Hebrew Bible, P. Bird nonetheless acknowledges the centrality of women in Ruth; see "Images of Women in the Old Testament," *Religion and Sexism* (ed. R. R. Ruether; New York: Simon & Schuster, 1974) 83.

29. E. Fuchs' discussion ("Status and Role of Female Heroines in the Biblical Narrative," *Mankind Quarterly* 23 [1982] 149–60) is among the most pointed.

30. See C. Meyers, "Women and the Domestic Economy of Early Israel," *Women's Earliest Records: From Ancient Egypt and Western Asia* (ed. B. S. Lesko; Brown Judaic Studies 166; Atlanta: Scholars Press, 1989) 269–70, for a discussion of the difficulty in evaluating "patriarchy" in a premodern society and in focusing on the role of individuals.

31. Campbell, *Ruth*, 64.

32. E.g., Sasson, *Ruth*, 23. The situations of other unmarried women (in Num 30:16, Deut 22:21, and Judg 19:2–3) also involve a connection to the "father's house." Cf. the quaint idea proposed by L. P. Smith (*The Book of Ruth* [IB 2; New York: Abingdon, 1953] 835) that "mother's house" is used, even though Ruth has a father (2:11), because Naomi is thinking of the "women's quarters," and the whimsical suggestion of P. Joüon, *Ruth: Commentaire philologique et exégétique* (Subsidia Biblica 9; Rome: Pontifical Biblical Institute, 1986 [orig. ed. 1953]) 36, that the use of mother is "plus délicat, plus féminin" and is appropriate because a woman is speaking.

33. So Campbell, *Ruth*, 60.

34. R. E. Murphy, *Wisdom Literature: Job, Proverbs, Ruth, Canticles, Ecclesiastes, Esther* (FOTL 13; Grand Rapids, MI: Eerdmans, 1981) 101–102; see also M. H. Pope, *Song of Songs* (AB 7C; Garden City, NY: Doubleday, 1977) 22–23, 432–33.

35. The other 13 percent of the text is spoken by choruses or consists of headings or verses of doubtful attribution. For an accounting of the distribution of verses by gender, see A. Brenner, *The Israelite Woman: Social Role and Literary Type in Biblical Narrative* (Sheffield: JSOT, 1985) 47–49.

36. Pointed out by Trible (*God and the Rhetoric of Sexuality*, 145), who also draws attention to other literary features signaling the prominence of the female.

37. Suggested by Brenner, *The Israelite Woman*, 45–50, among others.

38. For an examination of this reversal of gender-stereotypical language, see C. Meyers, "Gender Imagery in the Song of Songs," *Hebrew Annual Review* 10 (1986) 209–23.

39. Note also the recurrent appearance of "mother," which is found seven (!) times, whereas "father" is never mentioned; see Trible, *God and the Rhetoric of Sexuality*, 158.

40. Author's translation, rendering *'el* as "to" (with Pope, *Song of Songs*, NAB, REB, and NEB) rather than "into" (so RSV, NRSV, and other translations).

41. See R. Alter, *The Art of Biblical Poetry* (New York: Basic Books, 1985) 62–84, for a discussion of structures of intensification in Hebrew poetry.

42. E.g., JPSV, KJV; cf. M. Falk, *Love Lyrics from the Bible* (Bible and Literature Series 4; Sheffield: Almond, 1982) 129. See the NAB for an example of a translation that reads the word as masculine, only by also changing the subsequent stich ("there you would teach me to . . .").

43. E.g., RSV, NRSV, NEB (which reads "embrace" for "teach" and also inserts another stich), REB.

44. See R. Gordis, *The Song of Songs and Lamentations* (New York: KTAV, 1974) 98, for a rather convoluted conjecture about how the Hebrew may have been corrupted into MT *tĕlammĕdēnî* by a scribe confusing the verb *hrh* ("to conceive"), an original "she bore me," with the hiphil of *yrh*, the presumed root of *tôrâ*. Others would delete the *m* of *tlmdny* to achieve *tēlĕdēnî*, "(who) bore me." T. J. Meek (*Song of Songs* [IB 5; New York:

Abingdon, 1956], 140) exemplifies those who assume that maternal instruction "makes no sense here." M. Fox (*The Song of Songs and Ancient Egyptian Love Songs* [Madison: University of Wisconsin Press, 1985] 165–66) favors an expansion as an emendation of *tlmdny* to *yldty*.

45. See Pope, *Song of Songs*, 659, and the works cited.
46. See Meyers, *Discovering Eve*, 149–54, for a discussion of the mother's role in socialization and education in the family household.
47. On the structure of the book, see *inter alia* R. B. Y. Scott, *Proverbs Ecclesiastes* (AB 18; Garden City, NY: Doubleday, 1965) 14–22, and Murphy, *Wisdom Literature*, 49–50. Scholars divide the various subsections in different ways, but there is general agreement about the discrete nature of Proverbs 1–9, followed by a group of subcollections and/or appendices, and ending with the poem about the worthy woman (*'ēšet ḥayil*).
48. The term is variously given architectural, mythological, and (literary) structural significance; so Scott, *Proverbs*, 76–77, and Murphy, *Wisdom Literature*, 52. See also the summary of scholarly perspectives in W. McKane, *Proverbs* (OTL; Philadelphia: Westminster, 1970) 362–63.
49. C. R. Fontaine ("Proverbs," *Harper's Bible Commentary* [San Francisco: Harper & Row, 1988] 509–10) sees one of these verses (14:1) as part of a midrash on the banquet scene of 9:1–6.
50. RSV, NAB, and the commentaries of Scott (*Proverbs*, 96) and McKane (*Proverbs*, 231, cf. 472) are among those that delete "women." Some retain it: NEB, "The wisest women build their homes"; JPSV, "Every wise woman buildeth her house"; and NRSV, "The wise woman builds her house."
51. Pointed out by C. V. Camp, *Wisdom and the Feminine in the Book of Proverbs* (Bible and Literature Series 11; Sheffield: Almond, 1985) 200–201.
52. This is the thesis of Camp's book, *Wisdom and the Feminine*. See also Fontaine's summary ("Proverbs," 501–503) of the various theories about the origin of the anomalous figure of personified wisdom.
53. See C. Newsom, "Woman and the Discourse of Patriarchal Wisdom: A Study of Proverbs 1–9," *Gender and Difference in Ancient Israel* (ed. P. L. Day; Minneapolis: Fortress, 1989) 142.
54. Ibid.
55. So Roth, "The Wooing of Rebekah," 180. He draws on the analysis of R. M. Hals (*The Theology of the Book of Ruth* [Biblical Series 23; Philadelphia: Fortress, 1969]), who discovers a similarity between the Ruth and Rebekah novellas.
56. As in Murphy's *Wisdom Literature*. He is careful to note that "Wisdom Literature" is not itself a genre and so can be an inclusive designation. The Song surely has many wisdom interests and connections—Solomon, nature, the individual, no direct divine involvement; cf. Terrien, *Till the Heart Sings*, 45–46.
57. Boaz is the father, and the Moabite Ruth is the mother; but Ruth 4:17 announces that "A son is born to Naomi"!
58. The theories linking *ḥokmâ* with mythological goddess figures (as reviewed by Camp, *Wisdom and the Feminine*, 23–68) retain some validity even if a human model for female Wisdom is accepted; after all, goddesses too were shaped by the data of the human realm.
59. The leadership of women viewed internally, in terms of their household roles, may be reflected in the use of the term *gĕberet* for Sarah, in reference to her relationship with Hagar (Gen 16:4, 9). The usual translation, "mistress," is too coy and sexist, because the male equivalent, in terms of external leadership, involves a man's power over others (see Gen 27:29, 37; cf. Josh 7:17).
60. See the discussion in Meyers, *Discovering Eve*, 154–55.
61. Camp's examination (*Wisdom and the Feminine*, 139) of the link between indirection (through speech) and wisdom is particularly relevant to this point.

CHAPTER 5: MICAH—A REVOLUTIONARY

1. M. Buber, *The Kingship of God* (New York: Harper & Row, 1973).
2. G. E. Mendenhall, "The Hebrew Conquest of Palestine," *BA* 25 (1962) 66–87 (repr. *BAR* 3 [1970] 100–20).
3. Amos called down the wrath of God on the crimes committed against the poor in Israel. He was little interested in exploring the means by which God's wrath would be executed or in suggesting alternative futures. He did not, so far as we know, call on the oppressed to band together in order to force a new social order. He is praised in a church that sees its greatest task as that of denouncing the evils committed by the powerful. And he is questioned by those who, like M. Silver (*Prophets and Markets: The Political Economy of Ancient Israel* [Boston: Kluwer-Nijhoff, 1983]), feel that only the "better" representatives of society can ever resolve its problems, and that their freedom to act must be preserved from well-intentioned but ill-informed moralists like Amos.
4. Modern prophetic scholarship since J. C. Eichhorn has operated on the assumption that the editors of the prophetic texts usually failed to share the radicality of the prophets, and often toned down their sayings to make them acceptable in the religious communities where they were read.
5. Thus it was a difficult text for the Greek translators of LXX, who were unable to provide a coherent reading. It was a difficult text also for Jerome, who took considerable liberties with MT, and only occasionally relied on LXX, to produce a coherent translation.
6. I have made a study of modern translations into Spanish, which shows that all are built on the assumption that the censored oracle was a denunciation of the landholders addressed in 2:1–5. See my "Miqueas 2.6–11: ¿Qué quiso silenciar la Casa de Jacob? Profetismo e insurrección," *Revista Biblica*, Vol. 33, 1989. It has not been possible for me to make a similar study of English translations, though at least the RSV follows the same pattern.
7. Albrecht Alt, in a late (1955) article ("Micha 2, 1–5, GES ANADASMOS in Juda," *Kleine Schriften* III [Munich: Beck, 1959] 373–81), departs from this procedure by taking 5:1–5 as reflecting the authentic perspective of the prophet. This article is very important because it reveals an awareness of the contrast between Judah and Jerusalem, although Alt does not root this opposition in anything deeper than administrative history. Once one raises the possibility of Micah representing a revolutionary outlook, the likelihood of 5:1–5 being authentic decreases. In any case, it is methodologically more conservative to build our portrayal of Micah exclusively on the basis of the primary collection of his sayings.
8. Ibid.
9. In a recent textbook for elementary theological students, I have attempted systematically to read the history of Israel as the history of the conflicts between its fundamental social classes. See *Historia sagrada, historia popular: Historia de Israel desde los pobres, 1220 a.C.– 135 d.C.* (Managua: CIEETS, 1989).

CHAPTER 6: "ENEMIES" AND THE POLITICS OF PRAYER

1. B. Duhm, *Die Psalmen, erklärt* (Kurzer Hand-Commentar zum Alten Testament; 2nd ed.; Freiburg: Mohr, 1922) 104, 53.
2. H. Gunkel and J. Begrich, *Einleitung in die Psalmen: Die Gattungen der religiösen Lyrik Israels* (Handbuch zum Alten Testament; Göttingen: Vandenhoeck & Ruprecht, 1933) 184. Cf. R. C. Culley, *Oral Formulaic Language in the Biblical Psalms* (Toronto: University of Toronto Press, 1967) 23–31.
3. H. Gunkel, *Ausgewählte Psalmen* (4th ed.; Göttingen: Vandenhoeck & Ruprecht, 1917) 46.
4. Gunkel and Begrich, *Einleitung in die Psalmen*, 206–208 and esp. 190–93.

5. E.g., in their commentaries, H.-J. Kraus accepted only Psalms 6, 22, 30, 38, 41, 69, and 88 as certain, and A. Deissler only 6, 30, 38, 41, 69, and 88 (with 31 and 55 as further possibilities).
6. O. Keel, *Feinde und Gottesleugner: Studien zum Image der Widersacher in den Individualpsalmen* (Stuttgarter biblische Monographien 7; Stuttgart: Katholisches Bibelwerk GmbH, 1969) 18–19.
7. S. Mowinckel, *Psalmenstudien I: Åwän und die individuellen Klagepsalmen* (2nd ed.; Amsterdam: Schippers, 1961) 1–2, 5, 29–30.
8. See the review by J. Hempel of S. Mowinckel's *Psalmenstudien* in *Orientalische Literaturzeitung* 29 (1926) 482–84.
9. H. Birkeland, *Die Feinde des Individuums in der israelitischen Psalmenliteratur* (Oslo: Dybwad, 1933) 19, 59–94, 146, 151, 171–72.
10. G. Widengren, "Early Hebrew Myth," *Myth, Ritual and Kingship: Essays on the Theory and Practice of Kingship in the Ancient East and Israel* (ed. S. H. Hooke; Oxford, Oxford University Press, 1958) 199–200.
11. L. Delekat, *Asylie und Schutzorakel am Zionheiligtum: Eine Untersuchung zu den privaten Feindpsalmen* (Leiden: Brill, 1967); Keel, *Feinde und Gottesleugner*; S. J. L. Croft, *The Identity of the Individual in the Psalms* (JSOTSup 44; Sheffield: JSOT, 1987) 20.
12. Delekat, *Asylie und Schutzorakel*, 5.
13. See the criticism of Keel, *Feinde und Gottesleugner*, 29.
14. Ibid., 216.
15. Croft, *The Identity of the Individual*, 20.
16. Ibid., 177–78.
17. See N. Frye, *The Great Code: The Bible and Literature* (New York: Harcourt Brace Jovanovich, 1982) xiii, and B. S. Childs, *Introduction to the Old Testament as Scripture* (Philadelphia: Fortress, 1979) 72–79. Regarding a premodern antecedent of "shape" in the older usage of the term "scope," see G. T. Sheppard, "Between Reformation and Modernity: The Perception of the Scope of Biblical Books," *William Perkins' Commentary on Galatians (1617): With Introductory Essays* (ed. G. T. Sheppard; New York: Pilgrim, 1989) xlii–lxxi.
18. N. K. Gottwald, *The Hebrew Bible: A Socio-Literary Introduction* (Philadelphia: Fortress, 1985); see the section entitled "A Common Ground in New Literary and Social Scientific Criticism" (pp. 29–31).
19. Ibid., 31.
20. Ibid., 302.
21. Ibid., 335.
22. Ibid., 525.
23. Ibid., esp. 377–87, 492–502. Although Gottwald acknowledges redactional complexity in Isaiah 1–39, he still treats Isaiah 40–66 as an isolated set of traditions and never really considers the implications of the exilic and postexilic editing of Isaiah 1–39 together with Isaiah 40–66 in a manner comparable to his treatment of the book of Psalms. Cf. C. R. Seitz, "Isaiah 1–66: Making Sense of the Whole," *Reading and Preaching the Book of Isaiah* (ed. C. R. Seitz; Philadelphia: Fortress, 1988) 105–26; Childs, *Introduction to the Old Testament*, 311–38; and G. T. Sheppard, "Isaiah 1–39," *Harper's Bible Commentary* (ed. J. L. Mays; San Francisco: Harper & Row, 1988) 542–70; R. Rendtorff, "Zur Komposition des Buches Jesajas," *VT* 34 (1984) 295–320.
24. Gottwald, *The Hebrew Bible*, 537–41.
25. Ibid., 538.
26. Ibid., 539.
27. Ibid., 539–40.
28. F. G. Bailey, "The Peasant View of the Bad Life," *Peasants and Peasant Societies* (ed. T. Shanin; New York: Penguin, 1971) 314.

29. I. M. Lewis, *Social Anthropology in Perspective: The Relevance of Social Anthropology* (New York: Penguin, 1976) 140.
30. Ibid., 141.
31. H. W. F. Saggs, *The Greatness that Was Babylon* (New York: Mentor, 1962) 366.
32. Lewis, *Social Anthropology*, 142. Cf. M. Gluckman, *Order and Rebellion in Tribal Africa: Collected Essays* (London: Routledge & Kegan Paul, 1963).
33. Lewis, *Social Anthropology*, 144.
34. E.g., "Die Grundprobleme der israelitischen Literaturgeschichte," *Reden und Aufsätze* (Göttingen: Vandenhoeck & Ruprecht, 1913) 33–34. In the same essay, Gunkel describes the sad consequence of this progression to learned, written poetry and the canonization of scripture under the following characterization: "Zum Schluss dann die Tragödie der israelitischen Literatur: der Geist nimmt ab . . ."(p. 36). For Gunkel, editors of scripture appear most frequently as clumsy and doctrinaire manipulators of the original, smaller, pristine unities of the oral *Gattungen*.
35. K. Grayson, "Murmuring in Mesopotamia" (forthcoming in a *Festschrift* for W. G. Lambert; London: School of Oriental and African Studies, 1992); J. Saenger, "Silent Reading: Its Import on Late Medieval Scripture and Society," *Viator* 13 (1982) 367–414. On the anecdote about Augustine and Ambrose, see Augustine's *Confessions*, Sect. VI, 3, lines 25–27.
36. C. Westermann, "Struktur und Geschichte der Klage im Alten Testament," *Forschung am Alten Testament* (TBü 24; Munich: Kaiser, 1964) 269–95.
37. The lament psalms frequently contain vows that promise to offer a thanksgiving psalm in the sanctuary and before the assembly of people there. So, Ps 35:18 promises that "I will praise you in the great congregation; in the mighty throng I will acclaim you" (v. 18, cf. 40:10; 22:22). Psalm 116:13–14 describes a ritual of lifting a cup at a banquet in the presence of friends. Psalms can expressly call upon the surrounding people to clap their hands, shout for joy, and join in the praise (e.g., 22:23; 33:1; 34:3–5; 47:1; 66:1–3, 8; 68:4), and sometimes prayers suggest the very words the listening congregation should say to God (e.g., 35:27; 66:3).
38. Cf. G. T. Sheppard, "The Anti-Assyrian Redaction and the Canonical Context of Isaiah 1–39," *JBL* 104 (1985) 204–11.
39. E. Gerstenberger properly detects in these psalms signs of a "dispute between opposing parties for individuals who are suffering" (*Psalms: Part 1. With an Introduction to Cultic Poetry* [FOTL 14; Grand Rapids: Eerdmans, 1988] 79). My proposal about the role of overhearing such prayers would, however, eliminate the need to speculate precariously, as Gerstenberger and other scholars have done, about the possibility of an open verbal accusation and response with an enemy as a formal part of worship activity. Speech addressed directly to the enemy certainly would invite a response, but prayer by its nature is addressed first to God and only secondarily to those who overhear. In the logic of prayer, God is always given the option to reply first!
40. This tendency is very common and might be grounds for criticizing, for example, Brevard Childs' discussion of psalms in the chapter "Life Under Threat" of his *Old Testament Theology in a Canonical Context* (Philadelphia: Fortress, 1986). Childs there explains the language of "death" by "the suffering community" solely in terms of the experience of one's own short life and of "illness" as a foretaste of each person's inevitable, natural death.
41. On a similar use of the psalms, see M. M. Fortune, "My God, My God, Why Have You Forsaken Me?" *Spinning a Sacred Yarn: Women Speak from the Pulpit* (ed. by the publisher; New York: Pilgrim, 1982) 65–71, and S. B. Thistlewaite, "Every Two Minutes— Battered Women and Feminist Interpretation," *Weaving the Visions: New Patterns in Feminist Spirituality* (ed. J. Plaskow and C. Christ; San Francisco: Harper & Row, 1989).
42. For more on this same subject, see my "Blessed Are Those Who Take Refuge in Him (Ps 2:11): Biblical Criticism and Deconstruction," *Religion and Intellectual Life* 5 (1988)

57–66, and "Psalms: How Do the Ordinary Words of Women and Men [to God] Become God's Word to Me?" *The Future of the Bible: How to Read a Book that Seems Intent on Reading You* (Toronto: The United Church Publishing House, 1990) 49–98.
43. D. Bonhoeffer, *Psalms: The Prayerbook of the Bible* (Minneapolis: Augsburg, 1970) 11–12.
44. Childs, *Old Testament Theology*, 231–32.
45. Ibid., 207–10.
46. Bonhoeffer, *Psalms*, 60.

CHAPTER 7: EXEGETICAL STORYTELLING

1. D. C. Morgan, *Between Text and Community* (Minneapolis: Fortress, 1990) 9.
2. Ibid., 10.
3. P. Trible, *God and the Rhetoric of Sexuality* (Philadelphia: Fortress, 1978) 9, and B. L. Mack, *Rhetoric and the New Testament* (Minneapolis: Fortress, 1990) 14, 17.
4. Trible, *God and the Rhetoric of Sexuality*, 12.
5. Ibid.

CHAPTER 8: ISRAELITE RELIGION AND THE FAITH OF ISRAEL'S DAUGHTERS

1. Two (unpublished) papers were presented in the SBL (-ASOR) "Social World" project: "Sexual Distinction in Israelite Personal Names: A Socio-Religious Investigation" (SBL Seminar on the Social World of Ancient Israel, 1976) and "Women's Religious Participation in the Monarchy" (SBL-ASOR Seminar on the Sociology of the Monarchy, 1986). Related work, stimulated in large measure by these seminars, includes the following articles: "The Place of Women in the Israelite Cultus," *Ancient Israelite Religion: Essays in Honor of Frank Moore Cross* (ed. P. D. Miller, P. D. Hanson, and S. D. McBride; Philadelphia: Fortress, 1987) 397–419; "The Harlot as Heroine in Biblical Texts: Narrative Art and Social Presupposition," *Semeia* 46 (1989) 119–39; " 'To Play the Harlot': An Inquiry into an Old Testament Metaphor," *Gender and Difference* (ed. P. L. Day; Minneapolis: Augsburg Fortress, 1989) 75–94; "Women's Religion in Ancient Israel," *Women's Earliest Records: From Ancient Egypt and Western Asia* (ed. B. Lesko; Brown Judaic Studies 166; Atlanta: Scholars Press, 1989) 283–98; "Women (OT)," *Anchor Bible Dictionary* (Garden City, NY: Doubleday, forthcoming). See also my earlier work, "Images of Woman in the Old Testament," *Religion and Sexism: Images of Women in the Jewish and Christian Traditions* (ed. R. R. Ruether; New York: Simon & Schuster, 1974) 41–88; reprinted in *The Bible and Liberation: Political and Social Hermeneutics* (ed. N. K. Gottwald; Maryknoll, NY: Orbis, 1983) 252–88.
2. See Bird, "The Place of Women," 398–99, for an initial statement of aims in reconstruction. The problem that concerns me is the continued segregation of women in the social reconstruction of ancient Israel—both topically (as subjects of research) and in division of research labor. Can we continue to analyze and reconstruct the society (social order, institutions, worldview, etc.) by reference to men's activities and symbolic constructions and then try to insert women into the picture we have drawn? Have we not already prejudiced the categories and the terms of analysis? Recognition of this conceptual and procedural problem does not lead to ready solutions, but rather to awareness of deeper problems. If we attempt to include women at the ground level of our analysis, we are immediately confronted with the problem of how to represent them when our sources deny them voice. We lack direct access to women's perceptual world through written sources, and our limited artifactual evidence, which is of undetermined "authorship," is mute. The obstacles to social analysis that would treat women as subjects of social processes alongside—and in interaction with—men are formidable. They are also most acute in the realm of articulation of meanings—and hence the area of religion. I have argued elsewhere that the obstacles are not insurmountable and that we must at least make a deliberate and disciplined effort to imagine the missing partners in any attempt

to describe "Israelite" society and religion ("The Place of Women," 399–400; cf. "Women's Religion," 284–88).

3. For the latter title, see n. 6 below; for the former, n. 2 above.

4. See, e.g., G. Fohrer, *History of Israelite Religion* (Nashville: Abingdon, 1972); H.-J. Kraus, *Worship in Israel: A Cultic History of the Old Testament* (Richmond: John Knox, 1966); H. Ringgren, *Israelite Religion* (Philadelphia: Fortress, 1966); H. H. Rowley, *Worship in Ancient Israel: Its Forms and Meaning* (Philadelphia: Fortress, 1967); R. de Vaux, *Ancient Israel: Its Life and Institutions* (New York: McGraw-Hill, 1961) 271–517. Although some treatments focus on cognitive-affective dimensions (theology and worship) and others on institutions, all of necessity include attention to both. The difficulties of integrating cognitive and institutional aspects in a single analytical system are illustrated by the variety of approaches and organization represented in these volumes.

I have listed here only those works that focus on religion as an institution and/or system of beliefs and practices, although conceptions of religion and analyses of religious institutions and ideas play a significant role in histories of Israel and introductions to the Old Testament/Hebrew Bible. Unique among the available treatments is Gottwald's effort to integrate sociology and theology in his analysis of Israel's religion; see *The Tribes of Yahweh: A Sociology of the Religion of Liberated Israel, 1250–1050 B.C.E.* (Maryknoll, NY: Orbis, 1979), and "The Theological Task after *The Tribes of Yahweh*," *The Bible and Liberation: Political and Social Hermeneutics* (ed. N. K. Gottwald; Maryknoll, NY: Orbis, 1983) 190–200. I find his insistence on the continuity of religion with other social and political processes appealing, even though I cannot fully accept his construct and would emphasize the complexity of religious symbols (with Bynum, n. 5 below). Gottwald's attention to social processes in the analysis of religion has allowed him to introduce women into the picture more frequently than do other general studies, but women are still not fully represented as subjects of the socio-historical processes he describes.

5. For a helpful survey and analysis of anthropological approaches, see B. Morris, *Anthropological Studies of Religion: An Introductory Text* (Cambridge: Cambridge University Press, 1987). See also M. Banton (ed.), *Anthropological Approaches to the Study of Religion* (New York: Praeger, 1986); and R. L. Moore and F. E. Reynolds (ed.), *Anthropology and the Study of Religion* (Chicago: Center for the Scientific Study of Religion, 1984). For a critique of one influential theory from the perspective of its ability to interpret women's experience, see C. W. Bynum, "Women's Stories, Women's Symbols: A Critique of Victor Turner's Theory of Liminality," *Anthropology and the Study of Religion* (ed. Moore and Reynolds) 105–25. Cf. Bynum, "Introduction: The Complexity of Symbols," *Gender and Religion: On the Complexity of Symbols* (ed. C. W. Bynum, S. Harrell, and P. Richman; Boston: Beacon, 1986: 1–20) 8–10, for a feminist analysis of the understanding of religious symbol in the theories of Victor Turner and Clifford Geertz. One could argue that Geertz's understanding of religion as a system of symbols ("Religion as a Cultural System," *Anthropological Approaches to the Study of Religion* [ed. Banton: 1–46] 4, 8–9) prejudices the analysis in favor of men's experience, because the construction of symbol systems is typically associated with the sphere(s) of male activity and reflects male perceptions and experience. Bynum focuses instead on Geertz's understanding of symbol, which she finds inadequate. Insisting that "no theory of symbol can be adequate unless it incorporates women's experience and discourse as well as men's" ("The Complexity of Symbols," 15), Bynum suggests that "women [may] have . . . certain modes of symbolic discourse different from those of men" (16), arguing that "even where men and women have used the same symbols and rituals, they may have invested them with different meanings and different ways of meaning." These conclusions anticipate some of my own, formulated independently (see below). See also n. 35 below.

6. See P. A. Bird, "Gender and Religious Definition: The Case of Ancient Israel," *Harvard Divinity Bulletin* 20 (1990) 12–13, 19–20. This essay is adapted from a lecture, but retains much of its original character. It attempts to speak broadly about issues I have addressed elsewhere in more narrowly focused and/or technical studies, to identify underlying problems and themes, and to link the analysis of women's religious lives in ancient Israel more explicitly with contemporary examples of women's piety and theoretical discussion in feminist anthropology and gender studies.

7. On the uses of anthropology for reconstructing women's roles and activities in ancient Israel, see Bird, "The Place of Women," 400–401 and 413–14, nn. 14–18, and "Women's Religion in Ancient Israel," 288–91. Carol Meyers (*Discovering Eve: Ancient Israelite Women in Context* [New York and Oxford: Oxford University Press, 1988]) also draws heavily on anthropological studies for her critique of common feminist misconstruals of Israelite patriarchy and for her reconstruction of gender relations in early Israel, though with conclusions and emphases that differ from my own at significant points.

8. E. Friedl, "Islam and Tribal Women in a Village in Iran," *Unspoken Worlds: Women's Religious Lives* (ed. N. A. Falk and R. M. Gross; Belmont, CA: Wadsworth, 1989) 127 (emphasis mine).

9. S. S. Sered, "Women as Ritual Experts: The Religious Lives of Sephardi Jewish Women in Israel" (Ph.D. dissertation, Hebrew University, 1986) 2–3.

10. Ibid., 54–55.

11. Ibid., 55.

12. Ibid., 56.

13. Ibid., 29, 34–36.

14. Ibid., 30, 141.

15. F. Mernissi, "Women, Saints, and Sanctuaries in Morocco," *Unspoken Worlds* (ed. Falk and Gross) 112–21.

16. Ibid., 112–13.

17. Sered, "Women as Ritual Experts," 75–77.

18. P. K. McCarter, Jr., *I Samuel: A New Translation with Introduction, Notes and Commentary* (AB 8; Garden City, NY: Doubleday, 1980) 58, n. 3, citing M. Haran, *VT* 19 (1969) 11–22.

19. Cf. Sered, "Women as Ritual Experts," 31, for the belief that the saint was physically present in his tomb.

20. P. Brown, *The Cult of the Saints: Its Rise and Function in Latin Christianity* (Chicago: University of Chicago Press, 1981) 44.

21. The two should be distinguished, although they have much in common and may at times coincide. On cults of the dead, see T. J. Lewis, *Cults of the Dead in Ancient Israel and Ugarit* (HSM 39; Atlanta: Scholars Press, 1989).

22. Bird, "The Place of Women," 397, n. 3.

23. K. van der Toorn, "The Nature of the Biblical Teraphim in the Light of the Cuneiform Evidence," *CBQ* 52 (1990: 203–22) 215–16, 222.

24. Despite the plural form of the noun, it appears to describe a single object in 1 Samuel 19 (van der Toorn, "The Nature of the Biblical Teraphim," 206).

25. Van der Toorn notes that Wellhausen had "noticed the predilection of women for the cult of the teraphim." Observing that a number of texts show Israelite women engaged in ritual activities of their own, he asks whether we should add the involvement with the teraphim to this list. "Women certainly had access to the teraphim, and the story of Rachel's theft is suggestive of an emotional attachment to the images," he argues, although he finds evidence in Laban's indignant response that "the cult of the teraphim was by no means the exclusive business of women" ("The Nature of the Biblical Teraphim," 210). In both of these texts involving women, the teraphim appear to belong to the sphere of "family devotion" or "domestic piety" (210). References to the teraphim in Judges 17–18 and Hos 3:4, however, in which the term is paired with ephod, suggest

to van der Toorn that they also had a place in the public cult (211–12), more particularly in divination (213, 215). Whatever role they may have played in later cultic practice— and/or cult polemic—the Genesis and Samuel texts point to a primary association with domestic religion.

26. This question has received considerable attention in Mesopotamian studies in relation to personal names, which constitute an important source for understanding personal, and family, piety as distinct from the state cult. Attention has focused on the particular deities mentioned in theophoric names, the content of the petitions and praise, and the interpretation of apparently generic references to "the god" or "my god" as evidence for a "personal god." See, e.g., R. A. DeVito, "Studies in Third Millennium Sumerian Onomastics: The Designation and Conception of the Personal God" (Ph.D. dissertation, Harvard University, 1986). Although personal names have been seen as a source for understanding popular religion in Israel (M. Noth, *Die israelitischen Personennamen* [Stuttgart: Kohlhammer, 1929] esp. 132–35), lack of dramatic disjunction between a state pantheon and the deities invoked in personal names has meant that little attention has been given to the relationship of personal or family piety to the state cult in Israel.

27. See Bird, "The Place of Women," 410–11. The medium of Endor (1 Samuel 28) is a well-known example of a female practitioner of necromancy in the OT, described in v. 7 by the expression *'ēšet ba'ǎlat 'ôb* ("woman possessing a familiar spirit/ghost"). Elsewhere the term *'ôb* is used alone to designate the medium, usually paired with the masculine term *yiddě'ōnî* (Deut 18:11 [singular]; Lev 19:31; 20:6, 27; 2 Kgs 21:6; 23:24 [plural]). A noteworthy feature of this pairing is the highly unusual feminine-masculine order (*'ōbôt-yiddě'ōnîm*), which appears to confirm the predominance of women among this class of specialists. In contrast, diviners, who used technical means of inquiry and in Assyria and elsewhere were organized in professional guilds and supported by the state, are designated in biblical sources only by masculine forms: *qōsēm, měnahēš, mě'ônēim* (the *qal* feminine participle in Isa 57:3 is not a professional designation, but a generalized term of slander).

28. See esp. I. M. Lewis, *Ecstatic Religion: An Anthropological Study of Spirit Possession and Shamanism* (New York: Penguin, 1971). See also the case studies in *Unspoken Worlds* (ed. Falk and Gross): M. B. Binford, "Julia: An East African Diviner" (3–14); Y. K. Harvey, "Possession Sickness and Women Shamans in Korea" (37–44); and R. S. Kraemer, "Ecstasy and Possession: Women of Ancient Greece and the Cult of Dionysus" (45–55). Cf. A. Spring, "Epidemiology of Spirit Possession Among the Luvale of Zambia," *Women in Ritual and Symbolic Roles* (ed. J. Hoch-Smith and A. Spring; New York: Plenum, 1978) 165–90.

29. For discussion of ancient Near Eastern evidence, see S. Rollin, "Women and Witchcraft in Ancient Assyria (c. 900–600 BC)," *Images of Women in Antiquity* (ed. A. Cameron and A. Kuhrt; Detroit: Wayne State University Press, 1983) 34–45. Cf. S. D. Walters, "The Sorceress and Her Apprentice: A Case Study of an Accusation," *JCS* 23 (1970) 27–38, and T. Abusch, "The Demonic Image of the Witch in Standard Babylonian Literature: The Reworking of Popular Conceptions by Learned Exorcists," *Religion, Science, and Magic in Concert and in Conflict* (ed. J. Neusner, E. S. Frerichs, and P. V. M. Flesher; New York and Oxford: Oxford University Press, 1989) 27–58.

30. T. A. Holland, "A Study of Palestinian Iron Age Baked Clay Figurines with Special Reference to Jerusalem: Cave 1," *Levant* 9 (1977) 121–55; M. D. Fowler, "Excavated Figurines: A Case for Identifying a Site as Sacred?" *ZAW* 97 (1985) 333–44; U. Winter, *Frau und Göttin: exegetische und ikonographische Studien zum weiblichen Gottesbild im Alten Israel und in dessen Umwelt* (Freiburg: Universitätsverlag/Göttingen: Vandenhoeck & Ruprecht, 1986) 128–29; J. S. Holladay, "Religion in Israel and Judah under the Monarchy," *Ancient Israelite Religion* (ed. Miller, Hanson, and McBride) esp. 270–82 and 291, n. 109.

Holladay distinguishes two religious traditions according to archaeological evidence: (1) an officially sanctioned aniconic cult associated with sanctuaries in the capital and neighborhood shrines connected with the residences of important officials (apparently concerned largely with formal sacrificial ritual, including probably the eating of ritual meals) (280), and (2) a "totally different form of religious expression," witnessed in both north and south, by "small clusters of cultic artifacts, heavily biased toward the iconographic, discontinuously distributed (both spatially and temporally) throughout domestic quarters and by larger clusters centered on extramural locations near major cities," with "smaller Judean ('local' or 'neighborhood') cult areas, featuring modest supersets of the domestic clusters" attested near cave mouths (281). Holladay suggests that "the primary participants in this cultus were women" (294, n. 126), but does not elaborate on the basis for this identification.

What is of particular interest in the second type of cultic evidence is the distribution of the figurines in both domestic and cult sites. Whether or not this denotes a cultic activity in which women were the major participants, it does describe a pattern attested cross-culturally for women's religious activity. Women's rituals tend to be centered in the home, and their participation in public rituals typically links the domestic realm to the public religious realm.

31. Friedl, "Islam and Tribal Women," 169.
32. Ibid., 163; cf. A. H. Betteridge, "The Controversial Vows of Urban Muslim Women in Iran," *Unspoken Worlds* (ed. Falk and Gross) 102–11.
33. I am struck (unexpectedly) by the power of sacred places—and to a lesser degree persons and objects—to define what is religious. Although the holy may be viewed as pervading all of life, it is hard to identify it, grasp it, or sense its presence when it is not embodied in some concrete form. It is concentrated at sanctuaries, where it is typically under male control. Men are its primary guardians, representatives, and interpreters. Where women have access to it, either as guardians or supplicants, it is normally in forms derived from their everyday roles and activities as mothers, daughters, and wives: baking cakes for the Queen of Heaven, weaving garments for the Asherah, weeping for Tammuz, bewailing the virginity of Jephthah's daughter, celebrating the victory of Yahweh's armies in song and dance, serving at the tent of meeting. Of these six examples, the first four describe religious expressions rejected by normative Yahwism—or by the tradition that received canonical status—whereas modern interpretations of the last two repeatedly question whether the acts are religious or secular, and in the last case, legitimate or illegitimate.
34. Asymmetry of religious symbolism may be seen in other Muslim ceremonies, such as the wedding, in which the groom, with his male companions, proceeds to the mosque before entering the bridal chamber (as a sanctified warrior). The bride has no corresponding religious act (analysis based on the film "Some Women of Marrakech" [Granada]).
35. Sered, "Women as Ritual Experts," 12–13. Sered states that she could find no definition of religion particularly relevant to her study "since all accepted definitions of religion were composed by scholars who were considering primarily male religious experience" (13). She chose to use as a working definition a combination of Eliade's idea of the "sacred" (M. Eliade, *The Sacred and the Profane* [New York: Harper & Row, 1961] 8–18) and the five-category model (religious experience, ideology, ritual, knowledge, and secular consequences) of C. Glock and R. Stark (*Religion and Society in Tension* [New York: Rand McNally, 1965]). This allowed her to consider issues such as food preparation "that would not normally lie within the sphere of the study of religion" (13).
36. I recognize that the notion of equivalence is fraught with hazards, because it always involves comparison of phenomena that are commonly defined as dissimilar. I nevertheless believe that comparison aimed at identifying unobserved or discounted commonalities is essential and constitutes one of the contributions of the outside observer to an

understanding of the way societies "work" (see below). A significant contribution to
the notion of equivalence as it relates to women's religious activity is drawn from
women's own self-understandings of the nature and worth of their distinct activities and
duties. See Sered, "Women as Ritual Experts," 13.

37. Cf. H. L. Moore, *Feminism and Anthropology* (Oxford: Polity, 1988) 3–5 and 199, n. 1.

38. See E. Jacob, "Mourning," *IDB* 3.452–54; and Bird, "Women's Religion in Ancient
Israel," 295–96.

39. The example of meal preparation may be taken as representative of the various situations
in which men's religious activity depends on support actions of women. In modern
observance of *kashrut*, the woman's critical role is invested with religious significance,
but this appears to be a special development reflecting the shift of religious focus in
diaspora Judaism from temple to home as the primary place of ritual action. Here we
need to ask how women are motivated to do their required part. Do they understand it
as religious duty comparable to men's religious duties—or simply as their allotted
work, or as an added burden? Although pilgrim feasts may be understood as family
meals, that pattern cannot be assumed for all cultic or communal meals. See Bird,
"Women's Religion in Ancient Israel," 293–94.

40. The funeral may be understood as essentially a family affair, even when it involves the
entire village.

41. Evidence for a primary identification of major (central) sanctuaries with male worshipers
might be seen in Eli's misinterpretation of Hannah's behavior—behavior that is precisely
typical of the women at the *marabout!*

42. See J. G. Westenholz, "Tamar, *Qĕdēšâ*, *Qadištu* and Sacred Prostitution in Mesopotamia," *HTR* 82 (1989) 245–65, and my forthcoming monograph on the *qĕdēšâ* and
qadištu.

43. Cf. Ruth 4:14–15, 17, where blessing—and naming(!)—is performed by a group of
women. Although this is an anomalous text, it does point to otherwise unattested
communal celebrations and rituals of women. On rituals of menarche we have even less
evidence, though the story of Jepththah's daughter (Judg 11:34–40) seems to presuppose
some such ritual.

44. For example, the Iranian village women understood religion as essentially a male affair
in which they could not participate on equal terms. Prevented by menstruation and
child care responsibilities from regular attendance at the mosque and segregated to a
place of marginal visibility and audibility when they did attend, they took little interest
in the mosque and appear to have cultivated no alternative religious life. The women of
the Day Center also recognized a realm of male religious activity (in this case the
yeshiva) into which they could not enter, but in which they took high interest, blessing
it and offering financial support, as essential to their own well-being. Unlike the
universalizing demands of Islam, however, their religious tradition, or at least these
women's interpretation of it, allowed for highly differentiated male and female expressions of religious obligation and fulfillment. As a consequence, the women invested
their required tasks with religious meaning and ritual actions—of their own devising—
insisting that they did not need to be instructed by the rabbi. At times, in fact, their
religious practices clearly conflicted with the demands of the religious authorities.

In both of these cases, the women accepted the legitimacy of the male-dominated
and -defined religion; but in the case of the Jewish women, they created a religion of
their own, within the structures of the male-dominated religion and society. In their
own differentiated practice—and in their support of the male activities—they affirm and
elaborate their role as mothers and caretakers, which appears to be critical for their own
self-understanding and for their standing/status within their social world.

An alternative response of women to male-dominated religion in a highly gender-
segregated world may be illustrated by urban women in Tehran—sharing the same Shiite
faith but living in a different social world (Betteridge, "The Controversial Vows," 102–

11). Here we find women's religious rituals that parallel men's and that may even be led by women ritual specialists trained in the same textual and liturgical traditions as their male counterparts. I am inclined to see this development of parallel institutions as a modern one related to the modern education of women and their entry into professions shared by men, or parallel to men's professions. I doubt that such developments should be projected into the ancient world. What is interesting to note, however, is that even in the case of parallel institutions, the women's celebration takes a distinctly female form.

CHAPTER 9: PROMETHEUS, THE SERVANT OF YAHWEH, JESUS

1. This paper takes up in a new (Iranian) context some of the materials of my "Techniques of Imperial Control: The Background of the Gospel Event," *The Bible and Liberation: Political and Social Hermeneutics* (ed. N. K. Gottwald; Maryknoll, NY: Orbis, 1983) 357–77.

2. For the chronology, see N. C. Debevoise, *A Political History of Parthia* (Chicago: University of Chicago Press, 1938) 270.

3. Pliny 5.88; Strabo 11.9.2, cited by G. Rawlinson, *The Sixth Great Oriental Monarchy, or The Geography, History and Antiquities of Parthia* (London: Longmans Green, 1873) vi, to illustrate the parity of Rome and Parthia, along with Dio Cassius 40.14.3, Herodian 4.18, Justin 41.1.7.

4. Valerius Maximus 2.7.12, and numerous other sources gathered by M. Hengel, *Crucifixion in the Ancient World* (Philadelphia: Fortress, 1977) 51–52.

5. Darius Beh. II.76, III.52 (Kent 91, 92).

6. Darius Beh. II.76 (Kent 122); this is sect. 60 of the Akkadian version as transcribed by L. W. King and R. C. Thompson, *The Sculptures and Inscription of Darius the Great* (London: British Museum, 1907) 182.

7. P. Veyne ("Y a-t-il eu un impérialisme romain?" *Mélanges de l'École française de Rome: Antiquité* 87 [1975] 793–855) says that Rome had no fixed policy of imperial expansion; W. V. Harris (*War and Imperialism in Republican Rome, 327–70 B.C.* [Oxford: Oxford University Press, 1979]) says that it did; M. I. Finley ("Empire in the Greek and Roman World," *Greece and Rome* [2nd ser., 25; 1978] 1–15) with nuances shifts the discussion onto the benefits of empire. See also the articles in the collective volumes edited by M. T. Larsen, *Power and Propaganda: A Symposium on Ancient Empires: Mesopotamia* (Copenhagen Studies in Assyriology 7; Copenhagen: Akademisk Forlag, 1979), and by P. D. A. Garnsey and C. R. Whitaker, *Imperialism in the Ancient World* (Cambridge: Cambridge University Press, 1978).

8. Early references to the "Parthians" (e.g., Herodotus 7.66.1) are to an Iranian group invaded by the Scythians some time before 250 BCE (Strabo 11.9.2); the Arsacid Parthians represent a fusion of the two peoples.

9. On the Greek side, see B. Hemmerdinger, "158 noms communs grecs d'origine iranienne, d'Eschyle au grec moderne," *Byzantinoslavica* 30 (1969) 18ff.; on the Rabbinic, S. Telegdi, "Essai sur la phonétique des emprunts iraniens en araméen talmudique: Glossaire," *Journal Asiatique* 226 (1935) 224–56.

10. E. N. Luttwak, *The Grand Strategy of the Roman Empire from the First Century A.D. to the Third* (Baltimore: Johns Hopkins University Press, 1976) xii.

11. Ibid., 81.

12. See D. Winston, "The Iranian Component in the Bible, Apocrypha and Qumran: A Review of the Evidence," *History of Religions* 5 (1965/6) 183–216; J. R. Hinnells, "Iranian Influence upon the New Testament," *Acta Iranica* 1st ser., 2 (1974) 271–84; F. König, *Zarathustras Jenseitsvorstellungen und das alte Testament* (Vienna: Herder, 1964) finds *no* Avestan influence on the eschatology of the Hebrew Bible.

13. M. Smith, "Second Isaiah and the Persians," *JAOS* 83 (1963) 415–21. Smith points out that the parallels in the doctrine of creation come in the same parts of Second Isaiah as its agreements with the Akkadian decree of Cyrus (*ANET* 315–16).

14. *Yasna* 44.13 (from S. Insler, *The Gāthās of Zarathustra* cited in *Acta Iranica* 3rd ser., 8 (1975) 1; Leiden: Brill and Tehran-Liège: Bibliothèque Pahlawi, 1975]).

15. The Avestan catechism seems inherited because its noun-pairs are an Indo-European inheritance, illustrated by translations of these Hebrew phrases into European languages. For "heaven and earth" see the Russian of Gen 1:1: "In the beginning God created *nebo i zemlyu*"; for "light and darkness" see the Vulgate of Isa 45:7, *formans lucem et creans tenebras.*

16. Xerxes' own Old Persian text (Kent 151); *Yasna* 32.1.

17. And so in later Syriac texts, e.g., *The Hymn of the Soul*, line 50 (A. A. Bevan, *The Hymn of the Soul* [Texts and Studies V.3; Cambridge: Cambridge University Press, 1897]).

18. Winston, "The Iranian Component," 194, traces the fortunes of Iranian *ga(n)za*, "treasure," which in later Zoroastrian texts seems to mean a "treasury of merit" in the hereafter. Besides its literal takeover in Greek, Hebrew, and Latin, see *b. B. Bat.* 11a, where king Monobazus (himself Iranian), says, "I have gathered up (*gnzty*) treasuries of souls"; the Syriac *Hymn of the Soul* (Bevan, 74, 79), which speaks of heavenly "treasurers" (*gzbr'*); the Mandaean sacred corpus *Ginza*. Compare further in a purely Greek form the Gospel "treasure in heaven," the ultimate source of Pope Clement VI's "treasury [of merit]," 1343 CE.

19. An excerpt from the otherwise unknown historian Aemilius Sura preserved in the manuscripts of Velleius 1.6.6.

20. See Hesiod *Works and Days* 109–201. There is extensive literature. See J. W. Swain, "The theory of the Four Monarchies: Opposition History Under the Roman Empire," *CP* 35 (1940) 1–21; S. K. Eddy, *The King Is Dead: Studies in the Near Eastern Resistance to Hellenism 334–31 BC* (Lincoln: University of Nebraska Press, 1961) 16; Winston, "The Iranian Component," 189–90; G. F. Hasel, "The Four World Empires of Daniel 2 Against Its Near Eastern Environment," *JSOT* 12 (1979) 17–30; M. L. West, *Hesiod: Works and Days* (Oxford: Oxford University Press, 1978) 172–77; D. Mendels, "The Five Empires: A Note on a Propagandistic *Topos*," *AJP* 102 (1981) 330–37, with extensive bibliography.

21. Quoting a lost book of Polybius at *Punica* (8) 132. Polybius, who was present at the scene and is our ultimate source, in his extant work at 1.2.7, makes Persia, Sparta, and Macedon the precursors of Rome in its drive "to make the whole world subject."

22. D. J. Wiseman, *The Vassal-Treaties of Esarhaddon* (London: The British School of Archaeology in Iraq, 1958 [= *Iraq* 20]) i.8; translation in *ANET* 534.

23. Further classical usages of the theme "empire from sunrise to sunset" are gathered by E. Frankel, *Horace* (Oxford: Oxford University Press, 1957) 451.

24. J. Jeremias (*New Testament Theology* [New York: Scribner's, 1971] 245–47) makes Matt 8:11 Jesus' appropriation of the prophetic theme "the pilgrimage of the nations."

25. J. Joyce, *Ulysses* (New York: The Modern Library, 1934) 294.

26. Sapor *Res Gestae* 56 (Maricq 323) (A. Maricq, "Res Gestae Divi Saporis," *Syria* 35 [1958] 259–360); Hesychius A.1441 (i.52 Latte), by error *azabarites* in Ctesias, *FGH* 688 frag. 15.46; *b. Sabb.* 139a.

27. Plutarch *Them.* 27; J. M. Cook, *The Persian Empire* (New York: Schocken, 1983) 143.

28. This usage since Polybius 1.23.1; see H. J. Mason, *Greek Terms for Roman Institutions* (American Studies in Papyrology 13; Toronto: Hakkert, 1974) 99–100.

29. G. A. Cooke, *A Text-Book of North-Semitic Inscriptions* (Oxford: Oxford University Press, 1923) no. 82 (dated 8 CE).

30. *Mek.* ii.150 (J. Z. Lauterbach, *Mekilta de-Rabbi Ishmael* [3 vols.; Philadelphia: Jewish Publication Society, 1933]).

31. Compare texts where Greeks refer to the invader in the singular as "the Mede": Herodotus 1.163, 5.77; Thucydides 5.89; etc.

32. Kent (8–9) further lists Median forms in the Old Persian texts themselves.

33. There are new spellings of "satrap" in the Greek, Aramaic, and Lycian versions of the Xanthos inscription: H. Metzger *et al.*, *La stèle trilingue du Létôon* (Fouilles de Xanthos VI, Institut français d'études anatoliennes; Paris: Klincksieck, 1979).

34. Darius *Beh.* III.14 (Kent 125), II.15; *Yasna* 30.8.

35. Greek text with partial transcription of the two Iranian ones in Maricq (see n. 26); Iranian texts in M. Back, *Die sassanidischen Staatsinschriften* (*Acta Iranica* 18, 3rd ser.; *Leiden: Brill*, 1978); unsatisfactory edition by M. Sprengling, *Third Century Iran: Sapor and Kartir* (Chicago: Oriental Institute, 1953). For the words cited, see sect. 62 (Maricq, 327).

36. J. Vogt, "The Structure of Ancient Slave Wars," *Ancient Slavery and the Ideal of Man* (Cambridge: Harvard University Press, 1975) 39–92, esp. 52, 67.

37. Diodorus 34/35.2.7, 24. But Vogt ("Ancient Slave Wars," 70) is more speculative when he suggests that Aristonikos of Pergamum (133–129 BCE), in calling his following of poor men and slaves "Heliopolitai" (Strabo 14.1.38), that is, "citizens of Sun City," had in mind Heliopolis-Baalbek of Syria.

38. A. J. Toynbee, *A Study of History* (12 vols.; London: Oxford University Press, 1934–61) 6.414.

39. A. J. Podlecki, *The Political Background of Aeschylean Tragedy* (Ann Arbor: University of Michigan Press, 1966) 101–22. M. Griffith, in *The Authenticity of "Prometheus Bound"* (Cambridge: Cambridge University Press, 1977), wishes to deny the play to Aeschylus on stylistic grounds. But I feel that Greeks would have retained some memory of a different author, and I call its maker "Aeschylus" without apology.

40. For the Persian "King's Eye" see Herodotus 1.114.2. Another internal intelligence agency, the "King's Ear" (Xenophon *Cyr.* 8.2.12, Aristotle *Pol.* 1287b30) is attested in Egyptian Aramaic as *gušky'* (A. Cowley, *Aramaic Papyri of the Fifth Century B.C.* [Oxford: Oxford University Press, 1923]) no. 27.9); cf. Old Persian *gauša* "ear" (Kent 182).

41. Aeschylus' Oceanus says that in Zeus "a harsh monarch, in no way accountable (*hypeuthynos*), is ruling" (*PV* 324); the Persian Otanes says that, in contrast with the monarch, when the majority is in charge it exercises "accountable" rule (same Greek, Herodotus 3.80.6). Prometheus refuses to flatter (*thōptein*) Zeus (*PV* 937); Otanes says that the tyrant will reject a flatterer (*thōps*, Herodotus 3.80.5). Prometheus says, "So the arrogant are accustomed to show their arrogance (*hybrizein*)" (*PV* 970); Otanes recalls the *hybris* of Cambyses (Herodotus 3.80.2).

42. Black-figured kylix from the Museo Gregoriano Etrusco. See Metropolitan Museum of Art, *The Vatican Collections: The Papacy and Art* (New York: Abrams, 1983) 185 no. 101; C. M. Stibbe, *Lakonische Vasenmaler des sechsten Jahrhunderts v. Chr.* (2 vols.; Studies in Ancient Civilization 1; Amsterdam: North-Holland, 1972) no. 196 pl. 63.

43. Aeschylus uses what was then the technical term for "crucify." Hephaistos says, "I will peg (*prospassaleuein*) you to this inhospitable rock" (Aeschylus *PV* 20); Herodotus (9.120.4) ends his history with a description of how, in reprisal for numerous crucifixions by the Persians, the Greeks took Artayctes to a hill overlooking Xerxes' pontoon bridge, where they "pegged [same verb] him to a plank and hung him up."

44. Shelley *Prometheus Unbound* III.iv.471. Shelley's work, along with numerous others, is discussed by J. Duchemin, *Prométhée: Histoire du Mythe, de ses Origines orientales à ses Incarnations modernes* (Paris: Belles Lettres, 1974).

45. K. Marx and F. Engels, *Collected Works* (London: Lawrence & Wishart, 1975–) 1.31.

46. Ibid., vol. 1, pl. facing p. 374.

47. K. Barth, *The Epistle to the Romans* (London: Oxford University Press, 1933) 236.

48. H. Küng, *On Being a Christian* (New York: Doubleday, 1978) 431.

49. "To kick against the goads": Pindar 2 *Pyth.* 94–96; Aeschylus *Agam.* 1624; Euripides *Bacchae* 795.

50. See the survey by J. Bentley, "Prometheus Versus Christ in the Christian-Marxist Dialogue," *JTS* 29 (1978) 483–94.
51. E. Bloch, *The Principle of Hope* (3 vols.; Cambridge: MIT Press, 1986) 3.1213.
52. J. M. Lochman, *Christ and Prometheus? A Quest for Theological Identity* (Geneva: World Council of Churches, 1988) 28–33. This reworks the materials in his *Christus oder Prometheus? Die Kernfrage des christlich-marxistischen Dialogs und die Christologie* (Hamburg: Furche, 1972) 58–65.
53. Toynbee, *A Study of History*, 12.617.
54. It is irrelevant whether or not crucifixion was in theory accepted by Jewish courts. See the scholars cited by D. J. Halperin, "Crucifixion, the Nahum Pesher, and the Rabbinic Penalty of Strangulation," *JJS* 32 (1981) 32–46.
55. Luke 22:37 cites Isa 53:12 LXX; the Ethiopian eunuch (Acts 8:22–23) cites Isa 53:7–8; 1 Pet 2:22–25 extensively uses Isa 53:5–12; Isaiah 53 is also quoted explicitly at John 12:38; Rom 10:16, 15:21. Isaiah 50:6 LXX, "and my cheek to blows," underlies Matt 5:39, "whoever gives you a blow on the right cheek," and is cited at Justin *Apol* 1.32.2. Mark 15:34 places the opening of Psalm 22 on Jesus' lips, and adds echoes of the psalm that are formalized by the other Evangelists: (a) Mark 15:24 "and they divided his garments" echoes Ps 21:19 LXX, which is formally cited by John 19:24; (b) Mark 15:29 "wagging their heads" probably echoes Ps 21:8 LXX, and Matt 27:43 "He trusted in God, let him deliver him" makes the connection explicit; (c) Mark 15:36 surely echoes Ps 68:22 "they gave me vinegar to drink." F. Stolz ("Psalm 22: Alttestamentliches Reden vom Menschen und neutestamentliches Reden von Jesus," *ZTK* 77 [1980] 129–48) summarizes: the christology in these echoes of Psalm 22 "is nothing other than a critical reconstruction of Old Testament anthropology."
56. C. H. Dodd, *According to the Scriptures: The Sub-Structure of New Testament Theology* (London: Nisbet, 1952) 108–10.
57. Psalm 22:17c is explicitly applied to Christ by Justin *Dial* 104.1.
58. C. R. North, *The Suffering Servant in Deutero-Isaiah: An Historical and Critical Study* (London: Oxford University Press, 1948).
59. J. Friedrich, *Staatsverträge des Hatti-Reiches in hethitischer Sprache* (2 Teil; MVAG 34; Leipzig: Hinrichs, 1930) 106, line 8.
60. Wiseman, *The Vassal-Treaties of Esarhaddon* (see n. 22) 52, sect. 301; also at *ANET* 537, sect. 71.
61. Inscription of Persepolis (Kent 136).
62. See D. J. McCarthy, *Treaty and Covenant: A Study in Form in the Ancient Oriental Documents and in the Old Testament* (2nd ed.; Analecta Biblica 21A; Rome: Pontifical Biblical Institute, 1978); also K. Baltzer, *The Covenant Formulary in Old Testament, Jewish and Early Christian Writings* (Philadelphia: Fortress, 1971).
63. T. B. Mitford, "A Cypriote Oath of Allegiance to Tiberius," *JRS* 50 (1960) 75–79, lines 17–21; also P. Herrmann, *Der römische Kaisereid: Untersuchungen zu seiner Herkunft und Entwicklung* (Hypomnemata 20; Göttingen: Vandenhoeck & Ruprecht; 1968) 214 (emphasis added). The comparison of loyalty oaths to the Roman Emperor with ancient Near Eastern oaths and Hebrew covenant formularies is due to Moshe Weinfeld, in his fundamental study "The Loyalty Oath in the Ancient Near East," *Ugarit-Forschungen* 8 (1976) 379–414.
64. The confession of the chief priests is self-evident in the Russian translation, where John 19:15 comes out "We have no *Tsar* but Caesar"; for *Tsar* is an earlier borrowing with different phonetics of the same word *Caesar*.
65. Roman imperial formulae applied to Christ. (a) His *euangelion* recalls an inscription of 9 BCE, "the birthday of the god [Augustus!] was the beginning for the cosmos of the good news (*euangelia*) concerning him"; see V. Ehrenberg and A. H. M. Jones, *Documents Illustrating the Reigns of Augustus and Tiberius* (2nd ed.; Oxford: Oxford University Press, 1955) no. 98 line 36 (= *OGIS* 458). The text is a letter of the

proconsul of Asia in numerous copies; some gaps in the text cited are elsewhere supplemented. (b) Christ is "savior of the world" (John 4:42), a title attributed to the Emperors since Augustus (Ehrenberg-Jones no. 702); see Craig R. Koester, " 'The Savior of the World' (John 4:42)," *JBL* 109 (1990) 665–80. (c) Jesus is called *dominus meus et deus meus* (John 20:28 Vg) as Domitian insisted on being called *dominus et deus noster* (Suetonius *Domit.* 13.2). That all three usages appear in the Fourth Gospel proves it more political than it seems. A movement to make Jesus "king" (*basileus*, John 6:15) thus suggests imperial claims, for at 1 Pet 2:17 "honor the king" can only mean the Emperor as elsewhere in the Greek East.

66. C. B. Welles, *Royal Correspondence in the Hellenistic Period: A Study in Greek Epigraphy* (New Haven: Yale University Press, 1934) 299 no. 75 line 1.
67. Headless statue of Darius at Susa with an honorific inscription in Akkadian, Elamite, Old Persian, and Egyptian on the folds of his robe. Illustrated in Cook, *Persian Empire*, pl. 15; see M. Kervran *et al.*, "Une statue de Darius découverte à Suse," *Journal Asiatique* 260 (1972) 235–66.
68. *Suda* S.86 (iv.319 Adler), historical fragment under Trajan, perhaps from Arrian's *Parthica*. *Sampser* also in a papyrus: O. Eger *et al.*, *Griechische Papyri im Museum des oberhessischen Geschichtsverein zu Giessen* (Leipzig: Teubner, 1910) I.ii, no. 47.11; the editors in an addendum (I.iii.166) explain Persian *šamšer* as a compound, *šam* "claw" + *šēr* "lion," but I cannot verify this.
69. B. B. Bat. 21b; Syriac *Odes of Solomon* 28.4; Matt 26:52 Peshitto, "Put the *spsr'* back into its sheath."
70. Sapor *Res Gestae* 64 (Maricq [see n. 26] 329).
71. Kent 140.
72. Kent 129; my "The Septuagint as a Source of the Greek Loan-Words in the Targums," *Biblica* 70 (1988) 194–216, esp. 202–203.
73. Photo in Cook, *Persian Empire*, pl. 8; Xenophon (*Cyr.* 8.3.13) says that Achaemenids wear the diadem over the tiara.
74. Suetonius *Tib.* 9.1, *Nero* 13. These dynasts with their Iranian names were surely of different language and likely of different blood from their true "Armenian" subjects.
75. H. Greeven (*TDNT* 6.759) thinks that *proskynein* originally implied respect to a *chthonic* deity, on the grounds that kissing one such would require prostration!
76. Relief from the Persepolis treasury (Cook, *Persian Empire*, pl. 9); the king has not been surely identified. The gesture of "blowing a kiss" is described by Apuleius *Met.* 4.28.
77. R. N. Frye, "Gestures of Deference to Royalty in Ancient Iran," *Iranica Antiqua* 9 (1972) 102–107, analyzes a variety of gestures shown on the monuments. Herodotus (1.134.1) shows how the rank of the one being saluted determined the gesture.
78. Herodotus 7.136, Xenophon *Anab.* 3.2.13; Arrian *Anab.* 4.10–12, Plutarch *Alex.* 74.
79. Syriac text in Bevan (see n. 17); Greek text in R. A. Lipsius and M. Bonnet, *Acta Apostolorum Apocrypha* 2.2, 219–24 (*Acts of Thomas* 108–13); see v. 104. Cf. H. Kruse, "The Return of the Prodigal: Fortunes of a Parable on Its Way to the Far East," *Orientalia* 47 (1978) 163–214.
80. The book of Esther is not a mere historical romance, for it has access to good tradition. Thus in Hegay (Esth 2:8), eunuch over Xerxes' harem, it records one Hegias, the sole historical Greek person named in the Hebrew Bible; he must be the "Hegias of Ephesus" named in Xerxes' court by Ctesias, *FGH* 688 frag. 13.27.
81. I have dealt with many of these texts piecemeal in my *The Lebanon and Phoenicia: Ancient Texts Illustrating Their Physical Geography and Native Industries*: Vol. I, *The Physical Setting and the Forest* (Beirut: American University Press, 1969), and R. Meiggs, (*Trees and Timber in the Ancient Mediterranean World* [Oxford: Oxford University Press, 1982]) has since covered much of the same ground. Besides his bibliography, for deforestation in Lebanon note now: E. W. Beals, "The Remnant Cedar Forests of Lebanon," *Journal of Ecology* 53 (1965) 679–94; M. W. Mikesell, "The Deforestation of

Mount Lebanon," *Geographical Review* 59 (1969) 1–28; O. Makkonen, *Ancient Forestry* (Acta Forestalia Fennica [Helsinki] 82 [1967] and 95 [1969]); H. Klengel, "Der Libanon und seine Zedern in der Geschichte des Alten Vorderen Orients," *Das Altertum* 13 (1967) 67–76; E. C. Semple, "Climatic and Geographic Influences on Ancient Mediterranean Forests and the Lumber Trade," *Annals of the Association of American Geographers* 9 (1919), 13–37 (= her *The Geography of the Mediterranean Region: Its Relation to Ancient History* [New York: Holt, 1931] 261–96).

82. P. Briant, *Rois, Tributs et Paysans: Études sur les formations tributaires du Moyen-Orient ancien* (Annales littéraires de l'Université de Besançon 269; Paris: Belles Lettres, 1982) 451–56 and 451 n. 109.

83. The ornamental and recreational side of the "paradise" is mostly seen by Meiggs, *Trees and Timber*, 271; also by J. D. Hughes with J. V. Thirgood, "Deforestation, Erosion and Forest Management in Ancient Greece and Rome," *Journal of Forest History* 26 (1982) 60–75, esp. 73.

84. See now J.-F. Breton, *Les Inscriptions Forestières d'Hadrien dans le Mont Liban* (Inscriptions Grecques et Latines de la Syrie VIII,3; Bibliothèque Archéologique et Historique 104; Paris: Geuthner, 1980). He lists 187 inscriptions and has an original theory to account for the numerals on many as a designation of sequence in cutting.

85. Xenophon *Oecon.* 4.20–24; W. Fauth, "Der königliche Gärtner und Jäger im Paradeisos: Beobachtungen zur Rolle des Herrschers in der vorderasiatischen Hortikultur," *Persica* 8 (1979) 1–53.

86. Kent 155.

87. *Videvdat* 3.18; C. Bartholomae, *Altiranisches Wörterbuch* (Strasbourg: Trübner, 1904) 865.

88. Hostilities are initiated when Cyrus cuts down the paradise of Dardes (Xenophon *Anab.* 1.4.10); when Agesilaus in 396 BCE cuts down the paradise of Tissaphernes in Sardes (Diodorus 14.80.2); and when the Sidonians at Tripolis of Phoenicia in 350 BCE cut down the royal paradise (Diodorus 16.41.5)—no doubt for their new fleet (Brown, *Lebanon and Phoenicia* [see n. 81] 204–205).

89. Fragment of an Old Babylonian version of Tablet V of the Gilgamesh Epic (*ANET* 504b). See F. Stolz, "Die Baüme des Gottesgartens auf dem Libanon," *ZAW* 84 (1972) 141–56.

90. Berossos, *FGH* 680 frag. 8.141 = Josephus *Ag. Ap.* 1.141, *Ant.* 10.226. The hanging gardens are listed as one of the "seven wonders of the world" in a poem by Antipater of Sidon *Greek Anthol.* 9.58.

91. G. Schäfer, *"König der Könige"—"Lied der Lieder": Studien zum paronomastischen Intensitätsgenitiv* (Abhandlungen der Heidelberger Akademie der Wissenschaften, Phil.-hist. Klasse, 1973, 2; Heidelberg: Winter, 1974). He much expands the materials, particularly the Egyptian, first noted by J. G. Griffiths in the seminal article *"Basileus basileōn:* Remarks on the History of a Title," *CP* 48 (1953) 145–54.

92. Contrary to what I wrote in my "Kingdom of God," *Encyclopedia of Religion* (New York: Macmillan, 1987) 8.304–12 (with 26.482), esp. 8.305a.

93. R. Borger, *Die Inschriften Esarhaddons, Königs von Assyrien* (Archiv für Orientforschung, Beiheft 9; Graz, 1956) 96 line 19; but mostly with a supplement, "king of the kings of Musur," etc., which makes it clear that the literal sense is intended.

94. Instances of *šar(ri) šarrāni* are listed in M.-J. Seux, *Epithètes royales akkadiennes et sumériennes* (Paris: Letouzey et Ané, 1967) 318–19.

95. Kent 95; cf. Schäfer, *König der Könige*, 43.

96. Ezra 7:12 of some Artaxerxes; an inscription of Darius from Memphis, 482 BCE (*KAI* no. 267).

97. R. Meiggs and D. Lewis, *A Selection of Greek Historical Inscriptions to the End of the Fifth Century B.C.* (corr. ed.; Oxford: Oxford University Press, 1980) no. 12, re-engraving in the Roman period of a letter from Darius.

98. Thus in Sapor *Res Gestae* 7.
99. Ammianus 19.2.11; I cannot explain *pirosen*.
100. Agathias *Hist.* 4.24 (Corpus Scriptorum Historiae Byzantinae 261.5).
101. Similarly Ammianus 17.5.3, 10 gives the respective titulatures in an imperial correspondence: Sapor is *rex regum* . . . , *particeps siderum, frater Solis et Lunae* "king of kings, fellow of the stars, brother of the Sun and Moon"; Constantius is *uictor terra marique* . . . *semper Augustus* "victor by land and sea, perpetual Augustus."
102. Schäfer, *König der Könige*. It can surely *not* mean "song composed of shorter songs."
103. Cooke, *North-Semitic Inscriptions* (see n. 29), no. 130.
104. Dio Chrysostom 2.75. There is an isolated use in archaic Latin attributed to the *Carmen Saliare*, "supplicate the god of gods," *diuum deo supplicate*; Varro *De lingua latina* 7.27, discussed by Schäfer, *König der Könige*, 84–85.
105. Iranian influence on the Pentateuch is surely proved by the man's name Parnak of Zebulun (Num 34:25), which can be nothing other than *Pharnaces*.
106. The "great king" of Ps 95:3 may reflect Iranian influence. Elsewhere ("Kingdom of God," see n. 92) I have discussed the beautifully exact parallel to Pindar *Olymp.* 7.34 (464 BCE), where Zeus is "great king of the gods," again no doubt under Iranian influence.
107. Similarly *Greek Enoch* 9.4.
108. H. Musurillo, *The Acts of the Christian Martyrs* (Oxford: Oxford University Press, 1972) 82 no. 6.
109. J. Griffin, *Homer on Life and Death* (Oxford: Oxford University Press, 1980) 46.
110. Menander *Sicyonian* fragment 4 (ed. F. H. Sandbach; Oxford: Oxford University Press, 1972), where the object of conscription may be a sailor himself.
111. *OGIS* no. 665, line 21: conscription of animals.
112. Ulpian says that the ships of veterans may be confiscated, *angariari posse* (*Digest* 49.18.4; CIC 1.892).
113. *M. B. Meş* 6.3, of a donkey. See D. Sperber, *Nautica Talmudica* (Ramat-Gan: Bar-Ilan University Press and Leiden: Brill, 1986) 114–18; "Angaria in Rabbinic Literature," *Antiquité Classique* 38 (1969) 164–68. Rabbinic *'ngry'* is a loan from Greek *angareia*.
114. G. E. M. de Ste. Croix, *The Class Struggle in the Ancient Greek World from the Archaic Age to the Arab Conquests* (Ithaca, NY: Cornell University Press, 1981) 14–16, with the bibliography in n. 8, pp. 539–40. He analyzes in detail Libanius *Orat.* 50, where farmers and their beasts who have come into Antioch are conscripted to haul off rubble.
115. *Angaros* is Greek for a Persian "courier": Theopompus, *FGH* 115 frag. 109; *angareios* appears earlier at Herodotus 3.126, and *angelos* "messenger" may be an earlier borrowing from the same original. Late Biblical *'grt* is "letter." Another Iranian word for "messenger" is attested in Greek *askandes* (Plutarch *Alex.* 18.4 incorrectly *astandes*) and Aramaic *'zgd'* (*Tg. Ps.-J.* Isa 18:2, Peshitto 2 Cor. 5:20).
116. C. P. Jones, "*STIGMA*: Tattooing and Branding in Graeco-Roman Antiquity," *JRS* 77 (1987) 139–55.
117. G. F. Hill, *Sources for Greek History* (2nd ed.; Oxford: Oxford University Press, 1951) 167 (from Photius). Plutarch *Per.* 25 through misunderstanding reverses the situation. See P. Ducrey, *Le traitement des prisonniers de guerre dans la Grèce antique des origines à la conquête romaine* (Travaux et Mémoires 17, Ecole française d'Athènes; Paris: Boccard, 1968) 214–15.
118. Athenaeus 13.612c; Cicero *de off.* 2.25; a female runaway tattooed, Aristophanes *Lys.* 331.
119. Plautus *Aul.* 325, speaking of a "three-letter man," *trium litterarum homo*.
120. Quintilian 7.4.14, *si quis fugitiuo stigmata scripserit*.
121. E. G. Kraeling, *The Brooklyn Museum Aramaic Papyri* (New Haven: Yale, 1953) no. 5 line 7.

122. G. R. Driver, *Aramaic Documents of the Fifth Century B.C.* (rev. ed.; Oxford: Oxford University Press, 1957) no. 3.6; note the accurate distinction between the two Avestan sibilants in this transcription.

123. *Hymn to Mithra* 109 (I. Gershevitch, *The Avestan Hymn to Mithra* [Cambridge: Cambridge University Press, 1959]).

124. *Mek.* ii.247 (see n. 30), and cf. *Lev. Rab.* 32.1. See my comments in Gottwald (ed.), *The Bible and Liberation*, 373.

125. *CAD* s.v. *zaqīpu*.

126. E.g., impaling (*ANET* 276a with an indistinct vignette in *ANEP* no. 373); flaying (*ANET* 295a); hanging up bodies (*ANET* 288a).

127. Griffin, *Homer on Life and Death* (see n. 109) 46.

128. "Ut et conspectu deterreantur alii ab isdem facinoribus et solacio sit cognatis et adfinibus interemptorum eodem loco poena reddita in quo latrones homicidia fecissent" (*Digest* 48.19.28.15; CIC 1.863).

129. Herodotus records the crucifixion of Magi (1.128), others of rank (4.43), rebellious Greeks (3.125, 6.30).

130. *Strom.* 5.108.2 (GCS 52[15] 308).

131. Hengel, *Crucifixion in the Ancient World* (see n. 4), 73–76.

132. Josephus *J.W.* 1.97; perhaps the event is recalled in a Qumran commentary on Nahum (J. M. Allegro in *JBL* 75 [1956] 89–95).

133. Polybius 1.11.5, 1.24.6; Diodorus 25.10.2. The Carthaginians were then imitated by mutineers (Polybius 1.79.4). Mago in 296 BCE enticed the suffetes of Gades into his hands and scourged and crucified them (Livy 28.37.2). One Hannibal crucified the runaway Campanian slave Spendius, but was himself captured by Spendius' allies, who took their friend down and put Hannibal up in his place (Polybius 1.86.4–6).

134. S. Frankenstein, "The Phoenicians in the Far West: A Function of Neo-Assyrian Imperialism," *Power and Propaganda* (ed. Larsen [see n. 7]) 263–94, esp. 272, referring to A. L. Oppenheim.

135. Livy 1.26.4, discussed by Hengel, *Crucifixion in the Ancient World*, 43.

136. Elsewhere I hope to discuss how the enforcement clauses of treaties mediated across national lines the self-imprecations and curses in which all ancient literatures agree.

137. *Iliad* 18.271, 22.42; see J. P. Brown and S. Levin, "The Ethnic Paradigm as a Pattern for Nominal Forms in Greek and Hebrew," *General Linguistics* 26 (1986) 71–105, esp. 75.

138. Jesus may also have in mind the eagle as the standard of the Roman legion, which Josephus (*J.W.* 3.123) says was so chosen as being "king of the birds."

139. (a) Wall-painting from Çatal Hüyük, 6200 BCE, vulture devouring headless corpses, thought to represent disposal of the dead (*CAH*, new ed., Plates to Vols. I & II, pl. 6). (b) Stele of king Eannatum, Lagash, 2500 BCE, showing vultures on enemy slain, now in the Louvre (*ANEP* no. 301; E. Vermeule, *Aspects of Death in Early Greek Art and Poetry* [Berkeley: University of California Press, 1979] 47). (c) Relief from the palace of Sennacherib, Nineveh, seventh century BCE, vultures picking at enemy slain, now in the British Museum (Vermeule, *Aspects of Death*, 104).

140. But see Vermeule, *Aspects of Death*, 103–109, for a few minor and ambiguous representations.

141. Etruscan pitcher of Corinthian style, 625 BCE, frieze of vultures on corpse, Rome, Villa Giulia (O. J. Brendel, *Etruscan Art* [Harmondsworth: Penguin, 1978] 67 no. 38).

142. Vermeule, *Aspects of Death*, 108.

143. We are naturally reminded of the Parsi "Tower of Silence" or *dakhma* where vultures feed on corpses, but they cannot be securely traced before 1500 CE; see M. Boyce, *Textual Sources for the Study of Zoroastrianism* (Totowa, N.J.: Barnes & Noble, 1984) 149.

144. W. Peek, *Griechische Vers-Inschriften* (Vol. I; Berlin: Akademie, 1955) no. 1120 (emphasis mine).

145. J. P. Brown, "The Role of Women and the Treaty in the Ancient World," *BZ* 25 (1981) 1–28, esp. 23–25. I there point out a further agreement: Prometheus and the Servant each appeal to the elements as treaty-witnesses to a broken covenant.
146. For all the works described here, see D. Elliott (ed.), *¡Orozco! 1883–1949* (Oxford: Museum of Modern Art, 1980).
147. J. P. Brown, "The Ark of the Covenant and the Temple of Janus: The Magico-Military Numen of the State in Jerusalem and Rome," *BZ* 30 (1986/7) 20–35, esp. 28–29.
148. As a postscript, the most current work on the Old Persian empire is to be found in the volumes of *Achaemenid History*, three to date, each edited in whole or in part by H. Sancisi-Weerdenburg (Leiden: Nederlands Instituut voor het Nabije Oosten, 1987–88), with much bibliographical information.

CHAPTER 10: DEBT EASEMENT IN ISRAELITE HISTORY

1. A short list of biblical passages might include Exod 21:1–11; 22:25–27 (Heb 24–26); Lev 25:8–55; Deut 15:1–18; 23:19–20 (Heb 20–21); 24:6, 10–13, 17–18; Jer 34:8–22; Neh 5:1–13; 10:31 (Heb 32). Note, too, Deut 31:10; 1 Sam 22:2; 2 Kgs 4:1–7; 8:1–6; Isa 61:1; Jer 32:6–15; Ezek 18:7, 8, 12, 13, 16, 17; 22:12; 33:15; Ps 15:5; 112:5; Job 24:3, 9; Prov 19:17; 28:8; Ruth 4:1–12. A list of passages that probably refer to these same phenomena would run much longer.

   A representative sample of secondary literature might include K. Baltzer, "Liberation from Debt Slavery After the Exile in Second Isaiah and Nehemiah," *Ancient Israelite Religion: Essays in Honor of Frank Moore Cross* (ed. P. D. Miller, P. D. Hanson, and S. D. McBride; Philadelphia: Fortress, 1987) 477–84; M. David, "The Manumission of Slaves Under Zedekiah: A Contribution to the Laws About Hebrew Slaves," *Oudtestamentische Studiën* 5 (1948) 63–79; H. Gamoran, "The Biblical Law Against Loans on Interest," *JNES* 30 (1971) 127–34; R. Gnuse, *You Shall Not Steal: Community and Property in the Biblical Tradition* (Maryknoll, NY: Orbis, 1985) 18–47; S. B. Hoenig, "Sabbatical Years and the Year of Jubilee," *Jewish Quarterly Review* 59 (1969) 222–36; M. Kessler, "The Law of Manumission in Jer 34," *BZ* 15 (1971) 105–108; N. P. Lemche, "The 'Hebrew Slave': Comments on the Slave Law Ex. xxi 2–11," *VT* 25 (1975) 129–44; idem, "The Manumission of Slaves—The Fallow Year—The Sabbatical Year—The Yobel Year," *VT* 26 (1976) 38–59; J. Lewy, "The Biblical Institution of Dᵉrôr in the Light of Akkadian Documents," *EI* 5 (1958) 21–31; R. P. Maloney, "Usury and Restrictions on Interest-Taking in the Ancient Near East," *CBQ* 36 (1974) 1–20; E. Neufeld, "The Prohibitions Against Loans at Interest in Ancient Hebrew Law," *HUCA* 26 (1955) 355–412; idem, "Socio-Economic Background of Yōbēl and Šᵉmiṭṭā," *Rivista degli studi orientali* 33 (1958) 53–124; idem, "Jus redemptionis in Ancient Hebrew Law," *RIDA* 8 (1961) 30–40; idem, "Inalienability of Mobile and Immobile Pledges in the Laws of the Bible," *RIDA* 9 (1962) 33–44; R. North, *Sociology of the Biblical Jubilee* (Analecta Biblica 4; Rome: Pontifical Biblical Institute, 1954); N. Sarna, "Zedekiah's Emancipation of Slaves and the Sabbatical Year," *Orient and Occident: Essays Presented to Cyrus H. Gordon on the Occasion of His Sixty-Fifth Birthday* (Altes Orient und Altes Testament 22; ed. H. A. Hoffner; Neukirchen: Neukirchener Verlag, 1973) 143–49; S. Stein, "The Laws on Interest in the Old Testament," *JTS* 4 (1953) 161–70; B. Z. Wacholder, "The Calendar of Sabbatical Cycles During the Second Temple and the Early Rabbinic Period," *HUCA* 44 (1973) 153–96; idem, "Chronomessianism: The Timing of Messianic Movements and the Calendar of Sabbatical Cycles," *HUCA* 46 (1975) 201–18; H. M. Weill, "Gage et cautionnement dans la Bible," *Archives d'histoire du droit orientale* 2 (1938) 171–241; C. J. H. Wright, "What Happened Every Seven Years in Israel?" *Evangelical Quarterly* 56 (1984) 129–38, 193–201; idem, *God's People in God's Land: Family, Land and Property in the Old Testament* (Grand Rapids: Eerdmans, 1990).

2. N. K. Gottwald, "Political Economy and Religion in Biblical Societies: Seeking the Connections" (unpublished paper presented to the AAR Liberation Theology Group, Atlanta, Nov. 1986).

3. Ibid.
4. M. L. Chaney, "Systemic Study of the Israelite Monarchy," *Semeia* 37 (1986) 60–74; idem, "Bitter Bounty: The Dynamics of Political Economy Critiqued by the Eighth-Century Prophets," *Reformed Faith and Economics* (ed. R. Stivers; Lanham, MD: University Press of America, 1989) 15–30.
5. Gottwald, "Political Economy"; cf. M. L. Chaney, "Ancient Palestinian Peasant Movements and the Formation of Premonarchic Israel," *Palestine in Transition: The Emergence of Ancient Israel* (ed. D. N. Freedman and D. F. Graf; The Social World of Biblical Antiquity Series 2; Sheffield: Almond, 1983) 52; R. B. Coote and K. W. Whitelam, *The Emergence of Early Israel in Historical Perspective* (The Social World of Biblical Antiquity Series 5; Sheffield: Almond, 1987) *passim*; R. B. and M. P. Coote, *Power, Politics, and the Making of the Bible: An Introduction* (Minneapolis: Fortress, 1990) *passim*; T. F. Carney, *The Shape of the Past: Models and Antiquity* (Lawrence, KS: Coronado, 1975) 47–82; J. H. Kautsky, *The Politics of Aristocratic Empires* (Chapel Hill, NC: University of North Carolina Press, 1982) *passim*.
6. The history of traditional Korea offers an instructive parallel to each of these factors and to their concatenation. As in Palestine, the arable land of Korea occurs in relatively small regional units that are separated from one another by various topographical impediments. City-states under the impress of a larger and older neighbor—in this case, China—dominated the earlier chapters of political history. Regional centers of power then emerged, vying with one another for control of the whole peninsula. National unification involved one region's dominating the others through a combination of military and diplomatic means. Whenever central control weakened in the resulting nation-state, however, regional loyalties born of the geographic environment proffered their own candidates for national leadership.

   This factionalization of the elites of agrarian Korea was further exacerbated by the fact that its geopolitical position in East Asia was comparable to that of Palestine in western Asia and northeast Africa. It occupied the "turf" where the regional superpowers—China and Japan, and latterly Russia, the powers of western Europe, and the United States of America—contested claims and influence. Specific links between any given Korean elite faction and one of the large, foreign powers usually proved ephemeral, but the generic pattern of such alliances describes a powerful constant in Korean history.

   Perhaps the most stimulating one-volume history of Korea (K.-B. Lee, *A New History of Korea* [Cambridge: Harvard University Press, 1984]) takes factionalized elites, so understood, as the single most salient factor in Korean history. In the Korean-language original, a concluding chapter, "The Ruling Elite and the Course of Korean History" (not translated in the English version of the book), develops the theoretical point at some length; (cf. p. vi of the English translation; note, too, J. B. Palais, *Politics and Policy in Traditional Korea* [Cambridge, MA: Harvard University Press, 1975], 15–16, 291–92, n. 30). Although this note can only hint at the sustained parallels between this phenomenon in Korea and comparable dynamics in agrarian Palestine, the nature and extent of those parallels strongly encourage a testing of the analytical category involved against the biblical evidence.
7. Cf. Stein, "Laws on Interest," 165; Neufeld, "Prohibitions Against Loans at Interest," 359–62, 407; idem, "Socio-Economic Background," 57, 69, 71, 75–76, 99; Gamoran, "Against Loans on Interest," 127–29.
8. Cf. Chaney, "Bitter Bounty," 25; B. Lang, *Monotheism and the Prophetic Minority: An Essay in Biblical History and Sociology* (The Social World of Biblical Antiquity 1; Sheffield: Almond, 1983) 120; R. Critchfield, *Villages* (New York: Anchor/Doubleday, 1983) 345.
9. Cf. J. A. Dearman, *Property Rights in the Eighth-Century Prophets: The Conflict and Its Background* (SBL Dissertation Series 106; Atlanta: Scholars Press, 1988) 85–87, 108–31; K. W. Whitelam, *The Just King: Monarchic Judicial Authority in Ancient Israel* (JSOTSup 12; Sheffield: JSOT, 1979) *passim*.

10. J. Bottéro, "Désordre économique et annullation des dettes en Mésopotamie à l'époque paléo-babylonienne," *Journal of the Economic and Social History of the Orient* 4 (1961) 113–64; J. J. Finkelstein, "Ammiṣaduqa's Edict and the Babylonian 'Law Codes,' " *JCS* 15 (1961) 91–104; idem, "Some New *Misharum* Material and Its Implications," *Studies in Honor of Benno Landsberger on His Seventy-Fifth Birthday* (Assyriological Studies 16; ed. H. G. Göterbock and T. Jacobsen; Chicago: University of Chicago Press, 1965) 233–46; Gnuse, *You Shall Not Steal*, 41–42; F. R. Kraus, *Ein Edikt des Königs Ammi-saduqu von Babylon* (Studia et Documenta ad Iura Orientis Antiqui Pertinentia 5; Leiden: Brill, 1958); idem, *Königliche Verfügungen in altbabylonischer Zeit* (Leiden: Brill, 1984); idem, "Ein Edikt des Königs Samsu-Iluna von Babylon," *Studies in Honor of Benno Landsberger* (ed. Göterbock and Jacobsen) 225–31; N. P. Lemche, "*Andurārum* and *Mīšarum*: Comments on the Problem of Social Edicts and Their Application in the Ancient Near East," *JNES* 38 (1979) 11–22; idem, "Manumission of Slaves," 38–41; Lewy, "Biblical Institution," 21–31; M. Weinfeld, *Deuteronomy and the Deuteronomic School* (Oxford: Oxford University Press, 1972) 148–57; R. Westbrook, "Biblical and Cuneiform Law Codes," *Revue biblique* 92 (1985) 247–64.
11. Kraus, *Ein Edikt des Königs Ammi-saduqu*, 194ff.; Finkelstein, "Ammiṣaduqa's Edict," 103–104; S. N. Kramer, *The Sumerians: Their History, Culture, and Character* (Chicago: University of Chicago Press, 1963) 79–83; C. J. Gadd, *CAH* 1/2.141–42, 2/1.195–96; D. O. Edzard, *The Near East: The Early Civilizations* (ed. J. Bottéro, E. Cassin, and J. Vercoutter; The Weidenfeld and Nicolson Universal History 2; London: Weidenfeld and Nicolson, 1965) 225–26.
12. *CAD* 1/2.115; Lewy, "Biblical Institution," 21–31; Finkelstein, "Ammiṣaduqa's Edict," 104, n. 19; Lemche, "Manumission of Slaves," 41, n. 11; idem, "*Andurārum* and *Mīšarum*," 11–22.
13. Lemche, "Manumission of Slaves," 41, n. 11; "*Andurārum* and *Mīšarum*," 11–22.
14. Finkelstein, "Some New *Misharum* Material," 243–45; Gnuse, *You Shall Not Steal*, 41.
15. Lewy, "Biblical Institution," 29; Bottéro, "Désordre économique," 160–61; A. L. Oppenheim, *Ancient Mesopotamia: Portrait of a Dead Civilization* (Chicago: University of Chicago Press, 1964) 157; Finkelstein, "Some New *Misharum* Material," 242; Edzard, *Near East*, 225; Gadd, *CAH* 2/1.195–96; Lemche, "Manumission of Slaves," 41; Gnuse, *You Shall Not Steal*, 41–42.
16. Finkelstein, "Ammiṣaduqa's Edict," 100–104.
17. Edzard, *Near East*, 225.
18. Finkelstein, "Some New *Misharum* Material," 245.
19. The following account of Solon's reforms is summarized from: M. M. Austin and P. Vidal-Naquet, *Economic and Social History of Ancient Greece: An Introduction* (Berkeley: University of California Press, 1977) 70–72, 210–15; J. B. Bury, *A History of Greece* (3rd ed.; London: Macmillan, 1959) 180–89; and G. E. M. de Ste. Croix, *The Class Struggle in the Ancient Greek World from the Archaic Age to the Arab Conquests* (London: Duckworth, 1981) 281–82. See also the literature they cite, and for the older literature, Neufeld, "Socio-Economic Background," 53, n. 2.
20. Bocchoris, a ruler in Egypt during the twenty-fourth dynasty, is also said to have prohibited the person of a debtor from being bonded. See Neufeld, "Socio-Economic Background," 54.
21. For the specifics of these factional conflicts, particularly the rather complicated situation regarding the aristocracy of the Eupatrids, most but not all of whom sought to sabotage Solon's program, see Bury, *A History of Greece*, 188–89, and Ste. Croix, *Class Struggle*, 282.
22. H. C. Boren, *Roman Society: A Social, Economic, and Cultural History* (Lexington, MA: Heath, 1977) 19.
23. P. A. Brunt, *Social Conflicts in the Roman Republic* (Ancient Culture and Society Series; New York: Norton, 1971) 56.

24. The following account is summarized from Brunt, *Social Conflicts*, 42–59; Boren, *Roman Society*, 17–24; and M. Cary, *A History of Rome Down to the Reign of Constantine* (2nd ed.; London: Macmillan, 1960) 72–85.

25. Brunt, *Social Conflicts*, 55.

26. For more recent treatments, giving access, in turn, to earlier works, see S. M. Paul, *Studies in the Book of the Covenant in the Light of Cuneiform and Biblical Law* (VTSup 18; Leiden: Brill, 1970); H. J. Boecker, *Law and the Administration of Justice in the Old Testament and Ancient Near East* (Minneapolis: Augsburg, 1980); F. Crüsemann, "Das Bundesbuch—historischer Ort und institutioneller Hintergrund," *Congress Volume: Jerusalem, 1986* (*VTSup* 40; ed. J. A. Emerton; Leiden: Brill, 1988) 27–41; L. Schwienhorst-Schönberger, *Das Bundesbuch (Ex 20,22–23,33): Studien zu seiner Entstehung und Theologie* (BZAW 188; Berlin: de Gruyter, 1990).

27. Coote and Coote, *Power, Politics, and the Making of the Bible*, 39–44; R. B. Coote, *In Defense of Revolution: The Elohist's History* (Minneapolis: Fortress, forthcoming).

28. Coote, *Elohist's History*, chap. 12; S. A. Kaufman, "The Second Table of the Decalogue and the Implicit Categories of Ancient Near Eastern Law," *Love and Death in the Ancient Near East: Essays in Honor of Marvin H. Pope* (ed. J. H. Marks and R. M. Good; Guilford, CT: Four Quarters, 1987) 111–16.

29. Lemche, "Hebrew Slave," 129–44; T. J. Turnham, "Male and Female Slaves in the Sabbath Year Laws of Exodus 21:1–11," *SBLSP* (1987) 545–49.

30. On the process, see Chaney, "Systemic Study," 70–71. On the meaning of "Hebrew" in this context, see Chaney, "Peasant Movements," 55–57, 72–83; and N. Na'aman, "Habiru and Hebrews: The Transfer of a Social Term to the Literary Sphere," *JNES* 45 (1986) 271–88.

31. G. E. Wright, "The Provinces of Solomon (I Kings 4:7–19)," *EI* 8 (1967) European languages section, 58–68.

32. Coote, *Elohist's History*, chap. 13. In addition to accounts of Hezekiah's reign by the standard histories, see. J. Rosenbaum, "Hezekiah's Reform and the Deuteronomistic Tradition," *HTR* 72 (1979) 23–43.

33. Although a complex legal and literary history almost certainly preceded Josiah's promulgation, explication of its details would far exceed the space available here. The reader is referred to the works listed in n. 1 above, particularly those of C. J. H. Wright.

34. On these dynamics of Josianic history, in addition to the standard histories, see W. E. Claburn, "The Fiscal Basis of Josiah's Reforms," *JBL* 92 (1973) 11–22; R. D. Nelson, *The Double Redaction of the Deuteronomistic History* (JSOTSup 18; Sheffield: JSOT, 1981); M. L. Chaney, "Joshua," *The Books of the Bible* (ed. B. W. Anderson; New York: Scribners, 1989) 1.103–12; Coote and Coote, *Power, Politics, and the Making of the Bible*, 59–66.

35. In addition to the works of David, Kessler, Sarna, Lemche, and Wright cited in n. 1 above, see J. Bright, *Jeremiah* (AB 21; Garden City, NY: Doubleday, 1965) 219–24; R. P. Carroll, *Jeremiah: A Commentary* (OTL; Philadelphia: Westminster, 1986) 643–50; and W. L. Holladay, *Jeremiah 2* (Hermeneia; Minneapolis: Fortress, 1989) 236–43.

36. On Leviticus 25, see the works of North, Neufeld, Wacholder, Lemche, and Wright in n. 1 above.

37. The seven-year "sabbatical" may have originated with fallowing practices for individual fields and/or with patterns of individual debt-slave manumission. If so, the linking of either or both with more general debt remission probably occasioned a secondary phenomenon of placing all debt-related matters within the national jurisdiction on the same cycle. Complications such as those addressed by Deut 15:9–10 and Lev 25:26–27, 50–52 were the result. For the specific biblical vocabulary referring to the several practices combined in various ways in Deuteronomy 15 and Leviticus 25, see particularly the works of Wright cited in n. 1 above.

38. J. Bright, *A History of Israel* (3rd ed.; Philadelphia: Westminster, 1981) 361–64.

39. If Sarna ("Zedekiah's Emancipation," 147–49) is correct, this timing would also correspond to a sabbatical cycle fixed by the Zedekiah incident in Jeremiah 34.
40. In addition to the standard works on "P," see R. B. Coote and D. R. Ord, *In the Beginning: Creation and the Priestly History* (Minneapolis: Fortress, forthcoming).
41. Coote and Coote, *Power, Politics, and the Making of the Bible*, 74–84.

CHAPTER 11: WHY IS ANAT A WARRIOR AND HUNTER?

1. For example, R. Oden (*The Bible Without Theology* [San Francisco: Harper & Row, 1987] 40–91) has documented the scholarly effort to define mythology out of the Hebrew Bible. B. Albrektson (*History and the Gods* [Lund: Gleerup, 1967]) has demonstrated that the attempt to characterize biblical religion as revelation in history, distinct from and superior to revelation in nature, is foundationless.
2. See, e.g., Oden, *The Bible Without Theology*, 131–53.
3. Oden (ibid., 135–40, 153) points out that scholarly bias against Canaanite religion is consistent with the biblical texts' invectives against Canaanite cult practice.
4. For background on this bias in the field of ancient Near Eastern studies, it is instructive to read W. R. Smith, *The Religion of the Semites* (3rd ed.; London: A. and C. Black, 1927) 52–59.
5. J. A. Hackett, "Can a Sexist Model Liberate Us? Ancient Near Eastern 'Fertility' Goddesses," *JFSR* 5 (1989) 68–74.
6. Ibid., 65–66, 75.
7. Notable exceptions are A. Caquot *et al.* (*TO* 1.89), who observe that nowhere in the Ugaritic texts is a sexual relationship between Baal and Anat explicit. H. L. Ginsberg ("The North-Canaanite Myth of Anath and Aqhat," *BASOR* 97 [1945] 8–9) also stated that Anat was not a reproductive goddess, but his judgment was based in part on a mistranslation of the epithet *btlt* as "virgin" (see nn. 44 and 45).
8. This is insinuated by L. R. Fisher and F. B. Knutson, "An Enthronement Ritual at Ugarit," *JNES* 28 (1969) 165–66.
9. J. C. de Moor, "An Incantation Against Infertility (*KTU* 1.13)," *UF* 12 (1980) 308–309. Cf. B. Margalit, "Two AQHT Passages," *Orientalia Lovaniensia Periodica* 19 (1988) 80, 84–88.
10. See e.g., N. Wyatt, "The 'Anat Stela from Ugarit and its Ramifications," *UF* 16 (1984) 331, 337.
11. See e.g., Fisher and Knutson, "Enthronement Ritual," 166.
12. See e.g., R. Stadelmann, *Syrisch-palästinensische Gottheiten in Ägypten* (Leiden: Brill, 1967) 89–90; H. Cazelles, "L'hymne ugaritique à Anat," *Syria* 33 (1956) 56; G. del Olmo Lete, *Mitos y Leyendas de Canaan* (Madrid: Ediciones Cristiandad, 1981) 488; A. Kapelrud, *The Violent Goddess: Anat in the Ras Shamra Texts* (Oslo: Universitetsforlaget, 1969) 42–44, 96–98.
13. P. L. Day, "Anat: Ugarit's 'Mistress of Animals' " (forthcoming in *JNES*).
14. So also *TO* 1.89. On the basis of a conversation with Neal Walls, it is my understanding that this position will be argued in detail in his forthcoming Johns Hopkins dissertation. I have not seen this study, but my conversation with Walls leads me to believe that he and I independently have reached a number of similar conclusions.
15. A prime example is E. Lipiński's "Les conceptions et couches merveilleuses de Anath" (*Syria* 42 [1965] 45–73). In this article, Lipiski argues that *KTU* 1.96 depicts Baal and Anat copulating. This interpretation rests on ascribing a sexual connotation to virtually every obscure word in the text. To demonstrate the plausibility of his interpretation, he presents (p. 63) a transliteration and translation of *KTU* 1.11 1–8. He reconstructs the names of Baal and Anat into lacunae in two lines where a sexual embrace is described and then cites the text as evidence that Baal and Anat copulate! Cf. M. C. Astour, "Remarks on KTU 1.96," *Studi Epigrafici e Linguistici* 5 (1988) 13–24, esp. 16–17, 19, 21.

16. All further references to the Ugaritic texts will be to *KTU*'s transliterations and numbering system.
17. H. A. Hoffner,"Symbols for Masculinity and Femininity," *JBL* 85 (1966) 326–34. Cf. D. R. Hillers, "The Bow of Aqhat: The Meaning of a Mythological Theme," *Orient and Occident* (ed. H. A. Hoffner; Alter Orient und Altes Testament 22; Neukirchen: Neukirchener Verlag, 1973) 73.
18. Hoffner, "Symbols for Masculinity and Femininity," 332. For further examples, see Hillers, "The Bow of Aqhat," 73–74.
19. Cf. S. B. Parker, *The Pre-Biblical Narrative Tradition* (Atlanta: Scholars Press, 1989) 137–38. The following presentation of Anat's association with hunting summarizes my lengthier treatment ("Anat," see n. 13).
20. She also may have offered to teach Aqhat how to hunt, if the restoration *d* in the phrase *almdk.ṣ*[d]* is correct (1.18 I 29).
21. W. G. E. Watson, "The Falcon Episode in the Aqhat Tale," *JNSL* 5 (1977) 74 and n. 30.
22. 'nt.ṣd.tštr.'pt.šmm.
23. (22)'nt*(23)*w* 'ttrt.tṣd*n*. This and the previous reference are also noted by F. O. Hvidberg-Hansen, *La déesse TNT: Une étude sur la religion canaanéo-punique* (Copenhagen: Gad, 1979) 87.
24. 1.11, an upper right side tablet-fragment, is generally accepted to be part of the missing portion of 1.10 III. Cf. *TO* 1.275.
25. See *TO* 1.276–77.
26. So also A. Caquot, "Remarques sur la tablette ougaritique RS 1929 No 6 (*CTA* 13)," *EI* 14 (1978) European languages section, 18. 1.10 and 1.11 are widely claimed as evidence that Baal and Anat have a sexual relationship and that Anat bears Baal's offspring. (Examples from works already cited are Kapelrud, *The Violent Goddess*, 95; Lipiński, "Les conceptions," 62–63; Stadelmann, *Syrisch-palästinensische Gottheiten*, 89–90; del Olmo Lete, *Mitos y Leyendas*, 466; Hvidberg-Hansen, *La déesse TNT*, 98; Wyatt, "The Anat Stela," 337.) That Baal mates with Anat in the form of a cow is nowhere explicit in 1.10 and 1.11. Indeed, the fact that she is clearly differentiated from the cow she encircles (1.10 II 26–29) militates against identifying her as Baal's bovine mate.
27. For bibliographical information, see G. del Olmo Lete, "Le mythe de la vierge-mère 'Anatu,'" *UF* 13 (1981) 49–62; *Mitos y Leyendas*, 487–94, and *TO* 2.19–27. Again, this text is often cited as evidence that Baal and Anat are sexual partners (e.g., del Olmo Lete, "Vierge-mère," 50–51, 61–62; *Mitos y Leyendas*, 488–89; Cazelles, "L'hymne ugaritique," 50, 56; Wyatt, "The Anat Stela," 337). This is not explicit in the text.
28. Del Olmo Lete ("Vierge-mère," 60) presents the various proposals.
29. Caquot, "Remarques," 18; *TO* 2.26 and n. 35. Caquot reads *azrt* (line 30) as a misspelling of *agzrt*.
30. She is represented as such on two Minet el Beida gold pendants: (1) C. F. A. Schaeffer, *Ugaritica II* (1949) 36, fig. 10; O. Negbi, *Canaanite Gods in Metal* (Tel Aviv: Institute of Archaeology, 1976) 100, fig. 119; U. Winter, *Frau und Göttin* (Göttingen: Vandenhoeck & Ruprecht, 1983) fig. 42; (2) *ANEP* no. 465; Negbi, *Canaanite Gods*, 99, fig. 118; Winter, *Frau und Göttin*, fig. 41.
31. Ivory pyxis lid, tomb 3, Minet el Beida: C. F. A. Schaeffer and R. Dussaud, "Les fouilles de Minet-el-Beida et de Ras Shamra," *Syria* 10 (1929) 291–93 and pl. LVI; cf. H. J. Kantor, "The Aegean and Orient in the Second Millennium B.C.," *AJA* 51 (1947) 86–89 and pl. XXII; L. Kahil, "Artemis," *Lexicon Iconographicum Mythologiae Classicae* II/1 (ed. P. Müller *et al.*; Zurich: Artemis, 1984) 624, 1.2 no. 10.
32. B. Margalit, *The Ugaritic Poem of AQHT* (New York: de Gruyter, 1989) 300, 347, 362, 406, 477. See pp. 476–85 for his interpretive overview of the Aqhat material.
33. Wyatt, "The Anat Stela," 330.
34. A. Eaton, The Goddess Anat: The History of Her Cult, Her Mythology and Her Iconography (Ph.D. dissertation, Yale University, 1964), 103.

35. Eaton, "The Goddess Anat," 102–103; W. F. Albright, "The Evolution of the West-Semitic Divinity 'An- 'Anat- 'Atta," *AJSL* 41 (1925) 86–87.
36. M. Dijkstra, "Problematical Passages in the Legend of Aqhatu," *UF* 7 (1975) 193. Cf. de Moor, "Incantation," 307 n. 10, and his "Studies in the New Alphabetic Texts from Ras Shamra 1," *UF* 1 (1969) 182. On the meaning of *k anšt*, which Dijkstra and de Moor translate "like a man," see M. Dietrich and O. Loretz, "anš(t) und (m)inš(t) im Ugaritischen," *UF* 9 (1977) 47–50.
37. S. E. Loewenstamm, "Did the Goddess Anat Wear a Beard and Side-Whiskers?" *Israel Oriental Studies* 4 (1974) 1–3.
38. De Moor, "Incantation," 307 n. 10.
39. S. E. Loewenstamm, "Did the Goddess Anat Wear Side-Whiskers and a Beard? A Reconsideration," *UF* 14 (1982) 119–23.
40. D. Marcus, "The Term 'Chin' in the Semitic Languages," *BASOR* 227 (1977) 53–60.
41. *Magical Papyrus Harris*, recto 3, 8–9. The passage refers to Anat and Astarte; and the relevant phrase, when quoted in secondary sources, is typically along the lines of Albright's translation, "the great goddesses who conceive but do not bear" (W. F. Albright, *Archaeology and the Religion of Israel* [Baltimore: Johns Hopkins University Press, 1942] 75). This phrase is usually quoted out of context, which has led to numerous misunderstandings, Dijkstra's and de Moor's among them. H. te Velde (*Seth: God of Confusion* [Leiden: Brill, 1977] 28–29) translates: "As the mouth of the womb of Anat and Astarte was closed, the two great goddesses who were pregnant but did not give birth, they were closed by Horus and they were opened by Seth." Te Velde notes that Seth, himself untimely born, was thought to be able to cause abortions. To close a womb, as Horus does, means to impregnate. "Opened by Seth" means that Seth caused them to abort. The text has nothing to do with genital irregularities (nor eternally renewed virginity, as Albright, [*Archaeology*, 75] speculated). Furthermore, Anat and Astarte are used here as names of Isis, and the use of the singular in the first clause ("womb," "was closed") may indicate that they are not thought of as two distinct goddesses. Thus it is precarious to infer anything about Anat as she was known at Ugarit from this text. (I would like to thank Thomas Lambdin for discussing with me this text and its translation.)
42. De Moor ("Incantation," 306, 309–10) reconstructs a very damaged portion of 1.13 to say that Anat's vulva was either nonexistent or too small for Baal to copulate with her. His treatment of the text is unpersuasive.
43. The theory that accounts for Anat's character by seeing her as a creation of primitive matriarchal society (e.g., A. Vincent in Kapelrud, *Violent Goddess*, 16) has been discredited. Cf. J. Bamberger, "The Myth of Matriarchy: Why Men Rule in Primitive Society," *Women, Culture, and Society* (ed. M. Z. Rosaldo and L. Lamphere; Stanford: Stanford University Press, 1974) 263–80.
44. *CAD* s.v. *batūltu*; B. Landsberger, "Jungfräulichkeit: Ein Beitrag zum Thema 'Beilager und Eheschliessung,'" *Symbolae Iuridicae et Historicae Martino David Dedicatae* (ed. J. A. Ankum *et al.*; Leiden: Brill, 1968) 57–58; cf. E. Cassin, *Le semblable et le différent: symbolismes du pouvoir dans le proche-orient ancien*, (Paris: Éditions la Découverte, 1987) 339–40.
45. M. Tsevat, "Bᵉthûlāh; bᵉthûlîm," *TDOT* 2.338–43; G. J. Wenham, "*Bᵉtûlāh* 'A Girl of Marriageable Age,'" *VT* 22 (1972) 326–48; C. Locher, *Die Ehre einer Frau in Israel* (Orbis Biblicus et Orientalis 70; Göttingen: Vandenhoeck & Ruprecht, 1986) 121–92; P. L. Day, "From the Child Is Born the Woman: The Story of Jephthah's Daughter," *Gender and Difference in Ancient Israel* (ed. P. L. Day; Minneapolis: Fortress, 1989) 59–60, 69 n. 13. Cf. also M. Bal, *Death and Dissymmetry: The Politics of Coherence in the Book of Judges* (Chicago: University of Chicago Press, 1988) 46–48.
46. Cassin (*Le semblable et le différent*, 356) agrees that childbirth is the termination of the status *bᵉtûlâ/batūltu*. She notes the importance placed on the firstborn in Israel and

Mesopotamia as the one who "opens the womb." For a discussion of the ancient Greek evidence that the transition from *parthenos* to *gynē* took place as a result of the birth of the first child, see H. King, "Bound to Bleed: Artemis and Greek Women," *Images of Women in Antiquity* (ed. A. Cameron and A. Kuhrt; Detroit: Wayne State University Press, 1983) esp. 121–22.

47. Cf. King, "Bound to Bleed," 122.

48. Cf. E. Fuchs, "The Literary Characterization of Mothers and Sexual Politics in the Hebrew Bible," *Semeia* 46 (1989) 151–66.

49. This form is hypothetical for biblical Hebrew, because only suffixed forms are attested. Cf. *TO* 1.90–92; Hvidberg-Hansen, *La déesse TNT*, 100, 138.

50. There may also be a fourth reason. Note that in 1.13 Anat seems to have a special relationship to firstlings, both animal and human. The text is too fragmentary to delineate the context with complete confidence, but lines 27–28 may present Anat saying, "I will bless your son like a royal firstborn" (*amr.bnkm.k bk*[r.]z*b*l). Line 31 specifies that the cattle (? *agzrt;* see n. 29) that will give birth as a result of Anat's blessing have never been pregnant before (*kbdh.l* yd* hrh).

51. Ginsberg describes "the Anath of the Ugaritic period" as "a beautiful, youthful, girlish, vigorous, hoidenish, bellicose, even vicious goddess, but not a voluptuous and reproductive one" ("The North-Canaanite Myth," 9).

52. Although the meaning of *btlt* obliges me to acknowledge the full range of the symbolic space that she occupies, I would note in addition that, in my reading of the Ugaritic material, she is, more specifically, an unmarried, virgin *btlt*. Understanding her as such allows us to jettison the proposal that she is a "virgin mother" (del Olmo Lete, "Vierge-mère," 49, 50, 62 and n. 14; Albright, "'An-'Anat-'Atta," 83) whose virginity is somehow ever-renewed (Kapelrud, *The Violent Goddess*, 30; Wyatt, "The Anat Stela," 331; Hvidberg-Hansen, *La déesse TNT*, 101; Eaton, "The Goddess Anat," 64 and n. 35).

53. Although for a different reason, Parker (*The Pre-Biblical Narrative Tradition*, 114) notes that Anat in the Aqhat story represents female power that knows no bounds. Stadelmann describes her as a "schreckliche, maßlose Kriegsgöttin" (*Syrisch-palästinensische Gottheiten*, 89). Indeed, her disregard for gender boundaries makes her both powerful and frightening. On liminality and the confusion of categories, see V. Turner, *The Forest of Symbols* (Ithaca: Cornell University Press, 1967) 97–98.

CHAPTER 12: THE EVIL EYE IN THE FIRST TESTAMENT

1. The terms "First Testament" and "Second Testament" are here used for "Hebrew Bible/ Old Testament" and "New Testament" respectively.

2. J. M. Roberts, "Belief in the Evil Eye in World Perspective," *The Evil Eye* (ed. C. Maloney; New York: Columbia University Press, 1976) 223–78.

3. J. H. Berke, *The Tyranny of Malice* (New York: Summit Books, 1988), 35–56; L. Blau, *Das altjüdische Zauberwesen* (Budapest, 1898; repr. Franborough, England: Gregg International, 1970); idem, "Evil Eye," *JE* 5.280–81; L. DiStasio, *Mal Occhio: The Underside of Vision* (San Francisco: North Point, 1981); K. M. D. Dunbabin and M. W. Dickie, "Invidia Rumpantur Pectora: The Iconography of Phthonos/Invida in Graeco-Roman Art," *JAC* 26 (1983) 7–37 and pls. 1–8; A. Dundes (ed.), *The Evil Eye: A Folklore Casebook* (New York: Garland, 1981); E. Ebeling, "Beschwörungen gegen den Feind und den bösen Blick aus dem Zweistromlande," *Archiv Orientalni* 17 (1949) 172–211; F. T. Elworthy, *The Evil Eye: An Account of This Ancient and Widespread Superstition* (London: Murray, 1895; repr. with an introduction by L. S. Barron, New York: Julian, 1958); idem, "The Evil Eye," *Hastings Encyclopaedia of Religion and Ethics* 5.608–15; J. Engemann, "Zur Verbreitung magischer Übelabwehr in der nichtchristlichen und Christlichen Spätantike," *JAC* 18 (1975) 22–48 and pls. 8–15; E. S. Gifford, *The Evil Eye: Studies in the Folklore of Vision* (New York: Macmillan, 1958); O. Jahn, *Über den*

Aberglauben des bösen Blickes bei den Alten (Berichte der Sächsischen Gesellschaft der Wissenschaften zu Leipzig, Phil. hist. Classe; Leipzig, 1855); R. Koebert, "Zur Lehre des Tafsir über den bösen Blick," *Islam* 28 (1948) 111–21; B. Koetting, "Böser Blick," *RAC* 2.474–82; D. Levi, "The Evil Eye and the Lucky Hunchback," *Antioch-on-the-Orontes: Publications of the Committee for the Excavation of Antioch and Its Vicinity*, vol. 3 (ed. R. Stillwell; Princeton: Princeton University Press, 1941) 220–32; A. Lykiardopoulos, "The Evil Eye: Towards an Exhaustive Study," *Folklore* 92 (1981) 221–30; R. C. MacLagan, *Evil Eye in the Western Highlands* (London: Nutt, 1902); Maloney (ed.), *The Evil Eye* (previous note); D. Noy, "Evil Eye," *Encyclopaedia Judaica* 6 (1971) 997–1000; R. Park, *The Evil Eye, Thanatology, and Other Essays* (Boston: Badger, 1912); J. Russell, "The Evil Eye in Early Byzantine Society: Archaeological Evidence from Anemurium in Isauria," *Jahrbuch der Österreichischen Byzantinistik* 32/3 (1982) 539–48; S. Seligmann, *Der Böse Blick und Verwandtes: Ein Beitrag zur Geschichte des Aberglaubens aller Zeiten und Völker* (2 vols.; Berlin: Barsdorf, 1910); idem, *Die Zauberkraft des Auges und das Berufen* (Hamburg: Barsdorf, 1922); idem, *Die magischen Heil- und Schutzmittel aus der unbelebten Natur, mit besonderer Berücksichtigung der Mittel gegen den Bösen Blick: Eine Geschichte des Amulettwesens* (Stuttgart: Streker & Schroeder, 1927); T. Siebers, *The Mirror of Medusa* (Berkeley: University of California Press, 1983); J. Trachtenberg, *Jewish Magic and Superstition* (New York: Behrmann, 1939; repr. New York: Atheneum, 1970).

4. C. R. Smith, "An Evil Eye (Mark 7,22)," *ExpT* 53 (1941/42) 181–82; idem, "The Evil Eye," *ExpT* 54 (1942/43) 26; C. Edlund, *Das Auge der Einfalt: Eine Untersuchung zu Matth. 6,22–23 und Luk. 11,34–35* (Acta Seminarii Neotestamentici Upsaliensis 19; Lund: Gleerup, 1952); H. J. Cadbury, "The Single Eye," *HTR* 47 (1954) 69–74; F. C. Fensham, "The Good and the Evil Eye in the Sermon on the Mount," *Neotestamentica* 1 (1967) 51–58; J. H. Neyrey, "Bewitched in Galatia: Paul and Cultural Anthropology," *CBQ* 50 (1988) 72–100; J. H. Elliott, "The Fear of the Leer: The Evil Eye from the Bible to Li'l Abner," *Forum* 4 (1988) 42–71; idem, "Paul, Galatians, and the Evil Eye," *Currents in Theology and Mission* 17 (1990) 262–73.

5. Elliott, "The Fear of the Leer"; idem, "Paul, Galatians, and the Evil Eye."

6. The following description summarizes salient features of Evil Eye belief and practice as elaborated in the literature listed in n. 3.

7. L. Blau, "Eye," *JE* 1.310–11; P. Wilpert [S. Zenker], "Auge," *RAC* 1.957–69.

8. Elliott, "The Fear of the Leer," 47–50.

9. For photographs, see C. Johns, *Sex or Symbol: Erotic Images of Greece and Rome* (Austin: University of Texas Press, 1982), and D. Mountfield, *Greek and Roman Erotica* (New York: Crescent, 1982).

10. Johns, *Sex or Symbol*; Mountfield, *Greek and Roman Erotica*.

11. See Elliott, "The Fear of the Leer," 48, 50, figs. 3, 4, 6, and the illustrative material in Johns, *Sex or Symbol*; Mountfield, *Greek and Roman Erotica*.

12. As illustrated by the seventh-century BCE Phoenician plaque from Arslan Tash in Upper Syria (F. M. Cross, "Leaves from an Epigraphist's Notebook," *CBQ* 36 [1974] 486–90). The second of its double incantations (p. 489) reads:

> Flee, O "Eyer" (with the evil eye), from (my) house,
> From (my) head, O "Consumer of Eyes,"
> From the head of the dreamer when he dreams;
> Let his eye see perfectly!
> This charm is from the scroll of the Enchanter.

13. See Elliott, "The Fear of the Leer," 63–67, and "Paul, Galatians, and the Evil Eye."

14. E. S. McCartney, "Praise and Dispraise in Folklore," *The Evil Eye* (ed. Dundes) 9–38.

15. V. Garrison and C. M. Arensberg, "The Evil Eye: Envy or Risk of Seizure? Paranoia or Patronal Dependency?" *The Evil Eye* (ed. Maloney) 286–328, esp. 294–97, summarizing the wealth of cross-cultural ethnographic data on Evil Eye cultures analyzed by Roberts, "Belief in the Evil Eye."

16. Ibid., 290.
17. Ibid., 295.
18. Garrison and Arensberg, "The Evil Eye," 295, following G. M. Forster, "Peasant Society and the Image of Limited Good," *American Anthropologist* 67 (1965) 293–315. On the association of the limited good perception and the Evil Eye, see also G. M. Foster, "The Anatomy of Envy: A Study in Symbolic Behavior," *Cultural Anthropology* 13 (1972) 165–202; and on limited good as characteristic of the biblical worldview in particular, see B. J. Malina, *The New Testament World: Insights from Cultural Anthropology* (Atlanta: John Knox, 1981) 71–93.
19. On ocular aggression and the Evil Eye, see D. D. Gilmore, "Anthropology of the Mediterranean Area," *Annual Review of Anthropology* 11 (1982) 175–205, esp. 197–200.
20. See Blau, *Zauberwesen*; O. Boecher, *Dämonenfurcht und Dämonenabwehr* (BWANT 5, Series 10; Stuttgart: Kohlhammer, 1970); J. D. M. Derrett, *Jesus' Audience: The Social and Psychological Environment in Which He Worked* (New York: Crossroad, 1973), esp. 114–28.
21. G. Delling, "Baskainō," *TDNT* 1.594–95.
22. See, e.g., *baskania/fascinatio* in Wis 4:12 LXX and Vg.
23. C. T. Lewis and C. Short, *A Latin Dictionary* (Oxford: Clarendon Press, 1955) s.v. *invidere*.
24. P. Walcot, *Envy and the Greeks: A Study in Human Behavior* (Warminster, England: Aris and Phillips, 1978); esp. pp. 77–90, on the Evil Eye and envy.
25. This suggests that Evil Eye belief may also lie behind 1 Sam 2:29, 32 ("look with greedy/envious eye on"); 18:9 ("Saul eyed David enviously"). Compare the British folk expression for injuring with the Evil Eye, "to overlook," recorded by MacLagen, *Evil Eye*.
26. See H. Schoeck, *Envy: A Theory of Social Behaviour* (Indianapolis: Liberty, 1987) on envy and the Evil Eye; G. F. de la Mora, *Egalitarian Envy: The Political Foundations of Social Justice* (New York: Paragon, 1987); Maloney (ed.), *The Evil Eye*.
27. Blau, *Zauberwesen*, 86–93; idem, "Amulet," *JE* 1.546–50; Koetting, "Böser Blick," cols. 474–76.
28. 4 Macc 1:26, 2:15 (*baskania*); T. *Iss.* 3:2–3, 4:1–6 (*baskanos, ophthalmous ponērous*); T. *Benj.* 4:2–4 (*skoteinon ophthalmon . . . phthonei . . . zēloi*), cf. T. *Dan* 2:5; *Test. Solomon* 18:39.
29. *De Cher.* 33; *De Mut.* 95, 112; *De Somn.* I, 107; *De Vita Mos.* I, 246; *De Virt.* 170; *In Flacc.* 29.
30. *J.W.* 1.208; *Ant.* 1.188, 200, 260; 3.268; 6.59; 10.212, 250, 257; 11.265; *Life* 425; *Ag. Ap.* 1.72; 2.285.
31. On the New Testament Evil Eye texts, see Elliott, "The Fear of the Leer," 60–67.
32. Elliott, "The Fear of the Leer," 63–67; "Paul, Galatians, and the Evil Eye."
33. See Koetting, "Böser Blick."
34. See Blau, *Zauberwesen*, 152–65; idem, "Evil Eye"; Noy, "Evil Eye"; Trachtenberg, *Jewish Magic*; L. W. Moss and S. C. Cappannari, "Mal'occhio, Ayin ha ra, Oculus Fascinus, Judenblick: The Evil Eye Hovers Above," *The Evil Eye* (ed. Maloney) 1–15; A. Brav, "The Evil Eye Among the Hebrews," *The Evil Eye* (ed. Dundes) 44–54; T. Schrire, *Hebrew Magic Amulets: Their Decipherment and Interpretation* (New York: Behrmann, 1982).
35. See Koetting, "Böser Blick"; Engemann, "Zur Verbreitung"; Dunbabin and Dickie, "Invidia"; Russell, "Evil Eye"; Levi, "Evil Eye." See also J. Naveh and S. Shaked, *Amulets and Magic Bowls: Aramaic Incantations of Late Antiquity* (2nd ed.; Jerusalem: Magnes, 1987) 40–41, 44–45, 98–99, 102–103, 120, 133, 172–73.
36. Among conventional English language biblical translations of this passage, only KJV and JPSV preserve the explicit reference to the Evil Eye contained in the original Hebrew: "his/her eye shall be evil." Other translations attempt to convey the assumed

sense or implication of the Evil Eye reference. RSV, NAB: "will (be)grudge (food)"; NEB, TEV: "will not share"; JB: "will glower at"; E. Goodspeed (*The Complete Bible: An American Translation* [Chicago: University of Chicago Press, 1944]): "will act (so) meanly toward." This translational procedure is typical for most of the biblical Evil Eye references. As a consequence, the modern reader is left unaware of the biblical appearances of the Evil Eye phenomenon. The commentaries likewise rarely accord it any attention.

37. RSV: "Do not eat the bread of a man who is stingy"; NEB: "Do not go to dinner with a miser" (variant: "a man with an evil eye"); JB: "Do not dine with a niggardly man"; NAB: "Do not take food with a grudging man"; TEV: "Don't eat at the table of a stingy man"; Goodspeed: "Dine not with a miserly man."

38. Similar fear of the Evil Eye at meals among the Greeks and of its leading to vomiting is also recorded by Aristotle. In explaining why the herb rue was considered an effective remedy against the Evil Eye and therefore taken before dining, he comments:

> Why is rue said to be a remedy against the Evil Eye (*baskania*)? Is it because men think they are victims of the Evil Eye (*baskainesthai*) when they eat greedily or when they expect some enmity and are suspicious of the food set before them? For instance, when they take anything for themselves from the same course, they offer some one else a portion, adding the words, "so that you may not cast the Evil Eye upon me (*hina mē baskanēs me*)." All therefore will take with agitation what is offered to them, whether liquid or solid, those foods, the constriction or vomiting forth of which causes the solids to be carried upwards and ejected or the flatulence from the liquid to occasion pain and writhing. Rue, therefore, being eaten beforehand since it is naturally warming, rarefies the organ which receives the food and the whole body, with the result that it drives out the flatulence enclosed within it (*Problemata* 20.34).

39. The Hebrew text contains the following lines that are lacking in the LXX but partly represented in the Syriac version: "The (man of) Evil Eye God hates, and He has created nothing more evil than him. For this—by reason of everything the eye quivers, and from the face it makes tears." On the redundancy of these lines, see the comments of Oesterley in *APOT* 1:419–20.

Again the translations render the sense rather than the specific terminology of the Evil Eye. RSV, JB, TEV: "a greedy eye (RSV variant: "evil eye") . . . greedier than the eye"; NEB: "a greedy eye . . . no greater evil in creation than the eye"; NAB: "gluttony is evil. No creature is greedier than the eye."

40. RSV: "a miserly man"; NEB: "The miser" (variant: "The man with the evil eye"); JB: "the man of greedy eye"; NAB, Goodspeed: "The avaricious man"; TEV: "Selfish people."

41. RSV: "the gift of a grudging man"; NEB: "a grudging giver"; JB: "a grudging man's gift"; NAB: "a grudging gift"; TEV: "a gift that you resent giving."

42. RSV: "envious man"; NEB, NAB: "miser"; JB: "covetous one"; TEV: "stingy person."

43. RSV, NEB: "who is grudging to himself"; NAB, TEV: "stingy with himself"; JB: "mean to himself."

44. RSV, NEB, JB: "man with (or "who has") a grudging eye"; TEV: "a selfish man" (NAB, following the Hebrew, omits).

45. Following I. Levi (ed.), *The Hebrew Text of the Book of Ecclesiasticus* (Leiden: Brill, 1951).

46. JB: "greed" (note: "lit. 'the evil eye' "); TEV: "greed"; NAB: "he refuses his neighbor" (cf. LXX: *adikia ponēra*); RSV: "mean injustice"; NEB: "greedy injustice."

47. RSV: "A stingy man's eye begrudges bread"; NEB: "A miser grudges bread"; NAB: "The miser's eye is rapacious for bread"; JB: "The miser is begrudging of bread"; TEV: "Some people are too stingy to put bread on their own table."

48. The Hebrew and Syriac add: "A good eye (*'ayin tôbâ*) causes bread to increase and a dry fountain sends forth water upon [his] table."

49. Dunbabin and Dickie, "Invidia."

50. The additional Hebrew of v. 10 contrasts the Evil-Eyed person and his lack of food with the good-eyed person and his abundance. For the "good eye," see also Prov 22:9: "He that has a good eye will be blessed, for he shares his bread with the poor." For further contrasts of good- and evil-eyed persons, see Matt 6:22–23 // Luke 11:34–35 and *m. 'Abot* 2:9, 5:19.

51. Limitations of space require omitting a discussion of two further explicit Evil Eye passages: Sir 37:7–15, involving a warning against seeking counsel from potentially hostile and envious counselors, and especially advice concerning generosity from an Evil-Eyed man (*'iš ra'; baskanou*); and Wis 4:10–11, which notes how righteous Noah was spared injury from the Evil Eye (*baskania*; Vulg. *fascinatio*), which existed from the outset of the creation. On the former, see Elliott, "The Fear of the Leer," 59.

52. Mss. Vaticanus and Alexandrinus. The translations vary in the mss. they render, but, except for TEV, which offers the opposite, positive, sense of v. 16, they agree on the sense of Evil Eye here as "begrudging" Eye: RSV: "do not let your eye begrudge"; NEB: "never give with a grudging eye"; NAB: (omits v. 7b) v. 16: "do not begrudge"; JB: (omits v. 7b) v. 16: "do not do it grudgingly"; TEV: (omits v. 7b) v. 16: "do it gladly."

53. G. von Rad, *Deuteronomy* (Philadelphia: Westminster, 1966) 104–108.

54. "In Deut 15:1–18," as S. H. Ringe observes, "there is no specific mention of the agricultural fallow year, but the terminology of 'release' and the reference to a seven-year period link the collection of laws to Exod 21:2–6 and 23:10–11. For a later reinterpretation see Lev 25:2–7" (*Jesus, Liberation, and the Biblical Jubilee: Images for Ethics and Christology* [Philadelphia: Fortress, 1985] 16–32; quotation p. 20).

55. Similarly, vv. 12–18 begin with an older legal ordinance concerning slavery (Exod 21:1–11), which is reinterpreted for new circumstances. No longer is the "Hebrew" slave to be set free a nonfree foreigner, but a "brother" Israelite, who once was free and had sold himself in slavery to a fellow Israelite. Thus, by the time of the codification of laws reflected in Deuteronomy, the term "Hebrew" had come to identify the ethnic community of Israel rather than an alien economic class (Ringe, *Biblical Jubilee*, 20). Along with other modifications (von Rad, *Deuteronomy*, 107; Ringe, *Biblical Jubilee*, 21), vv. 12–18 focus, as do vv. 1–11, on the generosity (vv. 13–14), emotions (vv. 16, 18), and experiential empathy (v. 15) of the agents. The same pattern recurs in vv. 19–23. An earlier legal maxim (v. 19a; cf. Exod 22:29b–30) is followed by "partly legal, partly homiletic accretion" (von Rad, *Deuteronomy*, 108).

56. RSV: "your eye be hostile to"; NEB: "look askance at"; NAB: "grudge help to"; JB: "look coldly on"; Goodspeed: "behave meanly to"; TEV: "Do not refuse to lend him something."

57. Garrison and Arensberg, "The Evil Eye," 294–304.

58. See Prov 23:6–8; Sir 14:2–3, 37:11–12; Matt 6:19–22; Mark 7:18–23.

59. Foster, "Anatomy of Envy"; Garrison and Arensberg, "The Evil Eye," 295–97.

CHAPTER 13: THE DEUTERONOMIC LAW CODE

1. A. Phillips, "Another Look at Adultery," *JSOT* 20 (1981) 3–25. Others who take this approach include M. Greenberg ("Some Postulates of Biblical Criminal Law," *The Jewish Expression* [ed. J. Goldin; New York: Bantam, 1970] 18–37) and S. M. Paul (*Studies in the Book of the Covenant in the Light of Cuneiform and Biblical Law* [VTSup 18; Leiden: Brill, 1970]).

2. In fact, this legislation receives even greater attention in the writings of C. M. Carmichael (e.g., *The Laws of Deuteronomy* [Ithaca: Cornell University Press, 1974]; *Law and Narrative in the Bible: The Evidence of the Deuteronomic Laws and the Decalogue* [Ithaca: Cornell University Press, 1985]). Cf. also his *Women, Law, and the Genesis Traditions* (Edinburgh: Edinburgh University Press, 1979). However, I have chosen not to address his prolific studies on the subject in this article because his attempts to harmonize law

with narratives appear to be reductionistic. Carmichael's approach to the Hebrew Bible seems to reflect his apologetics toward ancient Israelite "patriarchy." Moreover, he asserts, "The premise is that the source of the problems taken up in the Deuteronomic legislation is not, as is most universally thought, matters that arose in the everyday life of the Israelites at various times and places, but matters that are found in the literary traditions available to the legislator in his time" (*Women, Law*, 4).

3. Phillips, "Another Look," 6.
4. Ibid., 7.
5. M. Weinfeld, *Deuteronomy and the Deuteronomic School* (Oxford: Oxford University Press, 1972) 284; S. D. McBride, "Deuteronomium," *Theologische Realenzyklopädie* 8 (1981) 534–35; "Polity of the Covenant People," *Int* 41 (1987) 242.
6. For a recent study arguing that the ethics of law in ancient Israel is no different from the ancient Near Eastern legal tradition, see R. Westbrook, *Studies in Biblical and Cuneiform Law* (Cahiers de la Revue biblique 26; Paris: Gabalda, 1988).
7. J. Goody, *The Development of the Family and Marriage in Europe* (Cambridge: Cambridge University Press, 1983).
8. Ibid., 221.
9. This situation stands in contrast to Exod 22:16–17, which legislates that a father may choose to block the marriage of his daughter to the individual who raped her—with the result that the father would still receive the marriage present for his daughter. Thus, a father could reap monetary gain from the rape of his daughter. The law is such that it would in fact be in the father's economic interest to stop such a marriage. Either he could then marry his daughter to someone else and receive a second marriage gift, or he could keep her at home and have the benefit of her labor.
10. R. de Vaux, *Ancient Israel* (2 vols.; New York: McGraw-Hill, 1961) 1.40.
11. Cross-cultural studies of societies that emphasize patrilineal inheritance suggest that the strongest family bond is between a mother and her son. The mother works to further the interests of her offspring as heir to his father, resulting in the son's feelings of indebtedness toward his mother. See E. J. Michaelson and W. Goldschmidt, "Female Roles and Male Dominance Among Peasants," *Southwestern Journal of Anthropology* 27 (1971) 338–39. For further information on the plight of the widow in ancient Israelite society, consult P. S. Hiebert (" 'Whence Shall Help Come to Me?': The Biblical Widow," *Gender and Difference in Ancient Israel* [ed. P. L. Day; Minneapolis: Fortress, 1989] 125–41).
12. N. P. Lemche, *Early Israel* (VTSup 37; Leiden: Brill, 1985) 259.
13. F. S. Frick, *The City in Ancient Israel* (SBLDS 36; Missoula: Scholars Press, 1977) 126–27.
14. This is demonstrated by H. Niehr (*Rechtsprechung in Israel: Untersuchungen zur Geschichte der Gerichtsorganisation im Alten Testament* [Stuttgarter Bibelstudien 130; Stuttgart: Kath-olisches Bibelwerk, 1987]), who provides an extensive study of the interaction and transformation of judicial spheres from prestate to postexilic Israel. For a sociological study of the political/leadership role of elders in adapting to structural and historical changes in ancient Israel, see D. L. Smith, *The Religion of the Landless* (Bloomington, IN: Meyer-Stone Books, 1989) 94–99.
15. M. Weber, *Ancient Judaism* (Glencoe: Free Press, 1952) 61–70.
16. Lemche, *Early Israel*, 279.
17. There is extensive bibliography on this topic. Recent studies include Frick (*City in Israel*, 114–27), Lemche, (*Early Israel*, 245–85), and Smith (*Religion of the Landless*, 94–99).
18. Y. A. Cohen, "Ends and Means in Political Control: State Organization and the Punishment of Adultery, Incest and the Violation of Celibacy," *American Anthropologist* 71 (1969) 658–87. See M. Weber, *The Protestant Ethic and the Spirit of Capitalism* (New York: Scribner's, 1930), and G. P. Murdock, "World Ethnographic Sample," *American*

Anthropologist 59 (1957) 664–87. Although one may find fault with the ethnographic data in this sampling, it is the only such source available for comparative study.

19. Cohen, "Ends and Means," 665.
20. Cohen (ibid., 667–68) uses the example of Gen 2:22–25, which he believes expresses the concerns of the Davidic monarchy to control marital relationships, to prove his point.
21. Ibid., 661.
22. This movement toward successful "vertical entrenchment" does not always follow the same course from state to state.
23. The same conclusion is reached by Goody, *Family and Marriage*.
24. Lemche, *Early Israel*, 269.
25. J. Bright, *A History of Israel* (3rd ed.; Philadelphia: Westminster, 1981) 221. However, recent works, such as Lemche's *Early Israel*, suggest that tribes were not as important as some have maintained.
26. This conclusion corresponds with Carol Meyers' argument concerning the diminution of women's social power with the advent of monarchy in Israel (*Discovering Eve* [Oxford: Oxford University Press, 1988] 189–96). This phenomenon is also evident in the contemporary world. Both Fascist and Communist regimes have promised women benefits that have not eventuated. For an account of women's perspectives on life in the Soviet Union that makes this same point, see the recent work by F. du Plessix Gray (*Soviet Women: Walking the Tightrope* [New York: Doubleday, 1989]).
27. For example, McBride, "Polity of the Covenant People," 242.
28. Cohen, "Ends and Means," 666–67.
29. Mentioned in 2 Chr 19:5. However, the historical accuracy of these details is questionable. See H. Donner, "The Separate States of Israel and Judah," in *Israelite and Judaean History* (ed. J. H. Hayes and J. M. Miller; Philadelphia: Westminster, 1977) 391–92.
30. L. Pospíšil, *Anthropology of Law: A Comparative Theory* (New York: Harper & Row, 1971) 95.
31. I would like to thank David L. Petersen for his helpful comments on earlier versions of this essay.

CHAPTER 14: REVOLUTIONS IN READING THE BIBLE

1. I have surveyed some of the influential social scientific expressions of this claim in "The Sociology of National Development and Salvation History," *Sociology and Human Destiny* (ed. G. Baum; New York: Seabury, 1980) 56–85.
2. Elsewhere I have sketched this framework and the collaboration of Christians in defining and institutionalizing it. See my "Christian Responsibility for the World of the Free Market? Catholicism and the Construction of the Post–World War II Global Order" (paper presented at an international conference on "500 Años del Cristianismo en America Latina," organized by the Universidad Academia de Humanismo Cristiano, in Santiago, Chile, July 1990).
3. For an excellent anthology of early writings, and critical commentaries, see G. Wilmore and J. Cone (ed.), *Black Theology: A Documentary History, 1966–1979* (Maryknoll, NY: Orbis, 1979). See also J. Evans, *Black Theology: A Critical Assessment and Annotated Bibliography* (New York: Greenwood, 1987).
4. Cain Felder notes even today the "alarming lack of books on the Bible in relation to Blacks" (C. H. Felder, *Troubling Biblical Waters: Race, Class, and Family* [Maryknoll, NY: Orbis, 1989] xiii).
5. For an example of this type of criticism, see C. W. Cone, *The Identity Crisis in Black Theology* (Nashville: AMEC, 1975). For a response that mined alternative black sources for theology, see J. Cone, *The Spirituals and the Blues* (New York: Seabury, 1972). For a general approach to the normal wisdom of the oppressed, and to the various subterfuges that they must normally adopt in order to survive under the noses of the defenders of the status quo, see J. Scott, *Weapons of the Weak: Everyday Forms of Peasant Resistance* (New Haven: Yale University Press, 1985).

6. C. Martin, "Womanist Interpretations of the New Testament: The Quest for Holistic and Inclusive Translation and Interpretation," *JFSR* 6 (1990) 58.
7. Cf. Felder, *Troubling Biblical Waters*, 6.
8. For an overview of the use of the Bible in the early stages of Latin American liberation theology, see A. McGovern, "The Bible in Latin American Liberation Theology," *The Bible and Liberation: Political and Social Hermeneutics* (ed. N. K. Gottwald; Maryknoll, NY: Orbis, 1983) 461–72.
9. I have tried to describe the extraordinary vitality, faith, and hope of the people I encountered in El Salvador in my "Holy Week in El Salvador," *The Ecumenist* 27 (1989) 81–85.
10. For a recent sympathetic yet critical reading of the use of the Bible in Latin American liberation theology, see N. K. Gottwald, "The Exodus as Event and Process: A Test Case in the Biblical Grounding of Liberation Theology," *The Future of Liberation Theology: Essays in Honor of Gustavo Gutiérrez* (ed. M. Ellis and O. Maduro; Maryknoll, NY: Orbis, 1989) 250–60. It should be noted, however, that recent exegetical work in Latin America, and elsewhere among liberation theologians, reflects evident attention to just these scholarly concerns. For references, see n. 13.
11. This attitude toward the Bible is widespread throughout the popular Christian communities in many Latin American countries. See C. Mesters, "The Use of the Bible in Christian Communities of the Common People," *The Challenge of Basic Christian Communities* (ed. S. Torres and J. Eagleson; Maryknoll, NY: Orbis, 1981) 197–210.
12. For example, Richard Horsley's *The Liberation of Christmas* offers an excellent scholarly confirmation of the parallels between the lives of the poor and oppressed in biblical times and today. He shows clearly how the infancy narratives, long neglected by mainstream exegetes as purely mythological, take on obvious meaning in terms of the experience of those at the bottom of a very exploitative and oppressive social order dominated by Jewish elites in collaboration with imperial Roman authorities. And, in separate chapters, he illustrates the growing mountain of evidence and analysis today that confirms the amazing parallels between the experiences of the poor and oppressed of the Roman empire of the first century and of the poor and oppressed of the American empire in Central America of the midtwentieth. See *The Liberation of Christmas: The Infancy Narratives in Social Context* (New York: Crossroad, 1989).

    Similarly, the Latin American exegete George Pixley testifies: "I believe that there is an affinity between the struggle of the Hebrew people against the forced labor and genocide imposed by the Egyptian state, and the current struggles of the popular classes in such places as Central America" (*Exodus: A Liberation Perspective* [Maryknoll, NY: Orbis, 1987] xiv).
13. For illustrations of more recent scholarly biblical exegesis from a liberationist perspective in Latin America, see L. Boff and G. Pixley, *The Bible, the Church, and the Poor* (Maryknoll, NY: Orbis, 1989). See also the *Revista de Interpretacion Biblica Latinoamericana*, published in Spanish by Ediciones Rehue, Argomedo 40, Santiago, Chile; and in Portuguese by Editora Vozes, Rua Frei Luís 100, 25689, Petrópolis, RJ, Brazil. Concerning the use of the Bible in black theology in South Africa, see I. J. Mosala, "The Use of the Bible in Black Theology," *The Unquestionable Right to Be Free: Black Theology from South Africa* (ed. I. J. Mosala; Maryknoll, NY: Orbis, 1986) 175–99. Concerning womanist approaches to biblical interpretation, see Martin, "Womanist Interpretations of the New Testament."
14. Thus, for example, Rosemary Radford Ruether asked of Christology: "Can a male savior save women?" See her *Sexism and God-Talk: Toward a Feminist Theology* (Boston: Beacon, 1983) chap. 5. For a positive answer to this question, see esp. E. Johnson, "Jesus, the Wisdom of God: A Biblical Basis for Non-Androcentric Christology," *Ephemerides Theologicae Louvanienses* 61 (1985) 261–94.

15. In this connection, some feminist scholars have argued that apparently exclusive, that is, generically masculine, language concerning God and the fact that Jesus was a man are not stumbling blocks for historically marginalized women. As Virginia Fabella has pointed out concerning some discussions among Asian women, "The fact that Jesus was a male was not an issue, for he was never seen as having used his maleness to oppress or dominate women. Nor does the fact of his maleness necessarily lead to the conclusion that God is male" ("A Common Methodology for Diverse Christologies?" *With Passion and Compassion: Third World Women Doing Theology* [ed. V. Fabella and M. A. Oduyoye; Maryknoll, NY: Orbis, 1988] 116). Elisabeth Schüssler Fiorenza refers to this observation in support of the argument that "so-called generic masculine language . . . is read differently by men and women," underlying the ambiguous reality that the Bible can be read by women as liberating and by men (or, more precisely, at least by ruling-class men and their priestly and scholarly supporters) as supporting a broader patriarchal social order ("The Politics of Otherness: Biblical Interpretation as Critical Praxis for Liberation," *The Future of Liberation Theology* [ed. Ellis and Maduro] 322).

16. As Susan Brooks Thistlethwaite notes in her illuminating article on reading the Bible in circles of battered women, the insight that women are included in the category of the poor, the oppressed, and the outcast means that "some biblical material that appears not to address women, or even appears hostile to them, can be reworked to bring out liberating themes for abused women" ("Every Two Minutes: Battered Women and Feminist Interpretation," *Feminist Interpretation of the Bible* [ed. L. Russell; Philadelphia: Westminster, 1985] 102).

    For illustrations of further feminist reflections on the authority of the Bible, see in the same volume R. R. Ruether, "Feminist Interpretation: A Method of Correlation" (pp. 111–24); E. Schüssler Fiorenza, "The Will to Choose or to Reject: Continuing our Critical Work" (pp. 125–36); L. Russell, "Authority and the Challenge of Feminist Interpretation" (pp. 137–46).

17. Concerning the professional middle-class biases of academic exegesis, see N. K. Gottwald, *The Tribes of Yahweh: A Sociology of the Religion of Liberated Israel, 1250–1050* B.C.E. (Maryknoll, NY: Orbis, 1979) chap. 2.

18. Gottwald provides a systematic statement of this approach; see his "Sociological Method in the Study of Ancient Israel," *The Bible and Liberation* (ed. N. K. Gottwald; Maryknoll, NY: Orbis, 1983) 26–37. Ched Myers also confirms the value of this approach for the study of Christian scriptures; see *Binding the Strong Man: A Political Reading of Mark's Story of Jesus* (Maryknoll, NY: Orbis, 1988) xxv, 459–72. See also R. Horsley, *Sociology and the Jesus Movement* (New York: Crossroad, 1989).

19. While I was living in Chile in 1986, I attended an introductory course in reading the Bible organized for lay pastoral agents in a poor neighborhood. The central theme was that historically the Bible, the house of the people, had been taken out of the hands of the poor by the scholars, and that only recently had the door and windows been opened again to the people, who should feel free to enter and use it as part of their daily lives. See C. Mesters, *Parabola de la Casa del Pueblo* (Santiago, Chile: Centro Ecuménico Diego de Medellín, 1986).

20. Gottwald, *The Tribes of Yahweh*.

21. As Gottwald pointed out, this god was similar to other Near Eastern gods in many respects. However, the members of the Canaanite federation also came to see this god in distinctive terms, as the sole high God concerned above all with their liberation. Gottwald, *The Tribes of Yahweh*, chaps. 53, 54.

22. Gottwald's effort in *The Tribes of Yahweh* to develop a coherent theoretical framework for interpreting Israelite religion must be seen in context. In the history of social science, there has been no greater challenge than how to conceptualize the relationships among religion, culture, economy, politics, psychology, history, technology, war, and other factors including climate and geography, i.e., in Christian terms how to interpret moral

and spiritual matters without neglecting all the other "material" factors like the economy and instincts like sex and aggression. This problematic has taken different forms in different contexts. In general, however, the widespread calls arising from the various liberation movements for perspectives that integrate insights concerning the racist, patriarchal, class-divided, imperialistic, and ecologically devastating character of the present social order require a paradigm shift cutting across the separate academic disciplines, precisely because exploitation and oppression cut across all the allegedly separate domains of culture, economy, and politics studied by the distinct academic disciplines, and because the churches have become such obviously important sites in these struggles. From the point of view of concern with religion in particular, the challenge has been how to avoid simply idealizing it, because such perspectives obviously screen out so much of the "economic" and "political" reality involved, as well as critical questions about the actual historical role of the churches. Gottwald's efforts are clearly inspired by this spirit.

The *Tribes of Yahweh* was written in the mid- and late 1970s. Against the background of the then-existing theoretical options—pure "idealism" or crude "materialism"—his achievement was, in my judgment, extraordinary. Not surprisingly, however, there remained a certain ambivalence concerning the irreducibility of religion and its centrality to the dynamics of history. Gottwald was struggling for a nonreductionist discourse of faith and economics and politics, which is still one of our greatest theoretical challenges, involving the most fundamental questions concerning basic theoretical frameworks and the whole academic organization of the production of knowledge.

23. As Willy Schottroff notes, the establishment of the permanent monarchy profoundly changed Israel. "The king was the head of the army, and the monarchy was intended primarily to ensure a united military leadership in defensive warfare. But it became in its turn the decisive factor in the evolution of society" ("The Prophet Amos: A Socio-Historical Assessment of His Ministry," *God of the Lowly: Socio-Historical Interpretations of the Bible* [ed. W. Schottroff and W. Stegemann; Maryknoll, NY: Orbis, 1985] 38).

24. See J. Kegler, "The Prophetic Discourse and Political Praxis of Jeremiah: Observations on Jeremiah 26 and 36," *God of the Lowly* (ed. Schottroff and Stegemann) 47–56.

25. As Felder notes, there remain persistent "ethnic and racial ambiguities" in the concept of Israel's election by Yahweh (*Troubling Biblical Waters*, 44).

26. See C. Meyers, "Procreation, Production, and Protection: Male-Female Balance in Early Israel," *JAAR* 51 (1983) 563–93. See also her "The Roots of Restriction: Women in Early Israel," *The Bible and Liberation* (ed. Gottwald) 289–306.

27. As Pixley points out, for example, in setting up a monarchy within Israel after the experience of egalitarianism in Canaan, David and his supporters appealed to Israelite ideology and the loyalty it inspired "for the novel purpose of supporting his kingship as the earthly representative of Yahweh's rule in Israel" (G. Pixley, *God's Kingdom: A Guide for Biblical Study* [Maryknoll, NY: Orbis, 1981] 40). And, beginning with Solomon, subsequent kings and their supporters further developed this interpretation of the tradition to legitimate their repressive and exploitative rule, "exactly the kind of labor which the Egyptian Pharaoh had imposed on the people of Yahweh and by reason of which Moses had led them to freedom in the desert" (p. 44).

The innovations and inventiveness of David and Solomon had their roots in non-Mosaic and pre-Mosaic royal traditions, focusing on the notions of fertility, creation, and continuity, and tending toward a universal comprehensiveness, as in the creation stories in Genesis. Some scholars suggest that this trajectory of biblical literature reflects an urban imperial consciousness and a radical rejection of the liberation consciousness of the Mosaic tradition. See, for example, W. Brueggemann, "Trajectories in Old Testament Literature," *The Bible and Liberation* (ed. Gottwald) 313. It is important to note, however, that many of these themes are not inherently monarchical, and that, in the spirit of indigenous groups around the world today, concern for creation and for oneness with the earth are compatible with concern for equality and justice.

In this spirit, see the strong criticisms of Bruggemann's position, and the alternate interpretation of Zion symbolism in the Jerusalem tradition as infused with a constant, pervasive concern for justice, and a consistent and radical criticism of royal attempts to pervert justice, in the perspective of a creation theology that places the liberation of the poor in Israel in the context of God's cosmic plan, in B. Ollenburger, *Zion the City of the Great King: A Theological Symbol of the Jerusalem Cult* (Sheffield: JSOT, 1987) 151–62. I am indebted to my colleague Anthony Ceresko for this reference.

28. For example, Pixley notes concerning this all-important notion, "There is no 'biblical concept' of the kingdom of God. . . . [T]he idea has no existence in its purity as an abstraction. It must always find expression in some particular historical project, a project that may well exclude other projects that also claim to embody the kingdom of God" (*God's Kingdom*, 2).

29. As Gutiérrez has pointed out, it is only when Job begins to see his situation from the point of view of poor and oppressed people that he is able to begin to make some sense of it, to gain deeper insight into the mysterious nature of God who promises the fullness of life to the poor, but who also "tolerates" historical periods where socially structured suffering and premature death are the norm for so many innocent people. See G. Gutiérrez, *On Job: God-Talk and the Suffering of the Innocent* (Maryknoll, NY: Orbis, 1987). Note, however, that, as profound as Gutiérrez' theological insights are, there is no reflection on the social context of the biblical text. In contrast, Crüsemann suggests that the Book of Koheleth is an expression of upper-class alienation, despair, and counsel to accept domination, which represents an enormous gulf dividing Koheleth from the disadvantaged. See F. Crüsemann, "The Unchangeable World: The 'Crisis of Wisdom' in Koheleth," *God of the Lowly* (ed. Schottroff and Stegemann) 57–77.

30. For background information, see D. Oakman, *Jesus and the Economic Questions of His Day* (Queenston, Ontario: Edwin Mellon, 1986); Horsley, *Sociology and the Jesus Movement*, esp. chaps. 5–7.

31. See R. Horsley and J. Hanson, *Bandits, Prophets, and Messiahs: Popular Movements at the Time of Jesus* (Minneapolis: Winston, 1985).

32. See J. Sobrino, *Christology at the Crossroads: A Latin American Approach* (Maryknoll, NY: Orbis, 1978) 195.

33. Cormie, "Holy Week in El Salvador."

34. E. Schüssler Fiorenza, *In Memory of Her: A Feminist Theological Reconstruction of Christian Origins* (New York: Crossroad, 1983) 121. This kind of claim has important theological implications. As Sobrino points out, "Following Jesus is the precondition for knowing Jesus" (*Christology at the Crossroads*, xiii, cf. 60).

35. I first wrestled with this issue in my "The Hermeneutical Privilege of the Oppressed: Liberation Theologies, Biblical Faith and Marxist Sociology of Knowledge," *Proceedings of the Catholic Theological Society of America* 33 (1978) 155–81.

36. See, for example, E. Hobsbawm, "Mass-Producing Traditions: Europe, 1870–1914," *The Invention of Tradition* (ed. E. Hobsbawm and T. Ranger; Cambridge: Cambridge University Press, 1983). See also Scott, *Weapons of the Weak*, esp. chap. 8.

37. For example, the author of a text on statecraft in India from the fourth century BCE argued that legends about the origin of kingship had propaganda value; he urged that the king's agents should spread the story that, as the alternative to anarchy at the dawn of history, people had elected the first king. See A. L. Basham, *The Wonder that Was India* (New York: Grove, 1959) 83.

38. See A. Ceresko, *Introduction to the Old Testament: A Liberation Perspective* (Maryknoll, NY: Orbis, forthcoming) chap. 22. This introductory overview of the Old Testament by my colleague is an excellent expression of the relevance of a "liberationist" perspective for reading the whole of the Bible; it will help significantly in advancing the

discussion beyond concern for individual texts, as central as these concerns must remain, to issues concerning the development of the Bible as a whole.

39. Schüssler Fiorenza, *In Memory of Her*, 33. She argues that "the revelatory canon for theological evaluation of biblical androcentric traditions and their subsequent interpretations cannot be derived from the Bible itself but can only be formulated in and through women's struggle for liberation from all patriarchal oppression" (p. 32). As a way of emphasizing current concrete experience and practice of women (and, by implication, of every oppressed group) as providing the focus and ultimate criteria for every interpretation, this statement is understandable.

Yet it seems to me that it is problematic in two ways. First, it might be read to imply that contemporary experience can be understood apart from reference to "tradition"— if not to the Bible, to some other traditional cultural, religious, and/or intellectual sources. But of course, there is no unmediated experience; every effort to name and to evaluate our experience, and to communicate about it to others, only proceeds with reference to inherited symbols, images, concepts, categories, frameworks, and so forth, even if they are combined in creative new ways. Indeed, for this reason, "tradition" is in a very real sense constitutive of our ways of feeling and thinking and being together, if never completely and in a closed way. Of course, the Bible is not the only source of such cultural/religious resources; it is irrelevant to many from other religious traditions and has been rejected by many, including some feminists. My point here, though, is that naming and evaluating our contemporary experience inevitably involves reference in some way to some "tradition(s)"; thus the issue is not tradition or contemporary experience, but which tradition(s), and how they are related to this experience.

Schüssler Fiorenza's claim is problematic in another way. It implies that the criterion she proposes for interpreting the Bible—namely, the concrete experience of contemporary women struggling for liberation—is not present in the Bible itself. With explicit reference to women's experience exclusively, it is not, I would agree. But in a more general form, in terms of the experience of the poor and oppressed, it is. In other words, the Bible itself offers grounds for the critical principles for interpreting biblical tradition. And in this sense, the issue is not the Bible or current experience, but, for us Christians, the complex, dynamic, critical, open, and creative interaction between the two in the service of the struggles for liberation of all the poor and oppressed.

As Schüssler Fiorenza herself says elsewhere, "Just as Jesus according to the Gospels realized freedom toward Scripture and tradition for the sake of human well-being and wholeness (cf. Mark 2:27), so too a feminist critical hermeneutics seeks to assess the function of the Bible in terms of women's liberation and wholeness" (*Bread Not Stone: The Challenge of Feminist Biblical Interpretation* [Boston: Beacon, 1984] 13–14).

40. Mesters, "The Use of the Bible," 208–209.

41. Of course, the same challenges are evident across all the academic disciplines. For a succinct expression of, for example, the range of feminist challenges to social scientists and their disciplines, see M. Westcott, "Feminist Criticism of the Social Sciences," *Harvard Educational Review* 49 (1979) 422–30.

42. Mesters, *Parabola de la Casa del Pueblo*.

43. Schüssler Fiorenza, "The Politics of Otherness," 315. In this connection, see also the womanist criticism of white feminist biblical interpretation in Martin, "Womanist Interpretations of the New Testament."

44. J. Cone, *For My People: Black Theology and the Black Church* (Maryknoll, NY: Orbis, 1984) 94.

45. Ibid., 133. In this connection, see K. G. Cannon, "The Emergence of Black Feminist Consciousness," *Feminist Interpretation of the Bible* (ed. Russell) 30–40.

46. J. Sobrino, *The True Church and the Poor* (Maryknoll, NY: Orbis, 1984) 137.

47. Leonardo and Clodovis Boff discriminate among a variety of ways for scholars to enter into solidarity with the poor; see *Introducing Liberation Theology* (Maryknoll, NY: Orbis, 1988) chap. 2.

48. For insight into the dialogues among Christians from countries in Africa, Asia, and Latin America, see K. C. Abraham (ed.), *Third World Theologies: Commonalities and Differences* (Maryknoll, NY: Orbis, 1990); concerning dialogues among theologians from the Third World and from the First World, see V. Fabella and S. Torres (ed.), *Doing Theology in a Divided World* (Maryknoll, NY: Orbis, 1985).

49. With great discipline and precision, Sandra Harding develops the implications for our understanding of the nature of science arising from the multiplication of standpoints and the claim that each group must interpret in terms of its own experiences—blacks, women, Third World peoples, indigenous people, gays and lesbians, and so forth. Her analysis is certainly relevant to theology, biblical exegesis, and ethics too, and has profound implications for every discussion of the nature of "authority" in our world. See *The Science Question in Feminism* (Ithaca, NY: Cornell University Press, 1986).

50. For an excellent analysis that explains how Reagan won two presidential elections without the support of the majority of Americans on most issues, see T. Ferguson and J. Rogers, *Right Turn: The Decline of the Democrats and the Future of American Politics* (New York: Hill and Wang, 1986).

51. Schüssler Fiorenza, "The Politics of Otherness," 318. This epistemological and hermeneutical point has important theological implications; as Cone points out, "God is more than what any one people can elaborate and express; no set of concepts or experiences can exhaust the significance of God. This is true of the experiences of all peoples, of course—including Hispanic, Asian-American, Amerindian, and African-American" (*For My People*, 173). And it is true for all white people and for people of all classes—above all, of the upper classes who so confidently assume that they have the truth and are willing, even eager, to mobilize police forces and armies, and to offer blood sacrifices, in defense of it.

52. Pixley, *God's Kingdom*, 17.

53. Cone, *For My People*, 151, 117.

54. Of course, there are other nonbiblical, nonreligious ways of grounding this perspective. For example, in my "Hermeneutical Privilege of the Oppressed," I examined grounds in Marx's thought for this kind of claim.

CHAPTER 15: UNRESOLVED ISSUES

1. There is virtually no bibliography on basic questions of epistemology in the fields of biblical and Syro-Palestinian archaeology; but see provisionally W. G. Dever, "Archaeology, Texts, and History-Writing," forthcoming in the H. Neil Richardson *Festschrift*. On epistemology in the larger sense, see the seminal, although radical, work of M. Shanks and C. Tilley, *Reconstructing Archaeology: Theory and Practice* (Cambridge: Cambridge University Press, 1987).

2. Among archaeologists, I seem to have been the most vocal proponent of such a dialogue; see W. G. Dever, "Syro-Palestinian and Biblical Archaeology," *The Hebrew Bible and Its Modern Interpreters* (ed. D. A. Knight and G. M. Tucker; Philadelphia: Fortress, 1985) 31–74; "The Contribution of Archaeology to the Study of Canaanite and Israelite Religion," *Ancient Israelite Religion: Essays in Honor of Frank Moore Cross* (ed. P. D. Miller, P. D. Hanson, and S. D. McBride; Philadelphia: Fortress, 1987) 209–47; "Archaeology," forthcoming in *The Anchor Bible Dictionary* (Garden City, NY: Doubleday); *Recent Archaeological Discoveries and Biblical Research* (Seattle: University of Washington Press, 1990) 3–36. For initiatives from the biblical side, also too infrequent, see references in n. 4.

3. On Dtr, see most recently R. Polzin, *Moses and the Deuteronomist: A Literary Study of the Deuteronomic History* (New York: Seabury, 1980); J. van Seters, *In Search of History: Historiography in the Ancient World and the Origins of Biblical History* (New Haven: Yale University Press, 1983); B. Halpern, *The First Historians: The Hebrew Bible and History* (New York: Harper & Row, 1988); G. Garbini, *History and Ideology in Ancient Israel* (New York: Crossroad, 1988).

4. See n. 2. Among biblical historians whose publications show them to be conversant with recent archaeological data, one can number only a few, such as N. K. Gottwald, *The Tribes of Yahweh: A Sociology of the Religion of Liberated Israel, 1250–1050 B.C.E.* (London: SCM, 1987); B. Halpern, *The Emergence of Israel in Canaan* (Chico, CA: Scholars Press, 1983); F. S. Frick, *The Formation of the State in Ancient Israel* (Sheffield: Almond, 1985); N. P. Lemche, *Ancient Israel: A New History of Israelite Society* (Sheffield: Almond, 1988); R. B. Coote and K. W. Whitelam, *The Emergence of Israel in Historical Perspective* (Sheffield: Almond, 1987); J. W. Flanagan, *David's Social Drama: A Hologram of Israel's Early Iron Age* (Sheffield: Almond, 1988); T. L. Thompson, *The Origin Tradition of Ancient Israel* (Sheffield: Almond, 1989). One might add, on broader topics, D. C. Hopkins, *The Highlands of Canaan: Agricultural Life in the Early Iron Age* (Sheffield: Almond, 1985). Thompson's call for a radically new approach to the question of Israel's origins, giving archaeological data perhaps as much weight as textual data, is closest to my own intuition; see *The Origin Tradition*, 25–32. This is despite my previously expressed skepticism about how Thompson has actually *used* archaeological data in the past.

5. See n. 4.

6. On this, Garbini's remarks, although caustic, need to be taken seriously; see *History and Ideology*, *passim*. He speaks of the "state of psychological subjection" of most biblical historians (p. 174).

7. See J. M. Barr, "Story and History in Biblical Theology," *JR* 56 (1976) 1–17; cf. L. Gilkey, "Cosmology, Ontology, and the Travail of Biblical Language," *JR* 41 (1961) 194–205; Halpern, *The First Historians*, 3–35; Garbini, *History and Ideology*, 1–20; and esp. Thompson, *The Origin Tradition*, 11–21.

8. A number of previous writers have noted the distinctions between *Geschichte* and *Historie*, but I am not aware that anyone has taken the arguments as far as I have here.

9. K. Stendahl, "Biblical Theology, Contemporary," *IDB* 1.418–32. I have found this distinction extremely helpful, although I hasten to add that the division of scholarly tasks I propose here, plus the third level of inquiry, is my own. For pertinent reflections from the Jewish side on Stendahl's "What did/does it mean?" see the provocative remarks of M. H. Goshen-Gottstein, "Tanakh Theology: The Religion of the Old Testament and the Place of Jewish Biblical History," *Ancient Israelite Religion* (ed. Miller, Hanson, and McBride) 617–44.

10. On possible connections between the decline of "biblical theology" and "biblical archaeology," especially over the "faith and history" issue, see W. G. Dever, "Biblical Theology and Biblical Archaeology: An Appreciation of G. Ernest Wright," *HTR* 73 (1981) 1–15.

11. On the mistaken notion that "philology + philosophy = history," which has so bedeviled biblical history, in my opinion, see further Halpern, *The First Historians*, 3–35. The cautionary remarks of R. Knierim are also pertinent; see "Criticism of Literary Features, Form, Tradition, and Redaction," *The Hebrew Bible and Its Modern Interpreters* (ed. D. A. Knight and G. M. Tucker; Philadelphia: Fortress, 1985) 123–28. Much of biblical scholarship, it seems to me, has been "hung up in the prolegomenon." Is this the direct result of inadequate methods, a certain deficiency in philosophy of history, or merely a failure of nerve?

12. On the question of philosophies of history, see further Halpern, *The First Historians*, 3–35. As a historian of sorts, I find myself in complete sympathy with the cogent remarks of Goshen-Gottstein, who states that "positivist historicism may be utopian, and reconstructing a base line of 'what it really meant' no more than a heuristic exercise. But this is precisely one of the rights and duties of modern critical scholarship: to exercise our own exegetical sovereignty in order to construct our understanding of the past" ("Tanakh Theology," 629). On the other hand, as an archaeologist I share Binford's caution: "Sometimes our questions about how it was in the past involve

finding out the roles which our ancestors played in their environment: The information required will therefore be behavioral and ecological, not ideological" (L. R. Binford, *In Pursuit of the Past: Decoding the Archaeological Record* [New York: Thames and Hudson, 1983] 31). On the latter basis, I have developed my own notion of the limitations of archaeology—at least often—to speak not of "causation" in history, but simply of the "ecology of socio-economic change." Both historians and archaeologists can now profit from the new "post-processualist" archaeology of Ian Hodder, which attempts to move beyond some of the rather naive notions of the "new archaeology," as well as the materialism and determinism of much recent archaeology. Hodder's is a welcome stress on the role of ideology, of culture, of *history*, in culture change. See *Reading the Past: Current Approaches to Interpretation in Archaeology* (Cambridge: Cambridge University Press, 1986).

13. See J. M. Miller, *The Old Testament and the Historian* (Philadelphia: Fortress, 1976) 40; "Old Testament History and Archaeology," *BA* 50 (1987) 60, 62. It is curious that Miller, when he writes history, employs so little of the archaeology of which he as a biblical scholar has unusual mastery. Thus, for instance, in J. M. Miller and J. H. Hayes, *A History of Ancient Israel and Judah* (Philadelphia: Fortress, 1986), the all-important and brilliant archaeological illumination of the conquest of Lachish by Sennacherib in 701 BCE is not even mentioned. Is this another case of a modern historian under the sway of the point of view of the biblical writers, for whom the fall of Lachish was simply irrelevant compared with the "miraculous" sparing of Jerusalem?

14. See W. G. Dever, "Syro-Palestinian and Biblical Archaeology"; "The Israelite Settlement" (forthcoming in *The Anchor Bible Dictionary*); *Recent Archaeological Discoveries*, 39–84; "Archaeological Data on the Israelite Settlement: A Review of Two Recent Works" and "Archaeology and Israelite Origins: A Review-Article" (both forthcoming in *BASOR*).

15. Here we are back to epistemology; cf. n. 1. The fundamental question, in my opinion, is this: What *are* "data"? Data, for the historian—at least the socioeconomic historian—are not simply *texts*, as so many biblical scholars presume (such as Miller, "Old Testament History and Archaeology"; cf. Halpern, *The First Historians*, 6–13 on "text biases"). I hope to address some of the issues in "Archaeology, Texts, and History-Writing."

16. See Dever, *Recent Archaeological Discoveries*, 3–11.

17. There is virtually no literature on this topic in our field, but see in general the seminal work of my colleague M. Schiffer, *Formation Processes of the Archaeological Record* (Albuquerque: University of New Mexico Press, 1987); cf. W. G. Dever, "The *Tell*: Microcosm of the Cultural Process," forthcoming in the G. van Beek *Festschrift*.

18. See further W. G. Dever, "Impact of the 'New Archaeology,' " *Benchmarks in Time and Culture: An Introduction to Palestinian Archaeology* (ed. J. F. Drinkard, G. M. Mattingly, and J. M. Miller; Atlanta: Scholars Press, 1988) 337–52.

19. Gottwald, *The Tribes of Yahweh*, xxv.

20. On Marx's "modes of production" as *social-evolutionary stages*, which includes not only material factors but conceptual systems, see M. Bloch, *Marxism and Anthropology: The History of a Relationship* (Oxford: Oxford University Press, 1983) 29ff. Our "Israelite mode of production" would be, of course, a variant of Marx's "Asiatic mode of production," but *not* to be confused with "oriental despotism"—indeed, its opposite. Gottwald has pursued these notions with more determination than have other biblical scholars. It is significant, on the other hand, that Hopkins concentrates precisely on the agrarian economy and social structure of early Israel, but does not contain a single reference to Marx's seminal notions. The same rather attenuated view of "economy" is found in O. Borowski, *Agriculture in Iron Age Israel: The Evidence from Archaeology and the Bible* (Winona Lake, IN: Eisenbrauns, 1987). These and other biblical scholars, for all their emphases otherwise on ideology, seem to be more "materialistic," closer to

economic determinism, than Marxists or Neo-Marxists (?) like Gottwald. For a pertinent discussion, which all the above have overlooked, see M. Sahlins, *Stone Age
Economics* (Chicago: Aldine, 1972) on the "domestic mode of production," based on
households. He describes this in detail, then goes on to observe "as the domestic
economy is in effect the tribal economy in miniature, so politically it underwrites the
condition of primitive society—society with a Sovereign" (p. 95). Could this not serve
as a most adept description of *early Israel*? The closest approximation to a treatment of
Israel's "mode of production" in the larger sense—incorporating archaeological data as
well—is L. E. Stager, "The Archaeology of the Family in Ancient Israel," *BASOR* 260
(1985) 1–35; but this, too, is only suggestive.

21. See, for instance, the strictures of F. M. Cross, "W. F. Albright's View of Biblical
    Archaeology and Its Methodology," *BA* 36 (1973) 2–5. Cross, however—an epigrapher
    and biblical scholar—in these remarks only reveals his own lack of understanding of
    current archaeology. See further my remarks in Dever, "Syro-Palestinian and Biblical
    Archaeology," 53–61; "The Contribution of Archaeology," 220–22; "Archaeology";
    "Archaeology, Texts, and History-Writing."

22. See n. 4; and add C. H. J. de Geus, *The Tribes of Israel: An Investigation into Some of the
    Presuppositions of Martin Noth's Amphictyonic Hypothesis* (Assen: Van Gorcum, 1976); D.
    N. Freedman and D. F. Graf (ed.) *Palestine in Transition: The Emergence of Ancient Israel*
    (Sheffield: Almond, 1983); G. Åhlström, *Who Were the Israelites?* (Winona Lake, IN:
    Eisenbrauns, 1986); R. G. Boling, *The Early Biblical Community in Transjordan* (Sheffield:
    Almond, 1988).

23. See especially I. Finkelstein's synthesis of his own and other Israeli surveys in *The
    Archaeology of the Israelite Settlement* (Jerusalem: Israel Exploration Society, 1988). In
    1991 there are scheduled to appear in English Z. Gal, *The Lower Galilee in the Iron Age*
    (Baltimore: ASOR, 1991); and A. Zertal, *The Israelite Settlement in the Hill Country of
    Manasseh* (Baltimore: ASOR, 1991). See also the more technical report of Finkelstein,
    "The Land of Ephraim Survey 1980–1987: Preliminary Report," *Tel Aviv* 15–16 (1988–
    89) 117–83. For the few excavated sites, see Finkelstein, *Izbet Sartah: An Early Iron Age
    Site near Rosh Ha'ayin, Israel* (Oxford: BARev International Series, 1986); J. A. Callaway
    and R. E. Coolley, "A Salvage Campaign at Radannah, in Bireh," *BASOR* 201 (1971)
    9–19; A. Mazar, "Giloh: An early Israelite Settlement Near Jerusalem," *IEJ* 31 (1981) 1–
    36; V. Fritz and A. Kempinski, *Ergebnisse der Ausgrabungen auf der Ḥirbet-el-Mšāš (Tēl
    Maśōś), 1971–1975* (Wiesbaden: Harrassowitz, 1983). For a review of the latter, see
    Dever, "Archaeology and Israelite Origins."

24. See n. 23. See also J. A. Callaway, "A New Perspective on the Hill Country Settlement
    of Canaan in Iron Age I," *Palestine in the Bronze and Iron Ages: Essays in Honor of Olga
    Tufnell* (ed. J. N. Tubb; London: Aris and Phillips, 1985); Dever, "The Contribution of
    Archaeology," and *Recent Archaeological Discoveries*, 39–84 (written in 1983); Stager,
    "Archaeology of the Family."

25. See J. Amitai (ed.), *Biblical Archaeology Today: Proceedings of the First International Congress
    on Biblical Archaeology, April 1984* (Jerusalem: Israel Exploration Society, 1985). Note
    especially the papers and responses of Callaway, Finkelstein, Gottwald, Herrmann,
    Kochavi, Mazar, and Stager.

26. See further W. G. Dever, "Biblical Archaeology: Death and Rebirth?" forthcoming in
    the Proceedings of the Second International Congress on Biblical Archaeology, Jerusa-
    lem, 1990.

27. See further W. G. Dever, "The Late Bronze–Early Iron I Horizon in Syria-Palestine:
    Egyptians, Canaanites, 'Sea Peoples,' and 'Proto-Israelites,' " forthcoming in *The Crisis
    Years—The Twelfth Century BCE* (ed. M. Joukowsky and W. A. Ward).

28. Fritz and Kempinski, *Ḥirbet-el-Mšāš*, 73–75; Callaway, "Hill Country Settlement";
    Mazar, "Giloh"; and add B. Wood, "Palestinian Pottery of the Late Bronze Age: An
    Investigation of the Terminal LB IIB Phase" (unpublished Ph.D. dissertation, University

348 Notes

of Toronto, 1985); W. G. Dever *et al.*, *Gezer IV: The 1968–71 Seasons in Field VI, the "Acropolis"* (Jerusalem: Hebrew Union College, 1987). See also Finkelstein, *Archaeology of the Israelite Settlement*, 270–91; and add V. Fritz, "Conquest or Settlement? The Early Iron Age in Palestine," *BA* 50 (1988) 84–100. The remarks of nonspecialists like Åhlström (*Who Were the Israelites?*) on ceramic developments may be partially accurate, but they carry little weight.

29. See also G. London, "A Comparison of Two Contemporaneous Lifestyles of the Late Second Millennium B.C.," *BASOR* 273 (1989) 37–55.
30. See Stager, "Archaeology of the Family."
31. See n. 20.
32. See, for instance, F. Barth, *Ethnic Groups and Boundaries: The Social Organization of Culture Differences* (Oslo: Universitetsforlaget, 1969) 9–38, esp. 17, 18.
33. Thus, for instance, Åhlström, *Who Were the Israelites?*, although this is much too negative in my opinion.
34. Boling's work *The Early Biblical Community* is a mixture of theological exercise, archaeological dilettantism, and nostalgia—a curious anachronism, rather than a new approach to "biblical archaeology." Elsewhere, I hope to review Boling in detail.

CHAPTER 16: NEW CONSTRUCTS IN SOCIAL WORLD STUDIES

1. F. White, *The Overview Effect* (Boston: Houghton Mifflin, 1987) 34.
2. J. Goody, *The Domestication of the Savage Mind* (Cambridge: Cambridge University Press, 1982); *The Interface Between the Written and the Oral* (Cambridge: Cambridge University Press, 1987); W. Ong, *Orality and Literacy* (New York: Methuen, 1982).
3. J. D. Bolter, *Turing's Man: Western Culture in the Computer Age* (Chapel Hill: University of North Carolina Press, 1984) 9.
4. P. M. McNutt, *The Forging of Israel: Iron Technology, Symbolism, and Tradition in Ancient Society* (Social World of Biblical Antiquity Series 8; Sheffield: Almond, 1990).
5. N. K. Gottwald, *The Tribes of Yahweh: A Sociology of the Religion of Liberated Israel, 1250–1050 B.C.E.* (Maryknoll, NY: Orbis, 1979).
6. Gottwald's relying on Marxist theory and interpretation jarred thinkers whose romanticism disposed them to eschew plain speaking about the Bible and its religions. Their disapproval was a distraction, but it did not thwart the advance toward both sociohistorical topics and social-scientific analyses that Gottwald's volume legitimated. On this list, I place apologetically a review that appeared in a volume published in a series under my general editorship (D. N. Freedman and D. F. Graf [ed.], *Palestine in Transition* [Social World of Biblical Antiquity Series 2; Sheffield: Almond, 1983]). The review was included belatedly without my knowledge. Nevertheless, its tone deserves a public apology comparable to the one offered in private as soon as the book appeared.
7. M. Godelier, *The Mental and the Material* (London: Verso, 1988). Emphasis his.
8. White, *The Overview Effect*.
9. McNutt, *The Forging of Israel*.
10. SBL, AAR, and ASOR.
11. J. Ziman, *Reliable Knowledge* (Cambridge: Cambridge University Press, 1978) 104–105; R. Harré, *Varieties of Realism* (Oxford: Basil Blackwell, 1986) 9–25.
12. J. Ziman, *Public Knowledge* (Cambridge: Cambridge University Press, 1968) 30–36.
13. Cf. G. A. Herion, "The Impact of Modern and Social Scientific Assumptions on the Reconstructions of Israelite History," *JSOT* 34 (1986) 3–33, and A. D. H. Mayes, "Sociology of the Old Testament," *The World of Ancient Israel* (ed. R. E. Clements; Cambridge: Cambridge University Press, 1989) 58.
14. Ziman, *Reliable Knowledge*, 23. Emphasis his.
15. P. C. Vitz and A. B. Glimcher, *Modern Art and Modern Science: The Parallel Analysis of Vision* (New York: Praeger, 1984) 11–44.
16. M. Levin, *Republican Art and Ideology in Late Nineteenth Century France* (Ann Arbor: UMI Research, 1986); *When the Eiffel Tower Was New: French Visions of Progress at the Centennial of the Revolution* (South Hadley: Mount Holyoke College, 1989).

17. See Harré below.
18. Cf. J. D. Martin, "Israel as a Tribal Society," *The World of Ancient Israel: Sociological, Anthropological and Political Perspectives* (ed. R. E. Clements; Cambridge: Cambridge University Press, 1989) 95–116; J. W. Flanagan, *David's Social Drama* (Social World of Biblical Antiquity Series 7; Sheffield: Almond, 1988) 53–76.
19. J. W. Flanagan, "Chiefs in Israel," *JSOT* 20 (1981) 47–73; F. S. Frick, *The Formation of State in Ancient Israel* (Social World of Biblical Antiquity Series 4; Sheffield: Almond, 1985).
20. R. B. Coote and K. W. Whitelam, *The Emergence of Early Israel in Historical Perspective* (Social World of Biblical Antiquity Series 6; Sheffield: Almond, 1987).
21. Flanagan, *David's Social Drama.*
22. Harré, *Varieties of Realism,* 73.
23. Ibid., 128.
24. Ibid., 316. Cf. D. Bohm, *Wholeness and the Implicate Order* (London: Routledge & Kegan Paul, 1980).
25. M. Curd, Review of Bohm, *Wholeness and the Implicate Order, Physics Today* 34 (1981) 58.
26. Bohm, *Wholeness and the Implicate Order,* 210.
27. J. T. Fraser, *The Genesis and Evolution of Time* (Amherst: University of Massachusetts Press, 1982) 25. Cf. J. Needham, *Time the Refreshing River* (London: Allen & Unwin, 1944).
28. Fraser, *The Genesis and Evolution of Time,* 29–30.

CHAPTER 17: SOCIOLOGICAL CRITICISM

1. Reprinted as "The Social World of Ancient Israel," *The Bible and Liberation: Political and Social Hermeneutics* (ed. N. K. Gottwald; Maryknoll, NY: Orbis, 1983) 150.
2. R. Morgan with J. Barton, *Biblical Interpretation* (Oxford Bible Series; Oxford: Oxford University Press, 1988) 151.
3. E. Schüssler Fiorenza, "The Ethics of Interpretation: De-Centering Biblical Scholarship," *JBL* 107 (1988) 3–4.
4. N. K. Gottwald, *The Hebrew Bible: A Socio-Literary Introduction* (Philadelphia: Fortress, 1985) 28–29.
5. N. K. Gottwald, "Literary Criticism of the Hebrew Bible: Retrospect and Prospect" (unpublished paper delivered to the Section on Biblical Criticism and Literary Criticism at the Annual Meeting of the SBL, November 24, 1986) 4.
6. Morgan, *Biblical Interpretation,* 147.
7. N. K. Gottwald, *The Tribes of Yahweh: A Sociology of the Religion of Liberated Israel, 1250–1050 B.C.E.* (Maryknoll, NY: Orbis, 1979).
8. Schüssler Fiorenza, "The Ethics of Interpretation," 4.
9. Ibid., 13.
10. T. Eagleton, *Literary Theory: An Introduction* (Minneapolis: University of Minnesota Press, 1983) 209.
11. Schüssler Fiorenza, "The Ethics of Interpretation," 14.
12. J. de Gruchy, *The Church Struggle in South Africa* (Grand Rapids: Eerdmans, 1979) 153.
13. L. Kretzschmar, *The Voice of Black Theology in South Africa* (Johannesburg: Ravan, 1986) 72. Emphasis mine.
14. I. J. Mosala, "The Use of the Bible in Black Theology," *The Unquestionable Right to Be Free: Essays in Black Theology* (ed. I. J. Mosala and B. Tlhagale; Johannesburg: Skotaville, 1986) 160.
15. Ibid., 181.
16. I. J. Mosala, *Biblical Hermeneutics and Black Theology in South Africa* (Grand Rapids, Eerdmans, 1989) 18.
17. Mosala, "The Use of the Bible," 178.

18. Mosala, *Biblical Hermeneutics*, 27. Emphasis mine.
19. Ibid., 39.
20. Ibid., 35.
21. F. Jameson, *The Political Unconscious: Narrative as a Socially Symbolic Act* (Ithaca, NY: Cornell University Press, 1981) 76.
22. Mosala, "The Use of the Bible," 187.
23. Jameson, *The Political Unconscious*, 36.
24. T. Eagleton, *Marxism and Literary Criticism* (Berkeley: University of California Press, 1976) 18.
25. E. Terray, "Classes and Class Consciousness in the Abron Kingdom of Gyaman," *Marxist Analyses and Social Anthropology* (ed. M. Bloch; London: Tavistock, 1984) 85–135.
26. E. Brumfiel, "Marxist Analysis and Structural Approaches to Social Change" (unpublished paper, 1985).
27. Mosala, *Biblical Hermeneutics*, 192–93.

CHAPTER 18: FEMINISM AND "MODE OF PRODUCTION"

1. In this volume, W. G. Dever, "Unresolved Issues in the Early History of Israel: Toward a Synthesis of Archaeological and Textual Reconstructions"; J. W. Flanagan, "New Constructs in Social World Studies"; B. J. Malina, "Interpretation: Reading, Abduction, Metaphor." Cf. also R. B. Coote and K. W. Whitelam, *The Emergence of Israel in Historical Perspective* (Sheffield: Almond, 1987); J. W. Flanagan, *David's Social Drama: A Hologram of Israel's Early Iron Age* (Sheffield: Almond, 1988); and other works cited in Dever, "Unresolved Issues," nn. 2, 4.
2. N. K. Gottwald, *The Hebrew Bible: A Socio-Literary Introduction* (Philadelphia: Fortress, 1985) 20–34. See my review article in *JSOT* 38 (1986) 85–93.
3. See M. Bal, *Murder and Difference: Gender, Genre and Scholarship on Sisera's Death* (Bloomington: Indiana University Press, 1988), esp. 111–34.
4. Unfortunately, the best statement of Bal's proposal has only recently been published in English, so that it has not been adequately clear even to those who know her biblical books well. See M. Bal, *On Story-Telling* (Sonoma, CA: Polebridge, 1991), chap. 1. The proposal undergirds the book on which I will draw most in this essay, *Death and Dissymmetry: The Politics of Coherence in the Book of Judges* (Chicago: University of Chicago Press, 1988); but the summary given there (pp. 32–38, 248–49) is not, in my view, adequate. See my review essay in *Religious Studies Review* 17 (1991) 1–10, esp. 7–9.

    So far as literary versus social-scientific is concerned, the proposals mentioned above (n. 1) are all from the side of the social sciences. From the literary side, I may mention my own "Writing the Wrongs of the World: The Deconstruction of the Biblical Text in the Context of Liberation Theologies," *Semeia* 51 (1990) 81–118.

    An exception to the lack of integrative proposals by women scholars is P. McNutt, *The Forging of Israel: Iron Technology, Symbolism, and Tradition in Ancient Society* (Sheffield: Almond, 1990). Her research design seems to me ideal, though I question the adequacy of her use of literature. Cf. also contributions to the work of the SBL/AAR/ASOR group on "Constructs of Ancient History and Religion" (1989–). C. V. Camp, *Wisdom and the Feminine in the Book of Proverbs* (Sheffield: Almond, 1985), seems to me a superb example of an interdisciplinary feminist approach resistant to systematicity; see my review article in *Union Seminary Quarterly Review* 44 (1990) 171–75.
5. The term is from Bal, *Death and Dissymmetry*, 5 and *passim*.
6. C. Meyers, *Discovering Eve: Ancient Israelite Women in Context* (New York and Oxford: Oxford University Press, 1988).
7. N. Steinberg, "The Deuteronomic Law Code and the Politics of State Centralization," in the present volume; R. Schwartz, "Adultery in the House of David: 'Nation' in the

Bible and Biblical Scholarship," forthcoming in *"Not In Heaven": Literary Readings of Biblical Texts* (ed. J. Rosenblatt and J. Sitterson; Bloomington: Indiana University Press), and in Schwartz's own book *Can These Bones Live?* (cited here in typescript provided by the author).

8. Gottwald, *The Hebrew Bible*, 595–609. Gottwald's espousal of "mode of production," is, if not unique, certainly rare among biblical scholars. In his essay in this volume, Dever complains of this lack, but notes that "Gottwald has pursued these notions with more determination than other biblical scholars" (Dever, "Unresolved Issues," n. 20).

9. N. K. Gottwald, "Political Economy and Religion in Biblical Societies: Seeking the Connections" (paper presented to the AAR Liberation Theology Group, Atlanta, GA, November 1986).

10. Ibid., 1B.

11. Such a scheme derives from the Marxist model of Louis Althusser, whose implications for literary theory are worked out by P. Macherey, *A Theory of Literary Production* (London: Routledge & Kegan Paul, 1978). Though Gottwald cites Althusser, he oddly neglects Macherey. Also to be mentioned here, because it concerns itself with premodern as well as modern literature, is F. Jameson, *The Political Unconscious: Narrative as a Socially Symbolic Act* (Ithaca, NY: Cornell University Press, 1981).

12. See esp. N. K. Gottwald, "Literary Criticism of the Hebrew Bible: Retrospect and Prospect," *The Bucknell Review* 37 (1990) 27–44, and "Social Class and Ideology in Isaiah 40–55: An Eagletonian Reading," *Semeia* (forthcoming). Note also Gottwald's extensive review of literary readings of biblical texts in *The Hebrew Bible*. He includes the literary theorists Mikhail Bakhtin, Jonathan Culler, Terry Eagleton, and Fredric Jameson in the bibliography to "Political Economy and Religion."

13. U. Melotti, *Marx and the Third World* (London: Macmillan, 1977) 8.

14. The unilinear scheme cannot accommodate such a move; classical society did not develop out of the "Asiatic" type. Some, therefore, have resorted to a "bilinear" scheme; but the much more powerful trend in recent Marxisms has been toward a less rigid, "multilinear" view. For all this, see Melotti, *Marx and the Third World*, 8–27. For ongoing theoretical rejection of the Asiatic mode, cf. B. Hindess and P. Q. Hirst, *Pre-Capitalist Modes of Production* (London: Routledge & Kegan Paul, 1975) 178–220.

15. Gottwald, "Political Economy and Religion," 4.

16. There is a serious question whether Israel could ever have been big enough for the tributary mode to be viable, because it seems most characteristic of large, imperial societies. Cf. D. Jobling, "Deconstruction and the Political Analysis of Biblical Texts: A Jamesonian Reading of Psalm 72," *Semeia* (forthcoming). Nonetheless, it seems to me useful to consider Israel's monarchy as a modified form of the tributary mode.

17. F. Engels, *The Origin of the Family, Private Property and the State* (Marxist Library 22; New York: International Publishers, 1942).

18. N. K. Gottwald, *The Tribes of Yahweh: A Sociology of the Religion of Liberated Israel, 1250–1050 B.C.E.* (Maryknoll, NY: Orbis, 1979) 323–27 and *passim*.

19. M. Sahlins, *Tribesmen* (Foundations of Modern Anthropology; Englewood Cliffs, NJ: Prentice-Hall, 1968), esp. 75–81. Cf. Sahlin's *Stone Age Economics* (Chicago: Aldine-Atherton, 1972), where he prefers the term "domestic mode." Dever asks, "Could this not serve as a most adept description of *early Israel?*" ("Unresolved Issues," n. 20). Meyers (*Discovering Eve*, 142) equates Sahlins' proposal with her own "household mode of production" (cf. p. 245). Cf. also L. E. Stager, "The Archaeology of the Family in Ancient Israel," *BASOR* 260 (1985) 1–35. (Dever's further comment, that Stager's article is "the closest approximation to a treatment of Israel's 'mode of production' in the larger sense—incorporating archaeological data as well," seems to disregard Meyers.)

20. Sahlins, *Tribesmen*, 78.

21. Ibid., 75.

22. A representative selection includes A. M. Bailey and J. P. Llobera (ed.), *The Asiatic Mode of Production: Science and Politics* (London: Routledge & Kegan Paul, 1981); Hindess and Hirst, *Pre-Capitalist Modes;* L. Krader, *The Asiatic Mode of Production: Sources, Development and Critique in the Writings of Karl Marx* (Assen: Van Gorcum, 1975); Melotti, *Marx and the Third World;* K. S. Newman, *Law and Economic Organization: A Comparative Study of Preindustrial Societies* (Cambridge: Cambridge University Press, 1983); K. A. Wittfogel, *Oriental Despotism* (New Haven: Yale University Press, 1963).

23. Engels, *The Origin of the Family*, on which see Krader, *The Asiatic Mode of Production*, 271–85, esp. 277–80.

24. K. Wittfogel, "The Stages of Development in Chinese Economic and Social History," *The Asiatic Mode of Production* (ed. Bailey and Llobera), 114–19, and esp. nn. 15, 40, 42 (legislation against families with multiple adult males), and 67.

25. Wittfogel, *Oriental Despotism*, 240, cf. 80, 202, 249, 258.

26. Newman, *Law and Economic Organization*, is an exception; but she disclaims any special interest in "the status of women" (p. 167).

27. Meyers, *Discovering Eve*, 43.

28. Ibid., 34–35, with reference to M. K. Whyte, *The Status of Women in Preindustrial Societies* (Princeton: Princeton University Press, 1978).

29. Meyers, *Discovering Eve*, 63.

30. Ibid., 56.

31. Ibid., 29. Cf. also pp. 64–71, where Meyers interprets demands for the total destruction of cities as evidence of plague, and the sparing of marriageable women as an indication that the value of their reproductive potential outweighed even the danger of disease.

32. Ibid., chap. 6.

33. Ibid., 140.

34. Meyers suggests (ibid., 135–37) that the incest laws of Leviticus 18 and 20 are based on such units, being designed to regulate sexual liaisons in kin-groups on just this scale.

35. Ibid., 143. Metal-work the only significant exception.

36. Ibid., 145–64.

37. Drawing on S. C. Rogers ("Female Forms of Power and the Myth of Male Dominance: A Model of Female/Male Interaction in Peasant Society," *American Ethnologist* 2 [1975] 727–56), Meyers lays out the conditions under which this sort of equation may be valid in societies where women are mainly concerned with domestic matters: namely, that the society be domestic oriented, and that men and women experience mutual interdependence. She believes that these conditions plausibly obtain for early Israel (*Discovering Eve*, 43–45, cf. 32–33).

38. Meyers, *Discovering Eve*, 189–96. Cf. her "The Roots of Restriction: Women in Early Israel," *The Bible and Liberation: Political and Social Hermeneutics* (ed. N. K. Gottwald; Maryknoll, NY: Orbis, 1983) 289–306.

39. Meyers, *Discovering Eve*, 16, 169.

40. Ibid., 28–29, referring to Engels, *The Origin of the Family*.

41. Ibid., 194. For extensive discussion, see Wittfogel, *Oriental Despotism*, 4, 78–86, 228–300.

42. Meyers, *Discovering Eve*, 142. For Sahlins, see n. 20.

43. Sahlins, *Tribesmen*, 75, 78.

44. Meyers, *Discovering Eve*, 60–61, 122–28. Nothing could be further from a mode of production approach than her appeal to Johannes Pedersen's romantic ideas of Israelite anthropology (pp. 123–24) in introducing her main discussion of the suprahousehold levels.

45. Steinberg, "The Deuteronomic Law."

46. Drawing on J. Goody, *The Development of the Family and Marriage in Europe* (Cambridge: Cambridge University Press, 1983).

47. "Thus one may question whether Deuteronomic justice is truly egalitarian in intent, as some have claimed. Women may have gained legal autonomy from their fathers and husbands through the legislation in Deuteronomy 19–25, but they were thrown on the defensive in ways that put them at a social disadvantage vis-à-vis men" (Steinberg "The Deuteronomic Law," 168).

48. Ibid.

49. "The laws of sexual behavior for commoners are not binding upon the royal court—despite what Deut 17:14–20 suggests. . . . The pattern of family dynamics consistently revealed in the Deuteronomic law code exists in obvious contrast to the actions of the Davidic house" (ibid., p. 169). Note the closeness of this to the discussion above (n. 25) of the tributary mode, and also, in its view of the biblical literature, to Schwartz's main thesis (pp. 248–49).

50. Meyers, *Discovering Eve*, 77.

51. P. Trible, *God and the Rhetoric of Sexuality* (Philadelphia: Fortress, 1978) 70–141.

52. Meyers, *Discovering Eve*, 81, 85.

53. Ibid., 95.

54. Ibid., 118. I will not deal here with the remainder of the verse.

55. Among a number of methodologically dubious points, I would single out the treatment of Gen 3:16a (pp. 99–109) as violating the principle of interpreting the more by the less obscure. The first line is much the more obscure, but it is made to determine the meaning of the clearer second line.

56. My reasons for generally preferring deconstructive to recuperative feminist approaches to Genesis 2–3 do not need to be rehearsed here (see my *The Sense of Biblical Narrative*, vol. 2 [Sheffield: JSOT, 1986] 40–43). Suffice it to say that Meyers' view of the Bible as enshrining male bias (pp. 11–12) is oddly absent from her treatment of the Garden of Eden. And some feminists will question how recuperative she has succeeded in being: e.g., the argument on p. 116 seems to give a man the right to rape his wife, provided it is "with the hope that conception will result."

57. Cf. J. P. Brown's essay in this volume, "Prometheus, the Servant of Yahweh, Jesus: Legitimation and Repression in the Heritage of Persian Imperialism."

58. Meyers, *Discovering Eve*, 91.

59. See n. 3 above.

60. Bal, *Death and Dissymmetry*, 3–4.

61. Ibid., 5.

62. But see ibid., 209.

63. Ibid., e.g., 99–104, 217–24. Cf. also my *The Sense of Biblical Narrative*, vol. 2, 66–84.

64. Steinberg, "The Deuteronomic Law Code," this volume. Cf. also the material from Wittfogel referred to in n. 24, above.

65. Schwartz, "Adultery in the House of David."

66. Ibid., 4–9.

67. Ibid., 11–14, with reference to M. Foucault, "Nietzsche, Genealogy, History," *Language, Counter-Memory, Practice: Selected Essays and Interviews* (ed. D. F. Bouchard; Ithaca, NY: Cornell University Press) 139–64, esp. 154. For "like the nations," see 1 Sam 8:5, 20.

68. There "are not separate spheres, public and private" (Schwartz, "Adultery in the House of David," 18). Cf. Abner and Rizpah (2 Sam 3:6–11), Adonijah and Abishag (1 Kgs 2:13–25).

69. Michal was, of course, married to David before her marriage to Paltiel.

70. Schwartz, "Adultery in the House of David," 23.

71. Ibid., 24–27, referring to 2 Sam 13:12. For rape as "folly in Israel," cf. Gen 34:7, Judg 20:6. For the distinctive sexual mores of ruling groups, cf. above, nn. 25, 49.

72. Bal, *Death and Dissymmetry*, 4, 237.

73. Ibid., e.g., 84–86, 118. Cf. Gottwald's well-known critique of the nomadic theory (e.g., *The Hebrew Bible*, 277–80).
74. See Bal, *Death and Dissymmetry*, chap. 4.
75. An interesting example of psychological input is the contrast between Bal's treatment of males' dependence on females and Meyers' *Discovering Eve*, 168–73, cf. 40–45. Meyers treats it in a positive way, as a very powerful social cement. Bal, although agreeing about interdependence as a social fact, insists also on the psychoanalytic dimension of male resentment of their dependence, which they cannot reconcile with their assumption of superiority. E.g., *Death and Dissymmetry*, 52–59; *Lethal Love: Feminist Literary Readings of Biblical Love Stories* (Bloomington: Indiana University Press, 1987) 95–103. For a possible correlation between cultural complexity and the level among men of ritualized fear of women, cf. Whyte, *The Status of Women*, 172.
76. As Meyers, for instance, does (*Discovering Eve*, esp. 37–40). She claims to find evidence for a tendency for intensive agricultural societies to be patrilineal and -local in M. K. Martin and B. Voorhies, *Female of the Species* (New York: Columbia University Press, 1975), but seems to me to read their data one-sidedly.

    Bal finds matrilocality (to revert to the traditional usage) not only in the story of "the Levite's concubine," but also in those of Achsah, Abimelech, Jephthah and his daughter, and Samson. Her suggestion that kinship is a major *differentium* between Judges and Genesis (pp. 111–13, 176, 279 n.12) is worth serious analysis. But her contribution here, I believe, remains at the level of "questions and hints." Her suggestion (sometimes) that matrilocal marriage functioned as a *system*, in coequal rivalry with the alternative, patrilocal system, seems to me to lead to inconsistency (e.g., she talks [p. 175] of the matrilocal wife's brothers as the ones who inherit their father's power; but if matrilocality were functioning as a total system, these brothers would be elsewhere, living with *their* fathers-in-law). But it is sufficient for Bal's case to show (as, for me, she has) that matrilocality "inhabits" the dominant patrilocal system of Judges, and that the resulting tension provides the basis for a view of the whole book, which explains at least as many of its details as any alternative proposal.
77. Bal draws extensively on Althusser in *On Story-Telling*, chap. 1 (sect. 3), and her option for "political . . . countercoherence" over "the comfortably justifiable position of the deconstructionist" (*Death and Dissymmetry*, 234) corresponds to Marxist critique of deconstruction. Schwartz, with her use of Foucault, is rhetorically more on the deconstructive side, but in a thoroughly historical mode. These are nuances in what both would see as essentially similar methods. On the issues, see my "Writing the Wrongs of the World," esp. 85–90.
78. See esp. "The Participation of Free Agrarians in the Introduction of Monarchy to Ancient Israel: An Application of H. A. Landsberger's Framework for the Analysis of Peasant Movements," *Semeia* 37 (1986) 77–106. Meyers, though alluding to unspecified internal factors, still puts the Philistine threat foremost (*Discovering Eve*, 189).
79. Bal, *Death and Dissymmetry*, 5.
80. Though it might gain support from the mode of production discussion, when F. Tökei, claiming to present the view of Marx and Engels, sees "patriarchal exploitation" less as a consequence of the Asiatic mode than as facilitating the transition to it ("The Asiatic Mode of Production," *The Asiatic Mode of Production* [ed. Bailey and Llobera] 257).Whyte's correlation (above, n. 75) could be reversed, so that increased fear of women leads to greater cultural complexity!
81. Gottwald, *The Hebrew Bible*, 595–609. The basic aim of Jameson, in *The Political Unconscious*, is to demonstrate correlations between contradictions in modes of production and in literary texts. For another example of what literary analysis may offer to socio-historical research, cf. my " 'The Jordan a Boundary': Transjordan in Israel's Ideological Geography," *The Sense of Biblical Narrative*, vol. 2, 88–134. It explores the murkiest waters of Israel's mythological geography, by a literary method that had to be

invented *ad hoc*. Yet its implications for Israel's attitude to Transjordan seem fairly direct (as noted by Flanagan, *David's Social Drama*, 233; cf. Gottwald, *The Hebrew Bible*, 256–57).

82. Cf. also the contributions to this volume by Meyers and Phyllis Bird.

83. I allude to Mieke Bal's review article, "The Bible as Literature: A Critical Escape," *Diacritics* 16 (1986) 71–79, now chap. 3 of *On Story-Telling*.

84. I wish to acknowledge the help of Margrét Kristjansson in the preparation of this essay.

CHAPTER 19: INTERPRETATION

1. Among these practitioners, I would like to thank the members of The Context Group: Project on the Bible in Its Cultural Environment, for their assessment of this paper at the group's first annual meeting in Portland, OR, March 22–24, 1990. As for the phrase "social-scientific criticism," it is the coinage of J. H. Elliott ("Social-Scientific Criticism of the New Testament: More on Methods and Models," *Semeia* 35 [1986] 1–33). I convinced him to drop the European "sociological, sociology," because the words in the European humanities usually refer to "social, social dimensions" (e.g., as in sociology of knowledge, sociology of mathematics). "Social-scientific" also points up the difference between present concerns and those of the early twentieth century and the "Chicago School," which essentially used the word "sociology" in the European sense and with the freight Comte *et al.* gave it (for Comte, see, e.g., E. Bréhier, *The History of Philosophy VI: The Nineteenth Century: Period of Systems, 1800–1850* [Chicago: University of Chicago Press, 1968; trans. dated 1932] 279–316); for Chicago, see C. W. Votaw, "Primitive Christianity: An Idealistic Social Movement," *American Journal of Theology* 22 (1918) 54–71, and especially C. A. Ellwood, "A Sociological View of Christianity," *Biblical World* 54 (1920) 451–57. It is unfortunate that some continue to speak of a sociological approach to the Bible when they mean social, historical, social-historical, and the like, e.g., H. C. Kee ("Sociology of the New Testament," *Harper's Bible Dictionary* [ed. P. J. Achtemeier; San Francisco: Harper & Row, 1985] 961–68). For an excellent overview, see C. Osiek, "The New Handmaid: The Bible and the Social Sciences," *TS* 50 (1989) 260–78. The most recent dictionary survey article (C. S. Rodd, "Sociology and Social Anthropology," *A Dictionary of Biblical Interpretation* [ed. R. J. Coggins and J. L. Houlden; Philadelphia: Trinity, 1990] 635–39) is about fifteen years behind in its description of the actual state of research, at least for the United States; while J. W. Rogerson's article in the same volume, "Anthropology" (pp. 26–28), totally ignores New Testament scholars.

2. The historian George E. Mendenhall recently accused Gottwald of fundamentalism in the latter's quest for relevant biblical meanings ("Ancient Israel's Hyphenated History," *Palestine in Transition: The Emergence of Ancient Israel* [ed. D. N. Freedman and D. F. Graf; Sheffield: Almond, 1983] 91–103). A seeker after relevance, yes; fundamentalist, hardly. After all, fundamentalism is premised on a biblical story constructed solely of unique elements in the biblical story, as unique as Israel itself. Granting such uniqueness to the Bible and all of its parts, singly and as a whole, fundamentalists then become too busy figuring out the meanings to put into the Bible to worry about what any author says or means, not unlike Israeli historiography in defense of recent claims to Palestine (see G. W. Bowersock, "Palestine, Ancient History and Modern Politics," *Blaming the Victim: Spurious Scholarship and the Palestinian Question* [ed. E. Said and C. Hitchens; London and New York: Verso, 1988] 181–91). Fundamentalists do not believe in inspired authors. And although they say they believe in an inerrant and inspired Bible text, they mean an inerrant and inspired reader, that is, they themselves, each with a dispensation from God from the normal ignorance and stupidity characteristic of pretentious human beings the world over. Because fundamentalists in fact deny inspired authors, the biblical authors have nothing to communicate to them. They can only be read into, like an inkblot or oil slick. By any reading, Norman Gottwald is not a fundamentalist.

356 Notes

3. For the value of this approach and the comparative approach in general, see C. Ragin, "New Directions in Comparative Research," *Cross-National Research in Sociology* (ed. M. L. Kohn; Newbury Park, CA: Sage, 1989) 57–76.
4. For the quality of interactive behavior at usual scholarly meetings, see A. W. Schaef and D. Fassel, *The Addictive Organization* (San Francisco: Harper & Row, 1988).
5. M. Csikszentmihalyi, *Beyond Boredom and Anxiety* (San Francisco: Jossey-Bass, 1975); idem, "Some Paradoxes in the Definition of Play," *Play as Context: 1979 Proceedings of the Association for the Anthropological Study of Play* (ed. A. T. Cheska; West Point, NY: Leisure Press, 1981) 14–36.
6. Following Sternberg, this definition points simply to the application of intelligence to a text from the past. "My definition of intelligence is that intelligence consists of those mental functions purposively employed for purposes of adaptation to and shaping and selection of real-world environments" (R. J. Sternberg, "Human Intelligence: The Model Is the Message," *General Systems* 30 [1987] 15).
7. By translation I mean the production of a dynamic or static equivalent meaning in another cultural system. Humans can indeed move from system to system and be understood within each system in terms of that system, but it does not seem they can mean systematically within an alien system, that is, cross-systemically. In other words, they cannot be understood without interpretation cross-systemically. Interpretation is the process that enables cross-systemic understanding. People within the same system do not need interpretation; they can usually understand quite directly, if not intuitively. After all, human beings, like their social systems, are finite.
8. See my "Reading Luke-Acts: Reading Theory Perspectives," *The World of Luke-Acts: A Handbook of Social Science Models for Biblical Interpretation* (ed. J. H. Neyrey; Peabody, MA: Hendrickson, forthcoming 1991). There are many learned exegetical and historical critics of the social science approach, as is well known. Yet we are never told by hesitant exegetes insisting on prior literary work just what is the reading theory behind their literary-critical method and its sense of textuality. And hesitant historians who insist on sifting all the facts first never mention just what is the reading theory behind their historical-critical method and its fact gathering and storytelling.
9. See T. Asad, "The Concept of Cultural Translation in British Social Anthropology," *Writing Culture: The Poetics and Politics of Ethnography* (ed. J. Clifford and G. E. Marcus; Berkeley: University of California Press, 1986) 183.
10. P. Rabinow, "Representations Are Social Facts: Modernity and Post-Modernity in Anthropology," *Writing Culture: The Poetics and Politics of Ethnography*, 239.
11. "Once the signifier is freed from a concern with its relation to an external referent it does not float free of any referentiality at all; rather, its referent becomes other texts, other images," notes Rabinow ("Representations Are Social Facts," 250). "If we attempt to eliminate social referentiality, other referents will occupy the voided position" (p. 251).
12. Concerning the inevitability of contemporary relevance in most storytelling, see B. J. Malina, *Christian Origins and Contemporary Anthropology* (Atlanta: John Knox, 1986) 166–84.
13. On the value of offering four categories instead of the usual dichotomy of us against them, see J. Gharajedaghi, "Social Dynamics: Dichotomy or Dialectic," *General Systems* 29 (1986) 143–53.
14. Rabinow, "Representations Are Social Facts," 253.
15. Ibid.
16. It seems that it is far better to argue from what exists to what is possible, than from what is possible to what should exist. Social science criticism, beginning with actual Mediterranean values and behavior, has a better starting point than the presumably well-tutored imagination of exegetes and historians who prefer to remain innocent of Mediterranean values and behavior in favor of some "inductive objectivity."

17. G. A. Miller and P. N. Johnson-Laird, *Language and Perception* (Cambridge: Belknap, 1976) 46, referring to M. Minsky and S. Papert, *Artificial Intelligence Progress Report* (Artificial Intelligence Laboratory A.I. memorandum 252, Jan. 1, 1972, Massachusetts Institute of Technology).

18. "Essentially a machine is a particular system of constraints. . . . More precisely, the system consists of four sets of constraints: (1) input conditions that determine the input of energy, (2) design conditions that prevent the energy from dissipating freely, (3) general boundary conditions that reinforce, weaken, or modify the design conditions, and (4) output conditions that engage and align (or disengage and misalign) the energy output with specific states of the environment. Energy is of course dissipated against all four sets of conditions. The proportion of energy used applying a load against the target states rather than dissipated in energy acquisition, struggle against design constraints, and compensation for boundary conditions is a measure of the efficiency of the machine, while the amount of the modification of the target states is a measure of its effectiveness" (R. Jung, "A Quaternion of Metaphors for the Hermeneutics of Life," *General Systems* 30 [1987] 29).

19. Ibid.

20. Ibid.

21. R. F. Ericson, "System-Induced Hypocricies [*sic*]: Our Quintessential Moral Dilemma," *General Systems* 30 (1987) 79.

22. For the latest such insistence, see S. R. Garrett, *The Demise of the Demonic: Magic and the Demonic in Luke's Writings* (Minneapolis: Fortress, 1989) e.g., 126, n. 108.

23. Such induction is based on a prior set of principles according to which recorded human experiences are perceived to be relevant data and then are categorized in some predetermined fashion. It is such induction used by most exegetes and historians that in fact involves passing whatever the historian is aware of through an implicit prefabricating "cookie cutter," thus producing data to be used in the story the historian wishes to tell. The story then serves to bolster the intuitive and implicit principles known to the researchers before they begin. To see how this works, see Malina, *Christian Origins and Cultural Anthropology*, 166–84. To demonstrate the claim that they are not processing information on the basis of some ethnocentric, contemporary scenario, critics of the social science methods might tell us what models they are in fact using. But as the guild knows so well, they do not use any models at all!

24. T. J. Scheff, "Shame and Conformity: The Deference-Emotion System," *American Sociological Review* 53 (1988) 402.

25. K. T. Fann, *Peirce's Theory of Abduction* (The Hague: Nijhoff, 1970) 4. The quotes from Peirce are from *Letters to Lady Welby* (ed. I. Lieb; New York: Whitlock's, 1953) 42, and *The Collected Papers of Charles Sanders Peirce* (ed. C. Hartshorne, P. Weiss, and A. W. Burks; Cambridge: Harvard University Press, 1931–58) 8.248 (par. 388).

26. F. E. Reilly, *Charles Peirce's Theory of Scientific Method* (Orestes Brownson Series on Contemporary Thought and Affairs 7; New York: Fordham University Press, 1970) 31. The quote from Peirce is from "The Laws of Nature and Hume's Argument Against Miracles," *Values in a Universe of Chance* (ed. P. P. Wiener; Garden City, NY: Doubleday, 1958) 320.

27. Fann (*Peirce's Theory*, 9) notes that induction "infers the existence of phenomena such as we have observed in cases that are similar," whereas abduction "supposes something of a different kind from what we have directly observed, and frequently something which it would be impossible for us to observe directly." He continues (p. 10): "For in induction we generalize from a number of cases of which something is true and infer that the same thing is probably true of a whole class. But in abduction we pass from the observation of certain facts to the supposition of a general principle to account for the facts. Thus induction may be said to be an inference from a sample to a whole, or from particulars to a general law; abduction is an inference from a body of data to an

explaining hypothesis, or from effect to cause. The former classifies, the latter explains. Abduction furnishes the reasoner with hypothesis while induction is the method of testing and verifying."

28. Reilly, *Charles Peirce's Theory*, 35.
29. Fann, *Peirce's Theory*, 10.
30. B. J. Lee, *The Galilean Jewishness of Jesus: Retrieving the Jewish Origins of Christianity* (New York: Paulist, 1988), esp. chap. 1, "An Historicist Conversation and Some of Its Grammar," 17–52; and see his "Two Process Theologies," *TS* 45 (1984) 307–19.
31. Lee, *Galilean Jewishness*, 48–49.
32. Jung, "A Quaternion of Metaphors," 25–31.
33. For examples, James V. Spickard contentiously insists that Mary Douglas's grid/group model is an ontological one ("A Guide to Mary Douglas's Three Versions of Grid/Group Theory," *Sociological Analysis* 50 [1989] 151–70). Douglas, in her response, seems to agree ("The Background of the Grid Dimension: A Comment," *Sociological Analysis* 50 [1989] 171–76), as does Robert Atkins in an unpublished paper ("Measuring the Strength of Social Boundaries in Paul," presented at the Social Sciences and New Testament Interpretation Section, SBL Annual Meeting, 1989). These proponents of ontology might benefit from reading F. L. Bates and W. G. Peacock, "Conceptualizing Social Structure: The Misuse of Classification in Structural Modeling," *American Sociological Review* 54 [1989] 565–77. After all, even Douglas (*Cultural Bias* [London: Royal Anthropological Institute of Great Britain and Ireland Occasional Paper No. 35, 1978] 15) describes her grid/group model as "polythetic classification," quite necessary because "without typologising there can be no generalising." On the other hand, we have historians of the Euro-American tradition, such as Wayne Meeks, who cryptically assures us "the aim [of the historical corpus he edits] is to understand those communities as they believed, thought, acted then and there—not to 'explain' them by some supposedly universal laws of social behavior" (cited from the editor's "Foreword" to each volume of *Library of Early Christianity* [Philadelphia: Westminster, 1986–]).

To see what an ontological model in this field might entail, I suggest a perusal of I. I. Mitroff and R. O. Mason, "Business Policy and Metaphysics: Some Philosophical Considerations," *The Academy of Management Review* 7 (1982) 361–70. It would seem the aforementioned critics might also benefit from both a Meyers-Briggs overview, such as I. I. Mitroff and R. H. Kilmann, *Methodological Approaches to Social Science* (San Francisco: Jossey-Bass, 1978), and some conspectus of models, such as the editor's initial essay in J. Richardson (ed.), *Models of Reality: Shaping Thought and Action* (Mt. Airy, MD: Lomond, 1984). To understand what is must reading in Euro-American schools and why, see also S. Nimis, "Fussnoten: Das Fundament der Wissenschaft," *Arethusa* 17 (1984) 105–34, and especially M. Lamont, "How to Become a Dominant French Philosopher: The Case of Jacques Derrida," *American Journal of Sociology* 93 (1987) 584–622. This latter might easily be applied to Gerd Theissen; see R. A. Horsley, *Sociology and the Jesus Movement* (New York: Crossroad, 1989).

34. Jung, "A Quaternion of Metaphors," 25.

CHAPTER 20: BIBLE AND LIBERATION IN SOUTH AFRICA

1. I. J. Mosala, *Biblical Hermeneutics and Black Theology in South Africa* (Grand Rapids, MI: Eerdmans, 1989) 193.
2. AZAPO (Azanian People's Organization); PAC (Pan Africanist Congress); ANC (African National Congress).
3. *Challenge to the Church: A Theological Comment on the Political Crisis in South Africa. The Kairos Document* (2nd ed.; repr. *The Kairos Covenant: Standing with South African Christians* [ed. R. J. Mouw et al.; New York: Friendship and Oak Park, IL: Meyer-Stone, 1988] 2–43). The implications of the government's propaganda war for the antiapartheid groups precluded a scientific critique of the Kairos document at the time of its

publication. Black theologians in particular, although disagreeing fundamentally with the theological implications, theoretical foundations, and ideological implications of the radical liberal theology of the *Kairos Document*, did not deem it good politics to provide the forces of reaction with ammunition that might have been used against the predominantly white but well-intentioned "Kairos theologians." This, however, indicates the danger of populism in the search for truth and liberation.

4. *Annual General Meeting Conference, (16–19 July, 1990) Institute for Contextual Theology* (Braamfentein: ICT, 1990) 1. (Hereafter *ICT Report*.)

5. See my comments on Tutu's hermeneutics in *Biblical Hermeneutics and Black Theology*, chap. 1.

6. See *ICT Report*, 3.

7. See the Confession section of *The Rustenburg Declaration* (National Conference of Churches in South Africa, 1990), 2.

8. Ibid.

9. Ibid., 6–7.

10. T. J. Byres, "Of Neo-Populist Pipe-Dreams: Daedalus in the Third World and the Myth of Urban Bias," *Journal of Peasant Studies* 6 (1979) 240. The quote is from V. I. Lenin, *Collected Works* (Moscow: Foreign Languages Publishing House, 1963–70) 18.560.

11. *Prophetic Fragments* (Grand Rapids, MI: Eerdinans, 1988) 30.

12. *ICT Report*, 10.

13. G. Arroyo, "Christians, the Church and Revolution," *Christians and Socialism: Documentation of the Christians for Socialism Movement in Latin America* (ed. J. Eagleson; Maryknoll, NY: Orbis, 1975) 229–46. Citation p. 231. Emphasis his.

14. Ibid., 244.

15. A. Mansueto, "From Historical Criticism to Historical Materialism" (unpublished paper presented to the Graduate Seminar on Social-Scientific Method in Biblical Studies, Graduate Theological Union, Berkeley, CA, 1983) 1.

16. *ICT Report*, 11.

CHAPTER 21: MARK'S GOSPEL IN THE INNER CITY

1. J. J. Vincent, *Doing Theology in the City* (Sheffield: Urban Theology Unit, 1977) 2.

2. J. J. Vincent, "The Evangelism of Jesus," *Journal of Bible and Religion* 23 (1955) 266–71.

3. J. J. Vincent, *Disciple and Lord: The Historical and Theological Significance of Discipleship in the Synoptic Gospels* (Sheffield: Academy, 1976).

4. N. K. Gottwald, *The Tribes of Yahweh: A Sociology of the Religion of Liberated Israel, 1250–1050 B.C.E.* (Maryknoll, NY: Orbis, 1979).

5. W. Brueggemann, *The Land: Place as Gift, Promise, and Challenge in Biblical Faith* (Philadelphia: Fortress, 1977).

6. G. R. Lilburne, *A Sense of Place: A Christian Ideology of the Land* (Nashville: Abingdon, 1989).

7. D. R. Edwards and J. A. Overman, "Who Were the First Urban Christians? Urbanisation in Galilee in the First Century" (unpublished paper given at the SBL International Meeting, Sheffield, August 1988).

8. Cf. my *Secular Christ* (Nashville: Abingdon, 1968) esp. 67–79; *Radical Jesus* (Basingstoke: Marshall Pickering, 1986) 13–19, esp. Jesus as "Northerner."

9. S. Freyne, "Land and Gospel," *Faith and the Hungry Grass: A Mayo Book of Theology* (ed. E. McDonagh; Blackrock, Dublin: Columba Press, 1990) 14–27.

10. N. K. Gottwald, "The Theological Task After *The Tribes of Yahweh*," *The Bible and Liberation* (ed. N. K. Gottwald; Maryknoll, NY: Orbis, 1983) 199.

11. J. Cardenas Pallares, *A Poor Man Called Jesus: Reflection on the Gospel of Mark* (Maryknoll, NY: Orbis, 1986) 2.

12. H. Waetjen, *A Reordering of Power: A Socio-Political Reading of Mark's Gospel* (Philadelphia: Fortress, 1989) xiv.

13. Ibid., 15.
14. H.-G. Gadamer, *Truth and Method* (London: Sheed & Ward, 1975).
15. The numerous "History of Interpretation" dissertations belong here, for a start.
16. C. Rowland and M. Corner, *Liberating Exegesis* (London: SPCK, 1990) 5.
17. Vincent, *Radical Jesus*, 23–25.
18. In my *Discipleship in the 90's* (London: Methodist Publishing House, 1991) 14.
19. J. J. Vincent, *Liberation Theology from the Inner City* (Edinburgh: Methodist Mission, 1989). Cf. my forthcoming *A British Liberation Theology* (London: Epworth, 1991).
20. N. Q. Hamilton, *Recovery of the Protestant Adventure* (New York: Seabury, 1981).
21. J. D. Davies and J. J. Vincent, *Mark at Work* (London: Bible Reading Fellowship, 1986) 14.
22. W. Wink, *Transforming Bible Study* (Nashville: Abingdon, 1980). The "Second Edition, Completely Revised and Expanded" (1990) has not altered the crucial elements of the method.
23. E. S. Kessler, *Radical Jesus in Parables* (Sheffield: Urban Theology Unit, 1973).
24. Cf. C. Brown, "The Year at UTU," *UTU in the 80's* (ed. M. Mackley; Sheffield: Urban Theology Unit, 1990) 5.
25. C. Boff, *Theology and Praxis: Epistemological Foundations* (Maryknoll, NY: Orbis, 1987).
26. Cf. my *Into the City* (London: Epworth Press, 1982) 121–40.
27. J. J. Vincent, *Britain in the 90's* (London: Methodist Publishing House, 1989) 44–45.
28. Cf. now "An Inner City Bible" in *Using the Bible Today*, ed. Dan Cohn-Sherbok (London: Bellew Publishing, 1991).
29. Rowland and Corner, *Liberating Exegesis*, 45.